PIMLICO

183

BRITAIN'S ROYAL FAMILIES

Alison Weir lives and works in Surrey. She is the author of *The Six Wives of Henry VIII, The Princes in the Tower* and *Lancaster and York.* Her forthcoming book, *Children of England*, is a study of Henry VIII's heirs.

BRITAIN'S ROYAL FAMILIES

The Complete Genealogy

———

ALISON WEIR

Revised Edition

PIMLICO

To Rankin, John and Kate

PIMLICO

An imprint of Random House
20 Vauxhall Bridge Road, London SW1V 2SA

Random House Australia (Pty) Ltd
20 Alfred Street, Milsons Point, Sydney
New South Wales 2061, Australia

Random House New Zealand Ltd
18 Poland Road, Glenfield
Auckland 10, New Zealand

Random House South Africa (Pty) Ltd
PO Box 337, Bergvlei, South Africa

Random House UK Ltd Reg. No. 954009

First published by The Bodley Head 1989
Pimlico edition, with revisions, 1996

7 9 10 8 6

Papers used by Random House UK Limited are natural,
recyclable products made from wood grown in sustainable
forests. The manufacturing processes conform to the
environmental regulations of the country of origin

Printed and bound in Great Britain by
Mackays of Chatham PLC, Chatham, Kent

ISBN 0 7126 7448 9

Author's Note

The reader may find it helpful to note the following points:

1. *Britain's Royal Families* covers the period from A.D. 800 to the present day. The monarchs belonging to each royal house appear in chronological order. Every member of the various royal dynasties of England, Scotland and Great Britain is included, even children who died in infancy. Since the succession has usually been invested in the male line, the descendants of female members of the royal families beyond the first generation have not been included, except where relevant to the succession. Likewise, the descendants of the illegitimate children of monarchs have not been included.

2. All names in the book have been Anglicised or Latinised for the sake of clarity. Where a person is known by more than one name, all the alternatives are given.

3. Where any fact or date is in dispute, this is indicated in the text, and all the possibilities are listed.

4. Many dates are either not known or disputed, and the following examples serve to illustrate how they appear in the text:

   Example 1 c.848 means around the year or date specified.
   Example 2 848/9 means during the period or years specified.
   Example 3 848? means the date has been estimated using circumstantial evidence and guesswork, and is purely conjectural.

5. The following rule applies to the listing of subjects by name:

   Example 1 Name followed by a question mark (?) means there is doubt that the person actually existed.
   Example 2 Name preceded by a question mark (?) means there is doubt that the name is correct.

6. A Select Bibliography is given at the end of the book. However, a short list of recommended reading is included at the end of each chapter, with the author's choice of books being listed in order of importance. Every effort has been made to trace the publishers of all the books listed, both in the bibliography and in the lists of recommended books; unfortunately, it has not always been possible to obtain this information, especially in the case of works published more than a century ago, and the author apologises for any significant omissions.

7. County boundaries given are those relevant to the period in question.

Foreword

In 1965, when I was fourteen, I read for the first time an adult historical novel. It was about Katherine of Aragon, and was entirely forgettable, except for the fact that it left me with a thirst to find out more about its subject. Subsequently, I read many more novels, and then many history books, and my interest expanded from the Tudor period to encompass the whole sweep of British, indeed, European, history. But from the first, my chief fascination was with the British monarchy, and it became my ambition to produce a book that would provide the reader with a complete genealogical record of all the royal families of England, Scotland and Great Britain.

It has taken me more than 22 years to research this book. Throughout this time I have consulted countless books and articles in various libraries, visited sites of interest, and revised the manuscript at least eight times. It may seem strange, but despite the fact that there are numerous and detailed books on the British monarchy, and even on royal genealogy, there is not one that gives a complete record of all the members of the various royal houses and families. To obtain such a record, I have had to research each person individually, cross-checking the facts where possible from alternative sources, and re-checking against new works as they were published. I have used original, contemporary sources for verification wherever possible.

The result is *Britain's Royal Families*, which I am convinced will prove an invaluable aid to the student of royal history, and will provide much of interest for even the most casual of royalty watchers.

Alison Weir
London, 1989

Note to the Pimlico Edition

The author wishes to extend her grateful thanks to all those who wrote offering information or pointing out errors in the text after the publication of the hardback edition. Where appropriate the text has been amended.

The author would also like to thank the staff at the Buckingham Palace Press Office for supplying the information needed to update the genealogical record of the present Royal family.

Alison Weir
Surrey, 1995

Contents

1. The Saxon and Danish Kings of England

There have been kings in England for more than 2,000 years, and yet this realm has been a monarchy for little more than half that time. Up until the Dark Ages, kingship was basically tribal, invested in chieftains of Celtic or Romano-British stock. Then, in the middle of the 5th century, England began to feel the impact of the Barbarian invasions that were changing the face of Europe. Angles, Saxons and Jutes came to these shores, settled, and then colonised the land. There then evolved 7 kingdoms, known to historians as the Heptarchy. The earliest kingdom was established in Kent by Hengist, son of a Germanic chieftain, in around A.D. 455. The other kingdoms were Essex, Sussex, East Anglia, Lindsey, Bernicia, Deira, Mercia and Wessex. Lindsey was centred around Lincoln; the names of its kings are not known to us, and it was very soon swallowed up by neighbouring kingdoms. Bernicia and Deira combined later on to form the kingdom of Northumbria, the first of the biggest three kingdoms to establish supremacy over the rest.

Christianity came to Kent in the late 6th century, and soon spread to the rest of the Heptarchy, although there were pagan influences still prevalent until the late middle ages. Not so welcome were the raids of the Vikings from Scandinavia, which were the scourge of England (and other countries also) from the 8th to the 11th centuries, and which found their ultimate achievement in the Norman Conquest of 1066.

Northumbria was the first kingdom to achieve supremacy, and during the 7th century it was a centre for the arts and religion. Unfortunately, the light of learning was extinguished during the following century because of the Viking raids. At that time, Mercia was in the ascendant. This kingdom comprised the Midlands and some of the southern counties. At its peak of supremacy, Mercia was governed by a king, Offa (d.796), who established firm government and overseas alliances. However, after his death, the kingdom declined because of ineffective leadership, leaving Wessex in the ascendant.

The kingdom of Wessex had been founded in A.D. 519 by a chieftain called Cerdic, who came to these shores from Germany in 494/5. His descendants, proud to bear his name, called themselves "Cerdingas". H.M. Queen Elizabeth II is a direct descendant of Cerdic. Later Saxon chroniclers would boastfully trace Cerdic's descent from Adam and Eve, via a mythical son born to Noah in the Ark, but of course this is pure fiction, and we must accept that Cerdic's ancestors were merely obscure Teutonic tribal chieftains and elders.

Anglo-Saxon kingship was a blend of the mystical and the practical. The function of the king was to protect his people, by making war if necessary, and by giving them laws to obey. He was also sanctified by holy rites, which evolved into the coronation as we know it, the modern form of which dates from the crowning of King Edgar in 973. Anglo-Saxon kings of the House of Wessex had from time immemorial been crowned upon the ancient coronation stone at Kingston-upon-Thames, in a simple ritual which was nowhere near as complicated as the European ceremony adapted for Edgar by Archbishop Dunstan. Hence, the king, set apart by his anointing and crowning, was a champion of the Church, and was deemed to hold his office from God.

The king was also expected to father sons for posterity, to ensure the succession and the stability of the kingdom. His wife was rarely accorded the title of "Queen" in Wessex; rather would she be known as "Lady". Succession was by primogeniture, supporting the right of the eldest son, although on several occasions the right of conquest prevailed over this.

As late as the 11th century, the Danes were still attempting to invade and conquer a by then united England, and they were ultimately successful, which is why our line of Anglo-Saxon monarchs is broken by four Danish interlopers. The succession in the 11th century was an ongoing problem as a result of this, and it was not finally resolved until 1066. In 1100, when Henry I married a princess of Saxon descent, the old and the new royal houses at last joined in blood.

This handbook is about the monarchy, and it begins with the first ruler who may properly be accorded the title of monarch, Egbert of Wessex. Egbert was acknowledged in his time as an outstanding ruler, who was recognised by other, lesser, kings as overlord of most of England by the end of his reign. For this reason, we must begin with Egbert. Unfortunately, his supremacy did not long survive his death, and the authority of his immediate descendants, the great Alfred included, was more or less confined to Wessex. It was not until more than a century after Egbert's death that the monarchy was properly established in England under King Athelstan.

KING EGBERT

FATHER: *Ealhmund, King of Kent.*
He was the son of Eafa of Wessex by a Kentish princess, whose identity is unknown. Ealhmund is known to have been reigning in Kent in 784 or 786. He died in 786 (?).
MOTHER: *Unknown.*
SIBLINGS: *St Alburga*
She was either the daughter of Ealhmund by his unknown wife, or the daughter of that wife by another husband. She is called the half-sister of Egbert.

Alburga married Wulfstan, who was perhaps Ealdorman of Wiltshire. Upon her widowhood, she entered her husband's religious foundation at Wilton, which she is said to have converted into a nunnery. She died and was buried there in c.800 or c.810.

Egbert did not have any brothers.

EGBERT
He was born around 769/80. He became "Subregulus" of Kent in 790/96, and succeeded Beorhtric as King of Wessex in 802. There is no record of his coronation. From 825 onwards, he had established his supremacy over all other rulers in England, and was effective overlord of all the south-eastern kingdoms. In 829, he succeeded Wiglaf as King of Mercia, although he was expelled the following year.

3

Egbert married (although no record exists of the date or the place):
Redburga

She is said to have been the sister of the King of the Franks (who, at that time, was Charlemagne), but her identity is uncertain, and hardly anything is known about her.

Issue of marriage:

1 *King Ethelwulf (see below).*

2 *Athelstan*

He became "Subregulus" of Kent, Essex, Sussex and Surrey in 839, and also reigned as King of East Anglia. He died in c.851.

Athelstan married a lady about whom no information exists, and had issue:

(i) *Ethelweard*

He was "Subregulus" of Kent. He died, probably unmarried, in 850.

3 *Edith*

She became a nun at Polesworth Abbey, Co. Warwick, where she later became Abbess. She died and was buried there, but the year is not recorded.

EGBERT

He died on 4th February (or after c.June), 839, and was buried in Winchester Cathedral. His bones are now in one of the mortuary chests there.

He was succeeded by his son Ethelwulf.

KING ETHELWULF

FATHER: *Egbert, King of Wessex (see page 3).*
MOTHER: *Redburga (see above, under King Egbert).*
SIBLINGS: *(see above, under King Egbert).*

ETHELWULF

He was born around 795/810. He became "Subregulus" of Kent, Essex, Sussex and Surrey in 825 or 828, and succeeded his father as King of Wessex on 4th February, 839. He was crowned, probably that same year, at Kingston-upon-Thames, Surrey. In 855/6, he resigned Wessex to his son Ethelbald, and confined his own authority to Kent, Sussex and Essex as "Subregulus".

Ethelwulf married firstly, in c.830 (although no record exists as to where):

Osburga

She was the daughter of Oslac of Hampshire or the Isle of Wight. She died in 846 or 852/5. (Osburga has sometimes been confused by historians with St Osburga, foundress of Coventry Abbey, who died c.1018).

Issue of marriage:

1 *Athelstan* (?)

Although some sources cite Athelstan as Ethelwulf's eldest son, he has almost certainly been confused with Athelstan, son of King Egbert, as the details of his life are identical. It is therefore improbable that Ethelwulf actually had a son called Athelstan.

2 *King Ethelbald (see page 6).*

3 *King Ethelbert (see page 7).*

4 *King Ethelred I (see page 8).*

5 *King Alfred (see page 9).*

6 *Ethelswitha*

She married, after 2nd April, 853 (or 854/5), Burgred, King of Mercia (d.874) at the Palace of Chippenham, Wiltshire. Shortly after her widowhood in 874, she became a nun. She went on a pilgrimage to Rome in 888/9, but died in Paris on the way there. She was buried at either Pavia or Ticino in Italy.

Ethelwulf married secondly, on 1st or 15th October, 856, at Verberie sur Oise, France:

Judith

She was the daughter of Charles I, King of the Franks, by Ermentrude, daughter of Odo, Count of Orléans. She was born in c.843/4, and was crowned Queen of Wessex on her wedding day.

In 860, she married secondly, her stepson, King Ethelbald (see page 6), at Chester, but the marriage was annulled that same year on grounds of consanguinity. She had no issue from either of these marriages.

In c.863, she married thirdly, Baldwin I, Count of Flanders (d.c.879), at Auxerre, France, and had issue:
1 Charles (died young).
2 Baldwin II, Count of Flanders (d.918), who married Elfrida of Wessex (see page 10, under King Alfred), and had issue. One of their descendants was Matilda, wife of William I.
3 Rudolf, Count and Abbot of Cambrai.
4 Gunhilda, who married Wilfred I, Count of Barcelona (d.897).
Judith's date of death is not known.

ETHELWULF
He died on 13th January (or late in the year), 858, and was buried in Winchester Cathedral.
He was succeeded by his son Ethelbald.

KING ETHELBALD

FATHER: *Ethelwulf, King of Wessex (see page 4)*.
MOTHER: *Osburga (see page 5, under King Ethelwulf)*.
SIBLINGS: *(see page 5, under King Ethelwulf)*.

ETHELBALD
He was born in c.834. He succeeded his father as King of Wessex on 13th January (or late in the year), 858, and was crowned soon afterwards at Kingston-upon-Thames, Surrey.
Ethelbald married, in 860 (although no record exists as to where):
Judith
    She was his father's widow, and the marriage was frowned upon. It was annulled that same year. There was no issue from it.
(Judith's details are given on pages 5 to 6, under King Ethelwulf).

ETHELBALD

He died on 20th December, 860, and was buried in Sherborne Abbey, Dorset.

He was succeeded by his brother Ethelbert.

KING ETHELBERT

FATHER: *Ethelwulf, King of Wessex (see page 4).*
MOTHER: *Osburga (see page 5, under King Ethelwulf).*
SIBLINGS: *(see page 5, under King Ethelwulf).*

ETHELBERT

He was born in c.836. He became "Subregulus" of Kent in 853 or 855, and succeeded his brother Ethelbald as King of Wessex on 20th December, 860. He was crowned soon afterwards at Kingston-upon-Thames, Surrey.

He died, unmarried and childless, in 865/6, and was buried in Sherborne Abbey, Dorset.

He was succeeded by his brother Ethelred.

ETHELRED I

FATHER: *Ethelwulf, King of Wessex (see page 4).*
MOTHER: *Osburga (see page 5, under King Ethelwulf).*
SIBLINGS: *(see page 5, under King Ethelwulf).*

ETHELRED I
He was born in c.840. He succeeded his brother Ethelbert as King of Wessex in 865/6, and was crowned shortly afterwards at Kingston-upon-Thames, Surrey.
Ethelred I married, in c.868 (although no record exists as to where): (?)*Wulfrida*
Nothing is known of her origin or dates.
Issue of marriage:
1 *Ethelwald*
He was born in c.868, and set himself up as King of York and Pretender to the throne of Wessex in 901, after the death of his uncle, King Alfred. He was killed defending his claims in 902/5 at the Battle of the Holm.

Ethelwald married a professed nun from Wimborne Minster, Dorset; her name is unknown.
2 *Ethelhelm*
He is perhaps to be identified with:
a) an Ealdorman of Wiltshire, or
b) an Archbishop of Canterbury who was consecrated in 919 and who died on 8th January, 923.

There is, unfortunately, no conclusive evidence to support either theory. It is possible that Ethelhelm died in 898.

ETHELRED I
He was killed on 23rd April (after Easter), 871, at the Battle of Merton, and was buried at Wimborne Minster, Dorset, although

some less reliable sources give his place of burial as Sherborne Abbey, Dorset. After his death, he was popularly reputed a saint.

He was succeeded by his brother Alfred.

KING ALFRED

FATHER: *Ethelwulf, King of Wessex (see page 4).*
MOTHER: *Osburga (see page 5, under King Ethelwulf).*
SIBLINGS: *(see page 5, under King Ethelwulf).*

ALFRED
Known as "the Great", he was born in 846/9 at Wantage, Dorset. He succeeded his brother Ethelred I as King of Wessex and Danish Mercia on 23rd April, 871, and was perhaps crowned at Kingston-upon-Thames, Surrey, although this is mere supposition, as there is no evidence for it.

Alfred married, in 868/9, at Winchester:
Ethelswitha

She was the daughter of Ethelred Mucel, Ealdorman of the Gainas (to be identified with Gainsborough, Lincolnshire?), by Edburga, a Princess of the Royal House of Mercia, perhaps the daughter of Coenwulf, King of Mercia, by his wife Elfrida.

After the death of King Alfred, Ethelswitha turned to religion, and became a nun at St Mary's Abbey, Winchester in c.901. She died in Winchester on 5th or 8th December, 905, and was buried there in St Mary's Abbey; her remains were later removed to Winchester Cathedral. After her death, she was popularly reputed a saint.

Issue of marriage:

1 *Ethelfleda*

Born c.869, she married Ethelred, Ealdorman of Mercia (d.911) in 886/7 (certainly by the end of 889), and had issue:

1 Elfwynn (904?—after 919).

Ethelfleda was recognised as Lady of the Mercians in 911, after the death of her husband. She died on 12th June, 918, at Tamworth, Staffordshire, and was buried in Gloucester Cathedral.

2 *Edmund*

No dates are recorded, but he was possibly the eldest son, born around 870, as he was crowned in the lifetime of his father, following a European precedent set by Charlemagne. Asser, King Alfred's biographer, says Edmund died in infancy.

3 *King Edward the Elder (see page 11).*

4 *Elfrida*

She married Baldwin II, Count of Flanders (d.918) between 893 and 899, and had issue:

1 Arnulf, Count of Flanders (d.964), who married Adela of Vermandois, and had issue. One of their descendants was Matilda of Flanders, wife of William I.
2 Adelulf, Count of Boulogne (d.933).
3 Daughter.
4 Daughter.

Elfrida died on 7th June, 929 (?), in Flanders, and was buried in St Peter's Abbey, Ghent.

5 *Ethelgiva*

She became a nun at Shaftesbury Abbey, Dorset, where she was elected the first Abbess in c.888. She died and was buried in Shaftesbury Abbey in c.896.

6 *Ethelweard*

Born c.880. Very little is known of his life. He died on 16th (?) or 26th October, 920/22.

Ethelweard married a lady about whom no information exists, and had issue:

(i) *Elfwine*
He was killed at the Battle of Brunanburgh in 937, and was buried in Malmesbury Abbey, Wilts.

(ii) *Ethelwine*
He was killed at the Battle of Brunanburgh in 937, and was buried in Malmesbury Abbey, Wilts.

(iii) *Thurcytel*
Born c.907, he became a monk at his own foundation at Croyland Abbey, Lincs. in c.946, and was later elected Abbot there. He died on 12th July, 975 at Croyland Abbey, and was buried there.

KING ALFRED

He died on 25th, 26th or 28th October, 899, and was buried in Newminster Abbey, Winchester. His remains were later removed to Hyde Abbey, Winchester, which was destroyed during the Reformation. The present site of his grave is unknown. His bones may possibly lie in one of the mortuary chests in Winchester Cathedral.

He was succeeded by his son Edward.

Recommended reading

The best biography, because it was written by a contemporary, is Asser's *Life of King Alfred*; the last edition, by D. Whitelock, was published in 1959 (Dent).

Eleanor Duckett's *Alfred the Great and his England* (Collins, 1957) is a good modern appraisal.

KING EDWARD THE ELDER

FATHER: *King Alfred (see page 9).*
MOTHER: *Ethelswitha (see page 9, under King Alfred).*
SIBLINGS: *(see page 9, under King Alfred).*

KING EDWARD

Known as "the Elder", he was born in c.871/2. He succeeded his father as King of Wessex on 25th, 26th or 28th October, 899, and was crowned on 31st May or 8th June, 900 at Kingston-upon-Thames, Surrey.

Edward married firstly (although no record exists of the date or the place):

11

Egwina

She is described as "a noblewoman", although her origins are unknown. William of Malmesbury, writing in the 12th century, states that her children were illegitimate, thereby suggesting that her marriage to Edward was uncanonical, but this is unlikely in view of the fact that her son succeeded Edward as undisputed king. She died in c.901/2.

Issue of marriage:

1 *King Athelstan* *(see page 15)*.

2 *Alfred*

No dates are recorded, and very little is known about him. He may have died young.

3 *St Edith*

She married Sihtric Caoch, King of Northumbria (d.927) on 30th January, 925/6 at Tamworth, Staffordshire. After her widowhood, she became a nun at Polesworth Abbey, Warwickshire in 927. That same year, she was transferred to Tamworth Abbey, Gloucestershire, where she was immediately elected Abbess. She died in c.927. After her death, she was canonised, and her Feast Day is 15th July.

Edward married secondly, in c.901/2 (although no record exists as to where):

Elfleda

She was the daughter of Ealdorman Ethelhelm by his wife Elswitha. She died in 920, and was buried in Winchester Cathedral.

Issue of marriage:

1 *Edwin*

He was perhaps "Subregulus" of Kent. In 933, he drowned in the English Channel, perhaps murdered on the orders of his half-brother, King Athelstan. He was buried in St Bertin's Abbey, Flanders.

2 *Elfweard*

Information about Elfweard is conflicting. One source states he married and had children, but gives no details. Another source, less trustworthy, states he was a hermit at Bridgenorth, Salop. What is certain is that he died on 1st August, 924 at Oxford, and was buried in Winchester Cathedral.

3 *Edfleda*

No dates are recorded. She was a nun, but her community is not named: it was perhaps Winchester. She was buried in Wilton Abbey, Wiltshire.

4 Edgiva *(or Ogive)*

She married Charles III, King of France (d.929) between 916 and 919, and had issue:

1 Louis IV, King of France (921?–954), who married Gerberga (d.984), daughter of Henry the Fowler of Saxony, Holy Roman Emperor, and had issue.

Edgiva married secondly, Heribert III, Count of Vermandois, Meaux, and Troyes (d.995) in c.951 at St Quentin, France, and had issue:

2 Stephen I, Count of Vermandois (b.952?–1021).

3 Agnes (b.953).

Edgiva died in c.953, perhaps in childbirth. Some sources state she died in 948, in which case her second marriage took place earlier than is generally supposed.

5 Edhilda

She married Hugh Capet, Count of Paris and Duke of the French (d.956) in 926/7, and had issue:

1 Hugh, King of France (938?–996), who married Adelaide (d.1004/5), daughter of William, Duke of Aquitaine, and had issue.

Edhilda died on 26th January, 947. (Some sources state she died in c.938, or even earlier, but this is improbable.)

6 Edith

She married Otto I, Duke of Saxony and German Emperor (d.973) in c.925/30, and had issue:

1 Liudolf, Duke of Swabia (d.957), who married Ida, daughter of Hermann, Duke of Almayne, Swabia, and had issue.

2 Liutgarde, married Conrad, Duke of Lorraine.

Edith died on 26th January, c.946/7 in Germany, and was buried in the Cathedral of St Maurice, Magdeburg.

7 Elfleda

She became a nun at Winchester, where she died in c.963. She was buried in Wilton Abbey, Wilts.

8 Elgiva

No dates are recorded. She married "a Prince near the Alps". He has recently been identified, with near certainty, as Boleslaw II, Duke of Bohemia (d.999). Other, less probable, identifications have been made with Conrad III, King of Burgundy (d.993); Alberic, son of Majolus, Count of Narbonne; and Charles Constantine, King of Arles, son of either the Emperor Louis the Blind or Louis II, King of Arles.

9 *Ethelfleda*

No dates are recorded. She was perhaps a nun at Romsey Abbey, Hampshire, and may have been elected Abbess of Romsey, where she was later buried.

10 *Ethelhilda*

No dates are recorded. She was a lay sister or recluse at Romsey Abbey, Hampshire. She was buried in Wilton Abbey, Wiltshire.

Edward married thirdly, in 920 (?) (although no record exists of the date or the place):

Edgiva

She was the daughter of Sigehelm, Ealdorman of Kent, and she was born before c.905. She died on 25th August, 968, and was buried in Canterbury Cathedral.

Issue of marriage:

1 *Edmund I* *(see page 16)*.

2 *St Edburga*

She became a nun at Nunnaminster Abbey, Winchester; she was possibly elected Abbess, but this is unlikely. She died on 15th June, 960, and was buried in Nunnaminster Abbey. After her canonisation, her remains were translated to Pershore Abbey, Worcs.

3 *Edgiva*

She was married in infancy to "Louis of Aquitaine, King of Arles", before 923. Her husband has not been successfully identified. He may have been Louis II, King of Arles, in which case the issue of the marriage may have been:

1 Charles Constantine, King of Arles (whose parentage is uncertain).

Louis may also be identified, with less credibility, with Louis the Blind, King of Lower Burgundy and Holy Roman Emperor (d.928). Some authorities cite Ebehard, Count of Nordgau (d.c.960) as the husband of Edgiva.

4 *King Edred* *(see page 17)*.

5 *Thyra*

She is said to have been a daughter of Edward by Edgiva, but there is some doubt about this. No dates are recorded. She married Gorm the Old, king in North Jutland, and had issue:

1 Harold I, King of Denmark (d.986), who also married and had issue.

Edward is also reputed to have had the following illegitimate issue, although this is in dispute:

1 Gregory, Abbot of Einsiedlen in Germany.

KING EDWARD THE ELDER
He died on 17th July, 924/5 at Farndon-on-Dee, and was buried in Winchester Cathedral.
    He was succeeded by his son Athelstan.

Recommended reading
The Chronology of the Reign of Edward the Elder by W. S. Angus (in *English Historical Review*, vol. 53, 1938). This is the only work on this king.

KING ATHELSTAN

FATHER: *King Edward the Elder (see page 11).*
MOTHER: *Egwina (see page 12, under King Edward the Elder).*
SIBLINGS: *(see page 12, under King Edward the Elder).*

ATHELSTAN
He was born in c.895. He succeeded his father as the first King of a united England on 17th July, 924/5, and was crowned on 4th September, 924/5 at Kingston-upon-Thames, Surrey. The monarchy in England may be said to have been properly established under King Athelstan. Athelstan never married, and had no issue. He died on 27th October, 939, at Gloucester, and was buried in Malmesbury Abbey, Wiltshire (his tomb dates only from the fifteenth century).
    He was succeeded by his half-brother Edmund.

EDMUND I

FATHER: *King Edward the Elder (see page 11).*
MOTHER: *Edgiva of Kent (see page 14, under King Edward the Elder).*
SIBLINGS: *(see page 14, under King Edward the Elder).*

EDMUND I
Known as "the Magnificent", he was born in c.920/22. He succeeded his half-brother King Athelstan as King of England on 27th October, 939, and was crowned on 29th November, 939 at Kingston-upon-Thames, Surrey. From 944 onwards, he was the effective ruler of the whole of England until his death.
Edmund I married firstly, in c.940 (although no record exists as to where):
St Elgiva
Her origins are unknown. She died in c.944 or 946 at Shaftesbury Abbey, Dorset, where she was probably buried (or, less probably, at Shipton Abbey). She has sometimes, erroneously, been described as Abbess of Wilton. After her death, she was popularly reputed a saint.
Issue of marriage:
1 *King Edwy (see page 18).*
2 *King Edgar (see page 19).*
3 *Daughter (name not known), who married Baldwin, Count of Hesdin.*
Edmund I married secondly, in c.946:
Ethelfleda
She was the daughter of Alfgar, Ealdorman of the Wilsaetas (Wiltshire?), and was perhaps born at Damerham, Wiltshire. After Edmund's death, she perhaps married secondly Athelstan, an Ealdorman. She later became a nun at Shaftesbury Abbey, Dorset,

where she died after 975, when her Will was dated. She was buried in Shaftesbury Abbey.

EDMUND I
He was murdered on 26th May, 946 at Pucklechurch, Dorset, when an outlaw named Liofa stabbed him whilst he was dining in his hall. He was buried in Glastonbury Abbey, Somerset.

He was succeeded by his brother Edred.

Recommended reading
King Edmund I and the Danes of York by M. L. R. Beaven (in *English Historical Review* vol. 33, 1918).

KING EDRED

FATHER: *King Edward the Elder (see page 11).*
MOTHER: *Edgiva of Kent (see page 14, under King Edward the Elder).*
SIBLINGS: *(see page 14, under King Edward the Elder).*

KING EDRED
He was born in c.923/5, and succeeded his brother Edmund I as King of England on 26th May, 946. He was crowned on 16th August, 946 at Kingston-upon-Thames, Surrey. He expelled the Danes from England in 954, thereupon establishing his authority throughout England.

One authority states that Edred had issue, but gives no details. I have found no other evidence to support this. There is no record of his having been married.

KING EDRED

He died on 23rd November, 955 at Frome, Somerset, and was buried in Winchester Cathedral. His bones are now in one of the mortuary chests there.

He was succeeded by his nephew Edwy.

KING EDWY

FATHER: *Edmund I (see page 16).*
MOTHER: *St Elgiva (see page 16, under Edmund I).*
SIBLINGS: *(see page 16, under Edmund I).*

KING EDWY

Known as "the Fair", he was born in c.941/3 (certainly before 943). He succeeded his uncle King Edred as King of England on 23rd November, 955, and was crowned at Kingston-upon-Thames c.26th January, 956. He was a weak king, and his authority was confined to Wessex from 958, his younger brother Edgar taking over the government of Northumbria and Mercia.

Edwy married, during the winter of 955/6 (although no record exists as to where):

Elgiva

Her father is unknown; her mother, Ethelgiva, of unknown origin, is said by some sources to have been Edwy's mistress. The marriage was certainly frowned upon by the Church. Late sources state that it was annulled around 958, and that Elgiva was banished from court, possibly to Ireland, but these sources may be too late to be reliable. Elgiva died around September, 959, at Gloucester.

KING EDWY

He died on 1st October, 959, at Gloucester, and was buried in Winchester Cathedral.

He was succeeded by his brother Edgar.

KING EDGAR

FATHER: *Edmund I (see page 16).*
MOTHER: *St Elgiva (see page 16, under Edmund I).*
SIBLINGS: *(see page 16, under Edmund I).*

KING EDGAR

Known as "the Peaceable", he was born in 942/4. He took over the government of Northumbria and Mercia from his brother King Edwy in 958, and was styled King of those realms from that date. He succeeded Edwy on 1st October, 959, but was not crowned until 11th May, 973, as St Dunstan, the Archbishop of Canterbury, would not agree to crown Edgar until he amended his way of life. The coronation, which took place in Bath Abbey, followed the new form of service devised by St Dunstan and based on European models. This is the form of Coronation Rite used, with modifications, in the 20th century.

Edgar married firstly, in c.961/2 (although no record exists as to where):

Ethelfleda

Known as "the Fair", she was the daughter of Ealdorman Ordmaer by his wife Ealda. Later sources allege that she was divorced by Edgar in c.964, so that he could marry his second wife, but this is probably a fabrication, and it is likely that Ethelfleda died in c.962/4, probably by 965 (although one unreliable source gives the date of her death as 972/3). She was buried in Wilton Abbey, Wiltshire, where she is said to have retired after her alleged divorce.

Issue of marriage:

1 *King Edward the Martyr (see page 21).*

Edgar married secondly, in c.964/5 (perhaps earlier) (although no record exists as to where):

Elfrida

Alternatively known as Alstrita or Elstrudis, she was the daughter of Ordgar, Ealdorman of Devon. She was born in c.945 at Lydford Castle, Devon. She married firstly, in c.962/3, Ethelwald, Ealdorman of East Anglia (d.963), and had issue:

1 Edgar.
2 (?) Ethelfleda (963?–1016?), Abbess of Romsey. She may have been Ethelwald's daughter by his first wife, although one account says she was his posthumous child.

Elfrida is said to have had an adulterous affair with King Edgar whilst still married to Ethelwald, and some sources allege that Ethelwald was murdered on Edgar's orders. Elfrida was crowned with her husband on 11th May, 973 at Bath Abbey: this was the first instance of the coronation of a Queen of England. She became a nun in c.986 at Wherwell Abbey, Hampshire, where she died, possibly on 17th November, 1002 (?); she was alive in 999, but had died before the end of 1002. She was probably buried in Wherwell Abbey.

Issue of marriage:

1 *Edmund*
He was born in c.965, and died in 970/72. He was buried in Romsey Abbey, Hampshire.

2 *Ethelred II (see page 22).*

King Edgar also had the following **illegitimate issue**:
By St Wulfrida (c.945–1000), Abbess of Wilton,
1 St Edith (962?–984), Abbess of Barking and Nunnaminster.

KING EDGAR

He died on 8th July, 975 at Winchester, and was buried in Glastonbury Abbey, Somerset.

He was succeeded by his son Edward.

Recommended reading

The Great Commendation of King Edgar by W. H. Stevenson (in *English Historical Review*, vol. 13, 1898).

The King and the Monks in the Tenth Century Reformation by E. John (in the *Bulletin of the John Rylands Library*, xlii, 1959/60).

KING EDWARD THE MARTYR

FATHER: *King Edgar (see page 19).*
MOTHER: *Ethelfleda (see page 19, under King Edgar).*
SIBLINGS: *Edward did not have any full brothers or sisters.*

KING EDWARD

Known as "the Martyr", he was born in c.962/3. He succeeded his father as King of England on 8th July, 975, and was crowned at Kingston-upon-Thames that same year (the date is unspecified). He was murdered on 18th March, 978 (not 979, as is sometimes stated), at Corfe Castle, Dorset, probably on the orders of his stepmother, Elfrida of Devon. He was buried in Wareham Abbey, Dorset; later on, his remains were moved to Shaftesbury Abbey, Dorset.

He was succeeded by his half-brother Ethelred.

Recommended reading
C. E. Fell's *Edward, King and Martyr* (1971) is the only biography on this monarch.

ETHELRED II

FATHER: *King Edgar (see page 19).*
MOTHER: *Elfrida of Devon (see page 20, under King Edgar).*
SIBLINGS: *(see page 20, under King Edgar).*

ETHELRED II

Known as "the Unraed" or "the Redeless" (both of which mean "without counsel"), he was born in c.966/9. He succeeded his half-brother Edward as King of England on 18th March, 978, and was crowned on 4th April, 978 (or 4th May, 979) at Kingston-upon-Thames, Surrey. He abdicated in favour of King Sweyn in the autumn of 1013, and fled to Normandy, but was restored to the throne after Sweyn's death on 3rd February, 1014.

Ethelred II married firstly, in c.980/85 (although no record exists as to where):

Elgiva

Alternatively known as Elfleda, she was the daughter either of Ealdorman Ethelbert, or of Thored, Ealdorman of York, by his wife Hilda. She was born in c.963, and died in February, 1002, at Winchester.

Issue of marriage:

1 *Athelstan*

He was born in c.986, and was killed in battle, fighting the Danes, in c.1012/15. One writer, Thietmar of Merseberg, states that Athelstan was alive late in 1016, but he is an unreliable source, and it is thought that Athelstan was almost certainly dead by the end of 1015.

2 *Edmund II* (see page 27).

3 *Edgar*

He died in 1012/15 (or, less probably, in c.1008).

4 *Edred*

He died in 1012/15.

5 *Edric (?)*

He has perhaps been confused with his brother Edred, and may not have existed. No dates are recorded.

6 *Edward (?)*

He is said to have died by c.1004. The evidence for his existence is very slender; charters said to have been attested by him have been proved spurious.

7 *Edwy*

He was murdered in 1017 on the orders of King Canute, and was buried in Tavistock Abbey, Devon.

8 *Egbert*

He died in c.1005.

9 *Edith*

She married Edric Streona, Ealdorman of Mercia (who was executed in 1017) in c.1007/9, and had issue:

1 Son; name not known (born before 1009).

Edith perhaps married secondly Thurcytel Thorgils Havi, a Danish Earl in England (who was killed in 1039), and perhaps had issue:

2 Harold, who married Gunhilda of Wendland, a granddaughter of King Sweyn. Harold died in 1042.

10 *Elgiva*

She married Uhtred, Earl of Northumbria (who was killed in 1016 or 1018), and had issue:

1 Edith (see page 178, under Malcolm II, King of Scotland). She married Maldred of Scotland, Lord of Allerdale, and had issue.

11 *Wulfhilda*

She married Ulfcytel Snylling, Ealdorman of East Anglia (who was killed in 1016).

12 *Daughter*

Her name is not known. She married one Athelstan (who was killed in 1010).

13 *Daughter*

Her name is not known. She became Abbess of Wherwell, and died after 1051.

Ethelred II married secondly, on 5th April, 1002, at Winchester Cathedral:

Emma

She was the daughter of Richard I, Duke of Normandy, by his wife Gunnora, and she was born in c.985/7 in Normandy. In 1017, after the death of Ethelred II, she married secondly King Canute, and had issue (see page 29, under King Canute). She died on 14th March, 1052, probably at Winchester, and was buried in Winchester Cathedral. Her bones now lie in one of the mortuary chests there.

Issue of marriage:

1 *King Edward the Confessor* (see page 33).

2 *Alfred*

Born before 1012, he was styled "Atheling". He was brutally murdered on 5th February, 1037 (or, less probably, 1036) at Ely, Cambridgeshire, probably on the orders of Earl Godwine (see page 34, under Harold II). He was buried in Ely Cathedral.

3 *Goda*

Alternatively known as Godgifu, she was born between 1004 and 1014. She married firstly Drogo (or Dreux), Count of Mantes and the Vexin (d.1035), and had issue:

1 Ralph, Earl of Hereford (d.1057), who married Gytha, perhaps the daughter of Osgood Clapa, and had issue.

2 Walter III, Count of Mantes and the Vexin (d. after 1063), who married Biota, daughter of Herbert, Count of Maine.

3 Fulk, Bishop of Amiens (1030–1058).

Goda married secondly Eustace II, Count of Boulogne (d.1093) in c.1036. It is possible that there was a child of this union, probably a daughter who married and had issue. The only evidence pointing to this is the fact that Eustace of Boulogne had a grandson who was given as hostage to William I in 1067.

Goda was dead by 1049.

ETHELRED II

He died on 23rd April, 1016 in London, and was buried in Old St Paul's Cathedral, London. His tomb was lost in the Great Fire of 1666.

He was succeeded by his son Edmund.

Recommended reading

There is no biography, as is the case with most Anglo-Saxon monarchs. The best work on the reign is:

English and Norse Documents relating to the Reign of Ethelred the Unready edited by M. Ashdown (1930).

KING SWEYN

FATHER: *Harold Bluetooth, King of Denmark.*
MOTHER: *Gunhilda, first wife of Harold, or Cyrid, his second wife, or Aesa, his concubine.*
SIBLINGS:
Thyra
She married Thorgils Sprakalegg, and had issue:
1 Gytha, mother of Harold II (see page 34).

KING SWEYN

Known as "Forkbeard", he was born in c.960 in Denmark. He succeeded his father as King of Denmark on 1st November, 986. He is said by some sources to have been deposed in 987 and restored in 1000. He usurped the throne of England in the autumn of 1013, having defeated and deposed Ethelred II; he claimed the throne by right of conquest, but had no dynastic claim to it. He was never crowned.

Sweyn married firstly, in c.990 (although no record exists as to where):
Gunhilda
She was probably the daughter of Mjeczislas I, Duke of Poland, by Dubrawka, daughter of Boleslaw I, Duke of Bohemia, or, less probably, the daughter of Boleslaw, King of Wendland. Sweyn later divorced her, probably before 1000. She died in c.1015. One source gives the date of her death as 992, but this must be wrong.
Issue of marriage:
1 *Harold*
He was born in c.994 in Denmark. He succeeded his father as King of Denmark on 3rd February, 1014, and died in 1018/19.
2 *King Canute (see page 29).*
The following were possibly the children of Gunhilda, although they may have been the issue of Sweyn by his second wife (see below):

25

3 Gytha

She married Erik Hakonson, a Danish Earl in England, and Earl of Hlathir in Norway in 1013, and had issue:

1 Haakon, Earl of Worcester (d.1029/30), who married Gunhilda, daughter of Wytgeorn, King of Wendland (see below).

4 Santslaue

Alternatively called Svantoslava, she was born and died in Denmark. No dates are recorded.

5 Thyra

She is said to have been born in c.993 in Denmark—probably the eldest child of Sweyn and Gunhilda, although this is open to doubt. She married Godwine, later Earl of Wessex (see page 34, under Harold II), and had issue, but no details of them are recorded. She died in 1018.

6 Daughter

Her name is not known. She married Wytgeorn, King of Wendland, and had issue:

1 Gunhilda; she married firstly Haakon, Earl of Worcester (d.1029/30) (see above), and secondly, Harold (d.1042), son of Edith, the daughter of Ethelred II.

Sweyn married secondly, probably before 1000 (although no record exists as to where):

Sigrid

Alternatively known as Sigrith or Syritha, and called "the Haughty", she was the daughter of Skogul Toste of Sweden, and was born in Sweden. She married firstly Eric VI, King of Sweden, (d.995), and had issue:

1 Olaf Svenski, King of Sweden (d.1022), who married a lady called Astrid, and had issue.

One source gives the date of Sigrid's death as 995, but this is impossible. It is likely that she died before 1013, as she has never been referred to as Queen of England.

Issue of marriage:

1 Astrid

Alternatively called Estrith, or Margaret. She married either Richard II, Duke of Normandy (d.1027) or Robert II, Duke of Normandy (see page 39, under William I) between 1017 and 1027. If her husband was Robert, then he repudiated her shortly after the marriage took place. She married secondly Ulf Thorgilson, a Danish Earl in England (d.1035; he was the brother of Gytha, mother of Harold II), and had issue:

1 Sweyn Estrithson, King of Denmark (d.1074/6), who married a lady called Gunhilda. He left illegitimate issue only.
2 Beorn, Earl of Danish Mercia. He was murdered in 1049.
3 Osbeorn (d.1086?).

Sigrid may also have been the mother of Sweyn's four other daughters (see above).

KING SWEYN

He died on 3rd February, 1014, at Gainsborough, Lincs., and was buried in England (location unknown). His remains were later moved to Roeskild Cathedral, Denmark.

He was succeeded by Ethelred II (see preceding chapter), who was in turn succeeded by Edmund, the son of Ethelred.

EDMUND II

FATHER: *Ethelred II (see page 22).*
MOTHER: *Elgiva (see page 22, under Ethelred II).*
SIBLINGS: *(see page 22, under Ethelred II).*

EDMUND II

Known as "Ironside", he was born between c.988 and 993. He succeeded his father as King of England on 23rd April, 1016, and was crowned during the same month at Old St Paul's Cathedral in London.

Edmund II married, in late summer (August?), 1015, at Malmesbury, Wiltshire:
Edith
Her origins are unknown. She married firstly Sigeferth (son of Earngrim), a Thane in East Anglia (he was murdered in 1015). The date of her death is not known.

Issue of marriage (who may have been twins):

1 Edward

He was born in 1016: he was aged 41 at his death. He was styled "Atheling", but spent the greater part of his youth in exile in Hungary. He died in 1057, in London, where he was buried in Old St Paul's Cathedral.

Edward married (no record exists of the date), in Hungary:

Agatha

She was probably the daughter of Bruno, Bishop of Augsburg and brother of Henry III, Emperor of Germany. With less probability, she was the daughter of Stephen, King of Hungary, by Gisela, daughter of Conrad II, Emperor of Germany, and sister of the Emperor Henry III. She is described as "a kinswoman" of the Emperor Henry III. Upon reaching old age, she became a nun at Newcastle-upon-Tyne, probably after the death of her daughter, Queen Margaret of Scotland, in 1093.

Issue of marriage:

(i) *Edgar*

He was born in c.1053 (certainly by 1058) in Hungary, and was styled "Atheling". In October, 1066, the Witan in London elected him King of England upon hearing of the death of Harold II at Hastings. He was not crowned, and by December, 1066, he had submitted to William I and abandoned all claims to the throne. He died after 1125, perhaps in 1130 (?).

(ii) *Margaret*

(See page 185, under Malcolm III, King of Scotland).

(iii) *Christina*

Born in Hungary, she became a nun, firstly—according to some authorities—at Wilton Abbey, Wiltshire, and then, in c.1086, at Romsey Abbey in Hampshire. She is sometimes called Abbess of Romsey, but only on very slender evidence. She died before 1102 (?).

2 Edmund

He was born either in 1016, or in 1017. He was taken to Hungary by his family in childhood, where he later died. Some sources state that he died young, but he must have lived at least into his teens.

Edmund married (no record exists of the date) in Hungary:

Hedwig

She was either the daughter of Stephen I, King of Hungary, by Gisela, daughter of Conrad II, Emperor of Germany, or the daughter of Henry II, Duke of Bavaria.

After Edmund's death, she married secondly Eppo, Count of Nellenburg.

EDMUND II

He died on 30th November, 1016, in Oxford or in London, and was buried in Glastonbury Abbey, Somerset.

He was succeeded by Canute, son of King Sweyn, who claimed the throne by right of conquest.

KING CANUTE

FATHER: *King Sweyn (see page 25).*
MOTHER: *Gunhilda of Poland (see page 25, under King Sweyn).*
SIBLINGS: *(see page 25, under King Sweyn).*

KING CANUTE

Alternatively called Cnut or Knud, and known as "the Great", he was born in c.995 in Denmark. He succeeded Edmund II as King of England on 30th November, 1016, claiming the throne by right of conquest, and is said to have been crowned on 6th January (?), 1017, at Old St Paul's Cathedral in London, although there is no contemporary evidence for this. He succeeded his brother Harold as King of Denmark in 1018/19, and became King of Norway by right of conquest in 1028.

Canute married, on 2nd July, 1017 (although no record exists as to where):

Emma

She was the widow of Ethelred II (see page 23, under Ethelred II).

Issue of marriage:

1 *King Harthacanute (see page 31).*

29

2 *Gunhilda*

Alternatively called Ethelfrida, she adopted the name Kunigunde upon her marriage. Born in c.1020, she married Henry III, Emperor of Germany (d.1056) on 10th June, 1036, at Nimeguen, Germany, and had issue:

1 Beatrice (b.1037), Abbess of Quedlinburg.

Gunhilda died on 16th or 18th July, 1038, on the Adriatic coast.

3 *Daughter*

Her name is not known, neither are her dates. She died aged about 8, and was buried in Bosham Church, Sussex.

Canute also had the following **illegitimate issue**:

By Elgiva (996?–1044?), daughter of Alfhelm, Ealdorman of Northampton, by his wife Wulfrun; some sources state that Elgiva was Canute's "handfast" wife, according to Danish custom; others state that she was his repudiated wife; at all events, their union was uncanonical. They had issue:

1 Sweyn, King of Norway (1015?–1036/7).

2 Harold I (see page 32).

There were contemporary doubts in certain court circles that Canute was the father of Elgiva's two sons.

KING CANUTE

He died on 12th November, 1035 at Shaftesbury, Dorset, and was buried in Winchester Cathedral. His bones now lie in one of the mortuary chests there.

He was succeeded by his son Harthacanute.

Recommended reading

Although it has long been out of print, the most useful book is:

L. M. Larson: *Canute the Great and the Rise of Danish Imperialism* (1912).

G. N. Garmonsway's *Canute and his Empire* (1964) is also a good biography.

KING HARTHACANUTE

FATHER: *King Canute (see page 29).*
MOTHER: *Emma of Normandy (see page 29, under King Canute).*
SIBLINGS: *(see page 29, under King Canute).*

KING HARTHACANUTE

Alternatively called Hardicanute, he was born in c.1018, and was designated titular King of Denmark in 1028. He succeeded his father as King of Denmark on 12th November, 1035, and as King of England on the same day, in his absence from that country. He remained in Denmark, and his authority in England was usurped by his half-brother Harold I in 1037. He was restored to the English throne on 17th March, 1040, upon the death of Harold I. He is said to have been crowned in June, 1040 at Canterbury Cathedral, Kent, but no contemporary evidence exists to show that he was consecrated at all.

KING HARTHACANUTE

He died unmarried (and childless), on 8th June, 1042, at Lambeth in London, and was buried in Winchester Cathedral.

He was succeeded by his half-brother Edward, the son of Ethelred II.

HAROLD I

FATHER: *King Canute (?) (see pages 29 to 30).*
MOTHER: *Elgiva of Northampton, Canute's concubine or handfast wife.*
SIBLINGS: *(see page 30, under King Canute).*

HAROLD I

He was born in c.1016/17, perhaps at Northampton. He was probably illegitimate, but contemporary doubts as to his paternity were probably mere political propaganda. In 1037, when King Harthacanute was still in Denmark, Harold usurped the throne of England and was recognised as King, being crowned that same year at Oxford.

Harold I married (although no record exists of the date or the place):
Elgiva
 Her origins are unknown, as are her dates.

Issue of marriage:

1 *Elfwine*
 He was born in London, but no dates are recorded for his life. Some sources infer he was illegitimate, but they are unreliable. He became a monk at Sainte-Foi Abbey, Conques, Aquitaine, his own foundation.

HAROLD I

He died on 17th March, 1040, at Oxford, and was buried, according to a faint tradition, in the old Abbey Church of St Peter at Westminster. It is less probable that he was buried in Winchester Cathedral, as is sometimes stated. His body, after a dishonourable exhumation, was reburied, probably in St Clement Danes Church, Strand, London (less probably, in St Olave's Church, Southwark, London). He was succeeded by his half-brother Harthacanute, whom he had once deposed (see previous chapter), who, in turn, was succeeded by Edward, son of Ethelred II.

KING EDWARD THE CONFESSOR

FATHER: *Ethelred II (see page 22).*
MOTHER: *Emma of Normandy (see page 23, under Ethelred II).*
SIBLINGS: *(see page 24, under Ethelred II).*

KING EDWARD

Known as "the Confessor", he was born around c.1003/4 (by 1005) at Islip, Oxon. When he succeeded his half-brother King Harthacanute, on 8th June, 1042, the crown of England reverted from the usurping Danish dynasty to the line of Cerdic once more, and for the last time. Edward was crowned on 3rd April, 1043, at Winchester Cathedral.
King Edward married, on 23rd January, 1045 (although no record exists as to where).
Edith
She was the daughter of Godwine, Earl of Wessex, by his wife Gytha (see page 34, under Harold II), and she was born in c.1020. Edith was perhaps anointed and crowned on her wedding day, but details of the ceremony have not been recorded. Her marriage to Edward was purely platonic, the King being unwilling, for religious reasons, to consummate it, hence there were no children. Edith died on 18th December, 1075, either at the Palace of Westminster or at Winchester, and was buried in Westminster Abbey.

KING EDWARD

He died on 4th/5th January, 1066, at the Palace of Westminster, and was buried in the new Westminster Abbey, built by his command and only recently consecrated.
He was succeeded by Harold, Earl of Wessex, his brother-in-law, to whom he left his throne, with the support of the Witan, there being no adult claimant to the crown of the line of Cerdic.

33

On 7th February, 1161, Edward the Confessor was canonised, thus becoming the only King of England to be made a saint.

Recommended reading
The best work, and the most authoritative, is:
Frank Barlow: *Edward the Confessor* (Eyre and Spottiswoode, 1970).
See also:
Frank Barlow: *Edward the Confessor and the Norman Conquest* (Eyre and Spottiswoode, 1966).

HAROLD II

FATHER: *Godwine*
He was the son of Wulfnoth, Cyld of Sussex, and was born in c.987. He married firstly Thyra, daughter of King Sweyn, and secondly, in c.1019/20, Gytha (see below). He was first created Earl in 1018, but his earldom is unknown. He was created Earl of Wessex and Kent in 1020. He died on 15th April, 1053, at Winchester Castle, of apoplexy, and was buried in Winchester Cathedral.

MOTHER: *Gytha*
She was the daughter of Thorgils Sprakalegg by Thyra, daughter of Harold Bluetooth, King of Denmark (and sister of King Sweyn); some authorities state that Thorgils was the son of Thyra, not her husband. Gytha was born in Denmark. She married Earl Godwine in c.1019/20. She died in exile, perhaps in Flanders, after June, 1069.

SIBLINGS:
1 *Edith*
(See page 33, under King Edward the Confessor).

2 *Sweyn*

He was born in c.1023, and was created Earl of Mercia in 1043. He died on 29th September, 1052, in exile, at Lycia, near Constantinople, in Byzantium.

Sweyn had the following illegitimate issue:

By Edgiva, Abbess of Leominster, a nun whom he abducted and with whom he contracted an uncanonical marriage:

1 Haakon (b.1046/7).

2 Tostig.

3 *Tostig*

He was born in c.1026, and was created Earl of Northumbria in c.1055. In that year, or later, he was also created Earl of Northampton and Nottingham. He was deprived of his earldoms on 3rd October, 1065. He was killed on 25th September, 1066, at the Battle of Stamford Bridge in Northumberland, fighting his brother Harold II in alliance with Harold Hardraada, King of Norway. Tostig was buried in York Minster.

Tostig married, in October, 1051 (although no record exists as to where):

Judith

Alternatively known as Fausta, she was the daughter of Baldwin IV, Count of Flanders, by Eleanor, daughter of Richard II, Duke of Normandy. After Tostig's death, she married secondly Welf IV, Duke of Bavaria.

Issue of marriage:

(i) *Skule*

He grew up, married, and had issue. No further details are recorded.

(ii) *Ketel*

He grew up, married and had issue. No further details are recorded.

4 *Gyrth*

He was created Earl of East Anglia in 1057, and was killed on 14th October, 1066 at the Battle of Hastings, Sussex.

5 *Leofwine*

He was created Earl of Kent, Surrey, Middlesex, Hertfordshire and Buckinghamshire in c.1057, and was killed on 14th October, 1066 at the Battle of Hastings, Sussex.

6 *Wulfnoth*

He died after 1087, either in Normandy, or at Salisbury, Wiltshire.

7 *Alfgar*

He is said to have been a monk at Rheims in France.

8 *Edgiva*

Nothing is known of her beyond her name.

9 *Elgiva*

She died in c.1066.

10 *Gunhilda*

She is said to have become a nun, either at St Omer in France, or at Bruges in Flanders. She died on 24th August, 1087 at Bruges, and was buried in Bruges Cathedral.

HAROLD II

Surnamed Godwineson, he was born in c.1020/22. He was created Earl of East Anglia in c.1045, and succeeded his father as Earl of Wessex on 15th April, 1053. He was created Earl of Hereford in 1058, and styled "Duke of the English" from 1064. He succeeded Edward the Confessor as King of England on 6th January, 1066, having been chosen by the King as his successor with the support of the Witan. Harold II was crowned on 6th January, 1066, probably at St Paul's Cathedral in London (some authorities state he was crowned at Westminster Abbey, but there is no evidence for this).

Harold II married, either in c.1064 or in March (?), 1066, at York:
Edith

She was the daughter of Alfgar, Earl of Mercia, by Edgiva or Elgiva Malet, or by Elfleda, daughter of Ealdred, Earl of Northumbria. She was born in c.1042. She married firstly Gruffydd ap Llywelyn, King of Wales (killed in 1063), either in c.1050 or in c.1056/7, and had issue:

1 Meredith (d.1070).
2 Idwal (d.1070).
3 Nesta, who married Osbern FitzRichard, Lord of Richard's Castle and Byton, and had issue.

After the death of Harold, Edith went into exile on the Continent where she died after 1070.

Issue of marriage, who may have been twins:

1 *Harold*

He was born in December, 1066 in Chester. He grew up in exile on the Continent, and died after 1098.

2 *Ulf*

He was perhaps born in December, 1066 in Chester, although some authorities have stated that he was an illegitimate son of Harold by his mistress Edith Swanneshals (see below). Ulf is said by some chroniclers to have drowned at sea before 1070, but he is recorded as being alive in 1087 in Normandy, after which he disappears from the records.

Harold II also had the following **illegitimate issue**:
Probably by Edith Swanneshals ("Swan Neck"):
1 Godwine.
2 Edmund.
3 Magnus.
4 Gunhilda; she became a nun at Wilton Abbey, Wiltshire.
5 Gytha; she married Vladimir II, Prince of Novgorod and Kiev (d.1125), and had issue. One of her descendants was Philippa, wife of Edward III.
6 Ulf (see above). He may have been Harold's legitimate son by his wife.

HAROLD II

He was killed on 14th October, 1066 at the Battle of Hastings, Sussex. He was not felled by an arrow between his eyes—this popular myth has been perpetrated by a misreading of the Bayeux Tapestry. He was, in fact, struck down by a blow from a sword wielded by a mounted Norman knight. Harold was buried on the seashore at Hastings, or on the battlefield—the latter is more likely. A stone memorial marks the spot within the grounds of Battle Abbey. Later on, Harold's remains were removed to Waltham Abbey in Essex.

He was succeeded by William, Duke of Normandy, the victor of Hastings.

Recommended reading
   Harold, the last of the Saxon Kings by E. Lytton (1948; Dent, 1970).
See also:
   A Visit of Earl Harold to Flanders in 1056 by P. Grierson (in *English Historical Review*, li, 1956).

2. The Norman Kings of England

Harold II was the last of the Saxon Kings of England. His successor, William I, based his claim to the English throne upon a promise made to him more than a decade before 1066 by Edward the Confessor, who is said to have told William that he, Edward, would make him his successor.

In 1064, Earl Harold was shipwrecked upon the coast of Normandy. William kept him in honourable captivity until he had sworn upon holy relics to do all in his power to enforce William's claim to the English throne. William knew very well that at that time it seemed that Harold, the most powerful man in England next to the king, would be designated Edward's successor, which was what in fact happened. When, in the autumn of 1065, Edward was seen to be dying, the Witan considered all the claimants and decided that Harold, as the only man with the strength and maturity that befitted him to rule England, was the natural choice. Edward, on his deathbed, accordingly left his crown to Harold, who seized power in defiance of his oath to William.

William thereupon gathered an army, sailed to England, and defeated Harold on 14th October, 1066 at the Battle of Hastings—it should actually be called the Battle of Senlac Ridge, as that was where it took place. Hastings is 11 miles away.

At that time, there was only one living male representative of the ancient line of the Kings of Wessex, and that was a child known as Edgar the Atheling. He was the grandson of Edmund II. The Witan in London set him up as king as soon as they received the news of William's victory at Hastings, but it quickly became obvious that Edgar's impeccable claim to the throne would be no match for William's determination to wear the crown of England. Edgar submitted to William within 6 weeks, and William was crowned King of England in Westminster Abbey on Christmas Day, 1066.

A new royal dynasty had been founded; the joining of England with Normandy brought England very much into the forefront of European affairs. William's followers received lands and honours, and thus founded aristocratic dynasties of their own in their new realm. A new order prevailed, England was feudalised, its Church overhauled, and its legal system; and all things Saxon were disdained by the conquering Normans.

William's claim to the English throne had very little basis in dynastic terms. His great-aunt Emma had been wife to both Ethelred II and Canute. William's wife Matilda was a descendant of King Alfred. And that was all. William's own ancestor, Rollo, who founded the duchy of Normandy in the 10th century, had been a Viking pirate. It was left to William's son, Henry I, to ally himself in blood to the ancient line of Cerdic: in 1100, he married Edith, the niece of Edgar the Atheling, much to the disgust of his Norman barons, who sneeringly referred to the royal couple as "Godric and Godgifu", old Saxon names now fallen into disrepute. Yet the marriage was popular with the common people, who were, after all, Saxon, and later Kings would acknowledge that it was fitting that the blood of Cerdic flowed in their veins.

WILLIAM I

FATHER: *Robert*

Known as "the Devil" or "the Magnificent", he was the son of Richard II, Duke of Normandy, by Judith of Brittany, and was born in c.1008 in Normandy. He perhaps married Astrid, daughter of King Sweyn, in c.1027, but repudiated her almost at once. He succeeded his brother Richard III as Duke of Normandy on 6th August, 1028, and died on 2nd or 22nd July, 1035, on pilgrimage at Nicea in Bithynia. William I was his illegitimate son.

MOTHER: *Herleva*

Alternatively called Arlette, she was the daughter of Fulbert, a tanner of Falaise in Normandy, by his wife Duxia. She was born in c.1012. She is said to have been noticed by Duke Robert as she sat washing clothes in a river. Their liaison produced two children (see below). Herleva married Herluin, Viscount of Conteville, between c.1029 and 1035, and had four (or perhaps as many as six) further children (see below). She died in c.1050, and was buried in the Abbey of St Grestain in France.

SIBLINGS:

Adeliza

She was born perhaps in 1029, before her mother's marriage to a Norman nobleman. She married firstly Enguerrand III, Count of Ponthieu (d.1053), and had issue:

1 Adelaide (alive in 1096).

Adeliza married secondly Lambert of Boulogne, Count of Lens in Artois (who was killed in battle in 1054) in c.1053, and had issue:

2 Judith (1054/5–after 1086); she married Waltheof, Earl of Northumbria and Huntingdon (who was executed in 1076), and had issue, including Matilda, wife of David I, King of Scotland.

Adeliza married thirdly Odo II, Count of Champagne (disinherited in 1071), and had issue:

3 Stephen, Count of Aumale (before 1070–1121/30), who married Hawise, daughter of Ralph de Mortimer of Wigmore, and had issue.

Adeliza was styled Countess of Aumale in her own right from 1082. She died between 1087 and 1090.

William did not have any full brothers.

HALF-SIBLINGS (the children of his mother's marriage):

1 *Robert*

He was born in 1030/1, and was created Count of Mortain in c.1049 or c.1056. He was probably created Earl of Cornwall in c.1066/7. He died on 8th December, 1090/1, and was buried in the Abbey of St Grestain, France.

Robert married, before 1066:

Matilda

She was the daughter of Roger of Montgomery, Earl of Shrewsbury, by Mabel, daughter of William, Seigneur of Alençon-Bellême. The date of her death is not known; she was buried in the Abbey of St Grestain in France.

Issue of marriage:

(i) *William*

He was born before 1084. He succeeded his father as Count of Mortain on 8th December, 1090/1, and married a lady called Adelaide, of whom nothing more is known. He died after 1140.

(ii) *Emma*

She married William IV, Count of Toulouse (d.1094), and had issue.

Robert married secondly:

Almodis

She was perhaps a sister of Boson, Count of La Marche. After Robert's death, she perhaps married Roger of Montgomery.

2 *Odo*

He was born between c.1031 and 1035. He entered the Church and was consecrated Bishop of Bayeux in Normandy around 1049 and before 23rd April 1050. He was created Earl of Kent in 1066/7; he was deprived of this earldom, which was not forfeited, in 1082, but restored in 1087. He was again deprived of the earldom of Kent in 1088, and this time it was declared forfeit, Odo being banished from England. He died in February, 1097 at Palermo, Sicily, and was buried in Palermo Cathedral.

Odo had the following illegitimate issue:

1 John.

3 *Emma* (?)

Historians now think she was probably fictitious. She is said to have married Richard of Goz, Viscount of Avranches (d.c.1082), and had issue:

1 Hugh, Viscount of Avranches, Earl of Chester (c.1047–1101), who married Ermentrude, daughter of Hugh, Count of Clermont, and had issue. Hugh died a monk.

4 *Muriel*

She married either William, Count of La Ferté-Macé, or, more probably, Eudo de Capello, Viscount of the Côtentin (it is possible that she had an unnamed sister who married William, Count of La Ferté-Macé—see below). Muriel perhaps had issue by Eudo:

1 Muriel; she is said to have married Robert de la Haia (although there is no firm evidence for this).

Muriel's date of death is not known; she was buried in the Abbey of Bury St Edmunds, Suffolk.

5 *Sister* (?)

Her existence is uncertain and her name unknown. She was possibly the sister who married William, Count of La Ferté-Macé.

6 *Isabella*

She married Henry, Count of Séez, and had issue:

1 St Osmund, Bishop of Salisbury (d.1099).

WILLIAM I

Known as "the Bastard", and later as "the Conqueror", he was born in c.1027/8 at Falaise Castle in Normandy. He succeeded his father as Duke of Normandy on 22nd July, 1035, despite his bastardy, as Duke

Robert had no legitimate son. William became Count of Maine by right of conquest in 1063. He defeated Harold II at the Battle of Hastings on 14th October, 1066, and claimed the crown of England by right of inheritance (according to William, Edward the Confessor had promised to make him his successor) and by right of conquest. William I formally acceded to the throne of England on 25th December, 1066, and was crowned on that same day in Westminster Abbey, his being the first coronation to take place in the Abbey, which set a precedent for (most) future coronations.

William I married, in c.1050/52 at the Cathedral of Notre Dame d'Eu in Normandy:

Matilda

She was the daughter of Baldwin V, Count of Flanders, by Adela, daughter of Robert II, King of France. She was born in c.1032, and was crowned Queen Consort on 11th May, 1068, either at Westminster Abbey or in Winchester Cathedral. Matilda died on 2nd November, 1083 at Caen in Normandy, and was buried in the Abbey of the Holy Trinity, her own foundation known as the Abbaye aux Dames, Caen, Normandy.

Issue of marriage:

1 *Robert*

Known as "Curthose", he was born in c.1052/4 in Normandy. He succeeded his father as Duke of Normandy on 9th September, 1087, but was deprived of the dukedom by his brother Henry I on 28th September, 1106, after losing the Battle of Tinchebrai in Normandy. Robert was henceforth a prisoner in England for the rest of his life. He died on 3rd, 10th or 15th February, 1134/5, still in captivity, at Cardiff Castle, and was buried in Gloucester Cathedral.

Robert married, in 1100, at Apulia, Sicily:

Sybilla

She was the daughter of Geoffrey, Count of Conversano. She died around February or March, 1103, at Rouen in Normandy, probably in childbed, although one chronicler states she was poisoned by a rival for her husband's affections. She was either buried at Caen in Normandy, or in Rouen Cathedral, Normandy.

Issue of marriage:

(i) *William*

Known as "Clito", he was born in 1101 at Rouen in Normandy. In the Spring of 1127, he was created Count of Flanders by right of inheritance through his grandmother Matilda of Flanders.

He died on 27th July, 1128 at the Abbey of St Bertin, St Omer, France, of wounds received at the Battle of Alost, and was buried in the Abbey of St Bertin, St Omer, France.

William married firstly, in 1123 (although no record exists as to where):

Sybilla

She was the daughter of Fulk V, Count of Anjou, by Aremburga, daughter of Hélias I, Count of Maine. She was born between 1112 and 1116. Her marriage to William Clito was annulled in 1124. She married secondly, Thierry of Alsace, Count of Flanders (d.1168) in 1134, and had issue, including:

1 Matthew I, Count of Flanders and Boulogne (d.1173), who married Mary, daughter of King Stephen, and had issue.

Sybilla retired in middle age to the Abbey of St Lazarus in Bethlethem, where she became a nun. She died and was buried there in 1165.

William married secondly, in January, 1128 (although no record exists as to where):

Joan (or Giovanna)

She was the daughter of Ranieri, Marquess of Montferrat, by Gisla, daughter of William I, Count of Burgundy. No dates are recorded.

(ii) *Henry*

He was born in 1102. He was killed whilst hunting in the New Forest in Hampshire; the year is not known.

Robert also had the following illegitimate issue:

By a priest's wife or mistress:

1 Richard (killed in the New Forest in 1100).

2 William (killed c.1110 at the Battle of Jerusalem, fighting the Infidel). He was Lord of Tortosa.

By an unknown woman:

3 Daughter (name not known); she married Hélias of Saint-Saëns, Count of Arques.

2 *Richard*

He was born before 1054 (or 1056?) in Normandy, and is said to have been created Duke of Bernay in Normandy. He was gored to death by a stag in 1075 or 1081, whilst hunting in the New Forest, Hampshire, and was buried in Winchester Cathedral.

3 *Cecilia*

She was born in c.1054/5 in Normandy, and entered the novitiate at the Abbey of the Holy Trinity, Caen, her mother's foundation, on

18th June, 1066. She was professed there as a nun on 5th April, 1075, and was elected Abbess of Caen in 1112. She died on 3rd July, 1126 at Caen, where she was buried in the Abbey of the Holy Trinity.

4 *Adeliza*

She was possibly born in 1055. Ordericus Vitalis states that she took religious vows early in life. Robert of Torigny states that she was at one time betrothed to Harold II when he was Earl of Wessex. She was probably dead by 5th January, 1066.

5 *William II* *(see page 45)*.

6 *Constance*

She was born in c.1057 or c.1061 in Normandy. She married Alan IV Fergant, Duke of Brittany (d.1119) at Caen, Normandy in c.1086. She died on 13th August, 1090, perhaps poisoned by her servants, and was buried in the Church of St Melans, near Rhedon, Brittany. Sandford, writing in the 17th century, perpetrated the myth that she was married 25 years and was buried in the Abbey of Bury St Edmunds, Suffolk.

7 *Adela* *(see page 51, under King Stephen)*.

8 *Henry I* *(see page 46)*.

9 *Agatha*

Alternatively called Elgiva, or Margaret, she may have been born in 1064. She was married by proxy to Alfonso VI (d.1109), King of Galicia and Léon, at the Abbey of the Holy Trinity, Caen, Normandy, but died before 1074, before the marriage could be consummated. She was buried in Bayeux Cathedral, Normandy.

10 *Matilda*

Very little is known of her. She died unmarried before 1112.

Note: There is no evidence that either William or Matilda were the parents of Gundrada, Countess of Surrey. Charters attesting this have been proved spurious.

WILLIAM I

He died on 9th September, 1087, at the Priory of St Gervais, Rouen, Normandy, of wounds received at the siege of Mantes. He was buried in St Stephen's Abbey, Caen, Normandy, his own foundation.

He was succeeded in England by his son William (and in Normandy by his son Robert).

Recommended reading

D. C. Douglas's *William the Conqueror* (Eyre and Spottiswoode, 1964) is still the best work.

Others worth consulting are:

Frank Barlow: *William I and the Norman Conquest* (Eyre and Spottiswoode, 1965), F. M. Stenton: *William the Conqueror* (1908), and A. Lloyd: *The Year of the Conqueror* (Longmans, 1966).

For William's sons, see:

L. G. Pine: *Heirs of the Conqueror* (Herbert Jenkins, 1965), G. Slocombe: *Sons of the Conqueror* (Hutchinson, 1960), and C. W. David: *Robert Curthose, Duke of Normandy* (1920).

WILLIAM II

FATHER: *William I (see page 39).*
MOTHER: *Matilda of Flanders (see page 42, under William I).*
SIBLINGS: *(see page 42, under William I).*

WILLIAM II

Known as "Rufus", he was born between c.1056 and 1060 in Normandy. He succeeded his father as King of England on 9th September, 1087, and was crowned on 26th September, 1087 in Westminster Abbey. He never married.

William is said by an unreliable 18th-century source to have had the following **illegitimate issue**:

1 Berstrand.

WILLIAM II

He was killed, perhaps murdered on the orders of his brother Henry, by an arrow in his back on 2nd August, 1100, in the New Forest, Hampshire. He was buried in Winchester Cathedral.

He was succeeded by his brother Henry.

Recommended reading
Two excellent works deal with the mystery surrounding William's death:
> D. Grinnell-Milne: *The Killing of William Rufus* (David and Charles, 1968), and J. Gilbert: *The Death of William Rufus* (in *History Makers*, no. 6, 1969).

The definitive full biography is:
> Frank Barlow: *William Rufus* (Methuen, 1983).

HENRY I

FATHER: *William I (see page 39).*
MOTHER: *Matilda of Flanders (see page 42, under William I).*
SIBLINGS: *(see page 42, under William I).*

HENRY I

Known as "Beauclerk" or "the Lion of Justice", he was born in September, 1068 at Selby, Yorkshire. He became Lord of Domfront in 1092, and Count of Coutances and Bayeux in 1096. He succeeded his brother William II as King of England on 3rd August, 1100, and was crowned on 5th/6th August, 1100 at Westminster Abbey. He usurped the duchy of Normandy on 28th September, 1106, after defeating his brother Robert, its lawful Duke, at the Battle of Tinchebrai.

Henry I married firstly, on 11th November 1100, at Westminster Abbey:

Matilda
She was christened Edith, but adopted the name Matilda upon her marriage as it was thought the Norman barons might not respect a queen with a Saxon name. She was the daughter of Malcolm III, King of Scotland, by St Margaret, a great-granddaughter of Ethelred II,

and her marriage to Henry I represented the union of Norman and Saxon royal lines. Matilda was born probably in the autumn of 1080, and was crowned Queen Consort on 11th or 14th November, 1100 at Westminster Abbey. She died on 1st May, 1118, at the Palace of Westminster, and was buried in Westminster Abbey.

Issue of marriage:

1 *Euphemia*

She was perhaps the child born in late July or early August, 1101 at Winchester, who died young.

2 *Adelaide*

She adopted the name Matilda upon her marriage. (See page 57, under Henry II).

3 *William*

He was born before 5th August, 1103 at Winchester. Styled "Atheling", he was designated Duke of Normandy in 1120. He drowned on 25th November, 1120, when the White Ship sank off Barfleur in Normandy.

William married, in June, 1119, at Lisieux in Normandy:

Matilda

She was christened Alice, but adopted the name Matilda upon her marriage, although she is sometimes called Isabella. She was the daughter of Fulk V, Count of Anjou, by Aremburga, daughter of Hélias I, Count of Maine, and sister to Sybilla, wife of William Clito, grandson of William I. She was born between c.1107 and 1111 in Anjou. After her husband drowned, she became in c.1121 a nun at Fontevrault Abbey in France, where she was elected Abbess in 1148. She died at Fontevrault Abbey in 1154, and was perhaps buried there. There was no issue of her marriage to William.

4 *Richard*

He drowned with his brother William on 25th November, 1120, when the White Ship sank off Barfleur in Normandy. Some sources state that the Richard who drowned in the White Ship was Henry I's natural son, and that his legitimate son Richard died in infancy. However, both Robert of Gloucester and the Saxon Chronicle state that Queen Matilda's son Richard drowned in the White Ship.

Henry I married secondly, on 29th January (or, less probably, 2nd February), 1121, at the Royal Chapel in Windsor Castle:

Adeliza

Alternatively known as Adelicia, Adela, Adelaide, Adeline or Alice, she was the daughter of Geoffrey VII, Count of Louvain, Duke of Lower Brabant and Lower Lorraine, by Ida, daughter of

Albert III, Count of Namur and Countess of Namur in her own right. There are no records of Adeliza's date of birth, but she was described as "nubile" in 1120, thus she was perhaps born between c.1103 and c.1106. She was crowned Queen Consort on 30th January (or, less probably, 3rd February), 1121 at Westminster Abbey. After the death of Henry I, she married secondly William d'Albini, Earl of Arundel (d.1176) after 1136 and before September, 1139, and had issue:

1 William, 2nd Earl of Arundel (before 1150–1193); he married Matilda, daughter of James de St Hilary du Harcourt, and had issue.
2 Reyner.
3 Henry.
4 Geoffrey.
5 Alice (d.1188); she married firstly John, Count of Eu, Lord of Hastings (d.1170), and had issue. She married secondly, Alvred de St Martin (d. after 1189).
6 Olivia. She died young, and was buried in Boxgrove Priory, Sussex.
7 Agatha. She died young, and was buried in Boxgrove Priory, Sussex.

Adeliza became a nun at Affligem Abbey, near Alost in South Brabant, in c.1149/50. She died on 23rd/24th March (or 23rd April), 1151 at Affligem Abbey, and was buried there.

Henry I also had the following **illegitimate issue**:

By Sybilla (also known as Adela or Lucy), daughter of Sir Robert Corbet of Alcester, Co. Warwick, and afterwards wife of Herbert FitzHerbert (d. by 1165):

1 Robert Fitzroy of Caen, Earl of Gloucester (1090/95–1147); he married Mabel (d.1157), daughter of Robert FitzHamon, Earl of Gloucester, and had issue. There is no certain evidence to show that Sybilla really was Robert's mother, who may have been an unknown woman of Caen.
2 Reginald or Rainald of Dunstanville, Earl of Cornwall (by 1110?–1175); he married Beatrice, daughter of William FitzRichard, and had issue.
3 William (by 1105–after 1187); he married a lady called Alice, of whom nothing more is known.
4 Sybilla (see page 191, under Alexander I, King of Scotland).
5 Gundrada (alive in 1130).
6 Rohese (d. after 1176); she married Henry de la Pomerai (d.c.1167), and had issue.

By Ansfrida, widow of Anskill, a knight and tenant of Abingdon Abbey:

7 Richard of Lincoln (drowned in the White Ship, 1120).

8 Fulk (b. before 1100); he either died young, or grew up and became a monk at Abingdon Abbey.

9 Juliana (1090?–after 1136); she married Eustace of Breteuil, Lord of Pacy (d.1136), and had issue. In widowhood, she became a nun at Fontevrault Abbey. There is some doubt that Ansfrida was her mother, but circumstantial evidence makes this likely.

By Nesta, Princess of Deheubarth (d.c.1114), daughter of Rhys ap Tewdwr, Prince of Deheubarth, by Gladys of Powys, and wife of Gerald de Windsor (d. by 1136):

10 Henry FitzHenry (1103? or 1105?; by 1109–killed 1157); he married an unknown lady and had issue.

By Edith, daughter of Forn Sigulfson, Lord of Greystoke, Cumberland (d.1173); afterwards wife of Robert d'Oilli:

11 Robert FitzEdith, Baron of Okenhampton (d.1172); he married Matilda, Dame du Sap, daughter of Robert d'Avranches, and had issue.

By Isabella of Meulan (b.c.1102/7), daughter of Robert de Beaumont, Earl of Leicester, and afterwards Countess of Pembroke:

12 Isabella or Elizabeth (b.1120?). Died unmarried.

By Edith, of unknown origin (d. after 1130):

13 Matilda or Mary (1090?–1120: drowned in the White Ship); she married Rotrou II, Count of Perche (d.1144), and had issue.

By unknown mothers:

14 William de Tracy (d.1136? or 1140?); he married an unknown lady and had issue.

15 Gilbert (1130?–1142).

16 Matilda; she married Conan III, Duke of Brittany (d. 1148), and had issue.

17 Constance or Matilda; she married Richard or Roscelin, Viscount of Beaumont-le-Maine, and had issue including Ermengarde, wife of William the Lyon, King of Scotland.

18 Eustacia; she married William Gouet III, Lord of Montmirail.

19 Alice or Aline; she married Matthew de Montmorenci, Constable of France, and had issue.

20 Matilda, Abbess of Montvilliers.

21 Daughter (name not known), who was betrothed at one time (c.1109) to William de Warenne.

22 Joan or Elizabeth; she married Fergus of Galloway, and had issue.

23 Emma; she married Guy de Laval.

24 Daughter (name not known), to be betrothed to Hugh FitzGervais in c.1110.

25 Sybilla of Falaise; she married Baldwin de Boullers.

HENRY I

He died on 1st/2nd December, 1135 at St Denis le Fermont in the Forest of Angers, near Rouen, Normandy, of food poisoning. He was **buried** in Reading Abbey, Berkshire, his own foundation. His tomb was destroyed during the Reformation.

He was succeeded by his nephew Stephen of Blois, although he had made his barons swear allegiance to his daughter Matilda as his successor.

Recommended reading
Henry I awaits his biographer. There are, however, some useful articles:

R. W. Southern: *The Place of Henry I in English History* (in *Proceedings of the British Academy*, xlviii, 1962), W. Farrar: *An Outline Itinerary of King Henry the First* (in *English Historical Review*, xxxiv, 1919), and also M. Neilson: *Matilda of Scotland* (in *The Lady*, November, 1968).

KING STEPHEN

FATHER: *Stephen Henry*

He was the son of Theobald III, Count of Blois; he married Adela of Normandy (see below) in 1080 at Breteuil in France, and again in 1081 at Chartres Cathedral, France. He succeeded his father as Count Palatine of Blois, Brie, Chartres and Meaux before 1090. He was killed on 19th May, 1102 during the siege of Ramula in the Holy Land, being slain by the Saracens after the battle of Ascalon.

Stephen had the following illegitimate issue:

1 Emma; she married Herbert II, Count of Maine, and had issue.

MOTHER: *Adela*

She was the daughter of William I by Matilda of Flanders, and she was born in c.1062 in Normandy. During her widowhood, she became a nun at the Cluniac Priory of Marigney-sur-Loire in the Diocese of Autun in France in c.1122. She died in 1137 or 1138 at Marigney, and was buried in the Abbey of the Holy Trinity, Caen, Normandy.

SIBLINGS:

1 Humbert, Count of Virtus (d. young).
2 William, Count of Chartres, Lord of Sulli (d. after 1104); he married Agnes (d. after 1104), daughter of Giles, Lord of Sulli, and had issue. William is described in the chronicles as an idiot, and was disinherited in favour of his younger brother Theobald in the succession to Blois.
3 Theobald IV, Count of Blois (1085/91?–1152); he also became Count of Champagne, and married Matilda, daughter of Ingelbert II, Duke of Carinthia, and had issue.
4 Henry; he was born in c.1099 at Winchester, and became a monk at the Priory of Cluny in France during his childhood. He later transferred to Bermondsey Abbey, Surrey, where he became Abbot. He was elected Abbot of Glastonbury in Somerset in 1126. He was nominated Bishop of Winchester on 4th October, 1129, and consecrated on 17th November, 1129. He died on 6th August, 1171 at Winchester, and was buried in Winchester Cathedral.
5 Philip, Bishop of Châlons (d. 1100).
6 Odo; he has perhaps been confused with Henry, who is referred to as Eudes in one charter.
7 Matilda or Lucy; she married Richard d'Avranches, 2nd Earl of Chester. Both were drowned in 1120 when the White Ship sank off Barfleur in Normandy.
8 Agnes; she married Hugh III de Puiset, and had issue.
9 Adela or Lithuise; she married Miles de Brai, Viscount of Troyes and Lord of Montlheri. The marriage was later annulled.
10 Eleanor (d. 1147); she married Raoul, Count of Vermandois.
11 Alice; she married Reginald III, Count of Joigni.

KING STEPHEN

He was born in c.1096/7 (before 1100) at Blois, France. He was created Count of Mortain before 1115, and became Count of Boulogne in right of his wife before 1125. On 22nd December, 1135, he usurped the throne of England upon the death of Henry I, who had left it to his daughter Matilda, to whom the barons had sworn allegiance. However, this had been given unwillingly, and it was generally felt that women were unfit to rule, hence Stephen met with little opposition, and was crowned on 26th December, 1135 at Westminster Abbey. By 1141, his weak government saw many of his nobles disillusioned and turning to Matilda, who invaded England that year. Stephen was deposed between 7th and 10th April, 1141, and imprisoned, while Matilda attempted to consolidate her claim to rule England. She failed in this, due to her haughtiness and high-handed approach to government, which alienated her supporters. Stephen was eventually released, and restored to the throne on 1st November, 1141; he was again crowned, on 25th December, 1141, at Canterbury Cathedral in Kent, and once again, in 1146, at Lincoln Cathedral.

King Stephen married, before 1125:

Matilda

She was the daughter of Eustace III, Count of Boulogne, by Mary, daughter of Malcolm III, King of Scotland, and sister to Matilda, wife of Henry I. Matilda was born around c.1103/5, and became Countess of Boulogne in her own right on the death of her father. She was crowned Queen Consort on 22nd March, 1136, at Westminster Abbey. She died on 2nd/3rd May, 1152 at Hedingham Castle, Essex, and was buried in Faversham Abbey, Kent. Her tomb was destroyed during the Reformation.

Issue of marriage:

1 *Baldwin*

He was born in c.1126, and died perhaps before 2nd December (?), 1135 (certainly before 1137) in the Tower of London. He was buried in the Priory of the Holy Trinity, Aldgate Without, London.

2 *Eustace*

He was born between c.1127/31, or perhaps in December, 1135. He was created Count of Boulogne at Christmas, 1146/7, and is said to have also been created Earl of Huntingdon, but this is unlikely. Eustace was crowned King of England in 1152, during his father's lifetime but he never lived to succeed him, dying on 10th or 16th August, 1153 at Bury St Edmund's, Suffolk. He was buried in Faversham Abbey, Kent.

Eustace married, in February, 1140, in Paris:

Constance

She was the daughter of Louis VI, King of France, by Adelaide, daughter of Umberto II, Count of Savoy and Maurienne, and she was born in c.1128. After Eustace's death, she married secondly Raymond V (d.1194), Count of Toulouse in 1154, and had issue:

1 Raymond VI, Count of Toulouse (1156–1222); he married firstly Ermensinda de Pelet (d.1176); he married secondly Beatrice of Beziers; he married thirdly a Princess of Cyprus, whom he divorced; he married fourthly, Joan, daughter of Henry II, and had issue.

2 William (or Alberic, or Alfonso), surnamed Taillefer (d.1183/4).

3 Baldwin (d.1212).

4 Alesia (d.1183); she married Roger, Viscount of Beziers.

5 Laura; she married Odo, Count of Comminger.

Constance died on 16th August, 1176 at Rheims in France.

3 *William*

He was born between c.1132 and 1137. He became Earl of Surrey in right of his wife before 1148/9. He succeeded his mother as Count of Boulogne on 17th August, 1153, and succeeded his father as Count of Mortain on 25th October, 1154. He was killed on 11th October, 1159 at the siege of Toulouse in France, and was buried in the Hospital of Montmorillon, Poitou, France.

William married, before 1148/9, although no evidence exists as to where:

Isabella

She was the daughter of William de Warenne, 3rd Earl of Surrey, by Adela, daughter of William Talvas, Count of Ponthieu, and she was born in c.1136/7. After the death of William, she married secondly Hamelin of Anjou, Earl of Surrey (1129?–1202), a bastard brother of Henry II. Hamelin adopted her surname "de Warenne" when the couple were married in April, 1164. They had issue:

1 William, 5th Earl of Surrey (d.1240); he married Matilda, who was perhaps a member of the Albini family. He married secondly, Matilda (d.1248), daughter of William Marshal, 4th Earl of Pembroke, and had issue. He also had illegitimate issue.

2 Matilda (d.c.1212); she married firstly Henry, Count of Eu and Baron Hastings (d.1183), and had issue, and secondly, Henry d'Estouteville of Eckington, Co. Derby (d. after 1231).

3 Isabella; she married firstly Robert de Lascy, and secondly Gilbert de l'Aigle, Lord of Pevensey, Sussex.

4 Ela; she married firstly Robert de Newburn, and secondly William FitzWilliam of Sprotborough.

5 Mary, Margaret or Matilda (d. after 1208); it may have been she, and not her sister Isabella, who married Gilbert de l'Aigle.

Isabella died on 13th July, 1199 or 1203, and was buried in the Chapter House, Lewes Priory, Sussex.

4 *Matilda*

She was born in c.1133/4, and was married in infancy at c.Easter, 1136 to Waleran de Beaumont, Count of Meulan (1104–1166). She died either before 1137 or in 1141 in the Tower of London, and was buried in the Priory of the Holy Trinity, Aldgate Without, London.

5 *Mary*

She was born in c.1136; she was dedicated to religion in her infancy and entered as a novice at Lillechurch Priory, Kent. She transferred to Romsey Abbey, Hampshire, where she was professed a nun between c.1148 and 1155. She was elected Abbess of Romsey after 1155. She succeeded her brother William as Countess of Boulogne on 5th October, 1159. She was abducted from her convent in 1160 by Matthew I, Count of Flanders and Boulogne (d.1173), who made her his wife in defiance of her religious vows around the same time. They had issue:

1 Ida, Countess of Boulogne (1161?–1216); she married firstly Gerard III, Count of Gueldres (d.1183), and secondly, Berthold IV, Duke of Zehringen (d.1186); and thirdly Reginald de Tree, Count of Dammartin, and had issue.

2 Matilda (1162?–c.1211); she married Henry I, Duke of Louvain and Brabant (c.1158–1235), and had issue.

Mary's marriage was annulled in c.1169, and she re-entered the religious life at the Benedictine nunnery of St Austrebert, near Montreuil, France, where she died and was buried in 1182.

King Stephen also had the following **illegitimate issue**:

By Dameta, a gentlewoman of Normandy:

1 Gervaise, Abbot of Westminster (c.1115/20–1160).

2 Almaric; he is called a brother of Gervaise in charters.

3 Ralph; he is called a brother of Gervaise in charters.

By unknown mothers:

4 William; he is mentioned only in 17th and 19th century genealogies.

5 Sybilla (d.c.1141); she married Hervey le Breton of Léon, Earl of Wiltshire (d.1168).

KING STEPHEN

He died on 25th October, 1154 in a monastery at Dover, Kent, and was buried in Faversham Abbey, Kent. His tomb was destroyed during the Reformation.

He was succeeded by his second cousin Henry, son of the Empress Matilda.

Recommended reading
There are two good modern biographies:
R. H. C. Davis: *King Stephen* (Longmans, 1967).
H. A. Cronne: *The Troubled Reign of King Stephen: Anarchy in England* (Weidenfeld and Nicolson, 1970).

3. The Angevin or Plantagenet Kings of England

When, in 1120, the *White Ship* sank off Barfleur in Normandy, Henry I lost to the sea, not only four of his children, but also both his legitimate heirs. His second marriage in 1121 produced no issue, and when he died in 1135, his only surviving child was a girl, the Empress Matilda, then wedded to her second husband, Geoffrey, Count of Anjou. Matilda was in Anjou when her father died, and the crown of England was seized by Stephen of Blois, her cousin, in defiance of the oath of allegiance that he and other magnates had taken to Matilda as Henry's successor. Matilda triumphed only briefly over Stephen, in 1141, when the crown came tantalisingly within her reach, but she alienated by her hauteur and overbearing manner many of her supporters, and eventually had to retire from the conflict. Yet she continued to promote the cause of her son Henry as heir to England, and in 1153, when faced by an invading army led by that young and very capable man, Stephen had to bow to public opinion and name him his successor. Thus came about the Treaty of Wallingford, which passed over the claims of Eustace and William, Stephen's sons, and recognised that of Henry of Anjou, who succeeded without hindrance to the throne of England the following year, Eustace having died some months previously, which most thought was very fortunate.

Thus was established the Angevin or Plantagenet dynasty. The name "Plantagenet" comes from the sprig of broom flower (Latin: *planta genista*) that Henry's father Geoffrey was accustomed to wearing in his hat. That name, however, was not formally adopted by the dynasty until the 15th century, when Richard, Duke of York was the first to use it as a surname to emphasise his claim to the throne during the Wars of the Roses.

The Plantagenets were a dynamic race, one of the most energetic and brilliant families of rulers the world has known. Reputedly descended from a witch, Melusine, who married an early Count of Anjou then vanished in a puff of smoke when he forced her to attend Mass—a tale the Angevin Kings were fond of relating—they ruled

England for over 300 years, and for more than 200 of those years the crown passed, usually peacefully, from father to son. What occurred to break this pattern will be related in the next chapter.

HENRY II

FATHER: *Geoffrey*

Surnamed Plantagenet after the broom flower he wore in his hat, he was the son of Fulk V, Count of Anjou, by Aremburga, daughter of Hélias I, Count of Maine; his sisters were married to a grandson of William I and the son of Henry I. Geoffrey was born on 24th August, 1113, and married the Empress Matilda on 3rd April, 22nd May or 17th June, 1128 at Le Mans Cathedral, Anjou. He succeeded his father as Count of Anjou in 1129, and was proclaimed Duke of Normandy on 19th January, 1144 after conquering the duchy. He died on 7th September, 1151 at Château du Loire, France, and was buried in Le Mans Cathedral, Anjou.

Geoffrey had the following illegitimate issue:

By Adelaide of Angers:

1 Hamelin, who adopted the surname "de Warenne" upon marriage, Earl of Surrey (1129?–1202); he married Isabella de Warenne, daughter-in-law of King Stephen, and had issue.

By unknown mothers:

2 Mary, Abbess of Shaftesbury, Dorset (d.c.1216).

3 Emma (d. before 1214?); she married firstly, Guy, Sire de Laval (d.1170/73), and secondly, David ap Owen, Prince of East Gwynnedd (d.1204), and had issue.

MOTHER: *Matilda*

Christened Adelaide, she adopted the name Matilda on her first marriage. She was the daughter of Henry I by Matilda of Scotland,

and she was born in c.February (by August), 1102, either at Winchester or in London. She married firstly Henry V, Emperor of Germany (d.1125) on 7th January, 1114, at Mainz in Germany, and was crowned there the same day. She was crowned again, with her husband, in 1117, in St Peter's Basilica, Rome, by the Pope. On 7th April, 1141, having deposed and imprisoned King Stephen in pursuance of her claim to the English throne (she was her father's rightful heir and Stephen an usurper), she assumed the title "Lady of the English", never officially being styled Queen of England. She was deposed in favour of Stephen on 1st November, 1141, having failed to consolidate her position. Matilda died on 10th September, 1167 at the Abbey of Notre Dame des Prés, near Rouen, Normandy, and was buried in Bec Abbey, Normandy, her remains later being removed to Rouen Cathedral.

SIBLINGS:

1 *Geoffrey*

He was born on 1st June, 1134 at Rouen or at Argentan, Normandy, and was created Count of Nantes in c.1150. He died unmarried on 26th July, 1157/8 at Nantes, Brittany, where he was buried.

2 *William*

He was born on 21st July, or in August, 1136, at Argentan in Normandy or at Angers, France, and was called Count of Poitou. He died unmarried on 30th January, 1163/4 at Rouen, Normandy, and was buried in Rouen Cathedral.

Henry II did not have any sisters.

HENRY II

Known as "FitzEmpress" or "Curtmantle", he was born on 5th March, 1133 at Le Mans, Anjou. He became Count of Touraine and Maine in 1151, and succeeded his father as Duke of Normandy and Count of Anjou on 7th September, 1151. He became Duke of Aquitaine in right of his wife on 18th May, 1152. He succeeded his second cousin Stephen as King of England on 19th December, 1154, and was crowned on that day in Westminster Abbey.

Henry II married, on 18th May, 1152 at Bordeaux Cathedral, Gascony:

Eleanor

She was the daughter of William X, Duke of Aquitaine, by Eleanor, daughter of Aimery I de Rochefoucauld, Viscount of Châtellérhault, and she was born around 1120/22, either at the Ombrière Palace, Bordeaux, or at Belin Castle, Guienne. She succeeded her father as Duchess of Aquitaine and Countess of Saintonge, Angoumois, Limousin, Auvergne, Bordeaux and Agen on 9th April, 1137. She married firstly Louis VII, King of France (1121?–1180) on 25th July, 1137 at Bordeaux Cathedral, and had issue:

1 Mary (1145–1198); she married Henry I, Count of Champagne (1127–1180), and had issue.

2 Alice (1150–1198); she married Theobald V, Count of Blois (d.1191), and had issue.

Louis divorced Eleanor on grounds of consanguinity on 18th March, 1152. She was crowned Queen Consort with her second husband Henry II on 19th December, 1154 at Westminster Abbey. Eleanor died on 1st April, 1204 at Fontevrault Abbey, France, where she was buried.

Issue of marriage:

1 *William*

He was born on 17th August, 1153, either at Poitiers in Aquitaine, or in Normandy, and was called Count of Poitiers. He died in c.April or June, 1156 at Wallingford Castle, Berkshire, and was buried in Reading Abbey, Berkshire.

2 *Henry*

He was born on 28th February, 1155 at Bermondsey Palace, Surrey. He was crowned King of England on 14th June, 1170 at Westminster Abbey, during the lifetime of his father, being styled King of England, Duke of Normandy, and Count of Anjou. Thereafter he was known as "the Young King". He was again crowned on 27th August, 1172 at Winchester Cathedral. He died on 11th June, 1183 at Martel Castle, Turenne, France, and was buried in Le Mans Cathedral, Anjou; his remains were later removed to Rouen Cathedral in Normandy.

Henry married, on 2nd November, 1160, at Newburgh in Normandy:

Margaret

She was the daughter of Louis VII, King of France, by Constance, daughter of Alfonso VII, King of Castile, and she was born in 1158. She was crowned Queen Consort with her husband on 27th August, 1172 at Winchester Cathedral. After the death of the Young King, she married secondly Bela III, King of Hungary (1148–1196) in 1185/6. She died in 1197/8 at Acre, whilst on a pilgrimage to the Holy Land.

Issue of marriage:

(i) *William*

He was born on 19th June, 1177, in Paris, and died there on 22nd June, 1177.

3 *Matilda*

She was born in June, 1156 at Windsor Castle. She married Henry V "the Lion", Duke of Saxony and Bavaria (1129–1195) on 1st February, 1168 at Minden Cathedral, Germany, and had issue:

1 Richenza (1172–1210); she married firstly Geoffrey III, Count of Perche (d.1202) and had issue, and secondly Enguerrand III, Lord of Coucy.

2 Henry, Duke of Saxony and Bavaria (1175–1227); he married Agnes (d.1204), daughter of Conrad of Hohenstaufen, Count Palatine of the Rhine, and had issue.

3 Lothaire (1181–1191).

4 Son (name not known) (b.&d.1182?).

5 Otto IV, Holy Roman Emperor, Earl of York and Count of Ponthieu (1183?–1218); he married firstly Beatrice of Swabia, daughter of Philip, Emperor of Germany, and secondly Mary, daughter of Henry I, Duke of Brabant.

6 William, Duke of Lüneberg and Brunswick (1184–1213); he married Helen, daughter of Waldemar I, King of Denmark.

7 Matilda.

8 Eleanor (?).

9 Gertrude (d.1197); she married Canute VI, King of Denmark (1163–1202).

10 Ingibiorg (?); she is said to have married Waldemar II, King of Denmark (1170–1241).

Matilda died on 28th June, 1189 at Brunswick in Germany, and was buried in Brunswick Cathedral.

4 *Richard I* *(see page 64).*

5 *Geoffrey*

He was born on 23rd September, 1158, and was styled Earl of Richmond and Duke of Brittany in right of his wife shortly after 6th September, 1181. He was trodden to death by his horse on 19th August, 1186, during a tournament in Paris, and was buried in the Cathedral of Nôtre Dame, Paris.

Geoffrey married, in July, 1181 (although no record exists as to where):

Constance

She was the daughter of Conan IV, Duke of Brittany and Earl of Richmond, by Margaret of Huntingdon, granddaughter of David I,

King of Scotland. Constance was born around 1160/62 in Brittany. After the death of Geoffrey, she married secondly Ranulf de Blundeville, 4th Earl of Chester (1172?–1232) on 3rd February, 1186, 1187 or 1188. This marriage was dissolved in 1199 after Constance deserted her husband. She married thirdly Guy of Thouars (d.1213) in 1199 at Angers in Anjou, and had issue:

1 Alice, Duchess of Brittany and Countess of Richmond (1201–1221); she married Peter of Dreux, Duke of Brittany (1187?–1250), and had issue.

2 Katherine (b.1201); she married Andrew de Vitre of Brittany.

Constance died in August or on 3rd, 4th or 5th September, 1201, at Nantes, Brittany, in childbirth, although some sources say she died of leprosy. She was buried in Villeneuve Abbey, Nantes, Brittany. Issue of marriage:

(i) *Eleanor*
She was born in 1184 or 1186, and was styled Countess of Richmond from 27th May, 1208. She spent most of her life in honourable confinement, King John realising that her claim to the throne was superior to his own. She died, perhaps murdered or starved to death, on 10th August, 1241 at Bristol Castle (or, less probably, at Corfe Castle, Dorset), and was buried in St James's Church, Bristol. Her remains were later removed to Amesbury Abbey, Wiltshire.

(ii) *Matilda*
She was born in 1185/6, and died young.

(iii) *Arthur*
He was born on 29th March, 1187 at Nantes, Brittany, and —as his father's posthumous son—was styled Duke of Brittany from birth. He was styled Earl of Richmond from 18th April, 1199. He is said, with good probability, to have been murdered by order of King John because of his (Arthur's) superior claim to the throne of England, probably on 3rd April, 1203, either at Rouen or Cherbourg in Normandy. He certainly disappeared before Easter, 1203. He was buried either at Notre Dame des Prés at Rouen, or in Bec Abbey, Normandy.

6 *Eleanor*
She was born on 13th October, 1162 (or 1161?) at Domfront Castle, Normandy. She married Alfonso VIII, King of Castile (1156–1214) in September, 1176 (or 1177?) at Burgos Cathedral, Castile, and had issue:

1 Sancho (b.&d.1180).
2 Berengaria, Queen of Castile (1181–1234); she married Alfonso IX, King of Léon (1173–1230), and had issue.
3 Urracca (1182–1220); she married Alfonso II, King of Portugal (1185–1223), and had issue.
4 Blanche (1183?–1253); she married Louis VIII, King of France (1187–1226), and had issue.
5 Henry (b.c.1184; d. young).
6 Ferdinand (1189–1209 or 1211).
7 Eleanor (1190–1253); she married James I, King of Aragon (1205–1276), and had issue. She was divorced in 1229.
8 Constance, Abbess of Las Huelgas, Castile (d.1243).
9 Sanchia (d. young).
10 Matilda (d. young).
11 Henry I, King of Castile (1204–1217); he married Matilda (d.1257), daughter of Sancho I, King of Portugal. The marriage was later annulled.
12 Constance (d. young).
Eleanor died on 31st October, 1214 at Burgos, Castile, and was buried there in the Abbey of Las Huelgas.

7 *Joan*

She was born in October, 1165 at Angers Castle, Anjou. She married firstly William II, King of Sicily (1154–1189) on 13th February, 1177 at Palermo Cathedral, Sicily, and had issue:
1 Bohemond, Duke of Apulia (b.&d.1181).
Joan was crowned Queen of Sicily on 13th February, 1177 at Palermo Cathedral. She married secondly Raymond VI, Count of Toulouse (1156–1222) (who was the son of Constance of France, daughter-in-law of King Stephen) in October, 1196 at Rouen, Normandy, and had issue:
2 Raymond VII, Count of Toulouse (1197?–1249); he married firstly Sanchia, daughter of Alfonso II, King of Aragon, and had issue. They were divorced in 1241. He married secondly Margaret, daughter of Hugh X de Lusignan, Count of La Marche, by Isabella, widow of King John.
3 Mary or Wilhelmina (b.1198); she married Berald of Elbine, Prince of Orange.
4 Richard (or, less probably, Bertrand) (b.&d.1199).
Joan died on 4th September, 1199, having been veiled as a nun on her deathbed at Fontevrault Abbey, France; she died in childbirth, and was buried at Fontevrault.

8 *King John (see page 66).*

Note: There is no contemporary evidence that Henry and Eleanor ever had a son called Philip, who is first mentioned in a 16th century source. He may have been confused with Richard I's bastard son Philip.

Henry II also had the following **illegitimate issue**:

By Ikenai, called "a common prostitute", but probably the daughter of a knight:

1 Geoffrey (1151/3?–1212), Archbishop of York.

2 William Longespée, Earl of Salisbury (before 1170–1226); he may have been the son of Ikenai, but this is doubtful. He married Ela (1196?–1261), daughter of William FitzPatrick, Earl of Salisbury, and had issue. Ela later became Abbess of Lacock in Wiltshire.

3 Peter, called a brother of Geoffrey.

By Alice, daughter of Louis VII, King of France (she was at that time betrothed to Henry's son Richard):

4 Daughter (name not known) (d. young).

5 Child (name and sex not known) (d. young).

6 Child (name and sex not known) (d. young).

7 Child (name and sex not known) (d. young).

By Nesta, wife of Sir Ralph Bloet or Blewer:

8 Morgan, Provost of Beverley, Yorkshire, and Bishop-Elect of Durham.

By Alice de Porhoët:

9 Child (name and sex not known) (b.1168?); its fate is unknown.

By unknown mothers:

10 Matilda, Abbess of Barking, Essex (d. by 1202).

11 Hugh of Wells (?), Bishop of Lincoln (d.1235).

12 Richard (?).

HENRY II

He died on 6th July, 1189 at Chinon Castle in France, and was buried in Fontevrault Abbey, France.

He was succeeded by his son Richard.

Recommended reading

The most exhaustive biography is:

W. L. Warren: *Henry II* (Eyre Methuen, 1973).

Others worth consulting are:

J. T. Appleby: *Henry II, the Vanquished King* (Bell, 1962).

R. Barber: *Henry Plantagenet* (Boydell Press, 1972).

Nesta Pain: *The King and Becket* (Eyre and Spottiswoode, 1966).
There is a wealth of other material on Henry, much of it out of date.
For Henry's family, see:

Alfred Duggan: *Devil's Brood: the Angevin Family* (Faber and Faber, 1957).

There is an excellent biography of Henry's mother:

Nesta Pain: *Empress Matilda, Uncrowned Queen of England* (Weidenfeld and Nicolson, 1978).

Eleanor of Aquitaine has attracted several biographers in recent years, including:

M. Meade: *Eleanor of Aquitaine* (Muller, 1978).

A. Kelly: *Eleanor of Aquitaine and the Four Kings* (Harvard University Press, 1952).

Régine Pernoud: *Eleanor of Aquitaine* (Collins, 1967).

RICHARD I

FATHER: *Henry II (see page 57)*.
MOTHER: *Eleanor of Aquitaine (see page 58, under Henry II)*.
SIBLINGS: *(see page 59, under Henry II)*.

RICHARD I

Known as "Coeur de Lion" ("the Lionheart"), he was born on 8th September, 1157 at Beaumont Palace, Oxford. He was invested with the duchy of Aquitaine in 1172. He succeeded his father as King of England and Duke of Normandy on 2nd September, 1189, being crowned on that day in Westminster Abbey. He was again crowned on 17th April, 1194, at Winchester Cathedral, following his release from a foreign captivity during the Crusades. Richard I spent only 10 months of his 10 year reign in England.

Richard I married, on 12th May, 1191, at the Chapel of St George, Limassol, Cyprus:

Berengaria

She was the daughter of Sancho VI, King of Navarre, by Beatrice or Sanchia, daughter of Alfonso VII, King of Castile, and she was born around c.1163/5 in Navarre. She was crowned Queen Consort on 12th May, 1191 in the Chapel of St George, Lemesnos, Limassol, Cyprus. It has often been said that Berengaria never set foot in England, but this was not so: she often visited the country of which she was Queen, particularly during her widowhood. In 1230, she founded the Abbey of L'Espan in Le Mans, Anjou, and probably took the veil there as a nun, possibly assuming the name in religion of Juliana. The date of her death is not recorded. She was buried in l'Espan Abbey, Le Mans, France; her remains were removed to Le Mans Cathedral in 1821. There was no issue of her marriage to Richard I.

Richard I had the following **illegitimate issue**:

By Joan de St Pol (?):

1 Fulk (?).

By an unknown mother:

2 Philip, Lord of Cognac (d. after 1201); he perhaps married Amelia of Cognac.

RICHARD I

He died on 6th April, 1199 at Chalus in the Limousin, France, of the effects of an arrow wound received during the siege of Chalus. He was buried in Fontevrault Abbey, France.

He was succeeded by his brother John.

Recommended reading

There have been several worthy biographies of Richard I in recent years:

John Gillingham: *Richard I* (Weidenfeld and Nicolson, 1973).

J. T. Appleby: *England without Richard, 1189–1199* (Bell, 1965).

J. Hampden: *Crusader King* (1956).

P. P. Henderson: *Richard Coeur de Lion* (Robert Hale, 1958).

Kate Norgate's *Richard the Lion Heart* (1924) is still one of the finest studies of the King.

KING JOHN

FATHER: *Henry II (see page 57).*
MOTHER: *Eleanor of Aquitaine (see page 58, under Henry II).*
SIBLINGS: *(see page 59, under Henry II).*

KING JOHN

Known as "Lackland" or "Softsword", he was born on 24th December, 1166 at Beaumont Palace, Oxford. He was designated King of Ireland in 1177, and created Count of Mortain in 1189. He was styled Earl of Gloucester in right of his first wife from 29th August, 1189. He succeeded his brother Richard I as King of England and Duke of Normandy on 27th May, 1199, being crowned on that day in Westminster Abbey.

John married firstly, on 29th August, 1189, at Marlborough Castle, Wiltshire:

Isabella

Also called Hawise, Joan and Eleanor, she was the daughter of William, Earl of Gloucester, by Hawise, daughter of Robert de Beaumont, 3rd Earl of Leicester, and she was born before 1176. She was never styled Queen of England, but was divorced before 30th August, 1199 on grounds of consanguinity. There was no issue of the marriage. She married secondly Geoffrey de Mandeville, Earl of Essex and Gloucester (and Sussex?) (d.1216) between 16th and 26th January, 1214. She married thirdly Hubert de Burgh, Earl of Kent (d.1243) around September/October, 1217. Isabella died, probably suddenly, on 14th October or c.18th November, 1217, and was buried in Canterbury Cathedral, Kent.

John married secondly, on 24th August, 1200, at Bordeaux Cathedral, Gascony:

Isabella

She was the daughter of Aymer Taillefer, Count of Angoulême, by

Alice, daughter of Peter de Courtenay, son of Louis VI, King of France, and she was born in c.1187. She was crowned Queen Consort on 8th October, 1200 in Westminster Abbey. She succeeded her father as Countess of Angoulême in the summer of 1202, but was not formally recognised as such until November, 1206. After the death of John, she married secondly Hugh X de Lusignan, Count of La Marche (d.1249) between 10th March and 22nd May, 1220, and had issue:

1 Hugh XI, Count of La Marche and Angoulême (1221?–1250/60); he married Yolande (d.1272), daughter of Peter Mauclerk, Count of Brittany, and had issue.

2 Aymer, Bishop of Winchester (d.1260).

3 Guy, Lord of Cognac and Archiac (d.1264).

4 Henry, Count of La Marche (d.1260); he married Yolande of Penthiévre, and had issue.

5 Geoffrey, Lord of Jarnac (d. before 1263); he married Joan, Viscountess of Châtellérhault, and had issue.

6 William, Earl of Pembroke and Wexford (1225/30–1296); he married Joan (d.1307), daughter of Warin de Munchesni, Lord of Swanscombe, and had issue.

7 Alice (d.1256); she married John de Warenne, 6th Earl of Surrey (1231?–1304), and had issue.

8 Margaret (d.1283); she married firstly Raymond VII, Count of Toulouse (son of Joan, daughter of Henry II). They were divorced in 1245. She married secondly Aymer, Viscount of Thouars, and thirdly Geoffrey, Seigneur de Châteaubriand.

9 Matilda; she married Humphrey de Bohun, 2nd Earl of Hereford and 1st Earl of Essex (1200?–1275), and had issue.

10 Isabella (d.1299); she married firstly Geoffrey, Seigneur de Taillebourg, and secondly Amaury, Seigneur de Craon.

11 Agatha or Agnes; she married William de Chauvigny, Seigneur de Châteauroux.

Isabella died on 31st May, 1246 at Fontevrault Abbey, France, where she was buried.

Issue of marriage:

1 Henry III (see page 73).

2 Richard

He was born on 5th January, 1209 at Winchester Castle, Hampshire. He was designated Count of Poitou before 14th August, 1225, and was first so styled on 21st August, 1227. He was created Earl of Cornwall on 30th May, 1227. He renounced the county of

Poitou in c.December, 1243. He was elected King of Germany (Almayne) and King of the Romans on 13th January, 1257, and was crowned on 17th May, 1257 at Aachen Cathedral, Germany. He died on 2nd April, 1272 at Berkhamstead Castle, Herts., and was buried in Hayles Abbey, Gloucs.

Richard had the following illegitimate issue:

By Jeanne de Valletort:

1 Richard de Cornwall (d. after 1280); he married and had issue.

By unknown mothers:

2 Walter de Cornwall.

3 Isabella de Cornwall; she married Maurice de Berkeley, and had issue.

Richard married firstly, on 13th or 30th March, 1231, at Fawley Church, Bucks.:

Isabella

She was the daughter of William Marshal, Earl of Pembroke, by Isabella, daughter of Richard FitzGilbert de Clare, 2nd Earl of Pembroke, and she was born on 9th October, 1200 at Pembroke Castle, Wales. She married firstly Gilbert de Clare, Earl of Hertford and Gloucester (1180?–1230) on 9th October, 1214 or 1217 at Tewkesbury Abbey, Gloucs., and had issue:

1 Amice (1220?–1284); she married firstly Baldwin de Redvers, 6th Earl of Devon, (d.1245) and secondly Robert of Guines.

2 Richard, Earl of Hertford and Gloucester (1222?–1262); he married firstly Margaret (Megotta) (d.1237), daughter of Hubert de Burgh, Earl of Kent. He married secondly Matilda (d. by 1289), daughter of John de Lacy, Earl of Lincoln, and had issue.

3 Agnes.

4 Isabella (1226–1254); she married Robert le Brus, Lord of Annandale (1210–1295), and had issue.

5 William (1228–1258).

6 Gilbert (b.1229); a priest (?).

Isabella died on 15th or 17th January, 1240, at Berkhamstead Castle, Herts., of jaundice contracted whilst in childbed, and was buried in Beaulieu Abbey, Hampshire.

Issue of marriage:

(i) *John*

He was born on 31st January or 2nd February, 1232 at Marlowe-on-Thames, Bucks., and died on 22nd/23rd September, 1233 at Marlowe-on-Thames, Bucks.; he was buried in Reading Abbey, Berkshire.

(ii) *Isabella*

She was born on 9th September, 1233 at Marlowe-on-Thames, Bucks., and died on 10th October, 1234, at Marlowe-on-Thames, Bucks.; she was buried in Reading Abbey, Berkshire.

(iii) *Henry*

He was born on 2nd, 4th or 12th November, 1235 at Haughley Castle, Suffolk. He was murdered by the sons of Simon de Montfort on 13th March, 1271, either in the Church of St Lorenzo, or the Church of St Silvestro, or the Cathedral of St Nicholas, Viterbo, Italy, and was buried in Hayles Abbey, Gloucs.

Henry married, on 5th or 15th May, 1269, at Windsor Castle:

Constance

She was the daughter of Gaston VII de Moncada, Viscount of Béarn, by Matilda, daughter of Boson de Mastas, Seigneur of Cognac. She married firstly Alfonso, Infante of Aragon (d.1260). Constance died in c.1299.

(iv) *Nicholas*

He was born on 17th January, 1240 at Berkhamstead Castle, Bucks., and died there the same day. He was buried in Beaulieu Abbey, Hampshire.

Richard married secondly, on 23rd November, 1243, at Westminster Abbey:

Sanchia

She was the daughter of Raymond Berenger V, Count of Provence, by Beatrice, daughter of Thomas I, Count of Savoy; her sister Eleanor was the wife of Henry III. Sanchia was born in c.1225 at Aix-en-Provence, France. She was crowned Queen of the Romans and Queen of Germany with her husband on 17th May, 1257 at Aachen Cathedral, Germany. She died on 5th or 9th November, 1261 at Berkhamstead Castle, Bucks., and was buried in Hayles Abbey, Gloucs.

Issue of marriage:

(i) *Richard*

He was born in July, 1246 at Wallingford Castle, Berkshire; he died there on 15th August, 1246, and was buried at Grove Mile.

(ii) *Edmund*

He was born on 26th December, 1249 or 5th December, 1250

at Berkhamstead Castle, Bucks., and was invested as Earl of Cornwall on 13th October, 1272. He died on 24th/25th September, or 1st October, 1300 at Ashridge Abbey, Herts., and was buried in Hayles Abbey, Gloucs.

Edmund married, on 6th October, 1272, at Ruislip Chapel, Middlesex:

Margaret

She was the daughter of Richard de Clare, Earl of Gloucester and Hertford, by Matilda, daughter of John de Lacy, Earl of Lincoln; her father was the son of Richard of Cornwall's first wife, Isabella Marshal. Margaret was born around 1249/50. She was either divorced or legally separated from her husband in February, 1293. She died in February, 1313 (or perhaps before 16th September, 1312), and was buried in Chertsey Abbey, Surrey. There was no issue of her marriage to Edmund.

(iii) *Richard (?)*

He may have been born in c.1252, although he has perhaps been confused with Richard de Cornwall, Earl Richard's illegitimate son. He was killed in 1296, at the siege of Berwick, by iron shot in his head.

Richard married thirdly, on 16th June, 1269, at the Stiftkirche, Kaiserslauten, Germany:

Beatrice

She was the daughter of Dirk II, Count of Falkenburg, by Joan van Loon. (Her parentage is sometimes erroneously given as either (i) Walram de Fauquemont, Lord of Mountjoye, by Jutta, daughter of Otto, Count of Ravensburg, Westphalia, or (ii) Lothaire, Count of Hostade and Dalem, or (iii) Philip von Falkenstein, Arch-Chamberlain of the Empire. She was no connection of any of these.) Beatrice was born in c.1253, probably at Falkenburg Castle, Germany. She died on 17th October, 1277, and was buried in the Church of the Franciscan Friars Minor, Oxford.

3 *Joan* (*see page 199, under Alexander II, King of Scotland*).

4 *Isabella*

She was born in 1214. She married Frederick II, King of Sicily, and Emperor of Germany (d.1250) on 20th July, 1235, at Worms Cathedral, Germany, and had issue:

1 Jordan (?) (b.&d.1236).

2 Agnes (b.&d.1237).

3 Henry, King of Jerusalem (1238–1253).

4 Margaret (1241–1270); she married Albert I, Margrave of Meissen and Landgrave of Thuringia and Misnes (1240–1315), and had issue.

Isabella was crowned Empress of Germany on 20th July, 1235, at Worms Cathedral. She died on 1st or c. 6th December, 1241, at Foggia, near Naples, Sicily, in childbirth, and was buried at Andria, Sicily.

5 *Eleanor*

She was born in 1215. She married firstly William Marshal, 2nd Earl of Pembroke (c.1190–1231) (brother of Richard of Cornwall's first wife Isabella) on 23rd April, 1224. Notwithstanding a vow of perpetual chastity entered into during her widowhood, she married secondly Simon de Montfort, Earl of Leicester (1208–1265: killed at the Battle of Evesham) on 7th January or 19th February, 1238, at the King's Chapel in the Palace of Westminster, and had issue:

1 Henry (1238–1265: killed at the Battle of Evesham).
2 Simon (1240–1271).
3 Guy, Count of Nola (1243?–1288?); he married Margaret, daughter of Aldobrandino Aldobrandeschi, Count of Anguillara, and had issue.
4 Amaury (d. after 1301); he was a canon at York, but later became a knight.
5 Richard (d. after 1266)
6 Eleanor (1252–1282); she married Llywelyn ap Gruffydd, Prince of Wales (killed 1282), and had issue.

After the death of her husband, Eleanor became a nun at Montargis Abbey in France. She died on 13th April, 1275 at Montargis Abbey, and was buried there.

King John also had the following **illegitimate issue**:

By a woman called Suzanne, or by a sister of William de Warenne, Earl of Surrey (Surrey's sister undoubtedly bore the King a child, but its identity is uncertain):

1 Richard FitzJohn of Dover, Baron of Chilham, Kent (d.1242/53); he married Rohese (d. by 1232), daughter of Fulbert of Dover, and had issue.

By Clementina, wife of Henry Pinel:

2 Joan (d.1237); she married Llywelyn ap Iorwerth, Prince of Wales (1173–1240), and had issue.

By Hawise, perhaps a member of the de Tracy family:

3 Oliver (d.1290); he was killed at the siege of Damietta, and was buried in Westminster Abbey.

By unknown mothers:
4 Osbert Gifford (d. after 1216).
5 Geoffrey FitzRoy (d.1205).
6 John FitzJohn or Courcy (d.1242); a knight; perhaps a clerk at Lincoln.
7 Odo or Eudo FitzRoy (d.1242?).
8 Ivo (confused with Odo?).
9 Henry; he married a minor heiress.
10 Richard, Constable of Wallingford Castle.
11 Matilda (?), Abbess of Barking.
12 Isabella la Blanche (?).

KING JOHN

He died on 18th/19th October, 1216, at Newark Castle, Lincs., and was buried in Worcester Cathedral.

He was succeeded by his son Henry.

Recommended reading
There have been several good recent biographies of King John:
W. L. Warren: *King John* (Eyre and Spottiswoode, 1962).
Maurice Ashley: *King John* (Weidenfeld and Nicolson, 1972).
J. T. Appleby: *John, King of England* (Bell, 1959).
A. Lloyd: *King John* (David and Charles, 1973).
S. Painter: *The Reign of King John* (J. Hopkins Press, 1949).
Kate Norgate's *John Lackland* (Macmillan, 1902) is still worth consulting.
Two good biographies deal with Richard of Cornwall:
N. Denholm-Young: *Richard of Cornwall* (Blackwell, 1947).
T. W. E. Roche: *The King of Almayne* (John Murray, 1966).
For Isabella of Angoulême, see:
H. G. Richardson: *The Marriage and Coronation of Isabella of Angoulême* (in *English Historical Review*, lxi, 1946) and *King John and Isabella of Angoulême* (in *English Historical Review*, 1946 and 1950).
F. A. Cazel and S. Painter: *The Marriage of Isabella of Angoulême* (in *English Historical Review*, lxii, 1948, and lxvii, 1952.

HENRY III

FATHER: *King John (see page 66).*
MOTHER: *Isabella of Angoulême (see page 66, under King John).*
SIBLINGS: *(see page 67, under King John).*

HENRY III
He was born on 1st October, 1207 at Winchester Castle, Hampshire. He succeeded his father as King of England and Duke of Normandy and Aquitaine on 28th October, 1216, being crowned on that day in Gloucester Cathedral with his mother's circlet, the Crown Jewels having been lost in the River Wash. He was again crowned on 17th May, 1220 at Westminster Abbey. In December, 1259, he formally renounced the duchy of Normandy under the terms of the Treaty of Paris.

Henry III married, on 14th January, 1236, at Canterbury Cathedral, Kent:

Eleanor
She was the daughter of Raymond Berenger V, Count of Provence, by Beatrice, daughter of Thomas I, Count of Savoy; her sister Sanchia later married Henry's brother Richard. Eleanor was born between 1217 and 1226, perhaps in c.1223, at Aix-en-Provence, France, and was crowned Queen Consort on 19th/20th January, 1236 at Westminster Abbey. She became a nun on 7th July, 1284 at Amesbury Abbey, Wiltshire. She died on 24th/25th June, 1291 at Amesbury Abbey, and was buried there.

Issue of marriage:
1 *Edward I (see page 81).*
2 *Margaret (see page 200, under Alexander III, King of Scotland).*
3 *Beatrice*
She was born on 25th June, 1242, at Bordeaux, Gascony. She married John de Montfort of Dreux, Earl of Richmond, afterwards

John II, Duke of Brittany (1239–1305) on 22nd January, 1260 at the Abbey of St Denis, Paris, and had issue:

1 Arthur II, Duke of Brittany (1262–1312); he married firstly Beatrice (1260–1291), daughter of Guy VI, Viscount of Limoges, and had issue. He married secondly Yolande, daughter of Robert IV, Count of Dreux, and widow of Alexander III, King of Scotland, and had issue.

2 John, Earl of Richmond (1266?–1334).

3 Peter, Count of Léon (d.1312).

4 Mary (1268–1339); she married Guy de Châtillon, Count of St Pol, and had issue.

5 Eleanor or Alice (1274–1329?); she became a nun at Amesbury Abbey, Wiltshire, and later Abbess of Fontevrault, France.

6 Blanche (d.1327); she married Philip, Count of Artois, Lord of Conches and Domfront (d.1298), and had issue.

7 Henry (d. young 1284).

Beatrice died on 24th March, 1275 in London; she was perhaps buried in Reading Abbey, Berkshire, and probably removed later to Greyfriars Church, Newgate, London. Her tomb was lost during the Reformation.

4 Edmund

Known as "Crouchback", he was born on 16th January, 1245 in London. He was nominated King of Sicily by the Pope on 7th January, 1254, but deprived of that kingdom in 1263. He was created Earl of Leicester on 26th October, 1265, and Earl of Lancaster on 30th June, 1267. He became Count of Champagne and Brie in right of his second wife in 1276. Edmund died on 5th June, 1296, at Bayonne, and was buried in Westminster Abbey.

Edmund married firstly, on 8th/9th April, 1269, in the newly-rebuilt Westminster Abbey:

Aveline

She was the daughter of William de Forz or Fortibus, 6th Earl of Aumale, by Isabella, daughter of Baldwin de Redvers, 7th Earl of Devon. She was born on 20th January, 1259 at Burstwick, Yorkshire, and succeeded her brother as Countess of Aumale before 6th April, 1269. She died on 10th November, 1274, at Stockwell, Surrey, and was buried in Westminster Abbey; hers was the first tomb in the new church. There was no issue of her marriage to Edmund.

Edmund married secondly, in January (before 3rd February),

1276, or between 27th July and 29th October, 1276 (although no evidence exists as to where):

Blanche

She was the daughter of Robert I, Count of Artois, by Matilda, daughter of Henry II, Duke of Brabant, and she was born around c.1245/50. She married firstly Henry I, King of Navarre and Count of Champagne (d.1274) in 1269, and had issue:

1 Joan, Queen of Navarre (1273–1305); she married Philip IV, King of France (1268–1314), and had issue, including Isabella, wife of Edward II.

2 Theobald (d.young).

Blanche died on 2nd May, 1302 in Paris, and was probably buried in the Minoresses Convent, Aldgate, London.

Issue of marriage:

(i) *Thomas*

He was born around 1277/80. He became Earl of Lincoln in right of his wife on or before 28th October, 1294. He succeeded his father as Earl of Lancaster and Leicester on 8th September, 1298. He was styled Earl Ferrers (Derby) from 1301. He renounced the earldom of Lincoln when he divorced his wife in c.1318. Thomas was executed on 22nd March, 1322, at Pontefract, Yorkshire, by order of Edward II. He was buried in the Priory of St John at Pontefract.

Thomas married, on or before 28th October, 1294 (?), or perhaps as late as c.1310 (although no record exists as to where):

Alice

She was the daughter of Henry de Lacy, 3rd Earl of Lincoln, by Margaret, daughter of Sir William Longespée of Amesbury, Wiltshire, a descendant of Henry II. Alice was born on 25th December, 1281, probably at Denbigh Castle, Denbighshire, and succeeded her father as Countess of Lincoln on 5th February, 1311; she succeeded her mother as Countess of Salisbury before 20th September, 1311. Lancaster divorced her in c.1318 on account of her adultery with the Earl of Surrey's squire, Sir Eubulo Lestraunge, whom she married as her second husband before 10th November, 1324. Eubulo died in 1335. Alice married thirdly Hugh de Freyne, Baron Freyne (d.1336/7) before 23rd March, 1336. She died on 2nd October, 1348, and was buried in Barlings Abbey, Birling, Kent. She had no issue from any of her marriages.

(ii) *Henry*

He was born in c.1281 at Grosmont Castle, Monmouthshire. He was restored to the earldom of Leicester on 29th March, 1324, two years after his brother's execution for treason, and styled Earl of Lancaster from 26th October, 1326, being restored formally to that earldom on 3rd February, 1327. He succeeded his brother John as Lord of Beaufort and Nogent in France in 1336 (?). Henry died on 22nd September, 1345, at Leicester, and was buried in Newark Abbey, Leicester.

Henry married, before 2nd March, 1297 (although no evidence exists as to where):

Matilda

She was the daughter of Sir Patrick de Chaworth of Kidwelly, by Isabella, daughter of William de Beauchamp, 1st Earl of Warwick. She was born in 1282 or 1288, and died before 3rd December, 1322, being buried at Mottisfont Priory.

Issue of marriage:

(a) *Henry*

He was born between 1299 and 1314 at Grosmont Castle, Monmouthshire. He was created Earl of Derby on 16th March, 1337, and succeeded his father as Earl of Lancaster, Earl of Leicester and Lord of Beaufort and Nogent on 22nd September, 1345. He was made a Knight of the Garter in 1348, created Earl of Lincoln on 20th August, 1349, and created Duke of Lancaster on 6th March, 1351. He was created Earl of Moray on 5th April, 1359, but never so styled. Henry died on 23rd/24th March, 1361, at Leicester Castle of the Black Death (bubonic plague), and was buried in Newark Abbey, Leicester.

Henry married, in c.1334/7 (although no record exists as to where):

Isabella

She was the daughter of Henry, 1st Baron de Beaumont and Earl of Buchan, by Alice, daughter of Sir Alexander Comyn. She died in 1361 at Leicester of the Black Death (bubonic plague), and was buried in Newark Abbey, Leicester.

Issue of marriage:

(i) *Matilda*

She was born on 4th April, c.1339 or 1341. She married firstly Ralph de Stafford (d.1347/9) on 1st

November, 1344. She married secondly William V, Duke of Bavaria, Count of Holland, Hainault and Zeeland (1327–1389) in 1352 at the King's Chapel in the Palace of Westminster. She succeeded her father as Countess of Leicester on 23rd March, 1361, but died on 10th April, 1362, in England, of the Black Death (bubonic plague) (although some sources say she was poisoned).

(ii) Blanche

She married John of Gaunt, Duke of Lancaster (see page 99, under Edward III).

(b) *Blanche*

She was born in c.1305, and married Thomas Wake, 2nd Baron Wake of Liddell (d.1349) before 9th October, 1316. She died on 10th July, 1380, and was buried in the Church of the Friars Minor, Stamford, Lincs.

(c) *Matilda*

She was born in c.1310. She married firstly William de Burgh, 3rd Earl of Ulster (1312–1333) after 1st May, 1327 (date of dispensation) and before 1330, and had issue:

1 Elizabeth; she married Lionel of Antwerp, Duke of Clarence (see page 95, under Edward III).

Matilda married secondly Ralph de Ufford (d.1346) before 8th August, 1343, and had issue:

2 Matilda (d.1413); she married Thomas de Vere, 8th Earl of Oxford (1336?–1371), and had issue.

Matilda became an Augustinian Canoness at Campsey Abbey, Suffolk (?) between 8th August, 1347 and 25th April, 1348; she transferred to the Poor Clares at Bruisyard Abbey, Suffolk (?) in 1364. She died before 5th May, 1377, at Campsey Abbey, Suffolk (?), and was buried in Bruisyard Abbey, Suffolk.

(d) *Joan*

She was born in c.1312. She married John, 3rd Baron Mowbray, Lord of Axholme, Bramber and Gower (1310–1361) after 28th February, 1327, and had issue:

1 John, 4th Baron Mowbray (1340–killed 1368); he married Elizabeth (1338–by 1368), daughter of John, 4th Baron de Segrave by Margaret, Duchess of Norfolk (see page 86, under Edward I), and had issue.

2 Blanche (d.1409); she either married John de Segrave of Folkestone (d.1349) and had issue, or married firstly Robert, Baron Bertram of Bothall (d.1363/4), secondly Thomas, Baron Poynings (d.1375), thirdly Sir John Worth (d.1391) and fourthly Sir John Wiltshire.

3 Eleanor (d.c.1387); she married firstly Roger, Baron de la Warre (1326–1370), and secondly Sir Lewis de Clifford (d.1404).

Joan died on 7th July, 1345 (?) or 1349 (?), and was buried in Byland Abbey, Yorkshire.

(e) *Isabella*

She was born in c.1317, and perhaps married Henry de la Dale in her youth. She became a nun at Amesbury Abbey, Wiltshire before 6th April, 1337, and was elected Prioress of Amesbury before 23rd March, 1344. She died after 1st February, 1347.

(f) *Eleanor*

She was born in c.1318. She married firstly John, 2nd Baron de Beaumont (d.1342) before June, 1337, and had issue:

1 Henry, 3rd Baron de Beaumont (1340–1369); he married Margaret (d.1398) daughter of John de Vere, 7th Earl of Oxford, and had issue.

2 Joan (d. after 1400).

Eleanor married secondly Richard FitzAlan, 10th Earl of Arundel (1306/13–1376) on 5th February, 1345 at Ditton Church, Stoke Poges, Bucks., and had issue:

3 Edmund (c.1346–c.1366).

4 Joan (c.1347–1419); she married Humphrey de Bohun, Earl of Hereford, Essex and Northampton (1342–1373), and had issue, including Mary, wife of Henry IV, and Eleanor, wife of Thomas, Duke of Gloucester (see page 113, under Edward III).

5 Richard, 11th Earl of Arundel (c.1348–executed 1397); he married firstly Elizabeth (d.1385), daughter of William de Bohun, Earl of Northampton, and had issue, and secondly Philippa Mortimer (see page 97, under Edward III).

6 Alice (c.1350–1414/16); she married Thomas Holland, 1st Earl of Kent (c.1355–1397), son of Joan, Princess of Wales (see page 93, under Edward III), and had

issue, including Eleanor, Countess of March (see page 96, under Edward III).

7 John, Baron of Arundel (c.1351–drowned 1379); he married Eleanor (1346?–1405), daughter of Sir John Maltravers, and had issue.

8 Thomas, Archbishop of Canterbury (1353–1414).

9 Mary.

10 Eleanor (c.1354/6–before 1366).

Eleanor died on 11th January, 1372 at Arundel Castle, Sussex, and was buried in Lewes Priory, Sussex.

(g) *Mary*

She was born around 1320/21. She married firstly Henry Percy, 3rd Baron of Alnwick (1322?–1368) in c. September, 1334 at Tutbury Castle, and had issue:

1 Henry, 1st Earl of Northumberland (1341–1408); he married Matilda (d.1372), daughter of Ralph, Baron Neville of Raby, and had issue. He married secondly Matilda (d.1398), daughter of Thomas, Baron Lucy of Cockermouth.

2 Thomas, Earl of Worcester (1344?–executed 1403). Had illegitimate issue.

3 Mary (b.1360); she married John, Baron Ros of Helmsley.

Mary died on 1st/2nd September, 1362, and was buried at Alnwick, Northumberland.

Henry, Earl of Lancaster, married secondly, after 1322 (although no evidence exists as to where):

Alice

She was the daughter of John de Joinville, Seneschal of Champagne, by Alice, daughter of Gautier, Seigneur de Risnel. She married firstly John, Seigneur of Arcis-sur-Aube and Chacenay (d. by 1307). Nothing more is known of her.

(iii) *John*

He was born before May, 1286, and became Lord of Beaufort and Nogent-Lartauld on the death of his mother in May, 1302. He died unmarried in c.1327 (?) or 1336 (certainly by 1337) in France.

(iv) *Mary*

No dates are recorded. She died young, in France.

5 *Richard*

He was born in c.1247, and died before 1256. He was buried in Westminster Abbey.

6 *John*

He was born in c.1250 at Windsor Castle, and died before 1256. He was buried in Westminster Abbey.

7 *William*

He was born in c.1250/51, and died either at birth or in 1256. He was buried in the New Church of the Knights Templars, Fleet Street, London.

8 *Katherine*

She was born on 25th November, 1252/3, at the Palace of Westminster. A mute child, she died on 3rd May, 1257 at Windsor Castle, and was buried in Westminster Abbey.

9 *Henry*

No dates are recorded. He died young, and was buried in Westminster Abbey.

HENRY III

He died on 16th November, 1272 at the Palace of Westminster, and was buried in Westminster Abbey.

He was succeeded by his son Edward.

Recommended reading

The definitive work is still:

F. M. Powicke: *King Henry III and the Lord Edward* (2 vols., Oxford University Press, 1947).

See also:

Kate Norgate: *The Minority of Henry III* (1912).

Tufton Beamish: *Battle Royal* (Muller, 1965).

EDWARD I

FATHER: *Henry III (see page 73).*
MOTHER: *Eleanor of Provence (see page 73, under Henry III).*
SIBLINGS: *(see page 73 under Henry III).*

EDWARD I

Known as "Longshanks" and "the Lawgiver", he was born on 17th/18th June, 1239, at the Palace of Westminster. He was created Duke of Gascony in 1254, and Earl of Chester on 14th February, 1254. He resigned the earldom of Chester on 24th December, 1264, but was restored to it on 4th August, 1265. He succeeded his father as King of England on 20th November, 1272, and was crowned on 19th August, 1274 at Westminster Abbey.

Edward I married firstly, between 13th and 31st October, 1254, at the Abbey of Las Huelgas, Burgos, Castile:

Eleanor

She was the daughter of Ferdinand III, King of Castile, by Joan, daughter of Simon of Dammartin, Count of Ponthieu and Aumale. Eleanor was born around 1244/5 in Castile. She was crowned Queen Consort on 19th August, 1274 at Westminster Abbey. She succeeded her mother as Countess of Ponthieu and Montreuil in March, 1279. Eleanor died on 28th November, 1290, at the manor of Harby, Notts., of a fever, and was buried in Westminster Abbey.

Issue of marriage:

1 *Eleanor*

She was born c.17th June, 1264 (or possibly as late as 1269, although the Issue Rolls of 1302 describe her as Edward's eldest daughter) at Windsor Castle. She married firstly Alfonso III, King of Aragon (d.1291) by proxy on 15th August, 1290 at Westminster Abbey. The marriage was not consummated because of the bridegroom's early death. Eleanor married secondly Henry III,

Count of Bar (d.1302) on 20th September, 1293 at Bristol, and had issue:

1 Edward I, Count of Bar (1294–1337); he drowned in a shipwreck. He married Mary (1298–c.1310), daughter of Robert, Duke of Burgundy, and had issue.
2 Joan (1295–1361); she married John de Warenne, Earl of Surrey (1286–1347) and had issue. She was divorced in 1315.
3 Eleanor (?); she is said to have married Llywelyn ap Owen of Deheubarth, and to have had issue, but this is doubtful.

Eleanor died on 12th October, 1298 at Ghent in Flanders, and was buried in Westminster Abbey.

2 *Joan*
She was born in the summer of 1265, either in Paris or perhaps at Abbeville, Ponthieu. She died before 7th September, 1265, in France, and was buried in Westminster Abbey.

3 *John*
He was born on 10th June or 10th July, 1266, either at Windsor Castle, or at Kenilworth Castle, Warwickshire, or at Winchester. He died on 1st or 3rd August, 1271/2 at the Palace of Westminster, and was buried in Westminster Abbey.

4 *Henry*
He was born on 13th July, 1267/8 at Windsor Castle. He died on 14th October, 1274, either at Merton, Surrey, or at Guildford Castle, Surrey, and was buried in Westminster Abbey.

5 *Alice*
She is said to have been born at Woodstock Palace, Oxon., but the date of her birth is unknown. The Harleian MSS. say she died at the age of 12. Some historians have identified her with the child born to the King and Queen in March, 1279, but this cannot be correct, as that infant's funeral at Westminster Abbey took place during the same year (see Isabella, below).

6 *Juliana or Katherine*
She was born in 1271 at Acre, Palestine, and died there on 28th May or 5th September, 1271. She is perhaps the daughter who is buried in the Church of the Friars Preachers, Bordeaux, Gascony.

7 *Joan*
She was born in Spring, 1272, at Acre, Palestine. She married firstly Gilbert de Clare, 3rd Earl of Gloucester and 7th Earl of Hertford (1243–1295) on 30th April, 1290, at Westminster Abbey, and had issue:

1 Gilbert, Earl of Gloucester and Hertford (1291–1314: killed at

the Battle of Bannockburn); he married Matilda (d.1320), daughter of Richard de Burgh, Earl of Ulster, and had issue.

2 Eleanor (1292–1337); she married firstly Hugh le Despenser (executed 1326), and had issue. She married secondly Sir William la Zouche de Mortimer of Ashby, Leics. (d.1337).

3 Margaret (1293–1342); she married firstly Piers Gaveston, Earl of Cornwall (1284?–executed 1312), and had issue. She married secondly Hugh de Audley, Earl of Gloucester (1289?–1347), and had issue.

4 Elizabeth (1295–1360); she married firstly John de Burgh (d.1313), and had issue. She married secondly Sir Theobald de Verdon of Alton, Staffs. (1278–1316), and had issue. She married thirdly Roger, Baron d'Amory (d.1322), and had issue.

Joan married secondly Ralph, 1st Baron de Monthermer, Earl of Gloucester and Earl of Atholl (d.1325) before July, 1297, and had issue:

5 Thomas, 2nd Baron Monthermer (1301–1340: killed at the Battle of Sluys); he married Margaret Teyes (d.1349), and had issue.

6 Edward, 3rd Baron Monthermer (1304–1340).

7 Mary (1298–after 1371); she married Duncan, 10th Earl of Fife (1285–1353), and had issue.

8 Joan (b.1299); a nun at Amesbury Abbey, Wilts.

Joan died on 23rd April, 1307 at her manor of Clare, Suffolk, and was buried in the Priory Church of the Austin Friars, Clare, Suffolk.

8 *Alfonso*

He was born on 24th November, 1273, either at Bayonne or at Bordeaux, Gascony, or in Maine. He was perhaps designated Earl of Chester in 1284. He died on 14th or 19th August, 1284, at Windsor Castle, and was buried in Westminster Abbey.

9 *Margaret*

She was born on 11th September, 1275 at Windsor Castle. She married John II "the Peaceful", Duke of Brabant (d.1312) on 8th July, 1290 at Westminster Abbey, and had issue:

1 John III "the Triumphant", Duke of Brabant (1300–1355); he married Mary (d.1335), daughter of Louis of France, Count of Evreux, and had issue.

Margaret died in 1318, and was buried in the Collegiate Church of St Gudule, Brussels.

10 *Berengaria* or *Berenice*

She was born in 1276 at Kennington Palace, Surrey, and died between 1276 and 1279. She was buried in Westminster Abbey.

11 *Mary*

She was born on 11th March or 22nd April, 1278 at Windsor Castle. She entered Amesbury Abbey, Wiltshire, as a novice in 1284, being there professed as a nun on 15th August, 1285. She died before 8th July, 1332, at Amesbury Abbey, where she was buried.

12 *Isabella*

She was born on 12th March, 1279, probably at Woodstock Palace, Oxon., or at Windsor Castle, or at Marlborough Castle, Wiltshire. She died in 1279, and was buried in Westminster Abbey.

13 *Elizabeth*

She was born in August, 1282 at Rhuddlan Castle, Flintshire, Wales. She married firstly John I, Count of Holland and Zeeland (d.1299) on 18th January, 1296/7 at Ipswich Priory Church, Suffolk. She married secondly Humphrey de Bohun, 4th Earl of Hereford and Essex (1276?–1322) on 14th November, 1302 at Westminster Abbey, and had issue:

1 Hugh or Humphrey (1303?–1305).
2 Eleanor (1304–1363); she married firstly James Butler, 1st Earl of Ormonde (1305?–1338), and had issue. She married secondly Sir Thomas de Dagworth (1276–murdered 1350), and had issue.
3 Mary or Margaret (b.&d.1305).
4 John, Earl of Hereford and Essex (1306–1336); he married firstly Alice, daughter of Edmund FitzAlan, Earl of Arundel, and had issue, and secondly Margaret (d. after 1347), daughter of Ralph, Lord Bassett of Drayton.
5 Humphrey, Earl of Hereford and Essex (1309–1361).
6 William, Earl of Northampton (1310/12–1360); he married Elizabeth (1313–1356), daughter of Bartholemew de Badlesmere, and had issue.
7 Edward, twin of William (1310/12–drowned 1334); he married Margaret (d.1341), daughter of William, Baron de Ros.
8 Edmund; he married Matilda, daughter of Nicholas de Segrave, Baron of Stowe.
9 Eneas (1313/15–before 1343).
10 Margaret (d.1391); she married Hugh de Courtenay, Earl of Devon (1303–1377), and had issue.

11 Isabella (b.&d.1316).
Elizabeth died on c.5th May, 1316 at Quendon, Essex, in child-birth, and was buried in Walden Abbey, Essex.

14 Edward II *(see page 89)*.

15 Beatrice
She was born after August, 1286, either in Gascony or in Aquitaine. She died young.

16 Blanche
She was born in 1289/90, and died young.

Edward I married secondly, on 8th or 10th September, 1299, at Canterbury Cathedral, Kent:

Margaret
She was the daughter of Philip III, King of France, by Mary, daughter of Henry III, Duke of Brabant, and she was born around 1279/82 in Paris. Margaret was never crowned. She died on 14th February, 1317/18, at Marlborough Castle, Wiltshire, and was buried in Greyfriars Church, Newgate, London. Her tomb was lost during the Reformation.

Issue of marriage:

1 Thomas
He was born on 1st June, 1300 at Brotherton, Yorkshire, and was created Earl of Norfolk on 16th December, 1312. He died between 4th August and 20th September, 1338, and was buried in the Abbey of Bury St Edmunds, Suffolk.

   Thomas married firstly, between c.1316 and 1320 (although no evidence exists as to where):

Alice
She was the daughter of Sir Roger Halys or Hales of Harwich, Essex. She died after 8th May, 1326, and before 1330.

Issue of marriage:

   (i) *Edward*
   He was born in c.1319/20, and died before 13th September, 1337, perhaps in 1332 (?).

      Edward married, in May/June, 1328 (although no evidence exists as to where):

   Beatrice
   She was the daughter of Roger Mortimer, Earl of March, by Joan, daughter of Peter de Genville. After the death of Edward, she married secondly Thomas de Braose, Lord Brewes, in c.1334 (before 13th September, 1337), and had issue:

1 Beatrice; she married William de Say, Baron Say (1340–1375), and had issue.

2 John, a knight (d.1367); he married Elizabeth de Montacute.

3 Thomas, a knight (d.1395).

4 Peter.

5 Elizabeth.

6 Joan.

Beatrice died on 16th October, 1383.

(ii) *Margaret*

Known as "Margaret Marshal", as the Dukes of Norfolk have always held the office of Earl Marshal of England, she was born around c.1320/22. She married firstly John de Segrave, 4th Baron de Segrave (1306 or 1315–1353) after 3rd March, 1327, and probably in 1337/8, and had issue:

1 Elizabeth (1338–1375/6); she married John, 4th Baron Mowbray of Axholme, Lincs. (1340–killed 1368), and had issue.

2 Anne, Abbess of Barking (d.c.1377).

Margaret succeeded her father as Countess of Norfolk between 4th August and 20th September, 1338. She married secondly Walter, 1st Baron de Mauny or Manny (d.1372) before 30th May, 1354, and had issue:

3 Thomas (drowned in infancy before 1371/2).

4 Anne (1354–1384); she married John Hastings, 2nd Earl of Pembroke (1347–1375), who had married previously Margaret, daughter of Edward III, and had issue.

Margaret was created Duchess of Norfolk for life on 29th September, 1397. She died on 24th March, 1399/1400, and was buried either in the Charterhouse, London, or in Greyfriars Church, Newgate, London.

(iii) *Alice*

She was born in c.1324. She married Edward de Montacute, 1st Baron Montacute (c.1304–1361) before 16th January, 1339, and possibly before 29th August, 1338, and had issue:

1 Elizabeth (b.1344): she married either Walter de Ufford or Sir John de Braose (d.1367).

2 Margaret (c.1347–before 1351/2).

3 Joan (1349–1375); she married William de Ufford, 2nd Earl of Suffolk (1339?–1382), and had issue.

4 Matilda (c.1350–1394); a nun, later Abbess of Barking.

Alice died probably between 14th November, 1351 and 30th

January, 1352 (certainly before 16th November, 1361), at Bungay, Suffolk, of wounds received as a result of an assault by her husband.

Thomas married secondly, in c.1328 (although no evidence exists as to where):

Mary

She was the daughter of Peter de Braose, and married firstly Ralph, Baron Cobham of Norfolk (d.1326), by whom she had issue:

1 John (1324–after 1378), Baron Cobham.

Mary died on 9th June, 1362 (or between 17th April, 1361 and 20th June, 1362).

Issue of marriage:

(i) *John*

No dates are recorded. He was a monk at Ely Abbey, Cambs.

2 *Edmund*

He was born on 5th August, 1301 at Woodstock Palace, Oxon., and was created Earl of Kent on 28th July, 1321. He was probably styled Earl of Arundel as well, as he held the castle and honour of Arundel, but he was never formally so created. He was executed for supporting his brother, the deposed Edward II, by order of the Regents Mortimer and Queen Isabella, on 19th March, 1330 outside Winchester Castle, and he was buried in the Church of the Dominican Friars, Winchester. His remains were later removed to Westminster Abbey.

Edmund married, in December, 1325 (after 6th October, date of dispensation) (although no record exists as to where):

Margaret

She was the daughter of John Wake, 1st Baron Wake of Liddell, by Joan, daughter either of William de Fenes or of John FitzBernard of Kingsdown, Kent. Margaret was born around c.1299/1300. She married firstly, John Comyn, Lord of Badenoch (killed 1314), and had issue:

1 Aymer (d. young before 1316).

Margaret succeeded her brother as Baroness Wake of Liddell on 30th/31st May, 1349, being first so styled on 20th August, 1349. She died on 29th September, 1349, of the Black Death.

Issue of marriage:

(i) *Edmund*

He was born in c.1326, and was restored to the earldom of Kent, which had been forfeited by his father, on 7th

December, 1330. He died before 5th October, 1331, or on 5th January, 1333 (?).

(ii) *Margaret*
She was born in 1327. She married Amanco, Seigneur d'Albret of Gascony, and died before 1352.

(iii) *Joan*
She married Edward of Woodstock, Prince of Wales (see page 93, under Edward III).

(iv) *John*
He was born on 7th April, 1330 at Arundel Castle, Sussex, his father's posthumous child. He succeeded his mother as Baron Wake of Liddell on 29th September, 1349. He was created Earl of Kent on 10th April, 1351. He died on 26th/27th December, 1352, and was buried in the Church of the Greyfriars, Winchester, Hants.

John married, after 3rd April, 1348 (date of dispensation) (although no evidence exists as to where):
Elizabeth
She was the daughter of William V, Margrave or Duke of Juliers, by Joan, daughter of William V, Count of Hainault and Holland, and sister of Philippa, wife of Edward III. After John's death, Elizabeth married secondly Sir Eustace d'Aubrécicourt (d.1372/3) on 29th September, 1360 at Wingham Church, Kent, and had issue:
1 Sanchez.
2 William.
After Eustace died, Elizabeth became a nun at Waverley Abbey. She died on 6th June, 1411, and was buried in the Church of the Greyfriars, Winchester, Hants. There was no issue of her first marriage.

Note: There is no contemporary evidence that the marriage of Edmund, Earl of Kent, and Margaret Wake produced two other sons, Robert and Thomas, who are mentioned in later sources.

3 *Eleanor*
She was born on 4th May, 1306 at Winchester. She died in 1311 at Amesbury Abbey, Wilts., and was buried in Beaulieu Abbey, Hants.

Edward I is reputed to have had the following illegitimate issue (according to the Hayles Abbey Chronicle), and while this is possible, it is still subject to some doubt:
By an unknown mother,

1 John Botetourt, Lord of Mendlesham, Suffolk (c.1265–1324); he married Matilda, daughter of Thomas FitzOates, and had issue.

EDWARD I

He died on 7th July, 1307 at Burgh-on-Sands, Northumberland, and was buried in Westminster Abbey.

He was succeeded by his son Edward.

Recommended reading
  L. F. Salzman: *Edward I* (Constable, 1968).
  F. M. Powicke: *King Henry III and the Lord Edward* (2 vols., Oxford University Press, 1947).
  T. F. Tout's *Edward I* (1893 and 1920) is now out of date.

EDWARD II

FATHER: *Edward I (see page 81)*.
MOTHER: *Eleanor of Castile (see page 81, under Edward I)*.
SIBLINGS: *(see page 81, under Edward I)*.

EDWARD II

He was born on 25th April, 1284 at Caernarvon Castle, Wales. He succeeded his mother as Count of Ponthieu and Montreuil on 28th November, 1290. He was created and invested as Earl of Chester and Prince of Wales on 7th February, 1301; he was the first English Prince of Wales, and since 1301 the title has usually been granted to the eldest son of the sovereign. The story of Edward being presented by his father to the Welsh on a shield, just after his birth in 1284, is a picturesque fabrication. He was created Duke of Aquitaine in May,

1306. He succeeded his father as King of England on 8th July, 1307, and was crowned on 24th/25th February, 1308, in Westminster Abbey.

Edward II was deposed by an illegally-convened "Parliament" on 20th January, 1327, and formally abdicated in favour of his son Edward on 25th January, 1327.

Edward II married, on 25th or 28th January, 1308, at Boulogne Cathedral, France:

Isabella

She was the daughter of Philip IV, King of France, by Joan I, Queen of Navarre, daughter of Blanche of Artois (see page 75, under Henry III). Isabella was born around c.1292/5 in Paris. She was crowned Queen Consort on 24th/25th February, 1308, in Westminster Abbey. She was instrumental in plotting the deposition and murder of her husband, and after his abdication she shared the Regency with her lover, Roger Mortimer, Earl of March. When Edward III attained his majority in 1330, the regents were overthrown. Mortimer was executed, and Isabella allowed an honourable retirement from public life. She died on 22nd August, 1358 either at Castle Rising, Norfolk, or at Hertford Castle, and was buried in Greyfriars Church, Newgate, London. Her tomb was lost during the Reformation.

Issue of marriage:

1 *Edward III (see page 92).*

2 *John*

He was born on c.15th or 25th August, 1316 at Eltham Palace, Kent, and was created Earl of Cornwall between 16th and 31st October, 1328. He died on 13th September, 1336, at Perth, Scotland, and was buried in Westminster Abbey.

3 *Eleanor*

She was born on 18th June, 1318 at Woodstock Palace, Oxon.; she married Reginald II, Count of Gueldres and Zutphen (d.1343) in May, 1332 at Nimeguen, Gueldres, and had issue:

1 Reginald III, Count of Gueldres (1334–1371); he married Mary (d.1398), daughter of John III, Duke of Brabant.

2 Edward, Count of Gueldres (1336–1371); he married Katherine (d.1401), daughter of Albert, Duke of Holland and Hainault.

Eleanor may also have been the mother of the following, although it is more probable that they were the children of Reginald's first wife, Sophia of Malines (d.1329):

3 Margaret (d.1344).

4 Matilda (d.1380); she married firstly Godfrey, Count of Hennenburg, and secondly John, Duke of Cleves; she married thirdly John, Count of Châtillon, Blois.

5 Mary (d.1405); she married William VI, Duke of Juliers (d.1393), and had issue.

6 Isabella, Abbess of Graventhal.

Eleanor died on 22nd April, 1355 at Deventer Abbey, Gueldres, where she was buried.

4 Joan *(see page 211, under David II of Scotland).*

Edward II also had the following **illegitimate issue**:

By an unknown mother:

1 Adam (c.1310–after 1322).

EDWARD II

He was murdered on 21st September, 1327 at Berkeley Castle, Gloucs., by having a red-hot spit thrust into his bowels; this was probably done on the orders of the Regent, Roger Mortimer, Earl of March, with the collusion of Queen Isabella, who was Mortimer's mistress. Edward was buried in Gloucester Cathedral.

He was succeeded by his son Edward, in whose favour he had abdicated on 25th January, 1327.

Recommended reading

There have been several recent works:

Natalie Fryde: *The Tyranny and Fall of Edward II* (Cambridge University Press, 1979).

C. Bingham: *Edward II* (Weidenfeld and Nicolson, 1973).

H. F. Hutchison: *Edward II, the Pliant King* (Eyre and Spottiswoode, 1971).

Hilda Johnstone: *Edward of Caernarvon* (1946).

For Isabella of France, see:

Hilda Johnstone: *Isabella, the She-Wolf of France* (in *History*, vol. 21, 1936).

C. G. Crump: *The Arrest of Roger Mortimer and Queen Isabel* (in *English Historical Review*, xxvi, 1911).

EDWARD III

FATHER: *Edward II (see page 89)*.
MOTHER: *Isabella of France (see page 90, under Edward II)*.
SIBLINGS: *(see page 91, under Edward II)*.

EDWARD III
He was born on 13th November, 1312 at Windsor Castle. He was created Earl of Chester on 24th November (?), 1312, and Count of Ponthieu and Montreuil on 2nd September, 1325. He was created Duke of Aquitaine on 10th September, 1325. He succeeded his father as King of England on 25th January, 1327, Edward II having abdicated in favour of his son on that day. Edward III was crowned on 1st February, 1327 in Westminster Abbey. On 20th October, 1330, he assumed personal rule after overthrowing the regents, his mother Queen Isabella and her lover Roger Mortimer, Earl of March. He formally assumed the title King of France, which he claimed through his mother, in January, 1340, thus starting the Hundred Years War.

Edward III married, on 24th January, 1328, at York Minster:
Philippa
She was the daughter of William V "the Good", Count of Hainault and Holland, by Joan, daughter of Charles of France, Count of Valois, and she was born in c.1313/14 either at Valenciennes or at Mons in Flanders. She was crowned on 2nd or 20th February, 1328 at Westminster Abbey, and again on 4th March, 1330, also at Westminster Abbey. She died on 15th August, 1369, at Windsor Castle, of a dropsy-like illness, and was buried in Westminster Abbey.

Issue of marriage:
1 *Edward*
Known from the 16th century onwards as "the Black Prince" (because of the colour of his armour), he was born on 15th June,

1330 at Woodstock Palace, Oxon. He was created Earl of Chester on 18th May, 1333, Duke of Cornwall on 3rd March, 1337, and Prince of Wales on 12th May, 1343, being invested with the principality on the same day. He was made a Knight of the Garter when his father first founded the Order in 1348. He was created Prince of Aquitaine on 19th July, 1362, and was created Lord of Biscay and Castro Urdiales in Castile by Peter I, King of Castile, on 23rd September, 1366. He resigned the principality of Aquitaine because of ill-health before 28th December, 1375. He died on 8th June, 1376 at the Palace of Westminster, and was buried in Canterbury Cathedral, Kent.

Edward married, on 10th/11th October, 1361, probably at St Stephen's Chapel in the Palace of Westminster, or—less probably —at Canterbury Cathedral or at Windsor Castle:

Joan

She was the daughter of Edmund, Earl of Kent, son of Edward I, by Margaret Wake, and she was born on 29th September, 1328. She married firstly Sir Thomas Holland or Holand of Broughton, Bucks. (d.1360) in c.1339 or in the Spring of 1340, according to her testimony of 1347. She then married secondly, and bigamously, William de Montacute, Earl of Salisbury (1328–1397), in c.1340/1 or 1346 (?) (probably before 10th February, 1341, and certainly by 15th October, 1348). Her marriage to Montacute was annulled by Papal Bull on 13th November, 1349, whilst her marriage to Holland was at the same time pronounced valid. The Pope accordingly ordered Joan to return to Holland and cohabit with him as his lawful wife, which she did around c.1349, and had issue:

1 Edmund (b. before 1352; d. young).

2 Thomas, Earl of Kent (c.1355–1397); he married Alice (c.1350–1414/ 16), daughter of Richard FitzAlan, 10th Earl of Arundel and a descendant of Henry III, and had issue.

3 Joan (c.1356–1384); she married John de Montfort IV, Duke of Brittany (1339–1399) (who afterwards married Joan, later the wife of Henry IV).

4 John, Duke of Exeter (c.1358–executed 1400); he married Elizabeth, daughter of John of Gaunt, Duke of Lancaster (see page 100, below), and had issue.

5 Matilda (c.1359–1391); she married firstly Sir Hugh de Courtenay (d.1377), and secondly Waleran of Luxembourg, Count of St Pol and Ligny (d.1415), and had issue by her second husband.

Joan succeeded her brother John (see page 88, under Edward I) as

Baroness Wake of Liddell and Countess of Kent on 26th/27th December, 1352, and was confirmed in her new titles on 22nd February, 1353. She was made a Lady of the Garter in 1378. She died on 7th, 8th or 21st August, 1385 at Wallingford Castle, Berks., and was buried in Greyfriars Church, Stamford, Lincs. It is likely that her remains were shortly afterwards removed to London, although the site of their final resting place is not recorded.

Issue of marriage:

(i) *Edward*

He was born on 27th January, 1365 at Angoulême in France, and died in January, 1371/2 at Bordeaux, Gascony. He was buried at Bordeaux, but later removed to the Church of the Austin Friars in London.

(ii) *Richard II (see page 116).*

Edward also had the following illegitimate issue:

By Edith de Willesford (d. after 1385):

1 Sir Roger de Clarendon (1345/60–executed 1402); he married Margaret (d.1382), daughter of John Fleming, Baron de la Roche.

By unknown mothers:

2 Edward (b.c.1349; d. young).

3 Sir John Sounders, or John de Galeis (Calais?).

2 *Isabella*

She was probably born in March (her mother was churched before 30th April), 1332, at Woodstock Palace, Oxon. She married Enguerrand II, Lord of Coucy, Count of Soissons and Earl of Bedford (1339?–1397) on 27th July, 1365 at Windsor Castle, and had issue:

1 Mary (1366–1404); she married Henry of Bar, Marquess of Pont-à-Mousson (d.1401), and had issue.

2 Philippa (1367–1411); she married Robert de Vere, Earl of Oxford and Duke of Ireland (1362–1392).

Isabella was made a Lady of the Garter in 1376. She died between 17th June and 5th October, 1382, and was buried in Greyfriars Church, Newgate, London.

3 *Joan*

She was probably born in February (certainly before 30th May), 1335 at Woodstock Palace, Oxon., not in the Tower of London as is sometimes stated. She died on 2nd September, 1348 at Loremo, Bordeaux, Gascony, of the Black Death (bubonic plague), and was buried either at Loremo, or Bordeaux, or in Bayonne Cathedral, Gascony.

4 *William*

He was born around 1334/6, certainly before 16th February, 1337, at Hatfield, Yorkshire, where he died before 3rd March, 1337. He was buried in York Minster.

5 *Lionel*

He was born on 29th November, 1338 at Antwerp in Brabant. He was styled Earl of Ulster in right of his wife from c.26th January, 1347. He was made a Knight of the Garter in c. April, 1361, and created Duke of Clarence on 13th November, 1362. He died on 17th October, 1368, at Alba, Piedmont, Italy, and was buried at Pavia, Italy. His remains were later removed to Clare Priory, Suffolk.

Lionel married firstly, on 15th August, 1342 in the Tower of London, and again on 9th September, 1342 at Reading Abbey, Berkshire:

Elizabeth

She was the daughter of William de Burgh, Earl of Ulster, by Matilda of Lancaster, a descendant of Henry III, and she was born on 6th July, 1332, probably at Carrickfergus Castle in Ulster. She succeeded her father as Countess of Ulster on 6th June, 1333. She died on 10th December (?), 1363, in Dublin, and was buried at Clare Priory, Suffolk.

Issue of marriage:

(i) *Philippa*

She was born on 16th August, 1355 at Eltham Palace, Kent. She married Edmund Mortimer, 3rd Earl of March (1352–1381) (grandson of the Regent Mortimer—see page 90, under Edward II) after 15th February, 1359, and probably in May, 1368 at the Queen's Chapel, Reading Abbey, Berkshire. Philippa died between 21st November, 1378 (date of Will) and 9th February, 1381, and was buried at Cork in Ireland. Her remains were later removed to Wigmore, Herefordshire.

The House of York would one day base its claim to the throne on its descent from Edward III through Philippa, therefore her issue is included here in full:

(a) *Elizabeth*

She was born on 12th February, 1371 at Usk, Monmouthshire. She married firstly Sir Henry ("Hotspur") Percy (1361–1403: killed at the Battle of Shrewsbury) before 1st May, 1380, and had issue:

95

1 Henry, 2nd Earl of Northumberland (1394–1455); he married Eleanor (d.1472), daughter of Ralph Neville, 1st Earl of Westmorland, and had issue. Eleanor was a granddaughter of John of Gaunt, Duke of Lancaster (see page 109, below).

2 Elizabeth (d.1436); she married firstly John, 7th Baron Clifford (d.1421/2), and had issue, and secondly Ralph Neville, 2nd Earl of Westmorland (1408–1485), and had issue.

Elizabeth married secondly Thomas, 1st Baron Camoys (d.1419), and had issue:

3 Son (name not known); he is said to have died young.

Elizabeth died on 20th April, 1417, and was buried at Trotton, Sussex.

(b) *Roger*

He was born on 1st September, 1373 or 11th April, 1374 at Usk, Monmouthshire. He succeeded his mother as Earl of Ulster between 21st November 1378 and 9th February, 1381, and his father as Earl of March on 27th December, 1381. He was killed on 20th July, 1398 at Kenlis during a skirmish with the Irish, and was buried at Wigmore, Herefordshire.

Roger married, on c.7th October, 1388 (although no record exists as to where):

Eleanor

She was the daughter of Thomas Holland, 1st Earl of Kent, by Alice, daughter of Richard FitzAlan, 10th Earl of Arundel and granddaughter of Eleanor of Lancaster, a descendant of Henry III, and she was born in c.1373. After Roger's death, she married secondly Edward de Cherleton, 4th Baron Cherleton of Powys (d.1421) after 19th June, 1399, and had issue:

1 Joan; she married Sir John Grey, Count of Tancarville (d.1421).

2 Joyce (1403?–1446); she married Sir John Tiptoft (d.1443), and had issue.

Eleanor died on 6th, 18th or 23rd October, 1405.

Issue of marriage:

(i) *Anne*

She married Richard, Earl of Cambridge (see page 111, below).

(ii) Edmund

He was born on 4th or 6th November, 1391 in the New Forest, Hampshire, and succeeded his father as Earl of March and Ulster on 20th July, 1398. He died on 18th/19th January, 1425 at Trim Castle, Co. Meath, Ireland, of plague, and was buried in the Collegiate Church of Stoke Clare, Suffolk.

Edmund married, in c.1415 (although no evidence exists as to where):

Anne

She was the daughter of Edmund, 5th Earl of Stafford, by Anne, Countess of Buckingham (see page 114, below), and was born in c.1398/1403. After the death of Edmund, she married secondly, John Holland, Earl of Huntingdon and 3rd Duke of Exeter (1395?–1447), grandson of John of Gaunt (see page 100, below) before 5th March, 1427, and had issue:

1 Henry (1430–1475), 4th Duke of Exeter; he married Anne Plantagenet, sister of Edward IV, and had issue. Afterwards divorced.

Anne died on 20th or 24th September, 1432, and was buried in the Church of St Katherine-by-the-Tower, London.

(iii) Roger

He was born on 24th March or 23rd April, 1393 at Netherwood, and died unmarried around c.1409/10.

(iv) Eleanor

She was born in c.1395. She married Edward, Baron Courtenay (d.1418) in 1408/9, and died after 1414, perhaps having become a nun after her husband's death.

(v) Alice

She is mentioned only by the Tudor chronicler Robert Fabyan, therefore her existence is doubtful.

(c) Philippa

She was born on 21st November, 1375 at Ludlow Castle, Shropshire. She married firstly John Hastings, 3rd Earl of Pembroke (1372–1389) in c.1385. She married secondly Richard FitzAlan, 11th Earl of Arundel (c.1348–executed 1397) (a descendant of Henry III) before 15th August, 1390, and had issue:

1 John (c.1394–d. young after 1397).

Philippa married thirdly Thomas Poynings, 5th Baron St John of Basing (d.1429) before 24th November, 1399. She died around 24th/26th September, 1400/1 at Halnaker, Sussex, and was buried in Boxgrove Priory, Lewes, Sussex.

(d) *Edmund*

He was born on 9th November, 1376/7 at Ludlow Castle, Shropshire, and was made a knight. He died before 13th May, 1411, possibly in 1409, at Harlech Castle, Wales.

Edmund married, in c. November, 1402, although no record exists as to where:

Katherine

She was the daughter of Owen Glendower by Margaret, daughter of Sir David Hanmer of Hanmer, Co. Flint. She died before 1st December, 1413, and was buried in St Swithun's Church, London.

Issue of marriage:

(i) Lionel (d. young).

(ii) Daughter (name not known) (d. young, 1413).

(iii) Daughter (name not known) (d. young, 1413).

(iv) Possibly more daughters who died young before 1413.

Lionel married secondly, on 28th May or 5th June, 1368, at the Church of St Maria Maggiore, Milan, Italy:

Yolande or *Violante*

She was the daughter of Galleazzo Visconti II, Duke of Milan, by Bianca Maria, daughter of Aimone, Count of Savoy, and she was born in c.1353. After the death of Lionel, she married secondly Ottone Paleologo, Marquess of Montferrat (murdered 1378) on 2nd August, 1377, at Pavia, Italy. She married thirdly Ludovico Visconti, Lord of Lodi (1358–1381) on 18th April, 1381, and had issue:

1 John (Giovanni).

Yolande died in November, 1386.

6 *John*

Known as John of Gaunt, he was born in February or March (certainly before 28th May), 1340 at St Bavon's Abbey, Ghent, Flanders, and was created Earl of Richmond on 20th September, 1342. He was made a Knight of the Garter in c. April, 1361. He was first styled Earl of Derby, a title he held in right of his first wife, on 21st July, 1361. He was created Earl of Lancaster in right of his first wife before 14th August, 1361, and Lord of Beaufort and Nogent, also in right of his first wife, on 14th August, 1361. He succeeded his sister-in-law, Matilda of Lancaster (see page 76, under Henry III) as Earl of Derby, Earl of Leicester and Earl of Lincoln on 10th April, 1362, and was created Duke of Lancaster on 13th November, 1362. He was created Lord of Bergerac and Roche-sur-Yon on 8th October, 1370. He surrendered the earldom of Richmond on 5th June, 1372. He assumed the style and title of King of Castile and Léon, in right of his second wife, before 6th October, 1372. He was created Duke of Aquitaine on 2nd March, 1390. He died on 3rd/4th February, 1399, probably at Leicester Castle, or—less probably—at Ely Place, Holborn, London, and was buried in Old St Paul's Cathedral, London.

John had the following illegitimate issue:

By Marie de St Hilaire (d. after 1399):

1 Blanche (before 1360–1388/9?); she married Sir Thomas Morieux.

John married firstly, on 19th May, 1359, at Reading Abbey, Berkshire:

Blanche

She was the daughter of Henry of Grosmont, Duke of Lancaster, by Isabella de Beaumont (see page 76, under Henry III), and she was born on 25th March, 1345. She died on 12th September, 1369, at Bolingbroke Castle, Lincs., of the Black Death (bubonic plague), and was buried in Old St Paul's Cathedral, London.

Issue of marriage:

(i) *Philippa*

She was born on 31st March, 1360 at Leicester Castle. She was made a Lady of the Garter in 1378. She married John I, King of Portugal (1357/8–1433) on 14th February, 1387 at Oporto Cathedral, Portugal, and had issue:

1 Blanche (1388–1389).

2 Alfonso (1390–1400).

3 Edward I, King of Portugal (1391–1438); he married Eleanor (d.1445), daughter of Ferdinand I, King of Aragon and Sicily, and had issue.

4 Peter, Duke of Coimbra (1392–1449); he married Isabella (1409–1443), daughter of James II, Count of Urgel, and had issue.

5 Henry "the Navigator", Duke of Viseu (1394–1460).

6 Isabella (1397–1471); she married Philip III, Duke of Burgundy (d.1467), and had issue.

7 John, Duke of Beja, Constable of Portugal (1400–1442); he

married Isabella (d.1445), daughter of Alfonso I, Duke of Braganza, and had issue.

8 Ferdinand, Grand Master of Aviz (1402–1443).

Philippa died on 19th July, 1415 at Odivelas, near Lisbon, Portugal, of plague, and was buried in Odivelas Abbey. Her remains were later removed to Batalha Abbey, Portugal.

(ii) *John*

He was born in c.1362 or c.1364, and died young. He was buried in St Mary's Church, Leicester.

(iii) *Elizabeth*

She was born before 21st February, 1363 at Burford, Shropshire. She was made a Lady of the Garter in 1378. She married firstly John Hastings, 3rd Earl of Pembroke (1372–1389) in 1380 at Kenilworth Castle, Warwickshire, but the marriage was annulled after 24th September, 1383. Hastings afterwards married Philippa Mortimer (see page 97, above). Elizabeth married secondly, John Holland, 1st Duke of Exeter (1352?–executed 1400) (son of Joan, Princess of Wales—see page 93, above) on 24th June, 1386, at Plymouth, Devon, and had issue:

1 John, 3rd Duke of Exeter (1395–1447); he married firstly Anne, daughter of Edmund, 5th Earl of Stafford, by Anne, Countess of Buckingham (see page 114, below), and widow of Edmund Mortimer, Earl of March and Ulster (see page 97, above), and had issue. He married secondly Beatrice of Portugal (d.1439). He married thirdly Anne (d.1457), daughter of John de Montacute, 3rd Earl of Salisbury, and had issue.

2 Richard (d.1400 or 1416).

3 Constance (1387–1437); she married Thomas Mowbray, Earl of Norfolk (1385–executed 1405), and had issue. She married secondly Sir John Grey (d.1439), and had issue.

4 Edward, a knight (c.1399–after 1413).

5 Alice (c.1392–c.1406), she married Richard de Vere, 11th Earl of Oxford (1385–1417), and had issue.

Elizabeth married thirdly John Cornwall, 1st Baron Fanhope (d.1443) before 12th December, 1400, and had issue:

6 Constance (d. by 1429); she was married or betrothed to John Maltravers, Earl of Arundel (1407–1435).

Elizabeth died on 24th November, 1425/6, and was buried in Burford Church, Shropshire.

(iv) *Edward*

He was born in c.1365, and died the same year. He was buried in St Mary's Church, Leicester.

(v) *John*

He was born before 4th May, 1366, and died young. He was buried in St Mary's Church, Leicester.

(vi) *Henry IV (see page 122).*

(vii) *Isabella*

She was born in c.1368, and died young.

John married secondly, on 21st September, 1371, probably at Roquefort, Guienne, or—less probably—at St Andrew, Guienne:

Constance

She was the daughter of Peter I "the Cruel", King of Castile, by Maria, daughter of John Garcias de Padilla, a handfast wife, and she was born in 1354 at Castro Kerez, Castile. She succeeded her father as "de jure" Queen of Castile on 13th March, 1369, but was never Queen "de facto", the throne having been usurped by Henry of Trastamara. She was made a Lady of the Garter in 1378. She died on 24th March, 1394, at Leicester Castle, and was buried in Newark Abbey, Leicester.

Issue of marriage:

(i) *Katherine*

She was born between 6th June, 1372 and 31st March, 1373 at Hertford Castle. She was made a Lady of the Garter in 1384. She married Henry III, King of Castile (1379–1406) in September, 1388 at the Church of St Antolin, Fuentarrabia, Castile, and had issue:

1 Mary (1401–1458); she married Alfonso V, King of Aragon and Sicily (1394–1458), and had issue.

2 John II, King of Castile (1406–1454); he married firstly Maria (d.1445), daughter of Ferdinand I, King of Aragon and Sicily, and had issue. He married secondly, Isabella (1428?–1496), daughter of John, Duke of Beja in Portugal, and son of Philippa of Lancaster (see page 99, above), and had issue, including Isabella I, Queen of Spain, mother of Katherine of Aragon, first wife of Henry VIII.

3 Katherine (1406–1439); married Henry of Aragon, Duke of Villena (d.1445).

Katherine died on 2nd June, 1418, and was buried at Toledo, Spain.

(ii) *John*

He was born in 1374 at Ghent in Flanders, and died in 1375.

John married thirdly, on 13th January, 1396 at Lincoln Cathedral:

Katherine

She was the daughter of Sir Payn Roët of Guienne, and she was born in c.1350. She married Sir Hugh Swynford of Coleby and Kettlethorpe, Co. Lincs. (1340–1372) before 1367 at St Clement Danes Church, Strand, London, and had issue:

1 Thomas (1368/72–1432) a knight; he married firstly Jane Crophill, and had issue. He married secondly Margaret (d.1454), daughter of Sir Henry Grey, and had issue.

2 Blanche (b.c.1370).

Katherine became the mistress of John of Gaunt in c.1371/2. She was made a Lady of the Garter in 1388. She died on 10th May, 1403 at Lincoln, and was buried in Lincoln Cathedral.

The issue of this marriage, all surnamed Beaufort after their father's French lordship, were all born before their parents were united in wedlock; they were legitimated by the Pope on 1st September, 1396, and also by Charter of Richard II on 9th February, 1397, but this same Charter also excluded them from the succession. Issue as follows:

(i) *John*

He was born around c.1371/3. He was made a Knight of the Garter in c.1397. He was created Earl of Somerset on 10th February, 1397, and Marquess of Somerset on 9th September, 1397. He was created Marquess of Dorset on 29th September, 1397, but deprived of this on 3rd November, 1399. He died on 16th March, 1410 at the Hospital of St Katherine-by-the-Tower, London, and was buried in Canterbury Cathedral, Kent.

John married, before 28th September, 1397 (although no evidence exists as to where):

Margaret

She was the daughter of Thomas Holland, 1st Earl of Kent, son of Joan, Princess of Wales (see page 93, above), by Alice, daughter of Richard FitzAlan, 10th Earl of Arundel, a descendant of Henry III, and she was born around c.1381/5. After the death of John, she married secondly Thomas, Duke of Clarence, son of Henry IV, after 10th November, 1411 (date of dispensation). She was made a Lady of the Garter in

1399. She died on 30th/31st December, 1439 at St Saviour's Abbey, Bermondsey, London, and was buried in Canterbury Cathedral, Kent.

Issue of marriage:

(a) *Henry*

He was born on 26th November or, less probably, on 16th October, 1401, and succeeded his father as Earl of Somerset on 16th March, 1410. He died on 25th November, 1418.

(b) *John*

He was born before 25th March or in c. April, 1404. He succeeded his brother Henry as Earl of Somerset on 25th November, 1418, and was made a Knight of the Garter in 1440. He was created Duke of Somerset and Earl of Kendal on 28th August, 1443. He died, perhaps by suicide, on 27th May, 1444, and was buried in Wimborne Minster, Dorset.

John had the following illegitimate issue:

1 John, Bastard of Somerset (d. after 1453).

2 Jacinda or Thomasine (1434?–after 1469); she married Reginald, Baron Grey de Wilton (1421–1494), and had issue.

John married, in 1439 or c.1442 (although no record exists as to where):

Margaret

She was the daughter of John, 3rd Baron Beauchamp of Bletsoe, by Edith, daughter of Sir John Stourton. She married firstly Sir Oliver St John of Bletsoe, Beds. (d.1437), and had issue:

1 John of Bletsoe, a knight; he married Alice, daughter of Thomas Bradshaigh of Haigh, Co. Lancs., and had issue.

2 Oliver of Lidiard Tregos or of Ewell, Surrey (d.1497); he married Elizabeth, daughter of Henry, Baron Scrope of Bolton, and had issue.

3 Agnes; she married David Malpas.

4 Edith; she married Sir Geoffrey Pole of Medmenham, Bucks. (d.1474), and had issue, including Sir Richard Pole, who married Margaret Plantagenet (see page 136, under Edward IV).

5 Elizabeth; she married William, Baron Zouche of Haryngworth.

6 Mary; she married Richard Frogenhall.

After the death of John Beaufort, her second husband, Margaret married thirdly Leo, 6th Baron Welles (killed 1461) in c. April, 1447, and had issue:

7 John, 1st Viscount Welles (d.1498); he married Cecilia of York, daughter of Edward IV, and had issue.

Margaret died on 8th August, 1482, and was buried in Wimborne Minster, Dorset.

Issue of marriage:

(i) Margaret (see page 148, under Henry VII).

(c) *Thomas*

He was born in 1405, and was called Earl of Perche, although there is no record of any formal creation. He died unmarried in 1432.

(d) *Edmund*

He was born in c.1406. He was created Count of Mortain on 22nd April, 1427, and made a Knight of the Garter before 5th May, 1436. He was styled Earl of Dorset from 1438, and formally created so on 18th or 28th August, 1442. He was created Marquess of Dorset on 24th June, 1443, and succeeded his brother John as Earl of Somerset on 27th May, 1444. He was created Duke of Somerset on 31st March, 1448. He was killed on 22nd May, 1455 at the Battle of St Albans, Herts., and was buried in St Albans Abbey.

Edmund married, around 1431/5, and before 7th March, 1436 (although no record exists as to where):

Eleanor

She was the daughter of Richard Beauchamp, 5th Earl of Warwick, by Elizabeth, daughter of Thomas, Lord Berkeley, and she was born in 1407/8 at Wedgenock, Co. Warwick. She married firstly, Thomas, 9th Baron de Ros (1406–1430), and had issue:

1 Thomas (1427–1461); he married Philippa, daughter of John, Baron Tiptoft, and had issue.

After the death of Edmund Beaufort, her second husband, Eleanor married thirdly Walter Rokesley. She died around 4th/6th or on 12th March, 1466/8 at Baynard's Castle, London.

Issue of marriage:

(i) Henry

He was born on 26th January or in c. April, 1436,

and was styled Earl of Dorset from 1448. He succeeded his father as Duke and Earl of Somerset, Marquess of Dorset and Count of Mortain on 22nd May, 1455. He was attained on 4th November, 1461, when all his honours and estates were declared forfeit, although he was restored to them all on 10th March, 1463. He was executed on 15th May, 1464 at Hexham, Northumberland, after the Battle of Hexham, and was buried either at Hexham Abbey or at Tewkesbury Abbey, Gloucs. He never married.

Henry had the following illegitimate issue:

By Joan Hill:

1 Charles Somerset, Earl of Worcester (1460?–1526); he married Elizabeth (1476?–1509/13), daughter of William Herbert, Earl of Huntingdon, and had issue. He married secondly, Elizabeth, daughter of Thomas West, 8th Baron de la Warre, and had issue. He married thirdly Eleanor (d. by 1549), daughter of Edward Sutton, 2nd Baron Sutton. The present Dukes of Beaufort are descended from Charles Somerset.

(ii) *Edmund*

He was born in c.1439, and by 1440. He was styled Duke of Somerset after his father's death in 1455, but never formally restored to the title. He was executed on 6th May, 1471 at Tewkesbury, Gloucs., after the Battle of Tewkesbury, and buried in Tewkesbury Abbey.

(iii) *John*

He was killed on 4th May, 1471 at the Battle of Tewkesbury, Gloucs., and was buried in Tewkesbury Abbey.

(iv) *Thomas*

He died young before 1463.

(v) *Margaret*

She married firstly Humphrey Stafford (d.1457/8) in 1455, and had issue:

1 Henry, Duke of Buckingham (1455?–executed 1483); he married Katherine Woodville, sister of Elizabeth, wife of Edward IV, and had issue. (See page 125 under Henry IV).

2 Son.

Margaret married secondly Sir Richard Dayrell or Dayre of Lillingstone Dayrell, Bucks., and had issue:

3 Margaret; she married James Touchet, Baron Audley, and had issue.

Margaret died in 1474.

(vi) Eleanor

She married firstly James Butler, 5th Earl of Ormonde and 1st Earl of Wiltshire (c.1422–executed 1461) perhaps in April, 1458 at Woodsford, Dorset. She married secondly Sir Robert Spencer of Spencercombe, Devon (d. after 1492) in c.1470, and had issue:

1 Katherine (d.1542); she married Henry Percy, 5th Earl of Northumberland (1478–1527), and had issue.

2 Margaret; she married Thomas Carey of Chilton Foliot, and had issue.

Eleanor died on 16th August, 1501.

(vii) Elizabeth

She married Sir Henry Lewes, and had issue:

1 Mary.

Elizabeth died before 1492.

(viii) Mary or *Margaret*

No dates are recorded. She married a man surnamed Burgh, and had issue:

1 Thomas.

2 Edward.

(ix) Anne

She married Sir William Paston of Norfolk (d.1496), and had issue:

1 William.

2 Mary (1469?–1489); she married Ralph Neville (d.1498).

3 Agnes. She is perhaps to be identified with Anne (see below).

4 Elizabeth; she married Sir John Saville of Thornhill, and had issue.

5 Margaret (b. & d.1474).

> 6 Anne; she married Sir Gilbert Talbot and had issue.

(x) Joan

She married first Robert Howth, Lord of Howth in Ireland, and secondly Sir Richard Fry. She died after 1492.

(e) Joan (see page 230, under James I, King of Scotland).

(f) Margaret

She married Thomas Courtenay, 5th Earl of Devon (1414–1458), and had issue:

1 Thomas, 6th Earl of Devon (1432–executed 1461).
2 John, 7th Earl of Devon (1435?–executed 1471).
3 Henry (executed 1466).
4 Joan; she married Sir Roger Clifford.
5 Elizabeth; she married Sir Hugh Conway.

(ii) Henry

He was born in c.1375, and entered the Church as a young man. He became Dean of Wells Cathedral, Somerset in 1397. He was provided to the See of Lincoln on 27th February, 1398, and was consecrated Bishop of Lincoln on 14th July, 1398. He was translated from Lincoln to Winchester on 19th November, 1404. He was nominated Cardinal-Priest of St Eusebius on 24th May, 1426. He died on 11th April, 1447 at Wolvesey Palace, Winchester, and was buried in Winchester Cathedral.

(iii) Thomas

He was born in c. January, c.1377. He was made a Knight of the Garter in c.1400. He was created Earl of Dorset on 5th July, 1411, and Duke of Exeter on 18th November, 1416. He was created Count of Harcourt and Lord of Lillebonne on 1st July, 1418. He died on 27th or 31st December, 1426 or on 1st January, 1427, at his manor of East Greenwich, Kent, and was buried in Bury St Edmunds Abbey, Suffolk.

Thomas married, before 15th February, 1403/4 (although no evidence exists as to where):

Margaret

She was the daughter of Sir Thomas Neville of Hornby, Lincs., by Joan Furnivall, and she was born in c. January, 1377, or in c.1383 (?). She was made a Lady of the Garter in 1408. She died between 1413 and 1426, probably before 9th April, 1424, and was buried in Bury St Edmunds Abbey, Suffolk.

Issue of marriage:

(a) *Henry*
No dates are recorded. He died young.

(iv) *Joan*
She was born in c.1379. She married firstly Robert, 2nd Baron Ferrers of Wemme (d.1396) before 30th September, 1394, and had issue:
1 Elizabeth (c.1394–1434); she married John de Greystoke, Baron Greystoke (1390–1436), and had issue.
2 Mary; she married Ralph Neville of Westmorland.

Joan married secondly Ralph Neville, 1st Earl of Westmorland (1364?–1425) before 29th November, 1396, and had issue:
3 Richard, Earl of Salisbury (1400?–killed 1460); he married Alice (1406–1462), daughter of Thomas de Montacute, 4th Earl of Salisbury, and had issue, including Richard Neville, Earl of Warwick, father of Anne, Queen of Richard III, and Isabella, Duchess of Clarence (see page 136, under Edward IV).
4 William, Baron Fauconberg, Earl of Kent (d.1463); he married Joan, Baroness Fauconberg (1406–1490), and had issue.
5 George, Baron Latimer (d.1469) (?); he married Elizabeth (1417–1480), daughter of Richard Beauchamp, Earl of Warwick, and had issue.
6 Robert, Bishop of Salisbury and Durham (1404?–1457).
7 Edward, Baron Bergavenny (d.1476); he married Elizabeth (d.1448), daughter of Richard Beauchamp, Earl of Worcester, and had issue. He married secondly Katherine (d. after 1478), daughter of Sir Robert Howard, and had issue.
8 Cuthbert (d. young).
9 Thomas (d. young).
10 Henry (d. young).
11 Katherine (d. after 1483); she married firstly John Mowbray, Duke of Norfolk (1392–1432), and had issue. She married secondly Thomas Strangeways. She married thirdly John, Viscount Beaumont (killed 1460). She married fourthly John Woodville (1445?–executed 1469), brother of Elizabeth, wife of Edward IV (see page 124, under Henry IV).
12 Joan; a nun.

13 Anne (d.1480); she married firstly Humphrey, Earl of Stafford (1402–killed 1460), and had issue. She married secondly Walter Blount, 1st Baron Mountjoy (1420?–1474).

14 Eleanor (d.1472); she married firstly Richard le Despenser, Baron Burghersh (1396–1414), and had issue. She married secondly Henry Percy, 2nd Earl of Northumberland (1392–killed 1455), and had issue.

15 Cecilia, Duchess of York (see page 134, under Edward IV).

16 One other, unnamed in the records.

Joan was made a Lady of the Garter in 1399. She died on 13th November, 1440 at Howden, Yorkshire, and was buried in Lincoln Cathedral.

7 *Edmund*

He was born on 5th June, 1341 at Abbot's Langley (now King's Langley), Herts. He was made a Knight of the Garter in c. April, 1361, and was created Earl of Cambridge on 13th November, 1362. He was created Duke of York on 6th August, 1385. He died on 1st August, 1402 at King's Langley, Herts., and was buried there in the Church of the Mendicant Friars.

Edmund married firstly, between 1st January and 30th April, 1372, at Hertford Castle (?):

Isabella

She was the daughter of Peter I "the Cruel", King of Castile, by Maria, daughter of John Garcias de Padilla, a handfast wife, and she was sister to Constance, wife of John of Gaunt (see page 101, above). Isabella was born in c.1355/6 at Morales or at Tordesillas, Castile. She was made a Lady of the Garter in 1379. She died on 23rd November, 1392/3, and was buried in the Church of the Dominican Friars, King's Langley, Herts.

Issue of marriage:

(i) *Edward*

He was born in c.1373, perhaps at Norwich, Norfolk. He was made a Knight of the Garter in 1387. He was created Earl of Cork between 25th February, 1390 and 15th January, 1395, and Earl of Rutland on 25th February, 1390. He was created Duke of Aumale on 29th September, 1397, but deprived of the dukedom on 3rd November, 1399. He succeeded his father as Duke of York on 1st August, 1402, and was confirmed in this dukedom on 5th November, 1402. He was restored to the dukedom of Aumale on 1st May, 1414. He was killed on 25th October, 1415 at the Battle of Agincourt, France, and was buried in the Collegiate Church of Fotheringhay, Northants.

Edward married, between 27th February, 1396 and 7th October, 1398:

Philippa

She was the daughter of John de Mohun, 2nd Baron of Dunster, by Joan, daughter of Sir Bartholemew de Burghersh of Ewyas Lacy, Co. Hereford. She married firstly Walter, 4th Baron FitzWalter (d.1386) before 27th June, 1385, and had issue:

1 Walter (d.1432); a knight; he married a lady called Elizabeth, and had issue.

Philippa married secondly Sir John Golafre of Langley, Oxon. (d.1396) before 13th November, 1389. She was made a Lady of the Garter in 1390. She died on 17th July, 1431, at Carisbrooke Castle, Isle of Wight, and was buried in Westminster Abbey.

(ii) *Constance*

She was born in c.1374. She married Thomas le Despenser, 1st Earl of Gloucester (1373–executed 1400) between 16th April, 1378 and 7th November, 1389 (possibly later, but certainly before 14th January, 1394), and had issue:

1 Edward (d. young).
2 Richard, Baron Burghersh (1396–1414); he married Eleanor (d.1472), daughter of Ralph Neville, 1st Earl of Westmorland by Joan Beaufort, daughter of John of Gaunt, Duke of Lancaster (see above, page 109).
3 Hugh (d. young, 1401).
4 Elizabeth (b.c.1398; d. young).
5 Isabella (1400–1439); she married firstly Richard de Beauchamp, Earl of Worcester (1397–1422) and had issue, and secondly Richard de Beauchamp, Earl of Warwick (1382–1439), and had issue.

Constance was made a Lady of the Garter in 1386. She died on 28th November, 1416, and was buried in Reading Abbey, Berkshire.

Constance may have had the following illegitimate issue, (although the daughter in question always held that her parents had married in c.1404; however, this claim failed against the petition of her father's sisters):

By Edmund Holland, Earl of Kent (1383–1408):

1 Eleanor (?) (b.1406?); she married James Touchet, Baron Audley
(1398?–1459), and had issue. She may have been the illegitimate
issue of Edmund Holland by Elizabeth Burghersh, but this is
unlikely.

(iii) *Richard*

He was born in c. September, c.1375/6, at Conisburgh Castle,
Yorkshire. He was recognised as hereditary Earl of Cambridge on 1st May, 1414, but forfeited all his honours and
estates on 5th August, 1415, on which day he was executed for
treason at Southampton Green, Hampshire. He was buried in
the Chapel of God's House, Southampton.

Richard married firstly, in c. May, 1406, or perhaps after
10th June, 1408 (date of dispensation) (although no record
exists as to where):

Anne

She was the daughter of Roger Mortimer, Earl of March, by
Eleanor Holland, and a great-great-granddaughter of Edward
III (see above), and it was through her that the House of York
derived its claim to the throne. She was born on 27th Decem-
ber, 1390, and died in September, 1411, perhaps in childbirth.
She was buried in King's Langley Church, Herts.

Issue of marriage:

(a) *Isabella*

She was born in 1409. She married firstly Sir Thomas Grey
of Werke or Heton (d. by 1443) after February, 1413, but
the marriage was annulled before 1426. She married
secondly Henry Bourchier, 1st Earl of Essex (c.1409–
1483) before 25th April, 1426, and had issue:

1 William, Viscount Bourchier (either killed 1471 or
d.1483?); he married Anne (1438?–1489), daughter
of Richard Woodville, 1st Earl Rivers, and sister of
Elizabeth, wife of Edward IV, and had issue.

2 Henry (d.1462); he married Elizabeth, Baroness
Scales (d.1473), daughter of Thomas, Baron Scales.

3 Humphrey (killed 1471); he married Joan (d.1490),
daughter of Sir Richard Stanhope of Rampton.

4 John (d.1485 or 1494); he married firstly Elizabeth,
Baroness Ferrers de Ruthyn, and secondly a daughter,
whose name is not known, of John Chichele.

5 Thomas (d.1492); he married Isabella Barre.

111

6 Edward (killed 1460).
7 Fulk (d. young).
8 Hugh (d. young).
9 Isabella (d. young).
10 Florence (d.1525/6).

Isabella died on 2nd October, 1484, and was buried in Beeleigh Abbey, Maldon, Essex; her remains were later removed to Little Easton Church, Essex.

(b) *Richard*

He inherited the dukedom of York, and was the first of his line to adopt the surname Plantagenet. His laying claim to the throne of England led to the Wars of the Roses. For a full entry, see under Edward IV.

Richard married secondly, around 1411/15 (although no record exists as to where):

Matilda

She was the daughter of Thomas, 6th Baron Clifford, by Elizabeth, daughter of Thomas de Ros, Baron Ros of Hamlake. After the death of Richard, she married secondly (?) John Neville, 5th Baron Latimer of Danby (d.1430), from whom she was later divorced. She died on 26th August, 1446, and was buried in Roche Abbey, Yorkshire.

Edmund married secondly, before 4th November, 1393:

Joan

She was the daughter of Thomas Holland, 1st Earl of Kent, son of Joan, Princess of Wales (see page 93, above), by Alice, daughter of Richard FitzAlan, Earl of Arundel, a descendant of Henry III. Her sister Margaret was married in turn to the sons of John of Gaunt (see page 102, above) and Henry IV. Joan was born in c.1380. She was made a Lady of the Garter in 1399. After the death of Edmund, she married secondly William, 5th Baron Willoughby d'Eresby (d.1409) before 9th August, 1404. She married thirdly Henry, 3rd Baron Scrope of Masham (executed 1415) on 6th September, 1410 at Faxflete Chapel, Yorkshire, and had issue, although no details are available. She married fourthly Henry Bromflete, 1st Baron de Vesci (d.1469) between Michaelmas, 1415 and 27th April, 1416. Joan died on 12th April, 1434.

8 *Blanche*

She was born in March, 1342 in the Tower of London, and died there the same month. Hence she was known as Blanche de la Tour. She was buried in Westminster Abbey.

9 *Mary*

She was born on 10th October, 1344 at Waltham, near Winchester, Hants. She married John de Montfort IV, Duke of Brittany (1339–1399) in the summer of 1361 at Woodstock Palace, Oxon. She died in the winter of 1361/2, and was buried in Abingdon Abbey, Oxon.

10 *Margaret*

She was born on 20th July, 1346, at Windsor Castle. She married John Hastings, 2nd Earl of Pembroke (1347–1375) on 19th May, 1359 at Reading Abbey, Berkshire. She died after 1st October, 1361, and was buried in Abingdon Abbey, Oxon.

11 *Thomas*

He was born probably in the summer of 1347, at Windsor Castle, and died young in 1348 (?). He was buried in King's Langley Church, Herts. Thomas has been overlooked by many historians who have confused him with his two brothers called William and his youngest brother, also called Thomas.

12 *William*

He was born before 24th June, 1348 at Windsor Castle, and died before 5th September, 1348. He was buried in Westminster Abbey.

13 *Thomas*

He was born on 7th January, 1355 at Woodstock Palace, Oxon. He was created Earl of Buckingham on 16th July, 1377, and became Earl of Essex in right of his wife on 22nd June, 1380. He was made a Knight of the Garter between April, 1380 and April, 1381. He was called Duke of Aumale from before 3rd September, 1385, although no record exists of his formal creation as such. He was created Duke of Gloucester on 6th August, 1385. He was murdered, probably on the orders of Richard II, at the Prince's Inn, Calais, France, on 8th/9th September, 1397, and was buried in the Collegiate Church of the Holy Trinity, Pleshy, Essex; his remains were later removed to Westminster Abbey.

Thomas married, before 8th February, 1376, perhaps in 1374 (?) (although no record exists as to where):

Eleanor

She was the daughter of Humphrey de Bohun, Earl of Hereford, Essex and Northampton, by Joan, daughter of Richard FitzAlan, Earl of Arundel, a descendant of Henry III, and she was born in c.1366. She was made a Lady of the Garter in 1384. After her

113

husband's murder in 1397, she is said to have lived as a nun at Barking Abbey, Essex, but she did not renounce her property. She died on 3rd October, 1399 at the Minoresses' Convent in Aldgate, London, and was buried in Westminster Abbey.

Issue of marriage:

(i) *Humphrey*

He was born in c. April, 1381/2, and styled Earl of Buckingham from his birth until his father's murder on 9th September, 1397. He died on 2nd September, 1399, either at Chester, or Coventry, or Anglesey, of plague, and was buried in Walden Abbey, Essex.

(ii) *Anne*

She was born in April, 1383. She married firstly Thomas, 3rd Earl of Stafford (1368?–1392) in c.1390. She married secondly Edmund, 5th Earl of Stafford (1377–1403: killed at the Battle of Shrewsbury) before 28th June, 1398, and had issue:

1 Anne; she married Edmund Mortimer, Earl of March and Ulster (see page 97, above).

2 Humphrey, Earl of Stafford (1402–1460: killed at the Battle of Wakefield); he married Anne (d.1480), daughter of Ralph Neville, 1st Earl of Westmorland by Joan Beaufort (see page 109, above), and had issue.

3 Philippa (d. young).

Anne was recognised as Countess of Buckingham, Hereford and Northampton, and Lady of Brecknock and Holderness from 1399, and was so styled from that date. She also styled herself Countess of Stafford. She was made a Lady of the Garter in 1405. She married thirdly William Bourchier, Count of Eu (d.1420) before 20th November, 1405, and had issue:

4 Henry, Viscount Bourchier, Count of Eu, 1st Earl of Essex (c.1409–1483); he married Isabella Plantagenet (see page 111, above), and had issue.

5 Thomas, Cardinal of St Cirac, Archbishop of Canterbury (1413–1486).

6 William, Baron FitzWaryn (c.1412–before 1469); he married Thomasine Hankeford, Baroness FitzWaryn (1423–1453), daughter of Sir Richard Hankeford, and had issue. He married secondly Katherine (d.1467), daughter of John Affeton of Afton, Devon.

7 John, Baron Berners (c.1415–1474); he married Marjorie, daughter of Richard, Baron Berners, and had issue.

8 Eleanor (c.1417–1474); she married John Mowbray, Duke of Norfolk (1415–1461), and had issue.

Anne died between 16th and 24th October, 1438, and was buried in Llanthony Priory, Monmouthshire.

(iii) *Joan*

She was born in 1384. She perhaps married (or was betrothed to) Gilbert Talbot, Baron Talbot of Goderick Castle and Blackmere (d.1419), but there was no issue of the marriage.

Joan died on 16th August, 1400, perhaps in childbirth, and was buried in Walden Abbey, Essex.

(iv) *Isabella*

She was born on 12th March, 1385/6, and became a nun at the Minoresses' Convent in Aldgate, London, on 23rd April, 1399. She died in c. April, 1402.

(v) *Philippa*

She was born in c.1389, and died before 3rd October, 1399.

Edward III also had the following **illegitimate issue**:

By Alice Perrers (1348?–1400), wife of William de Windsor:

1 John de Southeray or Surrey (c.1364/5–after 1383: 1384?); knighted 1377; he married Matilda, called a sister of Lord Henry Percy.

2 Joan; she married Robert Skerne of Kingston-upon-Thames, and perhaps had issue.

3 Joan or Jane; she married Richard Northland.

Perhaps by an unknown mother:

4 Nicholas Lytlington (?), Abbot of Westminster (d.1386). He did not claim to be the King's son, and was probably a member of the Despenser family.

EDWARD III

He died on 21st June, 1377, at Sheen Palace, Surrey, of a stroke, and was buried in Westminster Abbey.

He was succeeded by his grandson Richard.

Recommended reading

There have been two recent biographies of Edward III:

M. Packe: *King Edward III* (Routledge and Kegan Paul, 1983).

P. Johnson: *Edward III* (Weidenfeld and Nicolson, 1973).

Prior to these, the definitive biography was:

W. Longman: *The Life and Times of Edward III* (2 vols., Longmans Green, 1869)—it is now very much out of date.

For Edward's family, see:

B. C. Hardy: *Philippa of Hainault and her Times* (1910).

Hubert Cole: *The Black Prince* (Granada, 1976).

J. Harvey: *The Black Prince* (Batsford, 1976).

B. Emerson, *The Black Prince* (Weidenfeld and Nicolson, 1976).

F. Chambers: *The Fair Maid of Kent* (1877).

M. Galway: *Joan of Kent and the Order of the Garter* (*University of Birmingham Historical Journal*, vol. 1, 1947).

Sidney Armitage-Smith: *John of Gaunt* (Constable 1904) (which has yet to be bettered).

R. T. Bodey: *Time Honour'd Lancaster* (1926).

F. George Kay: *Lady of the Sun* (Muller, 1966), a superb study of Alice Perrers.

Anya Seton's *Katherine* (Hodder and Stoughton, 1954), a novel about Katherine Swynford, is so well researched and presented that I have included it here for light reading about the period.

RICHARD II

FATHER: *Edward, Prince of Wales (see page 92, under Edward III).*
MOTHER: *Joan of Kent (see page 93, under Edward III).*
SIBLINGS: *(see page 94, under Edward III).*

RICHARD II

He was born on c.6th January, 1367 (or 1366?) at Bordeaux, Gascony, France. He was created Prince of Wales, Earl of Cornwall and Earl of Chester on 20th November, 1376, and made a Knight of the Garter on 23rd April, 1377. He succeeded his grandfather Edward III as King of England on 22nd June, 1377, and was crowned at Westminster Abbey on 16th July, 1377.

Richard II was deposed on 19th August, 1399 by Henry of Bolingbroke, who usurped the throne as Henry IV when Richard formally abdicated on 29th September, 1399.

Richard II married firstly, on 14th, 20th or 22nd January, 1382 at St
Stephen's Chapel in the Palace of Westminster:
Anne
She was the daughter of Charles IV, Holy Roman Emperor, by
Elizabeth, daughter of Bogislaw V, Duke of Pomerania. Anne of
Bohemia, as she was known, was born on 11th May, 1366 at Prague,
Bohemia. She was crowned on 22nd January, 1382 at Westminster
Abbey, and was made a Lady of the Garter that same year. She died
on 7th June, 1394, at Sheen Palace, Surrey, of the plague, and was
buried in Westminster Abbey. There was no issue of the marriage.
Richard II married secondly, probably on 4th (less probably, 1st)
November, 1396, at St Nicholas' Church, Calais, France:
Isabella
She was the daughter of Charles VI, King of France, by Isabella,
daughter of Stephen II, Duke of Bavaria-Ingolstadt. Her sister
Katherine later married Henry V. Isabella was born on 9th November, 1389 at the Palace of the Louvre in Paris. She was made a Lady of
the Garter in 1396, and was crowned on 5th, 7th or 8th January, 1397
at Westminster Abbey. After the death of Richard II, she married
secondly Charles of Valois, Duke of Orléans (1394–1465) on 29th
June, 1406 at Compiégne, France, and had issue:
1 Joan (1409–1432); she married John II, Duke of Alençon (1409–1476),
and had issue.
Isabella died on 13th September, 1409 at the Château of Blois,
France, in childbirth, and was buried in St Laumer's Abbey, Blois.
Her remains were later removed to the Church of the Celestines,
Paris. There was no issue of her marriage to Richard due to her
extreme youth.
Richard II is said to have had the following **illegitimate issue**, but this
is unlikely on chronological grounds:
1 Richard Maudelyn.

RICHARD II
He was probably murdered, perhaps by starvation, and certainly by
17th February, 1400, whilst in captivity at Pontefract Castle,
Yorkshire. He was buried in King's Langley Church, Herts., but was
removed to Westminster Abbey in 1413.
He was succeeded by his cousin Henry of Bolingbroke.

Recommended reading
A. Steele: *Richard II* (Cambridge University Press, 1941).
G. Mathew: *The Court of Richard II* (John Murray, 1968).
H. F. Hutchison: *The Hollow Crown: A Life of Richard II* (Eyre and Spottiswoode, 1961).
J. J. N. Palmer: *The Background to Richard II's Marriage to Isabel of France* (*Journal of the British Institute for Historical Research*, vol. iv, 1971).

4. The Later Plantagenets: The Houses of Lancaster and York

The prolific Edward III sired eight sons, four of whom grew to maturity and had sons of their own. The eldest was the Prince of Wales, that Edward known to history as the Black Prince, who was the father of Richard II. Richard, although his entitlement to the throne was without dispute, was nevertheless a weak and unstable ruler. This led to his deposition by Henry of Bolingbroke in 1399, Bolingbroke's usurpation of the throne, and Richard's own probable murder the following year.

Bolingbroke, henceforth known as Henry IV, was the son of John of Gaunt, Duke of Lancaster, third surviving son of Edward III. In 1399, when he staged his successful coup, the rightful heir to the throne of England was Edmund Mortimer, Earl of March and Ulster, a child of nearly eight. Edmund was the great-grandson of Lionel of Antwerp, Duke of Clarence, second son of Edward III. It was true that Lionel's only child had been a daughter, Philippa, who was Edmund's grandmother, but in England there was no Salic Law to prevent the crown passing by way of inheritance to or through a female, and there is no doubt that Edmund had a better claim to the throne than Bolingbroke. However, Edmund was a child and Bolingbroke a grown man and a proven soldier: England needed a firm ruler, and so the claim of Edmund Mortimer was set aside while the House of Lancaster usurped the throne. Edmund died in 1425, and his claim to the throne was inherited by his surviving sister Anne's child, Richard, Duke of York. It was he who first used the surname Plantagenet.

For half a century, the House of Lancaster ruled England under Henry IV, Henry V, and Henry VI. Henry V executed Richard, Earl of Cambridge, who was the husband of Anne Mortimer and the son of Edmund of Langley, Duke of York, fourth surviving son of Edward III; Richard of Cambridge had plotted to overthrow the fifth Henry, but his treason was discovered and he was eliminated on the eve of the campaign that would see the English victorious at Agincourt. Henry V died young, and the House of Lancaster came to grief under his son

119

Henry VI, who was fitted rather for sainthood than kingship. Henry VI married the energetic and passionate Margaret of Anjou, but the marriage produced no children to begin with. Then, in 1453, the queen produced a son whilst her husband was suffering one of his periodic fits of insanity. The child was created Prince of Wales the following year, but many who supported the Duke of York questioned the infant's paternity. Yet it was Henry VI's misgovernment, rather than this, that precipitated the dynastic struggle which was known as the Wars of the Roses because the main protagonists, whilst hotly disputing the question of the succession in the gardens of the Inns of Temple in London, are said to have plucked roses from a bush to be their emblems in the struggle: a white rose for York, and a red rose for Lancaster.

York deeply resented the court party headed by the Queen, and promoted himself as the champion of good government; only later did he assert his superior claim to the throne. Thirty years of intermittent strife followed the outbreak of hostilities in 1455. Early battles in the conflict were indecisive. Then, in 1460, York was killed at the Battle of Wakefield, and his cause taken up by his son, Edward, Earl of March, who won a decisive victory at Towton the following Spring. This led to him being accepted as King of England and crowned at Westminster Abbey. Henry VI went into hiding, but was later taken into custody and imprisoned in the Tower.

Edward IV was a strong King, but he made the fatal mistake of making a very unpopular marriage to a commoner called Elizabeth Woodville, who brought as her dowry a host of rapacious relatives, eager for lands, honours and wealth. This marriage alienated the great Earl of Warwick, known as "the kingmaker", who had been Edward's staunchest supporter. Warwick allied himself with Margaret of Anjou and brought about the "readeption" of Henry VI, while Edward fled to the Low Countries. But he soon returned to raise an army and march for the final time upon his enemies. Warwick was killed at the Battle of Barnet in April, 1471, and Margaret's Lancastrian forces routed in the bloody Battle of Tewkesbury in May, 1471. During that same month, Henry VI died in mysterious circumstances in the Tower of London. At last, the House of York was securely established upon the throne.

Edward IV died in 1483, worn out prematurely by the pleasures of the table and the bedchamber, leaving as his heir Edward V, a boy of twelve. The government of the realm was placed in the capable hands of Edward IV's brother, Richard, Duke of Gloucester. Almost immediately, Gloucester announced that his brother's marriage to Elizabeth Woodville had been bigamous, and that their children were therefore bastards and unfit to inherit the crown. This information had been given to the Protector by a priest who said he had evidence that Edward had been precontracted to another lady at the time of his marriage to Elizabeth. As a result of this, the crown was offered to Gloucester, who accepted it, and was crowned as Richard III in July, 1483. Edward V and his brother, who had been living in the Tower of London as was customary before a King was to be crowned, suddenly disappeared from the scene, and controversy has raged ever since as to their fate. The evidence points overwhelmingly to their having been murdered on the orders of Richard III.

Richard III did not long enjoy his crown. His son died in 1484, and his wife in 1485. His heir was his sister's son, John de la Pole, Earl of Lincoln. Yet England was never destined to have a King John II. For although the great families descended from Edward III and having a strong claim to the crown of England had either died out or been barred from the succession by Act of Attainder, there yet remained in exile in France a scion of the Beauforts, who were the issue of John of Gaunt by his mistress (and later wife) Katherine Swynford. The Beauforts might have been legitimated after their parents' marriage, but they were barred from the succession by Letters Patent of Henry IV. This minor technicality did not, however, deter the "unknown Welshman" called Henry Tudor, who in 1485 invaded England with a foreign army, defeated Richard III at the Battle of Bosworth, and had himself crowned on the battlefield as King Henry VII with the circlet that had fallen from the head of the last Plantagenet King of England and rolled under a hawthorn bush near to where Richard fell, hacked to death in the midst of the fray.

Thus was the Tudor dynasty founded, of whom we shall hear more in the next chapter. Henry VII united the rival Houses of York and Lancaster by marrying Elizabeth, daughter of Edward IV. The Wars of the Roses ended in 1487 with the Battle of Stoke, when John, Earl of Lincoln, perished. But the tragedy of the House of York would not play itself out for another half a century, when most of its members had been brutally eliminated by the usurping Tudors.

HENRY IV

FATHER: *John of Gaunt, Duke of Lancaster (see page 98, under Edward III).*

MOTHER: *Blanche of Lancaster (see page 99, under Edward III).*

SIBLINGS: *(see page 99, under Edward III).*

HENRY IV

He was born probably on 3rd April, or—less probably—on 30th May, 1367, at Bolingbroke Castle, Lincs. He was made a Knight of the Garter on 23rd April, 1377, and styled Earl of Derby from 16th July, 1377. He was created Earl of Northampton and (probably) Earl of Hereford in right of his wife on 22nd December, 1384. He was created Duke of Hereford on 29th September, 1397, and succeeded his father as Duke of Lancaster, Earl of Leicester and Earl of Lincoln on 3rd February, 1399. He usurped the throne of England upon the abdication of Richard II on 30th September, 1399, and was crowned on 13th October, 1399 at Westminster Abbey.

Henry IV married firstly, between 20th July, 1380 and 10th February, 1381 either at Rochford, Essex, or at Arundel Castle, Sussex:

Mary

She was the daughter of Humphrey de Bohun, Earl of Hereford, Essex and Northampton, by Joan, daughter of Richard FitzAlan, Earl of Arundel, a descendant of Henry III. Her sister Eleanor was married to Henry IV's uncle, Thomas, Duke of Gloucester (see page 113, under Edward III). Mary was born around 1369/70. She was made a Lady of the Garter in 1388. She died on 4th June, 1394, at Peterborough Castle, in childbirth, and was buried in St Mary's Church, Leicester. Her remains were later removed to Trinity Hospital, Leicester.

Issue of marriage:

1 *Edward*

He was born in April, 1382, and died aged 4 days. He was perhaps buried in Monmouth Castle Chapel.

2 *Henry V* *(see page 128).*

3 *Thomas*

He was born on 29th September, 1388, either at Kenilworth Castle, Co. Warwick, or in London. He was made a Knight of the Bath on 12th October, 1399, when the Order was founded by his father, and a Knight of the Garter in c.1400. He was created Duke of Clarence and Earl of Aumale on 9th July, 1412. He was killed on 22nd March, 1421 at the Battle of Baugé, France, and was buried in Canterbury Cathedral.

Thomas had the following illegitimate issue:

1 John de Clarence; he was a knight, and was sometimes known as the Bastard of Clarence.

Thomas married, after 10th November, 1411 (date of dispensation) (although no evidence exists as to where):

Margaret

She was the daughter of Thomas Holland, Earl of Kent, son of Joan, Princess of Wales (see page 93, under Edward III), by Alice, daughter of Richard FitzAlan, Earl of Arundel, a descendant of Henry III. Margaret was born in c.1381/5. She married firstly John Beaufort, Marquess of Somerset, son of John of Gaunt, Duke of Lancaster (see page 102, under Edward III), and had issue. She was made a Lady of the Garter in 1399. She died on 30th/31st December, 1439 at St Saviour's Abbey, Bermondsey, London, and was buried in Canterbury Cathedral, Kent.

4 *John*

He was born on 20th June, 1389. He was made a Knight of the Bath on 11th October, 1399, when the Order was founded by his father, and a Knight of the Garter in c.1400. He was created Earl of Kendal and Duke of Bedford on 16th May, 1414, and Earl of Richmond on 24th November, 1414. He died on 14th/15th September, 1435 at his house called "Joyeux Repos" at Rouen, Normandy, and was buried in Rouen Cathedral, Normandy.

John had the following illegitimate issue:

1 Richard.

2 Mary (d. after 1458); she married Peter of Montferrat.

John married firstly, by proxy on 13th or 17th April, 1423 at Montbar, France, and in person on 14th June, 1423 at Troyes Cathedral, France:

Anne

She was the daughter of John the Fearless, Duke of Burgundy, by Margaret, daughter of Albert of Bavaria, Count of Hainault, Holland and Zeeland, and she was born around 1404/5 at Arras, Burgundy, France. Anne died on 14th November, 1432, at the Hôtel de Bourgogne, Paris, in childbirth, and was buried in the Church of the Celestines, Paris. Her remains were later removed to the Chartreuse de Champnol, Dijon, Burgundy, France.

Issue of marriage:

(i) *Unnamed child*

It was born in November, 1432 in Paris, and died shortly after its birth.

John married secondly, on 20th or 22nd April, 1433, at the Bishop's Palace, Thérouanne, France:

Jacquetta

She was the daughter of Peter of Luxembourg, Count of St Pol, by Margaret, daughter of Francis del Balso or Baux, Duke of Andria, and she was born in 1416 (?). After the death of Bedford, she married secondly Richard Woodville or Wydeville, 1st Earl Rivers (1405?–executed 1469) between 16th September, 1435 and 23rd March, 1436, and had issue:

1 Elizabeth; she married Edward IV (see page 138).

2 Anne (1438?–1489); she married firstly William, Viscount Bourchier (killed 1471 or d.1483?), son of Isabella Plantagenet (see page 111, under Edward III) and cousin of Edward IV, and had issue. She married secondly Sir Edward Wingfield, and thirdly George Grey, Earl of Kent (d.1503).

3 Margaret (1439?–1490/1); she married Thomas Maltravers, Earl of Arundel (1450?–1524).

4 Anthony, 2nd Earl Rivers (1440/2?–executed 1483); he married firstly Elizabeth (1436?–1473), daughter of Thomas, Baron Scales of Neucelles. He married secondly Mary, daughter of Sir Henry Fitz-Lewes. Anthony had illegitimate issue.

5 Mary (1443?–by 1481); she married William Herbert, Earl of Pembroke and Huntingdon (d.1491), and had issue.

6 Jacquetta (1444/5?–1509); she married John le Strange, Baron Strange of Knockin (d.1479), and had issue.

7 John (1445–executed 1469); he married Katherine (d. after 1483), daughter of Ralph Neville, 1st Earl of Westmorland, by Joan Beaufort (see page 108, under Edward III).

8 Lionel, Bishop of Salisbury (1446?–1484).

9 Edward (killed 1488).

10 Richard, 3rd Earl Rivers (d.1491).

11 Thomas; he married Anne Holland.

12 John (d. young).

13 Lewis (d. young).

14 Katherine, Duchess of Buckingham and Bedford (see page 130, under Henry V).

15 Martha; she married Sir John Bromley.

16 Eleanor or Joan; she married Anthony Grey, Baron de Ruthin (d.1480), and had issue.

Jacquetta was made a Lady of the Garter in 1435. She died on 30th May, 1472.

5 *Humphrey*

He was born around August/September, or on 3rd October, 1390. He was made a Knight of the Garter in c.1400, and created Duke of Gloucester and Earl of Pembroke on 16th May, 1414. In March, 1423, he assumed the style Count of Holland, Zeeland and Hainault in right of his first wife. He was created Count of Flanders on 30th July, 1436. He died, or was perhaps murdered, on 23rd February, 1447 at Bury St Edmunds, Suffolk, and was buried in St Albans Abbey, Herts.

Humphrey had the following illegitimate issue:

1 Arthur (d.1447).

2 Antigone; she married firstly Henry Grey, Lord of Powys and Count of Tancarville in Normandy (1419?–1450), and had issue. She married secondly John d'Amancier.

Humphrey married firstly, before 7th March (perhaps in February?), 1422/3, at Hadleigh, Essex (?):

Jacqueline

She was the daughter of William IV, Duke of Bavaria, Count of Holland, Zeeland and Hainault, by Margaret, daughter of Philip the Hardy, Duke of Burgundy, and she was born on 25th July, 1401, at The Hague, Holland. She married firstly John of Viennois, Dauphin of France (1398–1417) in July, 1406 at Compiégne, France, and again in 1415 at The Hague, Holland. She succeeded her father as Duchess of Bavaria and Countess of Holland, Zeeland and Hainault in 1417. She married secondly John IV, Duke of Brabant (1400/3–1426) on 10th March, 1418. This marriage was annulled by the Anti-Pope, Benedict XIII, in 1421/2. She was made a Lady of the Garter in 1423. Her marriage to Humphrey was annulled on 9th July, 1428, by Papal Decree, which also pronounced as valid her marriage to Brabant. She married fourthly Francis or Floris van Borselen, Count of Ostrevant (d.1470), in July, 1432 at Ostende, Flanders. She was dispossessed by the Duke of Burgundy of all her territories save Ostrevant in 1433. She underwent a second marriage ceremony with her fourth husband in July, 1434 at Martensdijk Castle, Holland. Jacqueline died on 8th/9th October, 1436, either at Leyden, or at Teilingen, Holland, and was buried at The Hague.

Issue of marriage:

(i) *Stillborn child*

It was born in 1424.

Humphrey married secondly, in 1428 (?) (before 1431) (although no record exists as to where):

Eleanor

She was the daughter of Sir Reginald Cobham of Sterborough, Kent, by Eleanor, daughter of Sir Thomas Culpeper of Rayal. She was perhaps born at Sterborough Castle, Kent. She became Humphrey's mistress some time before their marriage, and may have borne him 2 bastard children, possibly those listed above, but no firm details are recorded, and the children, if they existed, may have died young before the marriage took place. Eleanor was made a Lady of the Garter in 1432. In 1441, she was convicted of practising witchcraft upon Henry VI, and was imprisoned for life. She died between 1446 and 1454 in prison at Peel Castle, Isle of Man, where she is said to have been buried.

6 Blanche

She was born in the spring of 1392 at Peterborough Castle. She married Louis "Barbatus", Duke of Bavaria and Count Palatine of the Rhine (d.1436) on 6th July, 1402 at Cologne Cathedral, Germany, and had issue:

1 Stillborn child (1407).

2 Rupert (1409–1426).

Blanche was made a Lady of the Garter in 1408. She died on 22nd May, 1409 at Neustadt, Alsace, in childbirth, and was buried in the Church of St Mary, Neustadt, Alsace.

7 Philippa

She was born on or just before 4th June (not July, as is sometimes stated—her mother died giving birth to her in June), 1394 at Peterborough Castle. She married Eric of Pomerania, King of Sweden (Eric XIII), Denmark (Eric VII), and Norway (Eric III) (1382–1459) on 26 October, 1406 at Lund, Sweden, and had issue:

1 Stillborn child (1429).

Philippa was crowned Queen Consort of Sweden, Denmark and Norway on 1st November, 1406 at Lund, Sweden. She was made a Lady of the Garter in 1408. She died on 5th January, 1430, in the convent of Waldstena, Lingkoping, Sweden, where she was buried.

Henry IV is also said to have had the following illegitimate issue, although there is no contemporary evidence for this:

1 Edmund Labourde (d. young in 1401).

Henry IV married secondly, by proxy on 3rd April, 1402 at Eltham Palace, Kent, and in person on 7th February, 1403 at Winchester Cathedral:

Joan

She was the daughter of Charles II, King of Navarre, by Joan, daughter of John II, King of France, and she was born in c.1370. She married firstly John de Montfort IV, Duke of Brittany (1339–1399) (who had previously been married to Mary, daughter of Edward III) either on 25th August, 1386 at Pampelina, Navarre, or on 11th September, 1386 at Saillé, Navarre, and had issue:

1 Joan (1387–1388).

2 Daughter (name not known) (b.&d.1388).

3 Peter, who took the name and style John V, Duke of Brittany (1389–1422); he married Joan (1391–1433), daughter of Charles VI, King of France, and sister to the wives of Richard II and Henry V, and had issue.

4 Mary (1391–1446); she married John I, Duke of Alençon (d.1415).

5 Arthur III, Duke of Brittany (1393–1458); he married firstly Margaret (d.1441), daughter of John the Fearless, Duke of Burgundy, and secondly, Joan d'Albret, and thirdly, Katherine of Luxembourg.

6 Giles, Lord of Chantocé (1394–1412).

7 Richard, Count of Éstampes (1395–1438); he married Margaret (d.1466), daughter of Louis of Valois, Duke of Orléans, and had issue.

8 Blanche (c.1396– c.1418); she married John or Lomagne, Count of Armagnac (d. after 1448).

9 Margaret (1397–1428); she married Alan, Viscount de Rohan.

Joan was crowned Queen Consort on 25th/26th February, 1403, at Westminster Abbey. She was made a Lady of the Garter in 1405. She died on 2nd, 9th or 10th July, 1437 at the Dower House known as Pirgo, on the royal manor of Havering-atte-Bower, Essex, and was buried in Canterbury Cathedral, Kent. There was no issue of her marriage to Henry IV.

HENRY IV

He died on 20th March, 1413, in the Jerusalem Chamber in West-minster Abbey, of a disease resembling leprosy, and was buried in Canterbury Cathedral.

He was succeeded by his son Henry.

Recommended reading

Marie Louise Bruce: *The Usurper King: Henry of Bolingbroke* (Rubicon Press, 1986).

J. L. Kirby: *Henry IV of England* (Constable, 1970).

For Henry's family, see:

A. R. Myers: *The Captivity of a Royal Witch: the Household Accounts of Queen Joan of Navarre, 1419–21* (*Bulletin of the John Rylands Library*, vol. 24, no. 2, and vol. 26, no. 1, 1940).

E. Carleton Williams: *My Lord of Bedford* (Longmans, 1963).

K. H. Vickers: *Humphrey, Duke of Gloucester* (1907).

R. Putnam: *A Mediaeval Princess* (1904), being a biography of Jacqueline of Hainault.

HENRY V

FATHER: *Henry IV (see page 122).*
MOTHER: *Mary de Bohun (see page 122, under Henry IV).*
SIBLINGS: *(See page 123, under Henry IV).*

HENRY V

He was born probably on 9th August or 16th September, 1387, or—less probably—in August, 1386, at Monmouth Castle. He was created Prince of Wales, Duke of Cornwall and Earl of Chester, and Prince of Aquitaine on 15th October, 1399, and invested with these honours the same day. He was made a Knight of the Garter in 1399. He was created Duke of Aquitaine on 23rd October or 10th November, 1399, and Duke of Lancaster on 10th November, 1399. He succeeded his father as King of England on 21st March, 1413, and was crowned on 9th April, 1413 in Westminster Abbey. He was designated heir to the throne of France on 21st May, 1420, but did not live to enjoy his inheritance.

Henry V married, on 2nd/3rd June, 1420, at Troyes Cathedral, France:

Katherine

She was the daughter of Charles VI, King of France, by Isabella, daughter of Stephen II, Duke of Ingolstadt-Bavaria. Her sister Isabella had been married to Richard II. Katherine was born on 27th October, 1401 at the Hôtel de St Pol, Paris. She was crowned in Westminster Abbey on 23rd/24th February, 1421. After the death of Henry V, she formed a liaison with, and perhaps secretly married (although there is no evidence for this) Owen or Owain, son of Meredith ap Tudor (Tewdwr) by his wife Margaret. This marriage, if it took place at all, was solemnised between 1425 and 1428. Owen Tudor was born in c.1400 at Plas Penmynydd, Wales, and he was executed on 2nd February, 1461 by the Yorkists at Hereford. He was buried in Grey Friar's Church, Hereford. His union with Katherine produced issue as follows, and details are given in full as they are relevant to the succession:

(a) *Owen* or *Thomas* or *Edward*

He was born on 6th November, 1429 at the Palace of Westminster, and is perhaps to be identified with Edward Bridgewater, a monk at Westminster Abbey from 1468/9 to 1471/2. He died in 1502 at Westminster, and was buried in Westminster Abbey.

(b) *Edmund (see page 148, under Henry VII).*

(c) *Jaspar*

He was born in c.1431 at Hatfield, Herts. He was created Earl of Pembroke probably on 23rd November, 1452, certainly before 30th January, 1453. He was made a Knight of the Garter before 23rd April, 1459. He was attainted as a traitor by Act of Parliament on 4th November, 1461, and forfeited all his honours, but was styled Earl of Pembroke from October, 1470 until May, 1471, during the readeption of Henry VI. He was created Duke of Bedford on 27th October, 1485, and formally restored to all his honours on 12th December, 1485. He died on 21st or 26th December, 1495, and was buried in Keynsham Abbey, Somerset.

Jaspar had the following illegitimate issue:

By Mevanvy (d. by 1485?), a Welshwoman:

1 Helen or Ellen; she married William Gardiner of London, and had issue.

Jaspar married, before 7th November, 1485:

Katherine

She was the daughter of Richard Woodville, 1st Earl Rivers, by Jacquetta of Luxembourg (see page 125, under Henry IV), and sister to Elizabeth, wife of Edward IV. She was born before 1458. She married firstly Henry Stafford, 2nd Duke of Buckingham (1455?–executed 1483) in c. February, 1466, and had issue:

1 Edward, 3rd Duke of Buckingham (1478–executed 1521); he married Eleanor (d.1530), daughter of Henry Percy, 4th Earl of Northumberland, and had issue.

2 Henry, Earl of Wiltshire (1479?–1523); he married firstly Muriel or Margaret, daughter of Edward Grey, Viscount de Lisle, and secondly Cecilia (d.1529), daughter of William Bonville, Baron Harington.

3 Humphrey (d. young).

4 Anne; she married first Sir Walter Herbert (d.1507), and secondly George Hastings, Earl of Huntingdon (1488–1544), and had issue.

5 Elizabeth (d.1532); she married Robert Radcliffe, Earl of Sussex (d.1542). She was also the first recorded mistress of Henry VIII.

After the death of Jaspar, Katherine married thirdly Sir Richard Wingfield of Kimbolton Castle, Hunts. (1468–1525). She died before 1513.

(d) *Daughter (name not known)*
Polydore Vergil, Henry VII's official historian, says she became a nun, and there is no reason to doubt this, although no other source mentions her.

(e) *Margaret* or *Katherine*
She was born in January, 1437 at the Abbey of St Saviour, Bermondsey, London, where she died shortly after her birth.

Katherine died on 3rd January, 1437, at the Abbey of St Saviour, Bermondsey, London, in childbirth, and was buried in Westminster Abbey.

Issue of marriage:

1 **Henry VI** *(see page 131).*

HENRY V

He died on 31st August/1st September, 1422 at the Castle of Bois-de-Vincennes, France, and was buried in Westminster Abbey.
He was succeeded by his son Henry.

Recommended reading

Margaret Wade Labargé: *Henry V, the Cautious Conqueror* (Secker and Warburg, 1975).
Peter Earle: *Henry V* (Weidenfeld and Nicolson, 1972).
H. F. Hutchison: *Henry V* (Eyre and Spottiswoode, 1967).

HENRY VI

FATHER: *Henry V (see page 128).*
MOTHER: *Katherine of France (see page 129, under Henry V).*
SIBLINGS: *Henry VI did not have any legitimate siblings.*

HENRY VI

He was born on 6th December, 1421 at Windsor Castle. He is said to have been designated Duke of Cornwall from birth. He succeeded his father Henry V as King of England on 1st September, 1422, and his grandfather, Charles VI of France, as King of France on 11th October, 1422, in accordance with the terms of the Treaty of Troyes (1420) which settled the French succession upon Henry V and his heirs. Henry VI was crowned at Westminster Abbey on 5th/6th November, 1429, and at the Cathedral of Notre Dame in Paris on 16th/17th December, 1431. He assumed personal rule on 12th November, 1437.

Henry VI was deposed in favour of Edward, Duke of York (Edward IV) on 4th March, 1461. He was restored to the throne on

30th October, 1470—this was known as "the Readeption"—but deposed again in favour of Edward IV on 11th April, 1471.

Henry VI married, by proxy on 24th May, 1444 at the Cathedral of St Martin, Tours, France, and in person on 23rd April, 1445 at Titchfield Abbey, Hampshire:

Margaret

She was the daughter of René, Duke of Anjou and King of Naples and Sicily, by Isabella, Duchess of Lorraine, daughter of Charles I, Duke of Lorraine, and she was born on 23rd March, 1429 at Pont-à-Mousson, Lorraine. She was crowned on 30th May, 1445 in Westminster Abbey. She died on 25th August, 1482 at Château Dampierre, Anjou, and was buried in St Maurice's Cathedral, Angers, Anjou.

Issue of marriage:

1 *Edward*

He was born on 13th October, 1453 at the Palace of Westminster, and was Duke of Cornwall from birth. He was created Prince of Wales and Earl of Chester on 15th March, 1454, and invested with the principality of Wales on 9th June, 1454 at Windsor Castle. He was also made a Knight of the Garter. He was killed on 4th May, 1471 at the Battle of Tewkesbury, and was buried in Tewkesbury Abbey, Gloucs.

Edward married, probably on 13th December, 1470, at Château d'Amboise, France:

Anne

She was the daughter of Richard Neville, Earl of Warwick, by Anne, daughter of Richard de Beauchamp, Earl of Warwick, and she was born on 11th June, 1456 at Warwick Castle. After the death of Edward, she married Richard, Duke of Gloucester (see page 143, under Richard III for further details of her life).

HENRY VI

He was murdered on 27th(?) May, 1471 in his prison in the Tower of London; later sources credit the future Richard III with the murder, but this is unlikely, although the perpetrator of the deed was certainly very near the throne, if not occupying it. Henry was buried in Chertsey Abbey, Surrey, but was removed to St George's Chapel, Windsor in 1485. He had already been succeeded by his distant cousin Edward IV.

Recommended reading
The definitive biography of the King is:
  B. Wolfe: *Henry VI* (Eyre Methuen, 1981).
See also:
  R. L. Storey: *The End of the House of Lancaster* (1966).
  Alison Weir: *Lancaster and York* (Jonathan Cape, 1995).
  M. E. Christie *Henry VI* (1922).
For Margaret of Anjou, see:
  J. J. Bagley: *Margaret of Anjou, Queen of England* (Herbert Jenkins, 1948).
  Philippe Erlanger: *Margaret of Anjou, Queen of England* (English version published by Elek Books 1970, although it was written in 1932).
  Jock Haswell: *The Ardent Queen* (Peter Davies, 1976).

EDWARD IV

FATHER: *Richard*
He was the son of Richard, Earl of Cambridge (son of the fourth surviving son of Edward III) by Anne Mortimer (great-granddaughter of the second surviving son of Edward III), and he was born on 21st September, 1411/12. He married Cecilia Neville before 18th October, 1424. He was first styled Duke of York on 24th February, 1425, although the actual date of his restoration to the title and dignity (which had been forfeited when his father was executed in 1415) is assumed to have been sometime before this. He was formally restored in blood to the dukedom of York on 19th May, 1426, and was recognised as Earl of March, Earl of Ulster and Earl of Cambridge by hereditary right on 12th May, 1432. He was made a Knight of the Garter on 22nd April, 1433. In 1448, he assumed the surname Plantagenet, which had not been used since it

was borne by Geoffrey of Anjou, father of Henry II, in the 12th century; he did this to emphasise that his claim to the throne of England was stronger than that of Henry VI: this would lead shortly to the Wars of the Roses. Richard was attainted on 20th November, 1459, and all his titles and honours were declared forfeit. The Attainder against him was nullified in October, 1460, when he was restored to all his titles and honours, but he continued to press his claim to the throne, and was killed on 30th December, 1460, at the Battle of Wakefield. He was buried at Pontefract, but was later removed to the Collegiate Church of Fotheringhay, Northants.

MOTHER: *Cecilia* or *Cecily*

She was the daughter of Ralph Neville, 1st Earl of Westmorland, by Joan Beaufort, daughter of John of Gaunt, Duke of Lancaster (see page 109, under Edward III), and she was born on 3rd May, 1415 at Raby Castle, Co. Durham. She died a Benedictine nun on 31st May, 1495 at Berkhamstead Castle, Herts., and was buried in the Collegiate Church of Fotheringhay, Northants.

SIBLINGS:

1 *Joan*

She was born in 1438, and died the same year.

2 *Anne*

She was born on 10th/11th August, 1439 at Fotheringhay Castle, Northants. She married firstly Henry Holland, 4th Duke of Exeter (1430–drowned at sea 1475) before 30th July, 1447, and had issue.

1 Anne (c.1455–1475); she married Thomas Grey, 1st Marquess of Dorset (1455?–1501), son of Elizabeth Woodville, wife of Edward IV.

Anne was divorced from her first husband on 12th November, 1472. She married secondly Sir Thomas St Leger (executed 1483) in 1472/3, and had issue:

2 Anne (1476?–1526); she married George Manners, Lord Roos (d.1513), and had issue.

Anne died on 12th or 14th January, 1476 (or 1482?), in childbirth (?), and was buried in St George's Chapel, Windsor.

3 *Henry*

He was born on 9th/10th February, 1441 at Hatfield, Herts., and died young.

4 *Edmund*

He was born on 17th or 27th May, 1443 at Rouen, France. He was created Earl of Rutland on 29th January, 1446. He forfeited his earldom by Act of

Attainder in 1459, but was restored to it in October, 1460. He was killed on 30th December, 1460 at the Battle of Wakefield, Yorks., and was buried at Pontefract. His remains were later removed to the Collegiate Church of Fotheringhay, Northants.

5 *Elizabeth*

She was born on 22nd April, 1444, at Rouen, France. She married John de la Pole, 2nd Duke of Suffolk (d.1491) in c.August, 1461 (or, less probably, before October, 1460), and had issue:

  1 John, Earl of Lincoln (1462/4?–1487: killed at the Battle of Stoke); he married Margaret (d. after 1493), daughter of Thomas FitzAlan, Earl of Arundel, and had issue.

  2 Edmund, Earl of Suffolk (1471/2?–executed 1513); he married Margaret (d.1515), daughter of Sir Richard Scrope, and had issue.

  3 Humphrey, Rector of Leverington, Cambs., and of Hingham, Norfolk (1474?–1513).

  4 Edward, Archdeacon of Richmond, Yorks. (d.1485?).

  5 Richard, styled "Earl of Suffolk" (killed at the Battle of Pavia in 1525).

  6 Geoffrey.

  7 William (1478?–1539), a knight; he married Katherine (d.1521), daughter of William, 2nd Baron Stourton.

  8 Anne (d. after 1495); she was a nun at Sion Abbey, Middlesex.

  9 Katherine; she is said to have married William, Baron Stourton (1457–1524).

  10 Elizabeth (d. after 1489); she married Henry Lovell, Baron Morley (d. 1489).

  11 Dorothy (d. unmarried).

Elizabeth died between 7th January, 1503 and 3rd May, 1504, and was buried in Wingfield Church, Suffolk.

6 *Margaret*

She was born on 3rd May, 1446 at Fotheringhay Castle, Northants., and married Charles the Bold, Duke of Burgundy (1433–killed at the Battle of Nancy, 1477) on 3rd July, 1468 at Damme, Flanders. She died on 16th April or 28th November, 1503 at Malines, Flanders, and was buried in the Church of the Cordeliers, Malines.

7 *William*

He was born on 7th July, 1447 at Fotheringhay Castle, Northants., and died young.

8 *John*

He was born on 7th November, 1448 at The Neyte, a house near Westminster, and died young.

9 *George*

He was born on 21st October, 1449 at Dublin Castle, Ireland. He was made a Knight of the Garter in 1461, and a Knight of the Bath on 27th June, 1461. He was created Duke of Clarence on 28th June, 1461. He was created Earl of Salisbury and Earl of Warwick, in right of his wife, on 25th March, 1472. He was attainted on 8th February, 1478, and by this Act of Attainder forfeited all his estates and titles and the rights of himself and his heirs to the succession. He was privately executed on 18th February, 1478, in the Tower of London: tradition has it that he was drowned in a butt of Malmsey wine. He was buried in Tewkesbury Abbey, Gloucs.

George married, on 11th July, 1469, at the Church of Our Lady, Calais, France:

Isabella

She was the daughter of Richard Neville, Earl of Warwick, by Anne, daughter of Richard de Beauchamp, Earl of Warwick; her sister Anne married firstly Edward, Prince of Wales, son of Henry VI, and secondly Richard III. Isabella was born on 5th September, 1451 at Warwick Castle. She died, it was rumoured by poison, on 12th, 21st or 22nd December, 1476, at Warwick Castle, and was buried in Tewkesbury Abbey, Gloucs. Issue of marriage:

 (i) *Anne* (?)

   She was born on 16th April, 1470, in a ship off Calais. She was either born dead or died soon after birth, and was buried at Calais. Some sources state that the child born at sea in 1470 was a son.

(ii) *Margaret*

   She was born on 14th August, 1473 at Farleigh Castle, near Bath, Wilts. She married Sir Richard Pole (d.1505) on 22nd September, 1494, and had issue:

   1 Henry, Marquess of Montagu (1495?–executed 1538); he married Jane (d.1538), daughter of George Neville, Lord Bergavenny, and had issue.

   2 Reginald, Cardinal-Archbishop of Canterbury (1500–1558).

   3 Geoffrey, a knight, of Lordington, Sussex (1501–1558); he married Constance, daughter of Sir John Pakenham, and had issue.

   4 Ursula (d. 1570); she married Henry, Lord Stafford (1501–1563), and had issue.

   5 Arthur (d.1570); he married Jane, daughter of Sir Roger Lewkmor, and had issue.

   Margaret was restored to her father's earldom of Salisbury on 14th October, 1513. She was attainted on 12th May, 1539, and all her titles were declared forfeit. She was executed, with appalling barbarity, on

28th May, 1541 in the Tower of London, and was buried in the Royal Chapel of St Peter ad Vincula within the Tower.

(iii) *Edward*

He was born on 21st or 25th February, 1475 (or 1474?) at Warwick Castle, and was styled Earl of Warwick from birth, in right of his mother. He succeeded his mother as Earl of Salisbury in December, 1476, but was never so styled. He was confirmed as Earl of Warwick in 1490. He spent the greater part of his life in confinement, Henry VII resenting his proximity to the throne, and was executed for treason on 24th or 28th November, 1499 on Tower Hill, London. He was buried in Bisham Abbey, Berks.

(iv) *Richard*

He was born on 6th October, 1476 at Tewkesbury Abbey, Gloucs., and died on 1st January, 1477 at Warwick Castle. He was buried in Warwick Church, by the Castle.

10 *Thomas*

He was born in 1450/1, and died young.

11 *Richard III* (see page 143).

12 *Ursula*

Described as the youngest child, she was born on 22nd July, 1455 at Fotheringhay Castle, Northants., and died young.

13 *Katherine* (?)

14 *Humphrey* (?)

Katherine and Humphrey are described by Cecilia as her children in her will, although they are not included in any other contemporary list of the children of Richard, Duke of York. The entry in Cecilia's will may therefore refer in fact to her grandchildren, Humphrey and Katherine de la Pole, the issue of Cecilia's daughter Elizabeth.

EDWARD IV

He was born on 28th April, 1442 at Rouen, France. He was styled Earl of March during his father's lifetime. In November, 1459 he forfeited all his honours by Act of Attainder, but was restored to them in October, 1460. He succeeded his father as Duke of York, Earl of Ulster and Earl of Cambridge on 30th December, 1460. He was proclaimed King of England by Parliament on 4th March, 1461 after the deposition of Henry VI, and was crowned on 28th June, 1461 at Westminster Abbey.

Edward IV was deposed in favour of Henry VI on 3rd October, 1470, but restored to the throne on 11th April, 1471.

Edward IV married, on 1st May, 1464, at the Manor of Grafton Regis, Northants.:

Elizabeth

She was the daughter of Richard Woodville or Wydeville, 1st Earl Rivers, by Jacquetta of Luxembourg (see page 124, under Henry IV), and she was born in c.1437 at Grafton Regis, Northants. She married firstly Sir John Grey of Groby (killed 1461) in c.1452, and had issue:

1 Thomas, Marquess of Dorset (c.1455–1501); he married firstly Anne (c.1455–1475), daughter of Henry Holland Duke of Exeter by Anne, sister of Edward IV, and had issue. He married secondly Cecilia, Baroness Bonville and Harington (d.1529), daughter of William Bonville, Baron Harington, and had issue.

2 Richard (1456?–executed 1483), a knight.

Elizabeth was crowned Queen Consort on 26th May, 1465 at Westminster Abbey. Her marriage to Edward IV was declared invalid on 25th June, 1483, by the Act of Parliament known as "Titulus Regius", because of Edward's alleged precontract to Lady Eleanor Butler (see below); her children were at the same time declared illegitimate, and unfit to inherit the crown. The marriage was ultimately recognised as valid in October, 1485 by the first Parliament of Henry VII, and its issue were restored in blood accordingly. Elizabeth died on 8th June, 1492 at St Saviour's Abbey, Bermondsey, London, and was buried in St George's Chapel, Windsor.

Issue of marriage:

1 *Elizabeth*

(See page 149, under Henry VII, whom she married).

2 *Mary*

She was born on 11th August, 1467 at Windsor Castle. She was made a Lady of the Garter in 1480. She died on 23rd May, 1482 at Greenwich Palace, Kent, and was buried in St George's Chapel, Windsor.

3 *Cecilia or Cecily*

She was born on 20th March, 1469 at the Palace of Westminster. She married firstly John Welles, 1st Viscount Welles, K.G. (d.1498) between 25th November, 1487 and 1st January, 1488, and had issue:

1 Elizabeth (d. young before 1498).

2 Anne (d. young in c.1499).

Cecilia married secondly Thomas Kyme, Kymbe or Keme, either of Wainfleet and Friskney, Lincs., or of the Isle of Wight, between 13th May, 1502 and January, 1504, by whom she may have had issue, although the earliest evidence for this is as late as 1602, and may be suspect:

3 Richard; he married a lady called Agnes, and had issue.

4 Margaret or Marjorie; she married John Wetherby, and had issue.

Cecilia was made a Lady of the Garter in 1480. She died on 24th August, 1507 at Quarr Abbey, Isle of Wight, where she was buried.

4 Edward V *(see page 142)*.

5 Margaret

She was born on 10th April, 1472 at Windsor Castle, and died on 11th December, 1472. She was buried in Westminster Abbey.

6 Richard

He was born probably on 17th August, 1473 at the Dominican Friary, Shrewsbury, Shropshire. He was created Duke of York on 28th May, 1474, thereby establishing the tradition (which continues to this day) that the second son of the sovereign is always made Duke of York. He was made a Knight of the Garter on 15th May, 1475, and a Knight of the Bath during that same year. He was created Earl of Nottingham on 12th June, 1476, and Duke of Norfolk and Earl of Surrey and Warenne on 7th February, 1477. He was declared illegitimate by Act of Parliament and deprived of his titles on 26th June, 1483. Richard was last seen alive in July, 1483 within the precincts of the Tower of London; he is believed to have been murdered with his brother (see page 142, under Edward V). In 1674, bones discovered in the Tower and thought to be Richard's were buried in Westminster Abbey.

Richard married, on 15th January, 1478, at St Stephen's Chapel in the Palace of Westminster:

Anne

She was the daughter of John Mowbray, Duke of Norfolk, by Elizabeth, daughter of John Talbot, 2nd Earl of Shrewsbury, and she was born on 10th December, 1472 at Framlingham Castle, Suffolk. She was recognised and styled as Countess of Norfolk in her own right on 16th/17th January, 1476, after the death of her father. She died between 16th January, and 19th November, 1481, at Greenwich Palace, and was buried in Westminster Abbey. When Henry VII's Chapel was under construction, her body was moved to the Minoresses' Convent at Stepney, where her coffin was found during excavations in 1965. She was then reburied in Westminster Abbey.

7 Anne

She was born on 2nd November, 1475 at the Palace of Westminster. She married Lord Thomas Howard (afterwards Earl of Surrey, then Duke of Norfolk) (1473–1554) on 4th February, 1495 at Greenwich Palace, and had issue:
1 Thomas (c.1496 or 1508–1508).
2 Son (d. young before baptism).
3 Daughter (d. young before baptism).
4 Daughter (d. young before baptism).
Anne died after 22nd November (23rd November?), 1511 and before 1513, and was buried in Thetford Priory, Norfolk. Her remains were later removed to Framlingham Church, Suffolk.

8 George

He was born perhaps in March, 1477 (certainly before January, 1478), either at Windsor Castle, or at the Dominican Friary, Shrewsbury, Shropshire, and was perhaps styled Duke of Bedford. He died in March, 1479 at Windsor Castle, and was buried in St George's Chapel, Windsor.

9 Katherine

She was born on 14th August, 1479 at Eltham Palace, Kent. She married William Courtenay, later Earl of Devon (1475–1511) in c. October, 1495, and had issue:
1 Henry, Marquess of Exeter (1496?–executed 1538); he married firstly Elizabeth (d.1516?), daughter of John Grey, Viscount Lisle, and secondly, Gertrude (d.1558), daughter of William Blount, 4th Baron Mountjoy, and had issue.
2 Edward (1497?–1502).
3 Margaret (1499?–1519?); she married William, Baron Herbert.
Katherine took a vow of perpetual chastity upon her widowhood in 1511. She died on 15th November, 1527 at Tiverton Castle, Devon, and was buried in Tiverton Parish Church.

10 Bridget

She was born on 10th or 20th November, 1480 at Eltham Palace, Kent. She became a nun at Dartford Priory, Kent in c.1487 (and certainly before 1492). She died probably before 1513. John Weaver, writing in the 17th century, states she died in 1517, but Thomas More, writing in 1513, does not say that she is alive, although he mentions that her only surviving sister, Katherine, was then still living. Bridget was buried in Dartford Priory, Kent.

Edward IV also had the following **illegitimate issue**:

By Eleanor Talbot or Butler (d.1468), to whom Edward is alleged to have been precontracted:
1 Edward de Wigmore (d. in infancy, 1468).
By Elizabeth Lucy (née Waite), or Elizabeth (sometimes, but erroneously, called Jane) Shore:
2 Arthur Plantagenet, Viscount Lisle (1461/4–1542); he married firstly Elizabeth Grey, Baroness Lisle (d.1525/6), and had issue. He married secondly Honora (1493/5–1566), daughter of Sir Thomas Grenville.
3 Elizabeth (b.c.1464); she perhaps married Thomas Lumley. It is thought that Elizabeth Lucy was her mother.
By an unknown mother:
4 Grace (alive in 1492).

EDWARD IV
He died on 9th April, 1483 at the Palace of Westminster, and was buried in St George's Chapel, Windsor.
He was succeeded by his son Edward.

Recommended reading
Charles Ross: *Edward IV* (Eyre Methuen, 1974).
Mary Clive: *This Sun of York: A Biography of Edward IV* (Macmillan, 1973).
For Elizabeth Woodville, see:
D. MacGibbon: *Elizabeth Woodville, 1437–92* (1938).
G. Smith: *The Coronation of Elizabeth Wydeville* (1935).
For George Plantagenet, Duke of Clarence, see:
J. R. Lander: *The Treason and Death of the Duke of Clarence: A Reinterpretation* (*Canadian Journal of History*, ii, 1967).

EDWARD V

FATHER: *Edward IV (see page 133).*
MOTHER: *Elizabeth Woodville (see page 138, under Edward IV).*
SIBLINGS: *(see page 138, under Edward IV).*

EDWARD V

He was born on 1st, 2nd or 4th November, 1470 in the Sanctuary, Westminster Abbey. He was created Prince of Wales and Earl of Chester on 25th/26th June, 1471, and Duke of Cornwall on 17th July, 1471. He was made a Knight of the Garter on 15th May, 1475, and created Earl of March and Earl of Pembroke on 8th or 18th July, 1479. He succeeded his father as King of England on 9th April, 1483.

Edward V was declared illegitimate (see under Edward IV) by Act of Parliament on 25th June, 1483, and deposed that same day. He was last seen alive in July, 1483 within the precincts of the Tower of London. Contemporary rumours accused Richard III of his murder within the Tower and that of his brother Richard (the boys were thereafter known as "the Princes in the Tower"), and circumstantial evidence suggests that the murders were committed on the night of 3rd September, 1483. Controversy has raged ever since over who was actually responsible for the deed. Although the evidence is at best circumstantial, Richard III seems to be the likeliest culprit. In 1674, bones believed to have been those of Edward V and his brother were discovered beneath a staircase during excavations in the Tower of London, and buried in 1678 in Westminster Abbey by order of Charles II. Edward V was succeeded by his uncle, Richard of Gloucester.

Recommended reading
Elizabeth Jenkins: *The Princes in the Tower* (H. Hamilton, 1978).
Alison Weir: *The Princes in the Tower* (Bodley Head, 1992).

RICHARD III

FATHER: *Richard Plantagenet, Duke of York (see page 133, under Edward IV)*.

MOTHER: *Cecilia Neville (see page 134, under Edward IV)*.

SIBLINGS: *(see page 134, under Edward IV)*.

RICHARD III

He was born on 2nd October, 1452 at Fotheringhay Castle, Northants. He was created Duke of Gloucester on 1st November, 1461, and made a Knight of the Garter before 4th February, 1466. He acceded to the throne of England on 26th June, 1483 after the deposition of his nephew, Edward V, and was crowned on 6th July, 1483, in Westminster Abbey.

Richard III married, on 12th July, 1472, in Westminster Abbey:

Anne

She was the daughter of Richard Neville, Earl of Warwick, by Anne, daughter of Richard de Beauchamp, Earl of Warwick, and she was born on 11th June, 1456 at Warwick Castle. She married firstly Edward, Prince of Wales, son of Henry VI, probably on 13th December, 1470 at the Château of Amboise, France. She was crowned Queen Consort on 6th July, 1483 at Westminster Abbey. She died on 16th March, 1485, at the Palace of Westminster, probably of tuberculosis, and was buried in Westminster Abbey.

Issue of marriage:

1 *Edward*

He was born in c. December, 1473 (or perhaps as late as 1476) at Middleham Castle, Yorkshire, and was created Earl of Salisbury on 15th February, 1478. He became Duke of Cornwall upon his father's accession to the throne on 26th June, 1483, and was created Prince of Wales and Earl of Chester on 24th August, 1483, being invested as such on 8th September, 1483 at York Minster. He died probably on 9th April (less probably on 31st March), 1484 at Middleham Castle, Yorkshire, and was buried in Sheriff-Hutton Church, Yorkshire.

Richard III also had the following **illegitimate issue**:

By unknown mothers:

1 John of Gloucester, or of Pontefract, Captain of Calais (c.1470–murdered? 1499?).
2 Richard (1469–1550).
3 Katherine; she married William Herbert, Earl of Huntingdon (1455?–1491).
4 Stephen Hawes (?).
5 Unnamed child (?).
6 Unnamed child (?).
7 Unnamed child (?).

RICHARD III

He was killed on 22nd August, 1485, defending his crown and his kingdom against the forces of Henry Tudor at the Battle of Bosworth Field in Leicestershire. He was buried in Greyfriars Abbey, Leicester. His grave was despoiled during the Reformation. Richard was the last Plantagenet King of England. He was succeeded by his distant cousin Henry Tudor.

Recommended reading
Several books were published to mark the quincentenary of the reign of Richard III, among them:
Desmond Seward: *Richard III: England's Black Legend* (Country Life, 1983).
The following biography has yet to be surpassed, however:
Paul Murray Kendall: *Richard the Third* (Allen and Unwin, 1955).

5. The Tudors

The Tudors came, it must be said, from bastard stock. Henry VII's mother, Margaret Beaufort, was a descendant of John Beaufort, the first of the bastard children born to John of Gaunt, Duke of Lancaster and his mistress, Katherine Swynford. Henry's father, Edmund Tudor, was the offspring of the liaison between Henry V's widow, Katherine of France, and the Welsh squire, Owen Tudor. It may be that these two actually married in secret, but no proof of this has ever been discovered; in the 15th century, their children were looked upon as bastards, with all the handicaps that imposed upon inheritance. Not for them a Statute conferring legitimacy, as had been the good fortune of the Beaufort bastards of Katherine Swynford when her lover Gaunt at long last made her his wife. Yet even to this there was a sting in the tail: for while the Beauforts were recognised as legitimate, they were at the same time debarred by the Statute from ever inheriting the throne.

Henry VII was the only child of his parents; his father died before his birth and his mother remarried (she had been but 13 years old at the time of his birth, and never bore another child). Henry was exiled from England by Edward IV, while still a child, and spent his youth in the courts of France and Brittany with his uncle and staunch supporter, Jaspar Tudor. Both were of course utterly loyal to Henry VI and the House of Lancaster, and after the death of Henry VI and his son Edward, Henry Tudor was seen by many as the natural heir to the Lancastrian claim to the throne of England, despite his legal ineligibility to fulfil such a rôle. There was simply no one else fitted for it of the blood of Lancaster. And it was the crown of England that Henry meant to have. On Christmas Day, 1483, in the Cathedral of Rennes in Brittany, he vowed to marry Elizabeth of York, daughter of Edward IV, and thus unite the red and white roses of Lancaster and York. Henry must have known at this date that Edward V and his brother were dead; Elizabeth had been declared a bastard, and if she was to be declared her father's legitimate heir, this could only be so if her brothers predeceased her. Two years later, in August, 1485, Henry Tudor defeated Richard III at the Battle of Bosworth and became King of England. In January, 1486, he kept his vow and married Elizabeth, who had been legitimated in his first Parliament; the slight delay between Henry's accession and his marriage served only to emphasise that Henry's crown was his by right of conquest and of descent, and not through union with Elizabeth of York.

Thus was founded the Tudor dynasty, a dynasty that, as if to compensate for its precarious claim to the throne, was to be the most splendid and successful of all the English Royal Houses. During the 118 years of Tudor rule, England emerged from the mediaeval world as a modern state, prosperous and proud of itself. It was, however, a revolutionary age and a brutal one. Henry VIII declared himself Head of the Church of England and severed for ever all links with the Church of Rome. Under Elizabeth, the Protestant Anglican Church became firmly established. Voyages of discovery were opening up the wider world and trade flourished. The old nobility found themselves being replaced by "new men" such as had their origins in merchant families and no connection with the Norman companions of William I. Yet in this same age of enlightenment, of humanism and the flowering of the English Renaissance, thousands were executed for heresy or treason, often with appalling barbarity. There was no "niceness" about the Tudor monarchs: they did what they saw as necessary thoroughly and ruthlessly, although by 1603, when Elizabeth I died, much of the power of government had devolved upon Parliament, so often consulted by successive Tudor monarchs to give legality to dubious or unpopular measures, and eventually demanding to be consulted and to give approval as a right.

Yet while they were powerful and capable monarchs, the Tudors were never quite secure on the throne. During the first fifty years of their rule, too many members of the House of York remained alive for the new dynasty to feel secure. Later, threats to the succession would be posed by the Grey family and by Mary, Queen of Scots. But it was the surviving members of the House of York who constituted the worst threat, as there was no doubt in the minds of many that their title to the throne was far more valid than that of the Tudors. In fact, in 1485, when Henry VII acceded to the throne, there were then living 18 people with a better right to it than he, including his own wife and mother. By 1510, this figure had increased by about 16 more persons, born with Yorkist blood in their veins.

Of course, many of these heirs of York were women. Although the Salic Law had no validity in England (unlike in France, where women were debarred from inheriting the throne), memories of the Empress Matilda, whose attempt in the 12th century to rule England had resulted in bloody civil war, had led to an enduring prejudice against the notion of a female sovereign. Women were considered unfit to rule over men, and no one seriously thought of espousing the cause of any of the Yorkist women. It would be left to the Tudors to prove that a woman sovereign could rule very successfully.

It was the male members of the House of York who were the thorn in the side of the Tudors. Some died young, and of the eight who survived to be serious contenders for the throne, two chose a life of retirement away from public life, and were not molested. Two died in battle, one of them an exile fighting under a foreign banner. Four were executed. Both Henry VII and Henry VIII were cognisant of the weakness of their claim to the throne, and dealt ruthlessly with any would-be rivals. Mention should be made of Margaret Pole, Countess of Salisbury, niece of Edward IV and Richard III, who, at the age of nearly 68, was beheaded in an horrific manner on the orders of Henry VIII, on a trumped-up charge of treason. Lesser members of her family were imprisoned by that monarch, and left to rot in the Tower. By that time, the House of York had been virtually eliminated.

Indeed, to give his dynasty a sound title to the throne, Henry VII had to go back beyond the Plantagenets, the Normans, and the Saxon Kings, to the legendary Arthur, the ancient British kings, and the Welsh Prince Cadwaladr, whose red dragon appeared on Henry's standard. He claimed descent from all these, through Rhys ap Tewdwr, Prince of Deheubarth in Wales, who died in 1093. Henry even named his eldest son after King Arthur to emphasise the link between the Tudors and ancient royalty. The message was clear: he was the true successor to Arthur and Cadwaladr and their ilk; all those who had come since were the real usurpers.

The dynasty survived, but it did not flourish. The succession was an ongoing problem, because the Tudors were not a fruitful dynasty: many of its members were sickly, or died young. Henry VIII took drastic measures to get a male heir, taking six wives in the process, divorcing two, and beheading two more, as well as creating a schism in the Church. He was not just a man of lusts: nobody wanted a return to the dynastic warfare of the previous century, and Tudor prosperity had done much to make the new dynasty popular. Henry's only surviving son Edward VI did not live to marry, and there was then no alternative but for the country to turn to a female to be its ruler. But Mary I did not live long, and her two pregnancies ended in disappointment. Her sister Elizabeth I had a long and glorious reign, but she never married, probably for political reasons, and kept her country guessing until the last whom she would name as her successor. It was, of course, her cousin, James VI of Scotland, a descendant of Henry VII, and founder of the House of Stuart in 1603.

HENRY VII

FATHER: *Edmund*

He was the son of Owen Tudor by his liaison (it may have been a marriage) with Katherine of France, widow of Henry V, and he was born in c.1430, either at Much Hadham Palace, Herts., or at Hadham, Beds. He was created Earl of Richmond on 23rd November, 1452. He married Margaret Beaufort in October, 1455 at Bletsoe Castle, Beds. He died on 1st November, 1456 at Carmarthen Castle, Wales, and was buried in the Church of the Grey Friars, Carmarthen. His remains were later transferred to St David's Cathedral, Wales.

MOTHER: *Margaret*

She was the daughter of John Beaufort, Duke of Somerset (see page 104, under Edward III), by Margaret de Beauchamp, and she was born on 31st May, 1443 at Bletsoe Castle, Beds. She married firstly John de la Pole, later Duke of Suffolk (d.1491) between 28th January, 1449 and 18th August, 1450, but the marriage was annulled before 24th March, 1453, and de la Pole later married Elizabeth, sister of Edward IV. Margaret married secondly Edmund Tudor. After his death, she married thirdly Sir Henry Stafford (d.1471) between c.1459 and 1464. She married fourthly Thomas Stanley, Earl of Derby (1435?–1504) before October, 1473 (or October, 1482?), although she had taken a vow of perpetual chastity. She was made a Lady of the Garter in 1488. She died on 29th June, 1509 at the Abbot's House, Cheyney

Gates, Westminster Abbey, and was buried in Westminster Abbey.

SIBLINGS: *Henry VII did not have any siblings.*

HENRY VII

He was born on 28th January, 1457 at Pembroke Castle in Wales, and was Earl of Richmond from birth, being his father's posthumous child. He was deprived of the earldom of Richmond before 12th August, 1462. He succeeded Richard III as King of England on 22nd August, 1485, after the Battle of Bosworth, and was crowned on 30th October, 1485 in Westminster Abbey.

Henry VII married, on 18th January, 1486, at Westminster Abbey:
Elizabeth
She was the daughter of Edward IV by Elizabeth Woodville, and she was born on 11th February, 1466 at the Palace of Westminster. She was crowned Queen Consort on 25th November, 1487 in Westminster Abbey. She died on 11th February, 1503, in the Tower of London, in childbed, and was buried in Westminster Abbey.

Issue of marriage:

1 *Arthur*
Called Arthur to emphasise the new dynasty's links with the Kings of ancient Britain, he was born on 19th/20th September, 1486 at St Swithun's Priory, Winchester. He was Duke of Cornwall from birth. He was made a Knight of the Bath on 29th November, 1489. He was created Prince of Wales and Earl of Chester on 29th November, 1489, and was invested as such on 27th February, 1490 at the Palace of Westminster. He was made a Knight of the Garter on 8th May, 1491. He died on 2nd April, 1502, at Ludlow Castle, Shropshire, and was buried in Worcester Cathedral.

Arthur married, by proxy on Whitsunday, 1499 at the manor of Bewdley, Worcs., again by proxy on 19th May, 1501 at Bewdley, and in person on 14th November, 1501 at St Paul's Cathedral, London:
Katherine
She was the daughter of Ferdinand V, King of Aragon, by Isabella I, Queen of Castile, a descendant of John of Gaunt, and she was born on 16th December, 1485 at Alcala de Henares in Spain. After the death of Arthur, she married secondly Henry VIII (see page 152, under Henry VIII for further details of her life).

2 *Margaret (see page 238, under James IV of Scotland, whom she married).*

149

3 Henry VIII *(see page 151).*

4 Elizabeth

She was born on 2nd July, 1492, and died on 7th October or 14th November, 1495 at Eltham Palace, Kent, of "atrophy". She was buried in Westminster Abbey.

5 Mary

She was born on c.18th March, 1495/6, either at Richmond Palace, Surrey, or at the Palace of Westminster. She married firstly Louis XII, King of France (1462–1515), by proxy on 13th or 25th August, 1514 at Greyfriars Church, Greenwich Palace, again by proxy on 2nd September, 1514 at the Church of the Celestines in Paris, and in person on 9th October, 1514 at Abbeville Cathedral, France. She was crowned on 5th November, 1514 at St Denis' Cathedral, Paris. She married secondly Charles Brandon, Duke of Suffolk (1484–1545), secretly between 4th and 20th February, 1515 at the Chapel in the Palace of Cluny in Paris, and again on 31st (?) March, 1515 at the Chapel in the Palace of Cluny, and in public on 13th May, 1515, at Greyfriars Church, Greenwich Palace, Kent, and had issue:

1 Henry, Earl of Lincoln (1516–1534).

2 Frances (see page 158, under Queen Jane).

3 Eleanor (1519/20–1547); she married Henry Clifford, Earl of Cumberland (1517–1570), and had issue.

Mary died around 24th/26th June, 1533 at Westhorpe Hall, Suffolk, and was buried in the Abbey of Bury St Edmunds, Suffolk; her remains were later removed to St Mary's Church, Bury St Edmunds.

6 Edmund

He was born on 21st February, 1499 at Greenwich Palace, Kent; he was perhaps styled Duke of Somerset from birth, but was never formally so created. He died on 19th June, 1500 at the Old Palace, Hatfield, Herts., and was buried in Westminster Abbey.

7 Edward

He was the fourth and youngest son. The dates of his birth and death are not known. He died very young, and was buried in Westminster Abbey.

8 Katherine

She was born on 2nd February, 1503 in the Tower of London, and died there on c.18th February, 1503. She was buried in Westminster Abbey.

Henry VII also had the following **illegitimate issue**:

By a Breton lady whose name is not known:

1 Roland de Velville, Constable of Beaumaris Castle, Anglesey; he married a Welshwoman, and had issue.

HENRY VII

He died on 21st April, 1509 at Richmond Palace, Surrey, and was buried in Westminster Abbey.

He was succeeded by his son Henry.

Recommended reading

S. B. Chrimes: *Henry VII* (Eyre Methuen, 1972).

Neville Williams: *Henry VII* (Weidenfeld and Nicolson, 1972).

R. L. Storey: *The Reign of Henry VII* (Barrie and Rockliff, 1968).

Eric N. Simons: *Henry VII: The First Tudor King* (Muller, 1968).

See also:

N. Lenz-Harvey: *Elizabeth of York, Tudor Queen* (Arthur Barker, 1973).

W. C. Richardson: *Mary Tudor, the White Queen* (Peter Owen, 1970).

HENRY VIII

FATHER: *Henry VII (see page 148).*

MOTHER: *Elizabeth of York (see page 149, under Henry VII).*

SIBLINGS: *(see page 149, under Henry VII).*

HENRY VIII

He was born on 28th June, 1491 at Greenwich Palace, Kent. He was made a Knight of the Bath on 31st October, 1491, and created Duke of York on 31st October, 1494. He was made a Knight of the Garter on 17th May, 1495. He succeeded his brother Arthur as Duke of Cornwall on 2nd April, 1502, and was created and invested as Prince of Wales and Earl of Chester on 18th February, 1504 at the Palace of Westminster. He succeeded his father as King of England on 22nd April, 1509, and was crowned on 24th June, 1509 in Westminster Abbey. In 1521, he added to the royal style the title "Fidei Defensor" ("Defender of the Faith"), conferred upon him by Pope Leo X. This title is still borne by the Queen today. Henry styled himself King of Ireland from 1542.

Henry VIII married firstly, on 11th June, 1509, at Greenwich Palace, Kent:

Katherine
She was the daughter of Ferdinand V, King of Aragon, by Isabella I, Queen of Castile, a descendant of John of Gaunt, and she was born on 16th December, 1485 at Alcala de Henares in Spain. She married firstly Henry's elder brother Arthur, Prince of Wales, in 1501 (see page 149, under Henry VII). She was crowned Queen Consort on 24th June, 1509 in Westminster Abbey. Her marriage to Henry VIII was annulled on 23rd May, 1533 by Thomas Cranmer, Archbishop of Canterbury, on the grounds that she had been the wife of her husband's brother and that, according to the Levitical Law, her second marriage was uncanonical and incestuous, and the Pope had no power to dispense in such a case. She died on 7th January, 1536, at Kimbolton Castle, Hunts., probably of cancer, and was buried in Peterborough Cathedral. Her original tomb was destroyed in 1642, but its site may still be seen, and her bones still lie beneath the flagstones.

Issue of marriage:

1 *Stillborn daughter*
She was born on 31st January, 1510.

2 *Henry*
He was born on 1st January, 1511 at Richmond Palace, Surrey, and was Duke of Cornwall from birth. He was also styled Prince of Wales. He died on 22nd February, 1511 at Richmond Palace, and was buried in Westminster Abbey.

3 *Unnamed son*
He was born in November, 1513 at Richmond Palace, Surrey, and was Duke of Cornwall from birth. He died in November, 1513, and was buried in Westminster Abbey.

4 *Henry(?)*

He was born in November, 1514, and died the same day. While he lived, he was Duke of Cornwall.

5 *Mary I (see page 160)*.

6 *Unnamed daughter*

She was born on 10th November, 1518, and died the same day.

Henry VIII married secondly, in secret, on 25th January, 1533, either at York Place, London, or at the Palace of Westminster:

Anne

She was the daughter of Thomas Boleyn or Bullen, 1st Earl of Wiltshire and Ormonde, by Elizabeth, daughter of Thomas Howard, 2nd Duke of Norfolk. She was born around 1500/1501 at Blickling Hall, Norfolk. She was created Lady Marquess of Pembroke in her own right (the first time a female had been created a peer in her own right) on 1st September, 1532. She was crowned Queen Consort on 1st June, 1533 in Westminster Abbey. On 15th May, 1536, Anne Boleyn was tried and found guilty of high treason, and condemned to death in the Great Hall of the Tower of London. Her marriage to Henry VIII was declared invalid on 17th May, 1536; the grounds for this are not known. She was executed on 19th May, 1536 on Tower Green, within the Tower of London, and was buried in the Royal Chapel of St Peter ad Vincula within the Tower of London.

Issue of marriage (declared illegitimate on 17th May, 1536):

1 *Elizabeth I (see page 162)*.

2 *Stillborn child (sex unknown)*.

It was born in August/September, 1534; this was nearly a full-term pregnancy, but details of the birth were kept secret.

3 *Miscarriage*

This occurred in the summer of 1535.

4 *Stillborn son*

He was born on 29th January, 1536 at Greenwich Palace.

Henry VIII married thirdly, on 30th May, 1536 at Whitehall Palace, London:

Jane

She was the daughter of Sir John Seymour by Margaret, daughter of Sir Henry Wentworth of Nettlestead, Suffolk, and she was born in c. 1508, probably at Wulfhall in Savernake Forest, Wiltshire. She was never crowned. She died on 24th October, 1537 at Hampton

Court Palace, in childbed, and was buried in St George's Chapel, Windsor.

Issue of marriage:

1 *Edward VI (see page 156).*

Henry VIII married fourthly, on 6th January, 1540, at Greenwich Palace:

Anne

She was the daughter of John III, Duke of Cleves, by Mary, daughter of William III, Duke of Jülich and Berg, and she was born on 22nd September, 1515 at Düsseldorf, Cleves, Germany. Her marriage to Henry VIII was not consummated, and it was annulled on 9th July, 1540, on the grounds of Anne's alleged precontract with the Duke of Lorraine. Anne died on 16th/17th July, 1557 at Chelsea Old Palace, London, and was buried in Westminster Abbey. There was no issue of the marriage.

Henry VIII married fifthly, on 28th July, 1540, at Oatlands Palace, Surrey:

Katherine

She was the daughter of Lord Edmund Howard by Joyce or Jocasta, daughter of Sir Richard Culpeper, and she was born in c.1525, either at Lambeth in London, or at Horsham, Sussex. She was never crowned. Katherine was attainted for high treason, and was executed on 13th February, 1542 on Tower Green within the Tower of London. She was buried in the Royal Chapel of St Peter ad Vincula within the Tower of London. There was no issue of the marriage.

Henry VIII married sixthly, on 12th July, 1543 at Hampton Court Palace:

Katherine

She was the daughter of Sir Thomas Parr by Maud, daughter of Sir Thomas Green of Green's Norton, Northants., and she was born around 1512/14, either at Kendal Castle, Westmorland, or at her father's house at Blackfriars, London. She married firstly Edward de Burgh, 2nd Baron Borough (d.1529) after 26th June, 1526. She married secondly John Neville, 3rd Baron Latimer (1493–1542) perhaps in 1530, and certainly before the end of 1533. After the death of Henry VIII, her third husband, she married fourthly Thomas Seymour, 1st Baron Sudely (1508?–executed 1549), brother of Queen Jane (see above), between April and the end of May, 1547, and had issue:

1 Mary (1548–?); she either died young in c.1560, or grew up and married Sir Edward Bushel, and had issue. However, the evidence for this

marriage dates from the 18th century only, and should therefore be regarded with caution.

Katherine died on 7th September, 1548 at Sudely Castle, Gloucs., in childbed, and was buried in Sudely Castle Chapel. There was no issue of her marriage to Henry VIII.

Henry VIII also had the following **illegitimate issue**:

By Elizabeth Blount (1502?–1539/41), daughter of Sir John Blount of Kinlet, Shropshire, afterwards wife of Gilbert, Lord Tailboys:

1 Henry FitzRoy, Duke of Richmond and Somerset (1519–1536); he married Mary, daughter of Thomas Howard, 3rd Duke of Norfolk. He was the only bastard acknowledged by Henry VIII.

By Joan Dobson or Dingley:

2 Ethelreda or Audrey (d.1555); she married John Harington, and had issue.

By Mary Berkeley (?):

3 Sir John Perrot (1527?–1592) (?).

By an unknown mother:

4 Thomas Stucley or Stukely (1525?–1578) (?); he married Anne Curtis. It is highly unlikely that Henry VIII was the father of Thomas or Sir John Perrot.

HENRY VIII

He died on 28th January, 1547 at Whitehall Palace, London, and was buried in St George's Chapel, Windsor.

He was succeeded by his son Edward.

Recommended reading

There is a vast amount of material on Henry VIII, who has been a popular subject with biographers. There are two outstanding recent works:

Jaspar Ridley: *Henry VIII* (Constable, 1984).

John Scarisbrick: *Henry VIII* (Constable, 1968).

See also:

Neville Williams: *Henry VIII and his Court* (Weidenfeld and Nicolson, 1971).

Lacey Baldwin Smith: *Henry VIII: The Mask of Royalty* (Jonathan Cape, 1971).

Marie Louise Bruce: *The Making of Henry VIII* (Collins, 1977).

Carolly Erickson: *Great Harry* (Dent, 1980).

For Henry's wives see:

Alison Weir: *The Six Wives of Henry VIII* (Bodley Head, 1991).

Antonia Fraser: *The Six Wives of Henry VIII* (Weidenfeld & Nicolson, 1992).

Mary M. Luke: *Catherine the Queen* (Muller, 1967).

Garrett Mattingly: *Catherine of Aragon* (Jonathan Cape, 1942).

M. A. Albert: *The Divorce* (Harrap, 1965).

John E. Paul: *Catherine of Aragon and her Friends* (1966).

E. W. Ives: *Anne Boleyn* (Blackwell, 1986).

Carolly Erickson: *Anne Boleyn* (Dent, 1984).

Hester W. Chapman: *Anne Boleyn* (Jonathan Cape, 1974).

Marie Louise Bruce: *Anne Boleyn* (Collins, 1972).

W. Seymour: *Ordeal by Ambition: An English Family in the Shadow of the Tudors* (Sidgwick and Jackson, 1972); this is the story of the Seymours, and is the only modern work to summarise the life of Jane Seymour.

Anne of Cleves has yet to find a biographer.

For Henry's last wives, see:

Lacey Baldwin Smith: *A Tudor Tragedy: The Life and Times of Katherine Howard* (Jonathan Cape, 1961).

A. Martiensson: *Queen Katherine Parr* (Secker and Warburg, 1973).

EDWARD VI

FATHER: *Henry VIII (see page 151)*.
MOTHER: *Jane Seymour (see page 153, under Henry VIII)*.
SIBLINGS: *Edward VI did not have any full siblings.*

EDWARD VI

He was born on 12th October, 1537 at Hampton Court Palace, Surrey, and was Duke of Cornwall from birth. He succeeded his father as King of England on 28th January, 1547, and was crowned on 20th or 25th February, 1547 in Westminster Abbey.

EDWARD VI
He died unmarried on 6th July, 1553 at Greenwich Palace, Kent, and was buried in Westminster Abbey.

He was succeeded by his second cousin Lady Jane Grey.

Recommended reading
Hester W. Chapman: *The Last Tudor King* (Jonathan Cape, 1958). W. K. Jordan: *Edward VI, the Young King* (Allen and Unwin, 1968) and *Edward VI: The Threshold of Power* (Allen and Unwin, 1970).

QUEEN JANE

FATHER: *Henry*
He was the son of Thomas Grey, Marquess of Dorset, by Margaret, daughter of Sir Robert Wotton, and he was born on 17th January, 1517. He married firstly Katherine (d. after 1552), daughter of William FitzAlan, Earl of Arundel, before 1530. He succeeded his father as Marquess of Dorset, Baron Ferrers of Groby, Baron Harington and Baron Bonville on 10th October, 1530. He repudiated his first wife before 1533, and married secondly Frances Brandon in March or early May, 1533 at Suffolk Place, Southwark, London. He was made a Knight of the Bath on 30th May, 1533, and a Knight of the Garter on 17th February, 1547, and was created Duke of Suffolk, in right of his wife, on 11th October, 1551. Henry was attainted, and his estates were declared forfeit, on 17th February, 1554, as a result of his treasonous involvement in

Wyatt's rebellion against Mary I; he was executed on 23rd February, 1554 on Tower Hill, London, and was buried in the Royal Chapel of St Peter ad Vincula within the Tower of London.

MOTHER: *Frances*

She was the daughter of Charles Brandon, Duke of Suffolk, by Mary, daughter of Henry VII, and she was born on 16th July, 1517, either at Bishop's Hatfield, Herts., or at Westhorpe Hall, Suffolk. After the execution of her first husband, the Duke of Suffolk, she married secondly Adrian Stokes (1533–1585), her Master of Horse, on 9th March, 1554, and had issue:

1 Elizabeth (b.&d.1554).

2 Son (d. young).

3 Son (d. young).

Frances died on 20th or 21st November, 1559 at the Charterhouse, Sheen, Surrey, and was buried in Westminster Abbey.

SIBLINGS:

1 *Unnamed brother*

He died young before 1537.

2 *Unnamed sister*

She died young before 1537.

3 *Katherine*

She was born in August, 1540, perhaps at Dorset House, Westminster. She married firstly Henry Herbert, 2nd Earl of Pembroke (after 1538–1601) on 21st May, 1553, either at Ely Place, Holborn, London, or at Durham House, Strand, London. The marriage was annulled in 1554, and Katherine married secondly Edward Seymour, 1st Earl of Hertford (1539–1621) in secret around November/December, 1560 at Hertford House, Cannon Row, Westminster, and had issue:

1 Edward, Baron Beauchamp (1561–1612); he married Honora (d. after 1608), daughter of Sir Richard Rogers of Bryanston, Dorset, and had issue.

2 Thomas (1563–1619); he married Isabella, daughter of Edward Onley of Catesby, Northants.

3 Edward (d.1602); his existence is doubtful.

4 Katherine (d. young); her existence is doubtful.

Katherine's union with Edward Seymour was declared "no marriage" on 12th May, 1561, and deemed never to have taken place; it was, however, declared valid in 1608. Katherine died on 26th/27th January, 1568 at Cockfield Hall, Yoxford, Suffolk, and was buried in Yoxford Church, Suffolk. Her remains were later removed to Salisbury Cathedral.

4 *Mary*

She was born in 1545, and was a hunchback. She married Thomas Keyes (d.1571) on 10th or 12th August, 1564/5 at the Water Gate Lodge, by the Palace of Westminster. She died on 20th April, 1578 at the Barbican, by Red Cross Street, London, and was buried either in St Botolph's Church, Aldersgate, London, or in Westminster Abbey.

QUEEN JANE

She was born in October, 1537 at Bradgate Manor, Leics. The Will of Henry VIII left the crown, in order of succession, to his children, Edward, Mary and Elizabeth, and then, if their lines failed, to the heirs of his sister Mary, Duchess of Suffolk. When Edward VI died on 6th July, 1553, the Duke of Northumberland, who had governed the country in the boy King's name as Lord Protector, wished to see the continuance of his own power and the maintenance of the newly-established Protestant religion in England. The next heir, Mary Tudor, was a staunch Catholic, therefore it had not been difficult for Northumberland to persuade the dying Edward—a fervent Protestant—to sign a Device changing his father's Will. Mary was set aside, and also Elizabeth, whose religious convictions were uncertain, and the crown was willed by Edward to Lady Jane Grey, bypassing her mother Frances, who was rightful Queen after Mary and Elizabeth. Jane was proclaimed Queen of England on 10th July, 1553.

Queen Jane married, on 21st May, 1553, either at Ely Place, Holborn, London, or at Durham House, Strand, London:

Guilford

He was the son of John Dudley, Duke of Northumberland, by Jane, daughter of Sir Edward Guilford, and he was born in 1536. He was executed on 12th February, 1554 on Tower Hill, London, and was buried in the Royal Chapel of St Peter ad Vincula within the Tower of London. There was no issue of the marriage.

QUEEN JANE

She reigned for only nine days. The people of England rallied to the cause of Mary Tudor, and Jane, the usurper, was deposed on 19th July, 1553. She was executed on 12th February, 1554 on Tower Green, within the Tower of London, in the aftermath of Thomas Wyatt's rebellion. Jane was buried in the Royal Chapel of St Peter ad Vincula within the Tower of London.

She had already been succeeded by her second cousin Mary.

Recommended reading
  Hester W. Chapman: *Lady Jane Grey* (Jonathan Cape, 1962).
  David Mathew: *Lady Jane Grey: The Setting of the Reign* (Eyre
  Methuen, 1972).
Lady Katherine Grey's story is told in:
  Hester W. Chapman: *Two Tudor Portraits* (Jonathan Cape, 1960).

MARY I

FATHER: *Henry VIII (see page 151).*
MOTHER: *Katherine of Aragon (see page 152, under Henry VIII).*
SIBLINGS: *(see page 152, under Henry VIII).*

MARY I
She was born on 18th February, 1516 at Greenwich Palace, Kent. She
was proclaimed Queen of England upon the deposition of Queen
Jane on 19th July, 1553, although her regnal years were dated from
24th July. She was crowned on 1st October or 30th November, 1553 at
Westminster Abbey. She assumed the title Queen of Spain upon the
accession of her husband, Philip II, to the throne of Spain on 16th
January, 1556.
Mary I married, on 25th July, 1554, at Winchester Cathedral:
Philip
He was the son of Charles V, Holy Roman Emperor and King of
Spain, by Isabella, daughter of Manuel I, King of Portugal, and he
was born on 21st May, 1527 at Valladolid, Spain. He married firstly

160

Mary (1527–1545), daughter of John III, King of Portugal, on 12th November, 1543, at Salamanca, Spain, and had issue:
1 Charles (Don Carlos) (1545–1568).
Philip was designated King of Naples, Jerusalem and Savoy in preparation for his marriage to Mary I (to give him equal rank), and was made a Knight of the Garter on 24th April, 1554. He succeeded his father as King of Spain on 16th January, 1556. After Mary's death, he married thirdly Elizabeth (1545–1568), daughter of Henry II, King of France, in 1559 at Toledo, Spain, and had issue:
1 Unnamed daughter (b.1564).
2 Unnamed daughter (b.1564).
3 Isabella Clara Eugenia (1566–1633); she married Albert, Archduke of Austria (1559–1621).
4 Katherine Michela (1567–1597); she married Charles Emmanuel I, Duke of Savoy (1562–1630).
5 Unnamed daughter (b.&d. 1568).
Philip married fourthly Anne (1549–1580), daughter of Maximilian II, Holy Roman Emperor, in 1570 at Segovia, Spain, and had issue:
1 Ferdinand (1571–1578).
2 Edward (1575–1582).
3 Philip III, King of Spain (1578–1621); he married Marianna (1584–1611), daughter of Charles, Archduke of Austria, and had issue.
4 Mary.
Philip became King of Portugal in 1580. He died on 13th September, 1598 at the Palace of the Escorial, Madrid, Spain, where he is buried in the mausoleum. There was no issue of his marriage to Mary I.

MARY I
She died on 17th November, 1558 at St James's Palace, London, and was buried in Westminster Abbey.
She was succeeded by her half-sister Elizabeth.

Recommended reading
    H. F. M. Prescott: *Mary Tudor* (Constable, 1940).
    Jaspar Ridley: *Mary Tudor* (Weidenfeld and Nicolson, 1973).
    David M. Loades: *Mary Tudor* (Basil Blackwell, 1989).

ELIZABETH I

FATHER: *Henry VIII (see page 151).*
MOTHER: *Anne Boleyn (see page 153, under Henry VIII).*
SIBLINGS: *Elizabeth I did not have any full siblings.*

ELIZABETH I

She was born on 7th September, 1533 at Greenwich Palace, Kent. She succeeded her half sister Mary I as Queen of England on 17th November, 1558, and was crowned on 15th January, 1559 at Westminster Abbey.

ELIZABETH I

She died unmarried and childless, and probably a virgin, on 24th March, 1603 at Richmond Palace, Surrey, and was buried in Westminster Abbey.

She was succeeded by her third cousin, James VI of Scotland.

Elizabeth I was the last Tudor monarch.

Recommended reading

There is a vast amount of material about Elizabeth I. The following are a few of the best works:

Jaspar Ridley: *Elizabeth I* (Constable, 1987).

J. E. Neale: *Queen Elizabeth I* (Jonathan Cape, 1934).

J. B. Black: *The Reign of Elizabeth, 1558–1603* (Oxford University Press, 1959).

Elizabeth Jenkins: *Elizabeth the Great* (Gollancz, 1958).

Mary M. Luke: *A Crown for Elizabeth* (Muller, 1971).

Lacey Baldwin Smith: *The Elizabethan Epic* (Jonathan Cape, 1966).

Anne Somerset: *Elizabeth I* (Weidenfeld & Nicolson, 1991).

6. The Kings and Queens of Scotland from the 9th century to 1603

Before proceeding chronologically to the royal House of Stuart, it is time to retrace our steps through history to the 9th century, when the kingdom of Scotland was first established. Prior to this date, details of the early rulers of Scotland are obscure; the Scottish monarchy is said to have been founded by Alpin, founder of the House of MacAlpin or MacAlpine, which provided Scotland with kings until 1034, when the succession passed to the House of Dunkeld via the marriage of Bethoc, daughter of Malcolm II. The House of Dunkeld held sovereignty until 1290, when Queen Margaret, "the Maid of Norway", perished at sea. Her death led to a great contest for the throne, with thirteen "competitors" all contending for the crown. Edward I of England was asked to arbitrate, and he chose John Balliol, a lightweight whom he could easily manipulate to England's advantage. The Scots naturally resented Edward's interference in their government, and Balliol was obliged to abdicate in 1296. There followed the Second Interregnum, when Scotland was without a King from 1296 until 1306. Edward I was making strenuous efforts to bring Scotland under English rule during this period, until the emergence of Robert le Bruce, who declared himself King of Scotland in defiance of Edward in 1306, and who was destined to be one of the finest of Scotland's rulers. Bruce's dynasty did not long survive him; when his son died in 1371, the throne passed to Bruce's grandson Robert II, son of Marjorie Bruce by Walter the Steward, who gave his name to the House of Stewart.

The Stewarts ruled Scotland for more than two centuries, and Great Britain for another century, yet their hold on the throne was often a tenuous one. Throughout the 15th and 16th centuries, each Scottish monarch succeeded to the throne whilst still a child or a minor, and the country was subjected to continuous faction fights amongst power-hungry nobles. That the dynasty survived at all was nothing short of a miracle. Even the abdication of Queen Mary in 1567 did not ruin it, for her son James VI was guided by the magnates from his infancy along the path they wanted him to tread, and

Elizabeth of England, of course, took care of the displaced Mary by first imprisoning and then executing her. Thus it was that the Stewarts —or Stuarts, as they had become when Mary had married into the French royal house—came to inherit also the throne of England. For Mary's grandfather, James IV, had married Margaret Tudor, daughter of Henry VII of England, and when Queen Elizabeth died without heirs in 1603, James VI of Scotland, the great-grandson of Margaret Tudor, was the English Queen's nearest surviving relative.

The succession of the earliest monarchs of Scotland is often confusing, as until Norman influence from England led to the adoption of succession by primogeniture in the late 11th century, the Scots favoured the ancient system of tanistry, whereby the crown passed back and forth from one branch of the family to the other. This system evolved in a time when life expectancy was short, society was violent, and a ruler might well die while his son was an infant: it ensured that the fittest, maturest male would inherit the throne. And until the reign of Malcolm II in the early 11th century, the kingdom of Scotland was shifting its borders all the time, incorporating earlier, smaller kingdoms, or being subdivided between rival rulers. Malcolm II could therefore be said to be the first monarch of modern Scotland. Yet our chapter begins two hundred years before his time, with Alpin, founder of the Scottish monarchy and its first dynasty.

Part One: The House of MacAlpine

KING ALPIN

FATHER: *Eochaid IV, King "of Scotland".*
MOTHER: *She was the sister and heiress of Constantine, King of the Picts.*
SIBLINGS: *Alpin is not known to have had any siblings.*

KING ALPIN
He succeeded his father as a King in Scotland, and became also King of Kintyre in March/August, 834, thus establishing his power over a wide area. There is no record of his coronation.
King Alpin married a Scottish Princess (whose name is not known) and had issue:
1 *Kenneth I (see page 166).*
2 *Donald I (see page 167).*

KING ALPIN
He died on 20th July or in August, 834; he was killed whilst fighting the Picts in Galloway. His place of burial is not recorded.
   He was succeeded by his son Kenneth.

KENNETH I

FATHER: *King Alpin (see page 165).*
MOTHER: *a Scottish Princess.*
SIBLINGS: *(see page 165), under King Alpin).*

KENNETH I

He succeeded his father as King of Galloway and other parts of Scotland on 20th July or in August, 834, and became King of the area known as Dalriada in 841. In 843/4, he became King of the Picts, thus uniting the old Gaelic kingdoms of Alba for the first time, and by 846 he was firmly established as King of Scotland. There is no record of his coronation.

Kenneth I married a lady about whom no information exists, and had issue:

1 *Constantine I (see page 167).*
2 *King Aedh (see page 168).*
3 *Daughter (name not known).*
   She married Run Macarthagail, King of Strathclyde, and had issue:
   1 King Eochaid (see page 169).
4 *Daughter (name not known).*
   She married Olaf the White, King of Dublin.
5 *Daughter (name not known).*
   She married Aedh Finnliath, King of Ireland.

KENNETH I

He died in 859 at Forteviot, Perthshire, and was buried on the Isle of Iona.

He was succeeded by his brother Donald.

DONALD I

FATHER: *King Alpin (see page 165).*
MOTHER: *a Scottish Princess*
SIBLINGS: *(see page 165, under King Alpin).*

DONALD I

He succeeded Kenneth I in 859 as King of Scotland. There is no record of his coronation.

He was either killed in 863 in a battle at Scone, Perthshire, or died that year in his palace at Kinn Belachoir. He died unmarried and childless. His place of burial is not recorded.

He was succeeded by his nephew Constantine.

CONSTANTINE I

FATHER: *Kenneth I (see page 166).*
MOTHER: *Unknown.*
SIBLINGS: *(see page 166, under Kenneth I).*

CONSTANTINE I

He succeeded Donald I as King of Scotland in 863. There is no record of his coronation.

He married a lady about whom no information exists, and had issue:
1 *Donald II (see page 169).*

CONSTANTINE I
He was killed in 877 in a battle against the Danes at Inverdorat, the Black Cove, Angus. He was buried on the Isle of Iona.
    He was succeeded by his brother Aedh.

KING AEDH

FATHER: *Kenneth I (see page 166).*
MOTHER: *Unknown.*
SIBLINGS: *(see page 166, under Kenneth I).*

KING AEDH
He succeeded Constantine I as King of Scotland in 877. There is no record of his coronation.
He married a lady about whom no information exists, and had issue:
1 *Constantine II (see page 170).*
2 *Donald*
    He became King of Strathclyde in 908.

KING AEDH
He was killed in 878 at Strathallan, and was perhaps buried at Maiden Stone, Aberdeenshire.
    He was succeeded by his nephew Eochaid.

KING EOCHAID

FATHER: *Run Macarthagail, King of Strathclyde.*
MOTHER: *A daughter of Kenneth I.*
SIBLINGS: *Eochaid is not known to have had any siblings.*

KING EOCHAID

He succeeded his father as King of Strathclyde before succeeding his uncle King Aedh as King of Scotland in 878. There is no record of his coronation.

King Eochaid was deposed in 889, and perhaps died unmarried and childless the same year. His place of burial is not recorded.

He was succeeded by his cousin Donald.

DONALD II

FATHER: *Constantine I (see page 167).*
MOTHER: *Unknown.*
SIBLINGS: *Donald II did not have any siblings.*

DONALD II

He succeeded his cousin Eochaid as King of Scotland in 889. There is no record of his coronation.

He married a lady about whom no information exists, and had issue:
1 *Malcolm I (see page 171)*.

DONALD II
He was killed in 900 at Dun-fother, and was buried on the Isle of Iona.
   He was succeeded by his cousin Constantine.

CONSTANTINE II

FATHER: *King Aedh (see page 168)*.
MOTHER: *Unknown*.
SIBLINGS: *(see page 168, under King Aedh)*.

CONSTANTINE II
He succeeded Donald II as King of Scotland in 900. There is no record of his coronation.
He married a lady about whom no information exists, and had issue:
1 *King Indulf (see page 172)*.
2 *Cellach*
   He was killed in 937 at the Battle of Brunanburgh.
3 *Daughter (name not known)*.
   She married Olaf Cuaran, King of Northumbria (d.981) in 937, and had issue:
   1 Gluniarainn, King of Dublin (d.989).
   2 Sihtric, King of Dublin (d.1042); he married and had issue.
   3 Reginald (killed 980); he married and had issue.

CONSTANTINE II
He abdicated in 942/3, and became a monk at the monastery of St Andrews, Fife, where he later became Abbot. He died at St Andrews in 952, and was probably buried there.
   He was succeeded by his second cousin Malcolm.

MALCOLM I

FATHER: *Donald II (see page 169).*
MOTHER: *Unknown.*
SIBLINGS: *Malcolm I did not have any siblings.*

MALCOLM I

He succeeded Constantine II as King of Scotland in 942/3. There is no record of his coronation.

He married a lady, about whom no information exists, and had issue:
1 *King Duff (see page 173).*
2 *Kenneth II (see page 175).*

Malcolm I is also said to have had the following **illegitimate issue**:
1 Kenneth (?).

MALCOLM I

He was killed in 954 by the men of Moray, and was buried on the Isle of Iona.

He was succeeded by his second cousin Indulf.

KING INDULF

FATHER: *Constantine II (see page 170).*
MOTHER: *Unknown.*
SIBLINGS: *(see page 170, under Constantine II).*

KING INDULF

He succeeded Malcolm I as King of Scotland in 954. There is no record of his coronation.

He married a lady about whom no information exists, and had issue:

1 *King Colin (see page 174).*
2 *Eochaid*
   He was killed in 971 by the King of Strathclyde.
3 *Olaf*
   He was killed in c.977 by Kenneth II.

KING INDULF

He abdicated in 962 and became a monk. He was killed the same year by Viking invaders at the Battle of the Bauds at the Muir of Findochty, Banffshire. His place of burial is not recorded.

He was succeeded by his third cousin Duff.

KING DUFF

FATHER: *Malcolm I (see page 171).*
MOTHER: *Unknown.*
SIBLINGS: *(see page 171, under Malcolm I).*

KING DUFF
He succeeded Indulf as King of Scotland in 962. There is no record of his coronation.
He married a lady about whom no information exists, and had issue:
1 *Kenneth III (see page 176).*
2 *Malcolm*
  Styled Prince of Cumbria (a title borne in the early middle ages by the sons of the Kings of Scotland) in his youth, he became King of Strathclyde in 973, and died in 990/1.

KING DUFF
He was killed in 967 at Forres by the men of Moray. His place of burial is not recorded.
  He was succeeded by his third cousin Colin.

KING COLIN

FATHER: *King Indulf (see page 172).*
MOTHER: *Unknown.*
SIBLINGS: *(see page 172, under King Indulf).*

KING COLIN
Also called Cuilean, he succeeded Duff as King of Scotland in 967.
There is no record of his coronation.
He married a lady about whom no information exists, and had issue:
1 *Constantine III (see page 176).*
2 *Malcolm*
   He was alive in 1002. Nothing more is known of him.

KING COLIN
He was killed in 971 by Riderch of Strathclyde. His place of burial is
not recorded.
   He was succeeded by his third cousin Kenneth.

KENNETH II

FATHER: *Malcolm I (see page 171)*.
MOTHER: *Unknown*.
SIBLINGS: *(see page 171, under Malcolm I)*.

KENNETH II
He succeeded Colin as King of Scotland in 971. There is no record of his coronation.

He is said to have married a Princess of Leinster (whose name is not known), and had issue:

1 *Malcolm II (see page 177)*.
2 *Dungal*
He was killed in 999 by his cousin Gillacomgain, son of Kenneth III.
3 *Donada (?)*
She is also described as the daughter of Malcolm II. She married firstly (?) Finlay (Findlaech) MacRory, Mormaer of Moray (d.c.1004/5), and had issue:
(i) *King Macbeth (see page 182)*.
Donada married secondly Sigurd II Digri, Jarl of Orkney and Caithness (killed 1014) in c.1005/8, and had issue:
1 Thorfinn, Jarl of Orkney and Caithness (c.1009–c.1056/65?); he married Ingibiorg of Halland, afterwards the wife of Malcolm III, and had issue.

KENNETH II
He died (perhaps murdered on behalf of his successor) in 995 at Finella's Castle, probably at Fettercairn, and was buried on the Isle of Iona.

He was succeeded by his fourth cousin Constantine.

CONSTANTINE III

FATHER: *King Colin (see page 174)*.
MOTHER: *Unknown*.
SIBLINGS: *(see page 174, under King Colin)*.

CONSTANTINE III
He succeeded Kenneth II as King of Scotland in 995. There is no record of his coronation.
He married a lady about whom no information exists. There was no issue of the marriage.

CONSTANTINE III
He was killed in 997 at Rathinveramon. His place of burial is not recorded.
He was succeeded by his fourth cousin Kenneth.

KENNETH III

FATHER: *King Duff (see page 173)*.
MOTHER: *Unknown*.
SIBLINGS: *(see page 173, under King Duff)*.

KENNETH III

He succeeded Constantine III as King of Scotland in 997. There is no record of his coronation.

He married a lady about whom no information exists, and had issue:

1 *Beoedhe*

Also known as Bodhe or Boite, he married a lady about whom no information exists, and had issue:

(i) *Son (name not known)*

He married a lady about whom no information exists, and fathered a son (name not known) who was murdered in infancy in 1033.

(ii) *Gruoch (see page 182, under King Macbeth, whom she married).*

Beoedhe died before 1033.

2 *Giric*

A Mormaer, or "Subregulus", he was killed on c.25th March, 1005 at the Battle of Monzievaird.

3 *Gillacomgain*

He lived to maturity, but nothing more is known of him.

KENNETH III

He was killed on c.25th March, 1005 at the Battle of Monzievaird (?). His place of burial is not known

He was succeeded by his cousin Malcolm.

MALCOLM II

FATHER: *Kenneth II (see page 175).*
MOTHER: *a Princess of Leinster.*
SIBLINGS: *(see page 175, under Kenneth II).*

MALCOLM II

He was born in c.954. In his youth, he was styled Prince of Cumbria.

He succeeded his cousin Malcolm, son of King Duff, as King of Strathclyde in c.990/1, and ruled Strathclyde until 995, when he was deposed. He was restored in 997, and succeeded Kenneth III as King of Scotland on 25th March, 1005. In c.1016, he became King of Lothian, thus becoming the first effective ruler of the whole of Scotland. There is no record of his coronation.

Malcolm II married a lady whose name is not recorded, said to have been an Irishwoman from Ossory, and had issue:

1 *Bethoc*

Known as the Lady of Atholl, she married Crinan the Thane, Mormaer of Atholl, Abthane of Dule, Steward of the Western Isles, and Lay Abbot of Dunkeld (c.975–killed 1045 in battle against Macbeth), son of Duncan, Mormaer of Atholl. The marriage took place before 1008, perhaps in 1000, and they had issue, through whom they were founders of the Royal House of Dunkeld:

(i) *Duncan I (see page 180)*.

(ii) *Maldred*

He was created Lord of Allerdale, and was appointed Regent of the Kingdom of Strathclyde in 1034. He was probably killed in battle in 1045.

Maldred married (no record exists of the date or the place):
Edith

She was the daughter of Uhtred, Earl of Northumbria, by Elgiva, daughter of Ethelred II, King of England.

Issue of marriage:

(a) *Gospatrick*

He was born in c.1040. He was created Earl of Northumbria before 1071, possibly in 1068, but was deprived of this earldom in 1072, when he was created Earl of Dunbar. He died on 15th December, but the year is unspecified, at Ubbanford (modern Norham), Scotland, and was buried in Norham Church; however, another tradition states that he became a monk at Durham Cathedral, where he died and was buried.

Gospatrick married an unknown lady, and had issue:

1 Dolfin, Earl of Cumberland (d. after 1092); he married an unknown lady and had issue.

2 Waltheof, 1st Baron of Allerdale, Abbot of Crowland (d.1138?); he married a lady called Sigrid, and had issue.

3 Gospatrick, 2nd Earl of Dunbar (killed at the Battle of

the Standard, 1138); he married an unknown lady, and had issue.

4 Octreda; she married Waldeve, son of Gillemin.

5 Gunhilda; she married Orm, son of Ketil.

6 Matilda; she married Dolfin, son of Aylward.

7 Ethelreda; she married Duncan II.

  (b) *Maldred*

He married a lady about whom no information exists, and had issue:

1 Robert.

2 Uhtred.

3 Ulkil (?).

  (iii) *Daughter (name not known)*

She married a man about whom no information exists, and had issue:

1 Moddan, Earl of Caithness (killed 1040).

  (iv) *Daughter (name not known)*

Nothing is known about her.

2 Donada *(?)*

She has also been described as the daughter of Kenneth II, and the details of her life appear on page 175.

3 Daughter *(name not known)*

This may have been the daughter married to Sigurd, Jarl of Orkney in c.1005/8; some sources identify her with Donada.

MALCOM II

He died on 25th November, 1034, at Glamis Castle, Angus, mortally wounded by his kinsmen, and was buried on the Isle of Iona. He was the last sovereign of the House of MacAlpine.

He was succeeded by his grandson Duncan.

Part Two: The House of Dunkeld

DUNCAN I

FATHER: *Crinan, Lay Abbot of Dunkeld (see page 178*, under Malcolm II).
MOTHER: *Bethoc, daughter of Malcolm II.*
SIBLINGS: *(see page 178, under Malcolm II).*

DUNCAN I

Known as the Gracious, he was born in c.1001, and became King of Strathclyde in 1018. He succeeded his grandfather, Malcolm II, as King of Scotland on 25th November, 1034, thus becoming the first sovereign of the House of Dunkeld, named after his father's abbacy. There is no record of his coronation.

Duncan I married, in c.1030 (although no record exists as to where):
Sybilla

She was either the daughter of Bjorn Bearsson and sister of Siward Digera, Earl of Northumbria, or the daughter of Siward by Elfleda, daughter of Ealdred, Earl of Northumbria.

Issue of marriage:
1 *Malcolm III (see page 184).*
2 *Donald III (see page 186).*
3 *Maelmuire*
  He was born in c.1035.
  Maelmuire married a lady about whom no information exists, and had issue:

180

(i) *Madach*

Also known as Matad, he was created Earl of Atholl before 1115 (or later, before 1136?). He died between 1139 and 1159, perhaps in 1152.

Malcolm married Margaret, daughter of Haakon Paulsson, and had issue:

(a) Malcolm, Earl of Atholl (d.1186/98); he married firstly an unknown lady, and had issue, and secondly, Hextilda, daughter of Huctred of Tynedale by Bethoc, daughter of Donald III.

(b) Harold, Jarl of Orkney, Earl of Caithness (d.1206); he married Afrika, sister of Duncan, Earl of Fife, and had issue. He married secondly Gormlath or Hvarlod, daughter of Malcolm MacHeth, 1st Earl of Ross.

Madach married secondly, in c.1133 (although no record exists as to where):

Margaret

She was the daughter of Haco, Jarl of Orkney. After the death of Madach, she married secondly Erland Ugni, Jarl of Orkney (killed 1156).

4 *Daughter* *(name not known)* *(?)*

Her existence is doubtful. She is said to have married one Bertolf or Bartholemew (d.1121?), and had issue.

DUNCAN I

He was either murdered by Macbeth, or killed in battle against him, on 14th August, 1040, at Bothganowan (now Pitgaveny), near Elgin, or at Burghead. He was buried on the Isle of Iona.

He was succeeded by his cousin Macbeth.

KING MACBETH

FATHER: *Finlay MacRory, Mormaer of Moray.*
MOTHER: *Donada, daughter either of Kenneth II or Malcolm II.*
SIBLINGS: *(see page 175, under Kenneth II).*

KING MACBETH
He was born in c.1005, and became Mormaer of Moray around 1029/32. He succeeded Duncan I as King of Scotland on 14th August, 1040. No record exists of his coronation.
Macbeth married, after 1032 (although no record exists as to where):
Gruoch
   She was the daughter of Beoedhe, son of Kenneth III. She was born in c.1015. She married firstly Gillacomgain, Mormaer of Moray (burned alive in 1032), and had issue:
(a) King Lulach (see page 183).
There was no issue of her marriage to Macbeth.

KING MACBETH
He was killed on 15th August, 1057 at the Battle of Lumphanan, Aberdeenshire, by the future Malcolm III, son of Duncan I, and was buried on the Isle of Iona.
   He was succeeded by his stepson Lulach.

KING LULACH

FATHER: *Gillacomgain, Mormaer of Moray.*
MOTHER: *Gruoch (see page 182, under Macbeth).*
SIBLINGS: *King Lulach did not have any siblings.*

KING LULACH

Known as "the Simple", he was born around c.1029/32. He succeeded his stepfather Macbeth as King of Scotland on 15th August, 1057, and was crowned that same month on the Coronation Stone at Scone Abbey, Perthshire. This is the first recorded instance of the coronation of a King of Scotland.

King Lulach married (no record exists of the date or place):
Finnghuala (?)
  She was the daughter of Sinill, Mormaer of Angus. Her dates are not recorded.

Issue of marriage:

1 *Malsnechtai*
  He was perhaps created Mormaer of Moray at some stage, although he certainly became a monk later on. He died in 1085.

2 *Daughter (name not known).*
  She married Aedh, Mormaer of Moray, and had issue:
  1 Gruaidh; she married William, Lord of Egremont (see page 188, under Duncan II).
  2 Angus, King of Moray (d.1130); he married and had issue.

KING LULACH

He was killed on 17th March, 1058 at Essie in Strathbogie by his distant cousin and successor, Malcolm III. He was buried on the Isle of Iona.

  He was succeeded by Malcolm, son of Duncan I.

MALCOLM III

FATHER: *Duncan I (see page 180)*.
MOTHER: *Sybilla of Northumbria (see page 180, under Duncan I)*.
SIBLINGS: *(see page 180, under Duncan I)*.

MALCOLM III

Known as "Canmore" (or "Bighead"), he was born in c.1031, and became King of Strathclyde and Prince of Cumbria in 1034. He succeeded Lulach as King of Scotland on 17th March, 1058, and was crowned on 25th April, 1058 at Scone Abbey, Perthshire.

Malcolm III married firstly, in c.1059 or c.1066 (although no record exists as to where):

Ingibiorg

She was the daughter of Finn Arnasson of Vrjar, Jarl of Halland, by Bergljot, daughter of Halfdan Sigurdsson. She married firstly Thorfinn II, Earl of Caithness and Jarl of Orkney (1009–1056/65?) before 1038, and had issue:

1 Paul, Jarl of Orkney (d.1099); he married an unnamed daughter of Haakon Ivarsson, and had issue.
2 Erlend, Jarl of Orkney (d.1099); he married Thora, daughter of Somerled Uspaksson, and had issue.

Ingibiorg died before 1070.

Issue of marriage:

1 *Duncan II (see page 187)*.
2 *Malcolm*
   He died in c.1094.
3 *Donald*
   He died in 1085.

Malcolm III married secondly, in c.1069, at Dunfermline Abbey, Fife:

184

St Margaret

She was the daughter of Edward the Atheling, son of Edmund II, King of England, by Agatha of Hungary, and she was born in c.1045/6 in Hungary. She died on 16th November, 1093 at Edinburgh Castle, and was buried in Dunfermline Abbey, Fife. Her remains were later translated to the Escorial in Madrid, Spain, her head being buried in the Jesuit College at Douai, France. She was canonised as a saint in 1250.

Issue of marriage:

1 *Edward*

He died on 16th November, 1093 at Edwardsisle, near Jedburgh, of wounds received at the Battle of Alnwick.

2 *King Edmund* *(see page 189).*

3 *King Edgar* *(see page 190).*

4 *Alexander I* *(see page 190).*

5 *Edith*, *later called* **Matilda**

(See page 46, under Henry I of England, whom she married).

6 *David I* *(see page 191).*

7 *Ethelred*

He became Lay Abbot of Dunkeld. He was also styled Earl of Fife, probably posthumously, and probably before 1107 (although the date is uncertain). He died before c.1097, and was buried in Kilremont Church.

8 *Duncan*

Nothing is known of him. He may have become confused with Duncan II, Malcolm's son by Ingibiorg.

9 *Mary*

She married Eustace III, Count of Boulogne in c.1101/2, and had issue:

1 Unnamed son (d. young).

2 Matilda; she married Stephen, King of England.

Mary died on 31st May, 1115/16, and was buried in the Abbey of St Saviour, Bermondsey, London.

MALCOLM III

He was killed on 13th November, 1093 in a battle near Alnwick, Northumberland, and was buried at Tynemouth. His remains were later removed to Dunfermline Abbey, Fife, and later still, to the Escorial, Madrid, Spain.

He was succeeded by his brother Donald, an usurper.

Recommended reading
There is no biography of Malcolm III. For St Margaret, see:
T. R. Barnett: *St Margaret of Scotland* (1926).
D. McRoberts: *St Margaret of Scotland* (1960).
S. Fest: *The Hungarian Origin of St Margaret of Scotland* (1940).
L. Menzies: *St Margaret, Queen of Scotland* (Dent, 1925).

DONALD III

FATHER: *Duncan I (see page 180).*
MOTHER: *Sybilla of Northumbria (see page 180, under Duncan I).*
SIBLINGS: *(see page 180, under Duncan I).*

DONALD III

Known as "Donaldbane", he was born in c.1033, and was probably created Mormaer or Earl of Gowrie in c.1060. He usurped the throne of Scotland on 13th November, 1093, upon the death of his brother, Malcolm III, but was deposed by Malcolm's son Duncan II in May, 1094. When Duncan II died on 12th November, 1094, Donald III was restored to the throne as joint monarch with his nephew King Edmund, Donald ruling north of the Forth/Clyde line, and Edmund ruling south of it. Both Donald and Edmund were deposed in favour of King Edgar in October, 1097. No record exists of Donald ever being crowned.

Donald III married a lady about whom no information exists, and had **issue**:

1 *Bethoc*
She married Huctred of Tynedale, and had issue:
1 Hextilda; she married firstly Richard Comyn, and had issue. She married secondly Malcolm, 2nd Earl of Atholl (d.1186/98).

DONALD III

He was deposed in October, 1097, and imprisoned. He died in 1099 in prison at Rescobie, Forfarshire, and was buried in Dunkeld Abbey. His remains were later removed to the Isle of Iona.

He was succeeded by King Edgar.

DUNCAN II

FATHER: *Malcolm III (see page 184).*
MOTHER: *Ingibiorg of Halland (see page 184, under Malcolm III).*
SIBLINGS: *(see page 184, under Malcolm III).*

DUNCAN II

He was born in c.1060. He proclaimed himself King of Scotland after deposing his uncle, Donald III, in May, 1094. There is no record of his coronation.

Duncan II married, in c.1090/94 (although no record exists as to where):

Ethelreda or *Octreda*

She was the daughter of Gospatrick, Earl of Northumbria and Dunbar, a great-grandson of Malcolm II. She was buried in Dunfermline Abbey, Fife.

Issue of marriage:

1 *William*

He adopted the surname FitzDuncan, and is said to have been created Earl of Moray. He became Lord of Skipton and Craven, in right of his wife, in 1138 (?). He died in c.1154.

William had the following illegitimate issue:

1 Donald

William married, in 1138 (?) (although no record exists as to where):

Alice

She was the daughter of William le Meschin, Lord of Copeland, by

Cecilia de Rumely, Lady of Skipton. She married firstly a man called William. She married secondly, Alexander FitzGerold. She succeeded her mother as Lady of Skipton and Craven.

Issue of marriage:

(i) *William*

He adopted the surname MacWilliam, and was called Lord of Egremont. He was drowned at Bolton Wharf after 1155.

William married firstly (no record exists of the date or place):

Gruaidh

She was the daughter of Aedh, Mormaer of Moray, by a daughter of King Lulach.

Issue of marriage:

(a) *Donald MacWilliam*

He was killed on 31st July, 1187 on Mangarnia Moor, Speyside. Donald married an unknown lady, and had issue:

(i) Godfrey MacWilliam (executed in 1213 at Kincardine).

(ii) Donald MacWilliam (killed on 15th June, 1215 in Morayshire).

(iii) Unnamed daughter; she married a man surnamed MacEwen, and had issue.

(b) *Gospatrick MacWilliam*

He was created Lord of Airton, Yorks. He married and had issue, but no details are available. He died before 1208.

William married secondly (no record exists of the date or place):

Octreda

She was the daughter of Alan, Lord of Allerdale.

(ii) *Cecilia*

She married William le Gros, 3rd Earl of Aumale (d.1179), and had issue.

(iii) *Amabel*

She married Reginald de Lucy (d.1179), and had issue, although no details are available.

(iv) *Alice*

She married firstly Gilbert Pipard, and secondly Robert de Courtenay. She died in 1215.

DUNCAN II

He was killed on 12th November, 1094 at the Battle of Monthechin (Mondynes), Kincardineshire, and was buried in Dunfermline Abbey, Fife.

He was succeeded by the man he had deposed, Donald III.

KING EDMUND

FATHER: *Malcolm III (see page 184).*
MOTHER: *St Margaret (see page 185, under Malcolm III).*
SIBLINGS: *(see page 185, under Malcolm III).*

KING EDMUND

He was styled Prince of Cumbria in his youth. He became joint King of Scotland with Donald III, his uncle, on 12th November, 1094, following the death of his half-brother, Duncan II. Edmund's authority was confined to the area south of the Forth/Clyde line, while Donald III ruled north of it. There is no record of Edmund's coronation.

KING EDMUND

He was deposed (along with Donald III) in October, 1097 in favour of his brother Edgar. Edmund became a monk at Montacute Abbey, Somerset, where he later died (the date of his death is unknown). He was probably buried in Montacute Abbey. He never married, or had children.

He was succeeded by his brother Edgar.

KING EDGAR

FATHER: *Malcolm III (see page 184).*
MOTHER: *St Margaret (see page 185, under Malcolm III).*
SIBLINGS: *(see page 185, under Malcolm III).*

KING EDGAR
He was born around c.1072/4. He succeeded Donald III and Edmund (joint rulers) as King of Scotland in October, 1097. There is no record of his coronation.

KING EDGAR
He died unmarried and childless on 8th January, 1107, either at Dundee, or at Edinburgh Castle, and was buried in Dunfermline Abbey, Fife.
   He was succeeded by his brother Alexander.

ALEXANDER I

FATHER: *Malcolm III (see page 184).*
MOTHER: *St Margaret (see page 185, under Malcolm III).*
SIBLINGS: *(see page 185, under Malcolm III).*

ALEXANDER I

Known as "the Fierce", he was born in c.1077/8. He succeeded his brother Edgar as King of Scotland on 8th January, 1107. There is no record of his coronation.

Alexander I married, in c.1107 (although no record exists as to where):

Sybilla

She was an illegitimate daughter of Henry I, King of England, by Sybilla Corbet, and she was born around c.1092 at Domfront, Normandy. She died on 12th/13th July, 1122 on the Island of the Woman (Eilean ham Bam), Loch Tay, Perthshire, and was buried in a church there. There was no issue of the marriage.

Alexander I had the following **illegitimate issue**:

1 Malcolm MacHeth, Earl of Ross (1105/15?–1168); he married a sister of Somerled, Lord of Argyll, and had issue.

ALEXANDER I

He died on 23rd, 25th or 27th April, 1124 at Stirling Castle, and was buried in Dunfermline Abbey, Fife.

He was succeeded by his brother David.

DAVID I

FATHER: *Malcolm III (see page 184).*
MOTHER: *St Margaret (see page 185, under Malcolm III).*
SIBLINGS: *(see page 185, under Malcolm III).*

DAVID I

He was born around 1080/85, and was designated Prince of Cumbria in 1107. He was styled Earl of Huntingdon in right of his wife, and possibly also Earl of Northampton from c.1113/14. He succeeded his brother Alexander I as King of Scotland on 23rd, 25th or 27th April, 1124. There is no record of his coronation.

David I married, in 1113/14 (although no record exists as to where): *Matilda*

She was the daughter of Waltheof, Earl of Huntingdon and Northampton, by Judith, daughter of Lambert of Boulogne, Count of Lens, by Adeliza, sister of William I, King of England, and she was born in c.1074. She married firstly Simon de St Liz, Earl of Huntingdon and Northampton (d. after 1111) in c.1090, and had issue:

1 Simon, Earl of Huntingdon and Northampton (after 1103–1153); he married Isabella, daughter of Robert de Beaumont, 1st Earl of Leicester, and had issue.
2 St Waltheof, Abbot of Melrose (c.1100–1159/60).
3 Matilda (d.1140); she married Robert FitzRichard (d.1134), and had issue.

Matilda died between 23rd April, 1130 and 22nd April, 1131 (although she appears in a charter of 1147, now thought to be spurious), and was buried in Scone Abbey, Perthshire.

Issue of marriage:

1 Malcolm

Probably the firstborn. He died young. He is said to have been strangled in infancy by Donald III, although this is chronologically impossible, as Donald died in 1099, and Malcolm was not born until 1113 or later.

2 Henry

He was born in c.1114/15, and succeeded to the earldom of Huntingdon upon his father's resignation in c. February, 1136. He was created Earl of Northumberland in 1139. He died on 12th June, 1152, and was buried in Kelso Abbey, Roxburghshire.

Henry had the following illegitimate issue:

1 Margaret or Marjorie; she married John de Lindsay, and had issue.

Henry married, in 1139 (although no record exists as to where): *Ada*

Also called Adama or Adeline, she was the daughter of William de Warenne, 2nd Earl of Surrey, by Isabella, daughter of Hugh, Count of Vermandois. She died in 1178.

Issue of marriage:

 (i) *Malcolm IV (see page 196).*
 (ii) *King William the Lyon (see page 197).*
 (iii) *David*
    He was born in c.1143/52. He succeeded his father as Earl of

Huntingdon, Earl of Northumberland, Earl of Carlisle and Earl of Doncaster on 12th June, 1152 (his succession being confirmed in 1185). He was created Earl of Garioch in c.1180, and Earl of Cambridge and Earl of Lennox in 1205. He was deprived of all his English honours in 1215/16, but restored to them on 13th March, 1218. He died on 17th June, 1219 at Yardley, Northants., and was buried in Sawtrey Abbey, Hunts.

David had the following illegitimate issue:

1 Henry of Stirling.

2 Henry of Brechin (d.1238); he married Juliana, probably the daughter of Ralph de Cornhill, and had issue.

3 Ada; she married Malise, son of Ferteth, Earl of Strathearn.

4 David (?).

David married, on 26th August, 1190 (although no record exists as to where):

Matilda

She was the daughter of Hugh de Kevilloc, Earl of Chester, by Bertrada, daughter of Simon de Montfort, Count of Evreux, and she was born in 1171. She died on 6th January, 1233.

Issue of marriage:

(a) *Robert*

He died young, and was buried in Lindores Abbey, Fife.

(b) *Isabella*

She was born in 1206, and was known as "Isabella the Scot".

She married Robert le Brus, "the Noble", Lord of Annandale (d.1245) and had issue:

1 Robert, Lord of Annandale, a Competitor for the Crown of Scotland in 1292 (1220–1295); he married firstly Isabella (1226–1254), daughter of Gilbert de Clare, Earl of Hertford and Gloucester, and secondly, Christina (d.c.1305), daughter of Sir William de Ireby, by whom he had issue:

1 Robert le Brus (see page 206, under Robert I).

2 Beatrice; she married Hugh de Neville.

Isabella died in c.1251, and was buried in Saltre Abbey, near Stilton, Gloucs.

(c) *John*

Known as "the Scot", he was born in c.1207, and succeeded his father as Earl of Huntingdon and Garioch on 17th June, 1219. He was created Earl of Chester on 21st November, 1232. He died shortly before 6th June, 1237 at Darnal, and was buried in the Church of St Werburg, Chester.

John married, in c.1220/22 (although no record exists as to where):

Helen

She was the daughter of Llywelyn ap Iorwerth, Prince of Wales, by Joan, illegitimate daughter of John, King of England. After the death of John the Scot, she married secondly Robert de Quincy (d.1257) in 1237, and had issue:

1 Hawise (1250?–1295?); she married Baldwin Wake (d.1282), and had issue.

2 Joan (d.1283); she married Humphrey de Bohun (d.1265).

Helen died in 1253.

(d) *Henry*

He died young after 1215, and was buried in Lindores Abbey, Fife.

(e) *Ada*

She married Henry de Hastings (d.1250?) before 7th June, 1237, and had issue:

1 Henry, 1st Baron Hastings (d.1269); he married Joan de Cantelou (d.1271), and had issue.

Ada died after 1241.

(f) *Margaret*

She married Alan, Lord of Galloway (d.1234) in 1209, and had issue:

1 Devorguilla (see page 203, under King John Balliol).

2 Christina (d.1246); she married William de Forz, 5th Earl of Aumale (d.1241).

Margaret died in 1228.

(g) *Matilda*

She died unmarried.

(iv) *Ada*

She was born after 1139. She married Florence III, Count of Holland (d.c.1191) in 1162, and had issue:

1 Florence IV, Count of Holland, and Competitor for the Crown of Scotland in 1292 (murdered 1206?).

Ada died after 1206.

(v) *Margaret*

She married firstly Conan IV, Duke of Brittany (d.1171) in 1159/60, and had issue:

1 Constance, Duchess of Brittany (see page 60, under Henry II of England).

Margaret married secondly Humphrey de Bohun (d.1182) before Easter, 1175, and had issue:

2 Henry, 1st Earl of Hereford (1176?–1220); he married Matilda (d.1236), daughter of Geoffrey FitzPiers, Earl of Essex, and had issue.

(vi) *Isabella*

She married Robert, Baron Ros of Wark (d.1174) and had issue, but no details are recorded.

(vii) *Matilda*

She died young in 1152.

(viii) *Marjorie (?)*

She is said to have been Earl Henry's daughter by his wife Ada, but is now thought to have been more probably the daughter of one of the bastard sons of David, Earl of Huntingdon (see above), both of whom were called Henry. In 1291, Robert de Pinkeney, one of the Competitors for the Crown of Scotland, claimed to be her great-grandson, but there is no contemporary evidence for her parentage. She is said to have married Sir David de Lindsay, Lord of Luffness (d.c.1214), and to have had issue:

1 David, a knight (d.1241); he married a lady called Christina.

2 Gerard, a knight (d.1249).

3 Walter; he is said to have married Christina Huse, and to have had issue.

4 William.

5 Alice; she married Sir Henry de Pinkeney, Lord of Wedon-Pinkeney, and had issue.

3 *Claricia*

She died unmarried.

4 *Hodierna*

She died young and unmarried.

DAVID I

He died on 24th May, 1153 at Carlisle in Cumbria, and was buried in

Dunfermline Abbey, Fife. He was known as "the Saint", and was popularly reputed as one after his death.

He was succeeded by his grandson Malcolm.

MALCOLM IV

FATHER: *Henry, Earl of Huntingdon (see page 192, under David I).*
MOTHER: *Ada de Warenne (see page 192, under David I).*
SIBLINGS: *(see page 192, under David I).*

MALCOLM IV

Known as "the Maiden", he was born on 20th March, 1141/2. He succeeded his grandfather David I as King of Scotland on 24th May, 1153, and was crowned soon afterwards (the date is unknown) at Scone Abbey, Perthshire.

Malcolm IV is said, with reservations, to have had the following **illegitimate issue:**

1 Henry (d.1152 sic.). His existence rests only upon very obscure evidence, and he has perhaps been confused with King Malcolm's father, Henry. The date of his death, 1152, is impossible, as his alleged father was then no more than 11 years old.

MALCOLM IV

He died unmarried on 9th December, 1165 at Jedburgh Castle, and was buried in Dunfermline Abbey, Fife.

He was succeeded by his brother William.

Recommended reading
Acts of Malcolm IV, King of Scots, 1153–1165 edited by G. W. S. Barrow (1960).

KING WILLIAM

FATHER: *Henry, Earl of Huntingdon (see page 192 under David I).*
MOTHER: *Ada de Warenne (see page 192, under David I).*
SIBLINGS: *(see page 192, under David I).*

KING WILLIAM
Known as "the Lyon", he was born in c.1142/3. He succeeded his father as Earl of Northumberland on 12th June, 1152, but surrendered this earldom in 1157. He succeeded his brother Malcolm IV as King of Scotland on 9th December, 1165, and was crowned on 24th December, 1165 at Scone Abbey, Perthshire.

King William married, on 5th September, 1186 at Woodstock Palace, Oxon.:

Ermengarde
She was the daughter of Richard, Viscount of Beaumont-le-Maine, by Constance, illegitimate daughter of Henry I, King of England. She died on 11th February, 1233/4, and was buried in Balmerino Abbey, Fife.

Issue of marriage:

1 *Margaret*
She was born in c.1193. She married Hubert de Burgh, 1st Earl of Kent (d.1243) on 19th June, 1221, and had issue:
1 Margaret (Megotta) (1222?–1237); she married Richard de Clare, Earl of Hertford and Gloucester (1222?–1262).
Margaret died in 1259, and was buried in the Church of the Black Friars, London.

2 *Alexander II (see page 199).*

3 *Isabella*
She married Roger Bigod, 4th Earl of Norfolk (1212?–1270) in May, 1225 at Alnwick, Northumberland. She was repudiated by her husband on grounds of consanguinity in 1245, but was recon-

ciled to him in 1253. The date of her death is not known. She was buried in the Church of the Black Friars, London.

4 *Marjorie*
She married Gilbert Marshal, 4th Earl of Pembroke (d.1241), either before 14th July, or on 1st August, 1235, at Berwick-upon-Tweed. She died on 17th November, 1244, and was buried in the Church of the Black Friars, London.

King William also had the following **illegitimate issue**:

By the daughter of Adam de Hythus:
1 Margaret (d. after 1226); she married Eustace de Vesci (1169–1216), and had issue.

By a daughter of Robert Avenal:
2 Isabella; she married firstly Robert le Brus (d. before 1191), and had issue. She married secondly Robert de Ros, 1st Baron Ros of Helmsley (d.1226), and had issue.

By unknown mothers:
3 Robert de London.
4 Henry Galightly; he married and had issue.
5 Ada (d.1200); she married Patrick, 4th Earl of Dunbar (1152–1232), and had issue.
6 Aufrica; she married William de Say and had issue.
7 Unnamed child.
8 Unnamed child.
9 Unnamed child. No information exists about these three children.

KING WILLIAM
He died on 4th December, 1214 at Stirling, and was buried in Arbroath Abbey, Scotland.

He was succeeded by his son Alexander.

Recommended reading
G. W. S. Barrow: *The Acts of William I, King of Scots, 1165–1214* (1971) and *The Reign of William the Lyon, King of Scotland* (*Historical Studies VII* edited by J. C. Beckett, 1969).

ALEXANDER II

FATHER: *King William the Lyon (see page 197).*
MOTHER: *Ermengarde de Beaumont (see page 197, under King William).*
SIBLINGS: *(see page 197, under King William).*

ALEXANDER II

He was born on 24th August, 1198 at Haddington, East Lothian. He succeeded his father as King of Scotland on 4th December, 1214, and was crowned on 6th December, 1214 at Scone Abbey, Perthshire.

Alexander II married firstly, on 18th or 25th June, 1221 at York Minster:

Joan

She was the daughter of John, King of England, by Isabella of Angoulême, and she was born on 22nd July, 1210 (or, far less probably, in 1203 in Normandy). She died on 4th, 5th or 12th March, 1238 at Havering-atte-Bower, Essex, and was buried in Tarrant Crawford Abbey, Dorset. There was no issue of the marriage.

Alexander II married secondly, on 15th May, 1239, at Roxburgh:

Mary

She was the daughter of Enguerrand III, Lord of Coucy, by Mary, daughter of John, Lord of Montmirel-en-Brie. After the death of Alexander II, she married secondly John of Brienne, son of the King of Jerusalem, before 6th June, 1257. The date of her death is not known. She was buried at Newbottle, Scotland.

Issue of marriage:

1 *Alexander III (see page 200).*

Alexander II also had the following **illegitimate issue**:

1 Marjorie; she married Alan Durward, and had issue.

ALEXANDER II

He died on 6th July, 1249 on the Isle of Kerrara in the Bay of Oban, and was buried in Melrose Abbey, Roxburghshire.

He was succeeded by his son Alexander.

ALEXANDER III

FATHER: *Alexander II (see page 199).*
MOTHER: *Mary de Coucy (see page 199, under Alexander II).*
SIBLINGS: *Alexander III did not have any legitimate siblings.*

ALEXANDER III

Known as "the Glorious", he was born on 4th September, 1241 at Roxburgh. He succeeded his father as King of Scotland on 8th July, 1249, and was crowned on 13th July, 1249 at Scone Abbey, Perthshire.

Alexander III married firstly, on 26th December, 1251 at York
  Minster:
Margaret
  She was the daughter of Henry III, King of England, by Eleanor of Provence, and she was born on 29th September or 5th October, 1240 at Windsor Castle. She died on 26th/27th February, 1275 at Cupar Castle, Fife, and was buried in Dunfermline Abbey, Fife.
Issue of marriage:
1 Margaret
  She was born on 28th February, 1261 at Windsor Castle. She married Eric II, King of Norway (1268–1300) on c.31st August, 1281 at Bergen, Norway, and had issue:
  (i) *Queen Margaret (see page 202).*
  Margaret died on 9th April, 1283 at Tönsberg, Norway, in childbed, and was buried in Christ Kirk, Bergen, Norway.

2 Alexander

He was born on 21st January, 1264 at Jedburgh, Roxburghshire. He died on 17th or 28th January, 1284 at Lindores Abbey, Fife, and was buried in Dunfermline Abbey, Fife.

Alexander married on 15th November, 1282, at Roxburgh:

Margaret

She was the daughter of Guy of Dampierre, Count of Flanders. After the death of Alexander, she married secondly Reginald I, Count of Gueldres in c.1290, and had issue:

1 Reginald II, Count of Gueldres (d.1343); he married firstly Sophia of Malines (d.1329) and had issue, and secondly, Eleanor, daughter of Edward II of England (see page 90), and had issue.
2 Margaret; she married Thierry VIII, Count of Cleves.
3 Isabella; a nun.
4 Philippa; a nun.
5 Guy (?).
6 Philip (?).

Margaret died in 1330.

3 David

He was born on 20th March, 1273. He died at the end of June, 1281 at Stirling Castle, and was buried in Dunfermline Abbey, Fife.

Alexander III married secondly, on 1st November, 1285 at Jedburgh Abbey:

Yolande or *Joletta*

She was the daughter of Robert IV, Count of Dreux. After the death of Alexander III, she married secondly Arthur II de Montfort, Duke of Brittany (1262–1312) in May, 1294, and had issue:

1 Joan (1294–1363); she married Robert, Lord of Cassel (d.1331).
2 Beatrice (1295–1384); she married Guy, Lord of Laval (d.1347).
3 John III, Duke of Brittany (d.1345); he married Joan of Flanders, and had issue.
4 Alice (1297–1377); she married Bouchard VI, Count of Vendôme (d.1353).
5 Blanche (b.1300; d. young).
6 Mary (1302–1371); a nun.

Yolande died in 1323. There was no issue of her marriage to Alexander III.

ALEXANDER III

He was killed on 16th or 19th March, 1286, when his horse plunged over a cliff between Burntisland and Kinghorn, Fife. He was buried in Dunfermline Abbey, Fife.

He was succeeded by his granddaughter Margaret.

Recommended reading
J. Fergusson: *Alexander III, King of Scotland* (Maclehose, 1937).

QUEEN MARGARET

FATHER: *Eric II, King of Norway.*
MOTHER: *Margaret, daughter of Alexander III.*
SIBLINGS: *Queen Margaret did not have any siblings.*

QUEEN MARGARET
Known as "the Maid of Norway", she was born before 9th April, 1283 at Tönsberg, Norway. She succeeded her grandfather Alexander III, as Scotland's first Queen Regnant on 19th March, 1286, but was never crowned.

QUEEN MARGARET
She died in May (?) or on c.26th September, 1290, on board a ship passing by the Orkneys, whilst on her way to Scotland. She was buried at Bergen, Norway.

The death of the Maid of Norway left Scotland without a monarch, and at the mercy of Edward I of England. In 1290 began the First Interregnum, and the contest for the throne between the 13 Competitors. From these, Edward I, called upon to decide which had the most lawful claim to the crown, chose John Balliol as Scotland's next king.

Part Three: The House of Balliol

KING JOHN

FATHER: *John*

He was the son of Hugh de Balliol of Barnard Castle. He married Devorguilla of Galloway in 1233. He died in 1268/9.

MOTHER: *Devorguilla*

She was the daughter of Alan, Lord of Galloway, by Margaret, daughter of David, Earl of Huntingdon, grandson of David I. She died on 28th January, 1290, and was buried in Sweetheart Abbey, Kirkland.

SIBLINGS:

1 *Hugh*

He was born in c.1238 at Barnard Castle, and rose to the rank of knight. He married Agnes (d.1310), daughter of William de Valence, Earl of Pembroke. He died in 1271.

2 *Alan*

He was born at Barnard Castle. His dates are not recorded.

3 *Alexander*

He was born at Barnard Castle, and rose to the rank of knight. He married Eleanor of Geneva (d.c.1303), a kinswoman of Henry III, King of England. He died in 1278.

4 *Eleanor* or *Mary*

She married Sir John Comyn of Badenoch, and had issue, although no details are recorded.

5 *Cecilia*

She married John de Burgh (d.1280), and had issue:

1 Devorguilla; she married Robert FitzWalter (d.1326), and had issue.

2 Hawise; she married Robert de Grelley (d.1282), and had issue.

3 Marjorie; a nun at Chicksands Priory.

Cecilia died before 1273.

6 *Ada*

She married William de Lindsay of Lamberton (1250–killed 1283), and had issue:

1 Christina; she married Enguerrand de Guisnes, Seigneur de Coucy.

KING JOHN

Known as "Toom Tabard" (or "Turncoat"), he was born either in c.1240, or in 1249/50. He was created Baron of Bywell in Northumberland, but forfeited this honour in 1285. He was elected King of Scotland by Edward I of England on 17th November, 1292, thus bringing to an end the First Interregnum. He was crowned on 30th November, 1292 at Scone Abbey, Perthshire.

King John married, before 7th February, 1281 (although no evidence exists as to where):

Isabella

She was the daughter of John de Warenne, 6th Earl of Surrey, by Alice, daughter of Hugh X de Lusignan, Count of La Marche, by Isabella of Angoulême, widow of John, King of England, and she was born in 1253. The date of her death is not known.

Issue of marriage:

1 *King Edward (see page 213).*

2 *Henry*

He was killed on 16th December, 1332 at the Battle of Annan.

3 *Margaret*

She died unmarried.

4 *Anne (?)*

There is doubt that she ever existed. She is said to have married Brian FitzAlan of Bedale.

KING JOHN

He abdicated on 10th/11th July, 1296 at Brechin. Scotland was left without a King, and thus began the Second Interregnum, which lasted until 1306, when Robert Bruce seized the throne in defiance of Edward I, who had tried during the years it stood vacant to take it himself, and make Scotland a fief of England.

King John died between 4th March, 1313 and 4th January, 1314, either at Château Gaillard, Normandy, or at Bailleut-en-Gouffern,

Normandy. He was probably buried in the Church of St Waast, Normandy.

For further details of the House of Balliol, see page 213, after the House of Bruce.

Part Four: The House of Bruce

ROBERT I

FATHER: *Robert*

He was the son of Robert le Brus, Lord of Annandale (d.1295) (who was the son of Isabella "the Scot" of Huntingdon, a great-granddaughter of David I), by Christina (d.c.1305), daughter of Sir William de Ireby, and he was born in July, 1243. He married Margaret, Countess of Carrick, in 1271 at Turnberry Castle, and became Earl of Carrick in right of his wife. He resigned this earldom in favour of his son Robert on 27th October, 1292. After Margaret died, he married secondly, after 1292, a lady called Eleanor, whose origins are unknown. (After his death, she married secondly Sir Richard le Waleys of Burgh Wallis, Yorks., (d. after 1336) between 2nd December, 1304 and 8th February, 1306, and had issue, although no details are available. She died between 13th April and 8th September, 1331.) Robert le Brus succeeded his father as Lord of Annandale before 4th July, 1295, and died shortly before 4th April, 1304, either in England or in Palestine. He was buried in the Abbey of Holm Cultram.

MOTHER: *Margaret* or *Marjorie*

She was the daughter of Neil, 2nd Earl of Carrick, by Margaret, daughter of Walter, High Steward of Scotland. She succeeded her father to the earldom of Carrick, in 1256. She married firstly Adam de Kilconquhar, 3rd Earl of Carrick (d.1268) before 4th October, 1266. She died before 9th November, 1292.

206

SIBLINGS:

1 *Isabella*

She was born in c.1275. She married Eric II, King of Norway (1268–1300) (who had previously been married to Margaret, daughter of Alexander III, and by her had been the father of the Maid of Norway) before 25th September, 1293, and had issue:

1 Ingibiorg (1297?–?); she married Waldemar, Duke of Finland (murdered 1318).

Isabella died in 1358.

2 *Edward*

He was created Lord of Galloway before 16th March, 1309, and Earl of Carrick before 24th October, 1313. He became King of Ireland, and was crowned on 2nd May, 1316. He was killed on 14th October, 1318 at the Battle of Dundall, Ireland.

Edward had the following illegitimate issue (and see also below):

1 Thomas de Bruce.

Edward is said to have married firstly (although no evidence exists as to where):

Isabella

She was the daughter of John of Strathbogie, Earl of Atholl, by Margaret, daughter of Donald, 6th Earl of Mar. There is little sound evidence for her marriage to Edward, and it is thought likely that she was only his mistress. She died before 1st June, 1317.

Issue of marriage or liaison:

(i) Alexander de Bruce, Earl of Carrick (killed 1333); he married Eleanor, daughter of Sir Archibald Douglas.

Edward married secondly, after 1st June, 1317 (date of dispensation) (although no evidence exists as to where):

Isabella

She was the daughter of William, 5th Earl of Ross. No further details of her are recorded.

3 *Neil*

He was executed in 1306 at Berwick by the English.

4 *Thomas*

He rose to the rank of knight, and was executed in 1307 at Carlisle Castle by the English.

Thomas married (although no record exists of the date or the place):

Helen

She was the daughter of Sir John Erskine. Her dates are not recorded.

207

5 *Alexander*

He was appointed Dean of Glasgow, and executed in 1307 at Carlisle Castle by the English.

6 *Mary*

She married firstly Sir Neil Campbell of Lochawe (d.c.1316), probably after Michaelmas, 1312, and had issue:

1 John of Lochawe, Earl of Atholl (1313?–killed 1333); he married Joan, daughter of Sir John Menteith of Rusky and Knapdale.

2 Dougal; he married and had issue.

3 Duncan (?); he is said to have married and had issue, but the evidence for his existence is unsatisfactory.

Mary married secondly Sir Alexander Fraser (killed 1332) in c.1316, and had issue:

1 John of Touch Fraser (1317?–died in early manhood); he married an unknown lady and had issue.

2 William, a knight (1318?–killed 1346); he married Margaret (d.1364), said to have been the daughter of Sir Andrew Moray of Bothwell, and had issue.

Mary died before 22nd September, 1323.

7 *Christina* or *Christian*

She married firstly Gartnait, Earl of Mar (d.1305) in c.1292, and had issue:

1 Donald, 8th Earl of Mar (killed 1332); he married Isabella (d.1347), perhaps the daughter of Sir Alexander Stewart of Bonkyll, and had issue.

2 Helen (d. after 1342); she married firstly Sir John Menteith, Lord of Arran, and had issue, and secondly Sir James Garioch (?).

Christina married secondly Christopher Seton (executed 1306) in 1305/6. She married thirdly Sir Andrew Murray of Bothwell (1298–1338) after 12th October, 1325 (date of dispensation), and had issue:

1 John, a knight (d.1352); he married Margaret Graham, Countess of Menteith (see page 216, under Robert II).

2 Thomas, a knight (d.1361); he married Joan, daughter of Maurice Moray, Earl of Strathearn.

Christina died in 1356/7 "at a great age".

8 *Margaret*

She married Sir William de Carlyle (d. by 1329), and had issue:

1 William, a knight (d.1347).

2 John (d.1347); married and had issue.

9 *Matilda*

She married Hugh, 6th Earl of Ross (killed 1333) in c.1308, and had issue:

1 Matilda or Marjorie (d. after 1350); she married Malise, Earl of Strathearn and Caithness (d.1344/57).

2 William, 7th Earl of Ross (d.1372); he married Mary, daughter of Angus Og, Lord of the Isles, and had issue.

Matilda died between 1323 and 1329, and was buried at Fearn, Scotland.

10 *Son (name not known).*

He probably died young.

ROBERT I

Known as "the Bruce", he was born on 11th July, 1274, probably at Writtle, near Chelmsford, Essex. He succeeded his father as Earl of Carrick on 27th October, 1292, and as Lord of Annandale either in 1295 (?) or in 1304. On 25th or 27th March, 1306, he assumed the Crown and Royal Dignity of Scotland, thus bringing to an end the Second Interregnum. This he did in defiance of Edward I of England, who had declared his English estates forfeit on 20th February, 1305/6. Robert I was crowned on 27th March, 1306 at Scone Abbey, Perthshire.

Robert I married firstly, in c.1295 (although no evidence exists as to where):

Isabella

She was the daughter of Donald, 6th Earl of Mar, by his wife Helen, who was said to have been an illegitimate daughter of Llywelyn the Great, Prince of Wales. Isabella was dead by 1302.

Issue of marriage:

1 *Marjorie*

She was born in c.1297. (See page 214, under Robert II).

Robert I married secondly, in c.1302 (although no evidence exists as to where):

Elizabeth

She was the daughter of Richard de Burgh, Earl of Ulster and Connaught, by Margaret, daughter of John de Burgh. She died on 26th October, 1327 at Cullen Castle, Banffshire, and was buried in Dunfermline Abbey, Fife.

Issue of marriage:

1 *Margaret*

She married William, 5th Earl of Sutherland (d.1371) between 2nd August and 28th September, 1345, and had issue:

209

1 John, Master of Sutherland (1346?–1361).

Margaret died between 30th March, 1346 and 9th November, 1347 in childbed.

2 *Matilda*

She married Thomas Isaac, and had issue:

1 Joan; she married John, Lord of Lorne.

2 Katherine.

Matilda died on 20th July, 1353 at Aberdeen, and was buried in Dunfermline Abbey, Fife.

3 *David II* *(see page 211).*

4 *John*

He was born in October, 1327, and died young. He was buried in Restennet Priory, Forfarshire.

Robert I also had the following **illegitimate issue**:

1 Robert, Baron of Liddesdale (killed 1332).

2 Neil or Nigel of Carrick, a knight (d.1346).

3 Walter of Odistoun (?); probably spurious.

4 Christina of Carrick.

5 Margaret (d. after 1364); she married Robert Glen.

6 Elizabeth; she married Sir Walter Oliphant of Aberdalgie (d. after 1378), and had issue.

ROBERT I

He died on 7th June, 1329 at Cardross Castle, Dumbartonshire, and was buried in Dunfermline Abbey, Fife.

He was succeeded by his son David.

Recommended reading

G. W. S. Borrow: *Robert Bruce and the Community of the Realm of Scotland* (Eyre and Spottiswoode, 1965).

A. M. Mackenzie: *Robert Bruce, King of Scots* (1954).

DAVID II

FATHER: *Robert I (see page 206).*
MOTHER: *Elizabeth de Burgh (see page 209, under Robert I).*
SIBLINGS: *(see page 209, under Robert I).*

DAVID II

He was born on 5th March, 1324 at Dunfermline Palace, Fife, and was created Earl of Carrick between 17th March and 17th July, 1328, thus establishing the tradition that the title of Earl of Carrick is always borne by the eldest son of the sovereign in Scotland. David succeeded his father as King of Scotland on 7th June, 1329, and was crowned on 24th November, 1331 at Scone Abbey, Perthshire. He was overthrown by Edward Balliol (see page 213) in August, 1332 at the Battle of Dupplin Moor, near Perth, but restored to the throne the following December. He was again deposed by Edward Balliol in 1333, and finally restored in 1336.

David II married firstly, on 17th July, 1328, at Berwick-upon-Tweed, Northumberland:

Joan

She was the daughter of Edward II, King of England, by Isabella of France, and she was born on 5th July, 1321 at the Tower of London. She was crowned Queen Consort on 24th November, 1331 at Scone Abbey, Perthshire, this being the first time that a Scottish Queen Consort was crowned. Joan died on 7th September, 1362 at Hertford Castle, and was buried in Greyfriars Church, Newgate, London. There was no issue of her marriage to David II.

David II married secondly, in April or December, 1363 (or, less probably, 13th or c.20th February, 1364), either at Inchmurdach Manor, Fife, or at Inchmahome Priory, Perthshire:

Margaret

She was the daughter of Sir Malcolm Drummond by a daughter of Sir

211

Patrick de Graham. She married firstly Sir John Logie, and had issue:
1 John of Logie.
David II divorced Margaret on c.20th March, 1370. She died soon after 31st January, 1375, perhaps at Avignon, France. There was no issue of the marriage.

DAVID II
He died on 22nd February, 1371 at Edinburgh Castle, and was buried in Holyrood Abbey, Edinburgh.

He was succeeded by his nephew Robert Stewart.

Continuation of Part Three: The House of Balliol

KING EDWARD

FATHER: *King John (see page 203).*
MOTHER: *Isabella de Warenne (see page 204, under King John).*
SIBLINGS: *(see page 204, under King John).*

KING EDWARD

His date of birth is unknown. He claimed the throne of Scotland as his father's successor, and defeated David II in August, 1332 at the Battle of Dupplin Moor, near Perth. He was crowned King of Scotland on 24th September, 1332 at Scone Abbey, Perthshire. He was deposed in favour of David II on 16th December, 1332, and expelled from Scotland, but was restored to the throne in March, 1333. He was again deposed in 1334, and fled to England, yet was restored once more in 1335. He was finally deposed in 1336. He never married, and had no children.

KING EDWARD

He surrendered all claims to the throne of Scotland on 20th January, 1356. He probably died between May, 1363 and September, 1365, perhaps in January, 1364, at Wheatley, near Doncaster, Yorks., but one source at least hints that he was still alive in 1370. His place of burial is not known. He was succeeded in 1336 by David II (see page 211), who was in turn succeeded by Robert Stewart.

213

Part Five: The House of Stewart

ROBERT II

FATHER: *Walter*

He was the son of James, 5th High Steward of Scotland, by Cecilia, daughter of Patrick, 7th Earl of Dunbar and March. He was born in 1292, and in due course succeeded his father as 6th High Steward of Scotland, from which title derived the royal surname of Stewart, adopted by his successors. Walter married firstly, it is said, Alice, daughter of Sir John Erskine (although there is no proof of this), by whom he is said to have had issue:

1 Jean; she married Hugh, 6th Earl of Ross (d.1333), and had issue.

Walter married secondly Marjorie Bruce in 1315, thus founding the Royal House of Stewart. He married thirdly Isabella, daughter of Sir John Graham of Abercorn, and had issue:

1 John of Railston or Cunningham, a knight; he married and had issue.

2 Andrew; a knight.

3 Egidia (d. by 1406); she married firstly Sir James Lindsay of Crawford (d.1358), and had issue. She married secondly Sir Hugh of Eglinton, and thirdly Sir James Douglas of Dalkeith (d.1420).

Walter died on 9th April, 1326/7.

MOTHER: *Marjorie*

She was the daughter of Robert I, King of Scotland, by Isabella of Mar, and she was born in c.1297. She died on 2nd March, 1316 at Paisley, Renfrewshire, in childbed, after falling from her horse, and was buried in Paisley Abbey.

SIBLINGS: *Robert II did not have any siblings.*

ROBERT II

He was born on 2nd March, 1316 at Paisley, Renfrewshire. He was created Earl of Atholl on 16th February, 1342, and Earl of Strathearn around 6th/13th November, 1357/8. He resigned the earldom of Atholl on 31st May, 1367, and either resigned, or was deprived of, the earldom of Strathearn on 18th April, 1369; he was formally deprived of it on 16th September, 1369, although he was restored in blood to the earldom of Strathearn around 4th/7th April, 1370. He succeeded David II as King of Scotland—the first Stewart King—on 22nd February, 1371, and was crowned either on 22nd February or 26th March, 1371 at Scone Abbey, Perthshire.

Robert II married firstly, in 1336, and again after 22nd November, 1347 (date of dispensation), perhaps in 1349 (because the first marriage ceremony was uncanonical) (although no record exists as to where):

Elizabeth

She was the daughter of Sir Adam Mure of Rowallan, Ayrshire, by Joan Cunningham, his first wife, or Janet Mure, his second wife. The children of this marriage, most of whom were born before the second ceremony of marriage, were looked upon by many as not quite legitimate, although one of the sons succeeded his father as King. This uncertainty surrounding their status led to bitter conflict in after years between them and the unquestionably legitimate children of their father's second marriage (see below). Elizabeth Mure died before 1355.

Issue of marriage:

1 *John, who styled himself Robert III (see page 226).*

2 *Walter*

He was styled Earl of Fife in right of his wife before 14th August, 1362. He died between 14th August, 1362 and 10th January, 1363.

Walter married, before 1362 (although no record exists as to where):

Elizabeth

She was the daughter of Duncan, 10th Earl of Fife, by Mary, daughter of Ralph de Monthermer, Earl of Gloucester, by Joan, daughter of Edward I, King of England, and she was born before 1332. She succeeded her father as Countess of Fife in 1353, and was so styled from 1359. She married firstly Sir William Ramsay of Colluthie, Earl of Fife (d. after 1360). Walter Stewart was her second husband; there was no issue of the marriage. After his death, she married thirdly Sir Thomas Bisset of Upsetlington, Earl

215

of Fife (d.1365) between 10th January, 1363 and April (?) or 8th June, 1363. She married fourthly John de Dunbar, Earl of Fife (d. by 1371). She resigned the earldom of Fife to Robert, Duke of Albany, her brother-in-law (see below), on 30th March, 1371, but was again created Countess of Fife before 6th March, 1372. She died after 12th August, 1389.

3 *Robert*

He was born in c.1340/41, and was created Earl of Menteith on 28th February, 1361, pending his forthcoming marriage to the heiress of Menteith. He was created Earl of Fife between 4th December, 1371 and 6th March, 1372, following the resignation of Elizabeth, his sister-in-law (see above), but resigned the earldom to her on 6th March, 1372. He was created Duke of Albany on 28th April, 1398. He was created Earl of Atholl for life on 2nd September, 1403, but was never so styled, so it may be that he resigned at once. He was created Earl of Buchan before 20th September, 1406, following the death of his brother, Alexander (see below), but resigned it the same day. Robert died on 3rd September, 1420 at Stirling Castle, and was buried in Dunfermline Abbey, Fife.

Robert married firstly, after 9th September, 1361 (date of dispensation) (although no record exists as to where):

Margaret

She was the daughter of Sir John Graham by Mary, Countess of Menteith, and she was born before 1334. She married firstly Sir John Murray, Lord of Bothwell (d.1352) (son of Christina, sister of Robert I) after 21st November, 1348 (date of dispensation). She married secondly Thomas, Earl of Mar (1330?–1374) between 15th August, 1352 and 29th May, 1354, but he divorced her in c.1359, on the grounds that she was barren. She married thirdly Sir John Drummond of Concraig (d.1360/61) in c.1359. She succeeded her mother as Countess of Menteith on 29th April, 1360. Robert Stewart was her fourth husband. She died between 20th July, 1372 and 4th May, 1380, and was buried in Inchmahome Priory, Perthshire.

Issue of marriage:

(i) *Murdoch*

He was born in 1362 (?), and succeeded his father as Duke of Albany, Earl of Fife and Earl of Menteith on 3rd September, 1420. He forfeited all his honours on 25th May, 1425, and was executed the same day on Castle Hill, Stirling. He was buried in the Church of the Black Friars, Stirling.

Murdoch had the following illegitimate issue:

1 Daughter (name not known) (?); she is said to have married Archibald Campbell (d. by 1440), son of Marjorie Stewart (daughter of Robert, Duke of Albany by his second wife), but the evidence for her existence is unsatisfactory.

Murdoch married, between 17th February and 8th November, 1392 (although no record exists as to where):

Elizabeth

She was the daughter of Duncan, 8th Earl of Lennox, by Helen, daughter of Gillespic Campbell of Lochawe, and she was born in c.1370. She was styled Countess of Lennox in her own right from 12th May, 1437. She died between 7th October, 1456 and 4th May, 1458 at Inchmurrah Castle, Loch Lomond.

Issue of marriage:

(a) *Robert*

He was known as the Master of Fife. He died between 1416 and July, 1421.

(b) *Walter*

He rose to the rank of knight. He was executed on 24th May, 1425 on Castle Hill, Stirling, and was buried in the Church of the Black Friars, Stirling.

Walter had the following illegitimate issue:

By a lady surnamed Campbell:

1 Andrew Stewart, Lord of Avandale (d.1488) (?); he married a lady about whom no information exists.

2 Arthur.

By an unknown mother:

3 Mariott (?); she is said to have married Colin Campbell, Earl of Argyll (1406?–1475), but there is little evidence to support this.

By Janet, daughter of Sir Robert Erskine (Walter was granted a dispensation to marry her on 24th April, 1424, but there is no evidence to show that the marriage ever took place):

4 Walter of Morphie; he married and had issue.

Note: All Walter's bastards were legitimated on 17th April, 1479.

(c) *Alexander*

He rose to the rank of knight. He was executed on 25th

May, 1425 on Castle Hill, Stirling, and was buried in the Church of the Black Friars, Stirling.

(d) *James*

He died before 18th May, 1451 in exile in Ireland.

James had the following illegitimate issue:

By an Irish lady surnamed MacDonald:

1 Andrew, Lord of Avandale (?).

2 Arthur.

3 Walter.

4 James Beg.

5 Matilda; she married William Edmonston of Duntreath.

6 Son (name not known).

7 Son (name not known).

(e) *Isabella*

She married Sir Walter Buchanan, and had issue, although no details are recorded.

(ii) *Janet*

She was contracted in marriage on 20th July, 1372 to David de Loen, but no evidence exists to show that the wedding ever took place. She probably died unmarried.

(iii) *Mary*

She married Sir William Abernethy of Saltoun (d.1420), and had issue:

1 Son.

2 Son.

3 etc. Other children.

(iv) *Margaret*

She married Sir John de Swinton of Swinton (killed in battle in 1402) in c.1392, and had issue, although no details are available. She perhaps married secondly Sir Robert Stewart, Lord of Lorne and Innermeath (d.1449), but she may have been confused in the records with her sister Joan (see below). Details of the issue of this possible marriage are not recorded.

(v) *Joan*

She married Robert Stewart, Lord of Lorne and Innermeath (d.1449) after 27th September, 1397 (date of dispensation), and had issue:

1 John, Lord of Lorne (killed 1463).

2 Walter, 1st Lord Innermeath (d. by 1488/9); he married Margaret Lindsay (d. after 1481), and had issue.

3 Alan (d.c.1463).

4 David.

5 Robert.

6 Daughter (name not known); she is said to have married Robert, 8th Lord Erskine (d. by 1452), but there is no evidence for this.

(vi) *Beatrice*

She married James Douglas, Earl of Douglas and Avandale (d.1443). She died in c.1424.

(vii) *Isabella*

She married firstly Alexander Leslie, 9th Earl of Ross (d.1402) (see page 221, under Euphemia, Countess of Ross) before 1398, and had issue:

1 Euphemia, Countess of Ross (d. after 1424); she became a nun at North Berwick, and renounced her inheritance.

Isabella married secondly Walter Haliburton of Dirleton between 1402 and 2nd February, 1408, and had issue:

1 Walter (d. by 1447); he married Marjorie (see page 227, under Robert III), daughter of Archibald Douglas, 3rd Earl of Douglas, and had issue.

2 Christina; she married George Leslie, 1st Earl of Rothes (1417?–1490), and had issue.

Robert married secondly, after 4th May, 1380 (date of dispensation) (although no evidence exists as to where):

Muriella

She was the daughter of Sir William Keith by Margaret, daughter of John Fraser. She died shortly before 1st June, 1449.

Issue of marriage:

(i) *John*

He was born in 1381 (?), and succeeded his father as Earl of Buchan before 20th September, 1406. He was killed on 17th August, 1424 at the Battle of Verneuil, France.

John married, in November, 1413 (although no evidence exists as to where):

Elizabeth

She was the daughter of Archibald Douglas, 4th Earl of Douglas and Duke of Touraine, by Margaret, daughter of Robert III. She married secondly Sir Thomas Stewart (d. by 1435), and thirdly William Sinclair, 3rd Earl of Orkney (d.1476/82), by whom she had issue:

1 William; he married Christina, daughter of George Leslie, Earl of Rothes, and had issue.

2 Katherine, Duchess of Albany (see page 234, under James II).
Elizabeth died before 1451.
Issue of marriage:

(a) *Margaret*

She married George Seton, 1st Lord Seton (d.1478)
before 1436, and had issue:

1 John, Master of Seton (d. by 1478); he married
Christina (d.1496), daughter of John, 1st Lord Lindsay
of the Byres, and had issue.

2 Dougal (?).

(ii) *Andrew*

He died before 1413.

(iii) *Robert*

He is said to have been killed on 17th August, 1424 at the
Battle of Verneuil, France, but this is impossible as he was
recorded as alive in 1431.

(iv) *Marjorie*

She married Duncan, 1st Lord Campbell of Lochawe
(d.1453), and had issue:

1 Archibald or Celestine (d. by 1440); he married Elizabeth,
daughter of John, 3rd Lord Somerville of Carwath. He is
said to have married secondly a daughter of Murdoch, Duke
of Albany (see above), but this is improbable.

Some sources name Marjorie as the mother of Colin, 1st Earl
of Argyll (1431?–1493), and state that she died, possibly in
childbed, before August, 1432. Colin was almost certainly the
son of Lord Campbell by his second wife whom he married
shortly after Marjorie's death in c.1406.

(v) *Elizabeth*

She married Sir Malcolm Fleming of Biggar and Cumbernauld
(executed 1440) before 28th June, 1413, and had issue:

1 Malcolm (d. after 1432).

2 Robert, Lord Fleming (d.1491); he married firstly Janet,
daughter of James Douglas, 7th Earl of Douglas, and had
issue. He married secondly Margaret, daughter of John
Lindsay of Covington.

3 Margaret; she married Patrick, Master of Gray.

4 Alexander

Known as "the Wolf of Badenoch", he was born in c.1343, and
created Lord of Badenoch on 30th March, 1371. He was created
Earl of Buchan on 22nd July, 1382, and was styled Earl of Ross in

right of his wife from July, 1382. Alexander died before 1406: a possible date is 24th July, 1394. However, he may have died as late as 25th March, 1406. Other possible dates are 20th February, 1395 (but here there is possible confusion with the date of his wife's death), 1st August, 1405, or any date between August, 1405 and March, 1406. He was buried in Dunkeld Cathedral, Perthshire.

Alexander had the following illegitimate issue:

By Margaret Atheyn:

1 Alexander, Earl of Mar (1375?–1435); he married Elizabeth, Countess of Mar (1360?–1408).

2 Duncan.

3 Andrew of Sandhauch, Banffshire; a knight.

4 Walter.

5 James.

6 Robert of Atholl.

7 Margaret; she married Robert, Earl of Sutherland (d.1427), and had issue.

Alexander married, on or before 22nd/24th July, 1382 (although no evidence exists as to where):

Euphemia

She was the daughter of William, 7th Earl of Ross, by Mary, daughter of Angus Og, Lord of the Isles, and she was born after 1342/5. She married firstly Sir Walter Leslie, Earl of Ross (d.1382) between 1357 and 13th September, 1366, and had issue:

1 Alexander, 9th Earl of Ross (d.1402); he married Isabella Stewart, daughter of Robert, Duke of Albany (see above), and had issue.

2 Mary, Countess of Ross (d.c.1435); she married Donald Macdonald, Lord of the Isles (d.1423) (son of Margaret, daughter of Robert II), and had issue.

Euphemia was styled Lady of Ross from 9th February, 1372, following the death of her father; she was styled Countess of Ross during her second marriage to Alexander Stewart. She died between 5th September, 1394 and 20th February, 1395, and was buried in Fortrose Cathedral, Ross and Cromarty. There was no issue of her marriage to Alexander.

5 *Elizabeth*

She married Sir Thomas de la Haye, 7th Lord of Erroll (d.1406) before 7th November, 1372, and had issue:

1 William, a knight (d.1436); he married Margaret, daughter of Sir Patrick Gray of Broxmouth, and had issue.

2 Gilbert of Dronlaw, a knight; he married Elizabeth Reid, and had issue.
3 Elizabeth; she married Sir George Leslie of Rothes (1350–after 1412), and had issue.
4 Alice; she married Sir William Hay of Locharret.
5 Daughter (name not known); she married Norman (?), son of Andrew Leslie, and had issue.

6 *Isabella*

She married firstly James Douglas, 2nd Earl of Douglas (1358?–killed 1388) after 24th September, 1371 (date of dispensation), perhaps in 1373 (?), and had issue:
1 Son (name not known) (d. young).
Isabella married secondly Sir John Edmondston of Duntreath in 1388/90, and had issue:
1 Son (name not known).
Isabella died in c.1410.

7 *Jean*

She married firstly Sir John Keith (d.1375) on 17th January, 1373/4, and had issue:
1 Robert (d. by 1404).
2 Robert, Lord of Strathkyn (d.1430); he married the heiress of Troup, and had issue.
Jean married secondly Sir John Lyon of Glamis (killed 1382) between 27th June and 4th October, 1376, and had issue:
3 John, a knight (d.1435); he married Elizabeth, daughter of Sir Patrick Graham of Dundaff and Kilpont), by Euphernia, Countess Palatine of Caithness and Strathearn (see page 223, below), and had issue.
Jean married thirdly Sir James Sandilands of Calder in c. November, 1384 and had issue:
4 James of Calder, a knight (d.c.1426); he married a lady called Janet, and had issue.
Jean died after 1404, and was buried in Scone Abbey, Perthshire.

8 *Katherine (?)*

She may have been a daughter of Robert II by Elizabeth Mure. She married Sir Robert Logan of Restalrig, by whom she may have had issue, although no details are recorded. She died after 1394 (?).

9 *Margaret*

She married John MacDonald, Lord of the Isles (1326?–1387) after 14th June, 1350 (date of dispensation), and had issue:
1 Donald, Lord of the Isles (d.1423); he married Mary (d.c.1435),

daughter of Sir Walter Leslie by Euphemia, Countess of Ross (see page 221 above), and had issue.

2 John, known as Ian Mor Tanisteir (murdered 1427); he married Marjorie, daughter of Sir Hugh Bisset, and had issue.

3 Alexander, known as Alastair Carrach; he married and had issue.

4 Angus.

5 Hugh, Thane of Glentilt; he married and had issue.

6 Marcus.

7 Mary; she married Lachlan Maclean of Duart.

8 Elizabeth or Margaret; she married Angus Duff Mackay of Strathnaver.

10 *Marjorie*

She married firstly John de Dunbar, Earl of Moray (d.1391/2) after 11th July, 1370 (date of dispensation), and had issue:

1 Thomas, Earl of Moray (d.1415/22); he married a lady called Margaret (d.1422), and had issue.

2 Alexander; he is said to have married Matilda, daughter of James Fraser of Frendraught, and to have had issue.

3 James (b.1390).

4 Euphemia; she married Alexander Cumming and had issue (?).

Marjorie married secondly Sir Alexander Keith of Grandown before 24th April, c.1403, and perhaps had issue:

5 Christina (?); she married Sir Patrick Ogilvy (drowned 1429), and had issue.

Marjorie died after 6th May, 1417.

Robert II married secondly, after 2nd May, 1355 (date of dispensation) (although no evidence exists as to where):

Euphemia

She was the daughter of Hugh, 6th Earl of Ross, by Margaret Graham. She married firstly John Randolph, 3rd Earl of Moray (d.1346). She was crowned Queen Consort in 1372 at Scone Abbey, Perthshire. She died in 1387.

Issue of marriage:

1 *David*

He was born around 1356/60. He was created Earl Palatine of Strathearn on 26th/27th March, 1371, and Earl of Caithness between 21st November, 1375 and 28th December, 1377. He died before 5th March, 1389, perhaps in February (?), 1389 (?), or perhaps as early as 1382.

David married a lady whose name is not recorded:

She was the daughter of Sir Alexander Lindsay of Glenesk, by Katherine, daughter of Sir John Stirling of Glenesk.

Issue of marriage:

(i) *Euphemia*

She was born before 1375, and succeeded her father as Countess Palatine of Caithness and Strathearn before 5th March, 1389. She resigned the earldom of Caithness before July, 1402. She married firstly Sir Patrick Graham of Dundaff and Kilpont (d.1413) before December (and perhaps by 24th August), 1406, and had issue:

1 Malise, Earl of Strathearn and Menteith (c.1407–1490); he married a lady called Janet (d.c.1477), and had issue. He married secondly Marion (d.1530), possibly a Campbell of Glenorchy, and had issue.

2 Euphemia (d.1468); she married firstly Archibald Douglas, 5th Earl of Douglas (1390–1439), and had issue. She married secondly James, 1st Lord Hamilton (1415–1479) (he married secondly Mary, daughter of James II).

3 Elizabeth or Anne; she married Sir John Lyon (d.1435) (son of Jean, daughter of Robert II).

Euphemia married secondly Sir Patrick Dunbar of Bele (d. after 1438), and had issue:

4 Patrick.

5 George.

Euphemia died on 15th October, c.1434.

2 *Walter*

He was born in c.1360, and was created Baron of Brechin in 1378. He was created Earl of Caithness before July, 1402, and Earl of Atholl on c.28th April, 1404. He was created Baron Cortachy on 22nd September, 1409, and Earl Palatine of Strathearn on 22nd July, 1427. He resigned the earldom of Caithness in favour of his son Alexander around c.1428/30: 13th December, 1429 is the most probable date. He succeeded Alexander as Earl of Caithness in late summer, 1431. His honours and estates were declared forfeit on 26th March, 1437, and he was executed with appalling barbarity on the same day in Edinburgh as punishment for his part in the murder of James I.

Walter married, before 19th October, 1378 (although no evidence exists as to where):

Margaret

She was the daughter of Sir David de Barclay, Lord of Brechin, by

Janet, daughter of Sir Edward Keith of Synton. She died before 1st August, 1404.

Issue of marriage:

(i) *Alexander* or *Alan*

He was created Earl of Caithness around c.1428/30. He was killed in 1431 in a foray at Inverlochy, Inverness-shire.

(ii) *David*

He died after February, 1433 in England.

David married an Englishwoman whose identity is unknown, and had issue:

(a) *Robert*

He rose to the rank of knight, and was known as the Master of Atholl. He was granted a dispensation to marry one Margaret Ogilvy on 29th January, 1428/9, but there is no evidence to show that the marriage ever took place. He was executed in March, 1437 in Edinburgh for his part in the murder of James I.

On 1st August, 1404, Walter Stewart was granted a dispensation to marry Elizabeth, daughter of Sir William Graham of Kincardine, but no evidence exists to show that the marriage actually took place. Elizabeth married Sir John Stewart of Dundonald, bastard son of Robert II, in 1407/8.

3 *Elizabeth*

She married David Lindsay, 1st Earl of Crawford (1360?–1407) in 1380 or 1384 (dispensation granted on 22nd February, 1374/5), and had issue:

1 Alexander, 2nd Earl of Crawford (1387?–1438); he married Marjorie Dunbar (d. after 1429), perhaps a daughter of the Earl of Dunbar, and had issue.

2 David, Lord of Newdosk; he later became a priest.

3 Gerard (d. before 1421).

4 Ingelram (?), Bishop of Aberdeen (d.1458).

5 Marjorie; she married Sir William Douglas of Lochleven.

6 Elizabeth; she married Sir Robert Keith.

7 Elizabeth; she married Robert, Lord Erskine (d.1451/2); she may have been confused with her sister of the same name, and it is possible that they were one and the same person.

8 Isabella; she married Sir John Maxwell of Pollok, and had issue.

4 *Egidia* or *Jill*

She married Sir William Douglas of Nithsdale in c.1387, and had issue:

1 William, Lord of Nithsdale (d. after 1419).
2 Egidia (d. after 1438); she married Henry St Clair, Earl of Orkney (d.1421), and had issue.
Egidia died after 1388.
Robert II also had the following **illegitimate issue**:
By Moira Leitch (according to tradition):
1 John Stewart of Dundonald, a knight (d.1445/9); he married firstly Janet, daughter of John Sympil of Elistoun, and had issue. He married secondly Elizabeth, daughter of Sir William Graham of Kincardine.
By unknown mothers:
2 John Stewart, Lord of Burley (killed 1425).
3 John Stewart of Cairdney, a knight.
4 Alexander Stewart, Canon of Glasgow.
5 Alexander Stewart of Inverlunan, a knight.
6 Thomas Stewart, Archdeacon of St Andrews, Dean of Dunkeld.
7 James Stewart of Kinfauns.
8 Walter Stewart.

ROBERT II
He died on 19th April, 1390 at Dundonald Castle, Ayrshire, and was buried in Scone Abbey, Perthshire.

He was succeeded by his son John, who took the name Robert upon his accession.

ROBERT III

FATHER: *Robert II (see page 214).*
MOTHER: *Elizabeth Mure (see page 215, under Robert II).*
SIBLINGS: *(see page 215, under Robert III).*

ROBERT III
He was christened John, and took the name Robert upon his ac-

cession. He was born around c.1337/40. He was created Earl of Carrick on 22nd June, 1368, and styled Earl of Atholl on 17th October (?), c.1379, for this occasion only. He succeeded his father as King of Scotland on 19th April, 1390, and was crowned on 14th August, 1390 at Scone Abbey, Perthshire.

Robert III married, in c.1366/7 (although no evidence exists as to where):

Annabella

She was the daughter of Sir John Drummond of Stobhall by Mary, daughter of Sir William Montifex, and she was born in c.1350. She was crowned Queen Consort on 15th August, 1390 at Scone Abbey, Perthshire. She died in c. October ("Harvest-tide"), 1401 at Scone Palace, Perthshire, and was buried in Dunfermline Abbey, Fife.

Issue of marriage:

1 *David*

He was born on 24th October, 1378. He was created Earl of Carrick between 19th April, 1390 and 2nd January, 1391, and Duke of Rothesay (a title borne henceforth by the eldest son of a Scottish sovereign) on 28th April, 1398. He was created Earl of Atholl on 6th September, 1398. He died on 26th/27th March, 1402 in prison at Falkland Palace, Fife; he is said to have been starved to death, but he probably succumbed to dysentery. He was buried in Lindores Abbey, Fife.

David married, in February, 1399/1400, at Bothwell Church:

Marjorie

She was the daughter of Archibald Douglas, 3rd Earl of Douglas, by Joan, daughter of Thomas Moray of Bothwell. David Stewart was her first husband. She married secondly Sir Walter Haliburton of Dirleton (d. by 1447) (son of Isabella Stewart of Albany, granddaughter of Robert II) in 1403, and had issue:

1 John, Lord Haliburton (d.1452/4); he married Janet (d. after 1493), daughter of Sir William Seton of Seton, and had issue.

2 Walter (d. after 1433); he married Katherine, daughter of Alexander Chisholme.

3 Robert.

4 William (d. after 1439).

Marjorie died before 11th May, 1421.

2 *James I* *(see page 230).*

3 *Robert*

He died young.

4 *Margaret*

Known as the Lady of Galloway, she married Archibald Douglas, 4th Earl of Douglas and Duke of Touraine (1370?–killed 1424) before 1390, and had issue:

1 Archibald, 5th Earl of Douglas (1390–1439); he married Euphemia (d.1468), daughter of Sir Patrick Graham by Euphemia, granddaughter of Robert II, and had issue.

2 William; he married Marjorie Stewart, and had issue.

3 Elizabeth; she married John Stewart, Earl of Buchan (see page 219, under Robert II).

4 James, a knight (killed 1424).

Margaret died between 26th January, 1449 and September, 1456, probably at Thrieve Castle, Galloway, and was buried in the Collegiate Church of Lincluden, Dumfries.

5 *Mary or Mariot*

She married firstly George Douglas, 13th Earl of Angus (d.1402/5) after 24th May, 1397 (date of dispensation and contract), and had issue:

1 William, Earl of Angus (1398?–1437); he married Margaret (d. after 1484), daughter of Sir William Hay of Yester, and had issue.

2 Elizabeth; she married Alexander Forbes, 1st Lord Forbes (d.1448), and had issue. She married secondly Sir David Hay of Yester.

Mary married secondly Sir James Kennedy of Dunure (killed 1408) in 1404 (?), and had issue:

3 James, Bishop of Dunkeld and St Andrews (1405/6–1465).

4 Gilbert, Lord Kennedy (1406?–1480?); he married firstly Katherine, daughter of Herbert, 1st Lord Maxwell, and had issue. He married secondly Isabella (d.1484), daughter of Sir Walter Ogilvy of Lintrathen.

5 John, a knight (d. after 1434).

In July, 1409, Mary was granted a dispensation to marry Sir William Cunningham (d.1413/15), but it is doubtful whether the marriage ever took place. She married thirdly William, 1st Lord Graham of Kincardine (d.1424) on 13th November (?), 1413 (?) (certainly before 15th May, 1416), and had issue:

6 Patrick, Archbishop of St Andrews (d.1478).

7 Robert of Strathcarron and Fintry; he married firstly Janet, daughter of Sir Richard Lovel of Ballumbie, and had issue. He

married secondly Matilda, daughter of Sir James Scrymgeour of Dudhope, and had issue.

8 Son (name not known).
9 Son (name not known).
10 Son (name not known).

Mary married fourthly Sir William Edmondston of Duntreath in 1425, and had issue, although no details are recorded. She died in c.1458, and was buried in Strathblane Church, Scotland.

6 *Egidia*
She died unmarried.

7 *Elizabeth*
She married Sir James Douglas, 1st Lord of Dalkeith (d.1441) before 10th November, 1387, and perhaps as early as 24th March, 1381/2, and had issue:

1 William (1390–1425); he perhaps married Margaret Borthwick, although this is unlikely.
2 James, 2nd Lord of Dalkeith (d.1456/8); he married Elizabeth (d. after 1456), daughter of James Gifford of Sheriffhall, and had issue, including James, who married Joan, daughter of James I.
3 Henry of Dalkeith (d. by 1456); he married Margaret (d.1473), daughter of James Douglas, 7th Earl of Douglas, and had issue.

Elizabeth died before 1411.

Robert III also had the following **illegitimate issue**:
1 James Stewart of Kilbride.

ROBERT III

He died on 4th April, 1406 at Dundonald Castle, Ayrshire, and was buried in Paisley Abbey, Renfrewshire.

He was succeeded by his son James.

JAMES I

FATHER: *Robert III (see page 226).*
MOTHER: *Annabella Drummond (see page 227, under Robert III).*
SIBLINGS: *(see page 227, under Robert III).*

JAMES I
He was born on 25th July (?) (or in December), 1394 at Dunfermline Palace, Fife. He was created Duke of Rothesay and Earl of Carrick on 10th December, 1404. He succeeded his father as King of Scotland on 4th April, 1406 (although he was not proclaimed until June), whilst being held in captivity in England. He was not released to govern his kingdom until 1424, when he was crowned on 2nd or 21st May at Scone Abbey, Perthshire.

James I married, on 2nd, 10th or 13th February, 1424, at the Priory Church of St Mary Overy, Southwark, London:

Joan
She was the daughter of John Beaufort, Earl of Somerset, a grandson of Edward III, King of England, by Margaret Holland. She was crowned Queen Consort on 2nd or 21st May, 1424 at Scone Abbey, Perthshire. She married secondly Sir James Stewart ("the Black Knight") of Lorne (d.c.1448) before 21st September, 1439, and had issue:

1 John, Earl of Atholl (1440?–1512); he married firstly Margaret (d.c.1475), daughter of Archibald Douglas, 5th Earl of Douglas, and had issue. He married secondly Eleanor (d.1518), daughter of William Sinclair, Earl of Orkney and Caithness, and had issue.

2 James, Earl of Buchan (d.1498/1500); he married Margaret, daughter of Sir Alexander Ogilvy of Auchterhause, and had issue.

3 Andrew, Bishop of Moray (c.1443–1501).

Joan died on 15th July, 1445, at Dunbar Castle, and was buried in the Monastery of the Charterhouse, Perth.

Issue of marriage:

1 *Margaret*

She was born around Christmas, 1424. She married Louis, Dauphin of Viennois (afterwards Louis XI, King of France: d.1483) on 24th June, 1436 at Tours Cathedral, France, and again on 25th June, 1436 at Rheims Cathedral, France. She died on 16th August, 1445 at Châlons, France, and was buried in Châlons Cathedral. Her remains were later removed to the Church of St Léon, Thouars, France.

2 *Isabella*

She married Francis I, Duke of Brittany (d.1450) on 30th October, 1442, and had issue:

1 Mary; she married John, Viscount de Rohan.

2 Margaret; she married Francis II, Duke of Brittany, and had issue.

Isabella died in 1494.

3 *Eleanor*

She was born on 26th October, 1427. She married Sigismund von Tirol, Archduke of Austria (d.1496) around 12th/24th February, 1449. She died in 1480.

4 *Joan*

A mute, she was born in c.1428. She is alleged to have married James Douglas, Earl of Angus (d.1446), and she was certainly contracted to him on 18th October, 1440, but there is no evidence to show that the marriage ever took place. She did marry James Douglas, Earl of Morton (d.1493) before 15th May, 1459, and had issue:

1 John, Earl of Morton (by 1466–1513); he married Janet (d. after 1515), daughter of Patrick Crichton of Cranston-Riddell, and had issue.

2 Janet (d. by 1490); she married Patrick Hepburn, 1st Earl of Bothwell, (d.1508) and had issue.

3 James (d. after 1480).

4 Elizabeth (d. after 1479).

Joan died after 16th October, 1486, and was buried in Dalkeith Church, Midlothian.

5 *Alexander*

He was born on 16th October, 1430 at Holyrood Palace, Edinburgh, the elder of twins. He was Duke of Rothesay from birth. He died in 1430.

231

6 James II *(see page 233).*

7 Mary

She was designated Countess of Buchan, either at birth or upon her marriage. She married Wolfert van Borssele, Count of Grandpré and Lord of Campveere in Zeeland (d.1487) in 1444 at ter Veere, Zeeland, and had issue:

1 Unnamed son (d. young).

2 Unnamed son (d. young).

Mary died on 20th March, 1465, and was buried at Sandenburg-ter-Veere, Zeeland.

8 Annabella or Jean

She married firstly Louis of Savoy, Count of Geneva, afterwards King of Cyprus (d.1482) on 14th December, 1447 (or possibly 1455) at Stirling Castle. They divorced in 1458. Annabella married secondly George Gordon, 2nd Earl of Huntly (d.1501) before 10th March, 1459/60, and had issue:

1 Isabella (d. by 1485); she married William Hay, 3rd Earl of Erroll (d.1507).

Annabella was also possibly, but improbably, the mother of the following:

2 Janet (d.1559); she married Alexander Lindsay, Master of Crawford (d.1489), and had issue. She married secondly Patrick Grey, 3rd Lord Grey (d.1541); they were later divorced. She married thirdly Patrick Butler of Gormock, and fourthly James Halkerstoun of Southwood.

3 Elizabeth (d. after 1525); she married William Keith, 2nd Earl Marischal (d.1527), and had issue.

4 Margaret; she married Patrick Hepburn, 1st Earl of Bothwell (d.1508), and had issue.

5 Agnes; she married Sir Gilbert Hay of Kilmalamak.

6 (Highly improbable) Alexander, Earl of Huntly (d.1524); he married firstly Janet (d.1510), daughter of John Stewart, 1st Earl of Atholl, and had issue. He married secondly Elizabeth (d.1529/30), daughter of Andrew, 2nd Lord Hay.

Annabella was divorced from her second husband on 24th July, 1471 on grounds of consanguinity.

JAMES I

He was assassinated on 21st February, 1437 in the monastery of the Friars Preachers at Perth (or at Edinburgh), and was buried at Perth, either in the monastery of the Carthusians, or the monastery of the Black Friars, or the monastery of the Dominician Friars.

He was succeeded by his son James.

Recommended reading

E. W. M. Balfour-Melville: *James I, King of Scots* (Methuen, 1936).

L. A. Barbé: *Margaret of Scotland and the Dauphin Louis* (1917).

JAMES II

FATHER: *James I (see page 230).*
MOTHER: *Joan Beaufort (see page 230, under James I).*
SIBLINGS: *(see page 231, under James I).*

JAMES II

He was born on 16th October, 1430 at Holyrood Palace, Edinburgh, the younger of twins. He succeeded his brother Alexander as Duke of Rothesay, probably in 1430, being first so styled on 22nd April, 1431. He succeeded his father as King of Scotland on 21st February, 1437, and was crowned on 25th March, 1437 at Holyrood Abbey, Edinburgh.

James II married, on 3rd July, 1449 at Holyrood Abbey, Edinburgh:
Mary

She was the daughter of Arnold, Duke of Gueldres, by Katherine, daughter of Adolf, Duke of Cleves, and she was born in 1433. She was crowned Queen Consort on 3rd July, 1449 at Holyrood Abbey, Edinburgh. She died on 16th November or 1st December, 1463, and was buried in Holy Trinity Church, Edinburgh.

Issue of marriage:

1 *Unnamed child*

It was born on 19th May, 1450, and died the same day.

2 *Mary*

She was probably born in the summer of 1451 (?), certainly before 16th May, 1452. She married firstly Thomas Boyd, 1st Earl of Arran (d.1473/4) before 26th April, 1467/8, and had issue:

1 James, 2nd Lord Boyd (killed 1484).
2 Margaret or Grizelda (1468/73–after 1516); she married Alexander Forbes, 4th Lord Forbes (d. by 1491). She married secondly David Kennedy, 1st Earl of Cassilis (killed at Flodden, 1513).

Mary's marriage to Arran was declared null and void in c. February/March, 1473/4 (or, much less probably, in 1469). She married secondly James, 1st Lord Hamilton (1398?–1479) in c. February/March, and before April, 1474, and had issue:

1 James, Earl of Arran (1475?–1529); he married firstly Elizabeth (d.1544), daughter of Alexander, 2nd Lord Home; they were later divorced. He married secondly Janet (d.1522), daughter of Sir David Beaton of Creich, and had issue.
2 Robert, Seigneur d'Aubigny (d.1543).
3 Elizabeth (d. after 1531); she married Matthew Stewart, 2nd Earl of Lennox (killed at Flodden, 1513), and had issue.

Mary died in c. May, 1488 (?).

3 *James III* *(see page 237)*.

4 *Alexander*

He was born in c.1454/5, certainly before 8th July, 1455. He was created Baron of Annandale and styled Earl of March before 4th August (on 8th July?), 1455, and was created Duke of Albany between 4th July, 1457 and 3rd July, 1458. His titles and estates were all declared forfeit on 4th October, 1479, but he was restored in blood between June and December, 1482, and was created Earl of Mar and Garioch between 29th September and 10th October, 1482. His titles and estates were again declared forfeit on 27th June, 1483. He was killed in 1485 (?) in France at a tournament, and was buried in the Church of the Celestines, Paris.

Alexander married firstly, in c.1475 (although no evidence exists as to where):

Katherine

She was the daughter of William Sinclair, 3rd Earl of Orkney and Caithness, by Elizabeth, daughter of Archibald Douglas, 4th Earl of Douglas, by Margaret, daughter of Robert III. She was divorced on 2nd or 9th March, 1478, on grounds of propinquity, and her issue declared illegitimate. The divorce was ratified by Act of Parliament on 15th November, 1516.

Issue of marriage:

 (i) *Margaret*

 She married Sir Patrick Hamilton of Kincavil (d.1520), and was said to have had issue, but this is improbable. She died after 5th July, 1542.

 (ii) *Andrew*

 Nothing is known of him.

 (iii) *Son (name not known)*

 He was born in 1477, and died before 1479.

 (iv) *Alexander*

 He was born in the late 1470s. He took Holy Orders, and was appointed Prior of Whitehorn. He later became Abbot of Inchaffray. He was nominated Bishop of Moray on 31st May, 1528, and consecrated on 16th April, 1532. He died on 19th December, 1537, and was buried in Scone Abbey, Pertshire.

 Alexander had the following illegitimate issue:

 1 Alexander; he was legitimated in 1550.

 2 Alexander.

 3 Margaret; she married first Patrick Graham of Inchbrakie (d.1536), and had issue. She married secondly Colin Campbell of Glenurchy.

Alexander married secondly, between 16th January and 4th December, 1479, (and not on 10th February, 1480, as is sometimes stated) in France:

Anne

She was the daughter of Bertrand de la Tour, Count of Auvergne, by Louise, daughter of George de la Trémouille, Seigneur of Trémouille in Poitou. After the death of Alexander, she married secondly Louis, Count of La Chambre in Savoy (d.1517) on 17th February, 1487. She died on 13th October, 1512 at La Rochette Castle, Savoy, and was buried in the Carmelite monastery at La Rochette.

Issue of marriage:

(i) *John*

 He was born around 1481/5. He was first styled Duke of Albany in June, 1505, and was formally restored to the duchy between 8th April, 1514 and May, 1515. He died on 2nd June, 1536 at Mirefleur in the Auvergne, France, and was buried in the chapel of the Palace of Vic-le-Comte, France.

 John had the following illegitimate issue:

 By Jean Abernethy:

235

1 Eleanor; she married John de l'Hôpital, Comte de Choisy, and had issue.

John married, after 13th July, 1505 (date of dispensation) (although no evidence exists as to where):

Anne

She was the daughter of John de la Tour, Count of Auvergne and Lauraguais, by Joan, daughter of John of Bourbon, Count of Vendôme, and she was born after 1495. She became Countess of Auvergne and Boulogne in her own right. She died in June, 1524 at the Castle of St Saturnin, France.

5 *David*

He was born after 1454 and before 12th February, 1456. He was created Earl of Moray on 12th February, 1456, and died before 18th July, 1457.

6 *John*

He was born after October, 1456, perhaps in c. July, 1457, or in 1459 (?). He was created Earl of Mar and Garioch between 21st June, 1458 and 25th June, 1459. He forfeited all his estates in 1479/80, and died, or was murdered, either on 9th July, 1479, or—more probably—some time in 1480, at Craigmillar Castle, Edinburgh.

7 *Margaret*

Some sources state that she became the wife of William, Lord Crichton (d.1493), but this is almost certainly a fabrication. He abducted and seduced her to spite her brother, James III; there is no contemporary evidence for their marriage. Their clandestine union produced the following illegitimate issue:

1 Margaret Crichton (d. by 1546); she married firstly William Todrik of Edinburgh (d. by 1507), and secondly George Halkerstoun (killed at Flodden, 1513), and had issue. She married thirdly George Leslie, 2nd Earl of Rothes (d.1513), and had issue.

James II also had the following **illegitimate issue**:

1 John Stewart of Sticks and Ballechin; he married and had issue.

JAMES II

He was killed on 3rd August, 1460 when a cannon burst at the siege of Roxburgh; he was buried in Holyrood Abbey, Edinburgh.

He was succeeded by his son James.

JAMES III

FATHER: *James II (see page 233).*
MOTHER: *Mary of Gueldres (see page 233, under James II).*
SIBLINGS: *(see page 233, under James II).*

JAMES III

He was born either in May, or on 10th July, 1452 (or, less probably, on 20th July, 1451), either at the Castle of St Andrews, Fife, or at Stirling Castle. He was Duke of Rothesay from birth. He succeeded his father as King of Scotland on 3rd August, 1460, and was crowned on 10th August, 1460 at Kelso Abbey, Roxburghshire.

James III married, on 10th or 13th July, 1469, at Holyrood Abbey, Edinburgh:

Margaret

She was the daughter of Christian I, King of Denmark, Norway and Sweden, by Dorothea, daughter of John III, Margrave and Elector of Brandenburg, and she was born in c.1456/7. She died on 14th July, 1486 at Stirling Castle, and was buried in Cambuskenneth Abbey, Stirlingshire.

Issue of marriage:

1 *James IV (see page 238).*
2 *James*

He was born in March, 1476 (?), and is said to have been created Marquess of Ormonde at his baptism that year. He was created Duke of Ross on 23rd January, 1481 or 29th January, 1488. He was created Earl of Ardmannoch and Baron of Brechin and Nevar, and perhaps Duke of Ross, on 29th January, 1488. He was nominated Archbishop of St Andrews on 20th September, 1497, but was never consecrated. He died around 12th/17th January, 1504 in Edinburgh, and was buried in St Andrews Cathedral, Fife.

3 *John*
He was born between 16th July, 1479 and 12th July, 1480, perhaps in December, 1479. He was created Earl of Mar on 2nd March, 1486. He died unmarried on 11th March, 1503.

JAMES III
He was assassinated on 11th June, 1488 in a cottage at Milltown, near Bannockburn, and was buried in Cambuskenneth Abbey, Stirlingshire.

He was succeeded by his son James.

JAMES IV

FATHER: *James III (see page 237).*
MOTHER: *Margaret of Denmark (see page 237, under James III).*
SIBLINGS: *(see page 237, under James III).*

JAMES IV
He was born on 17th March, 1473, and was Duke of Rothesay, Earl of Carrick and Lord of Cunningham probably from birth. He succeeded his father as King of Scotland on 11th June, 1488, and was crowned on 26th June, 1488 at Scone Abbey, Perthshire.

James IV married, by proxy on 25th January, 1502 at Richmond Palace, Surrey, and in person on 8th August, 1503 at Holyrood Abbey, Edinburgh:

Margaret
She was the daughter of Henry VII, King of England, by Elizabeth of York, and she was born on 28th, 29th or 30th November, 1489, at the Palace of Westminster. She was crowned Queen Consort on 8th August, 1503 at Holyrood Abbey, Edinburgh. After the death of James, she married secondly Archibald Douglas, 6th Earl of Angus

(1490?–1557) on 4th, 5th or 6th August, 1514 at Kinnoul Church, and had issue:

1 Margaret (1515–1578); she married firstly Lord Thomas Howard (d.1537). She married secondly Matthew Stewart, 4th Earl of Lennox (1516–murdered 1571), and had issue, including Henry, Lord Darnley, who married Mary, Queen of Scots.

Margaret divorced her second husband on 11th March, 1527/8. She married thirdly Henry Stewart, 1st Lord Methven (1495/1500?–1552) 1552) before 2nd April, perhaps in March, 1528, and may have had issue (although this is improbable):

1 Dorothea (?); (d. young).

Margaret died on 8th or 18th October, or on 24th November, 1541 at Methven Castle, Perthshire, of "palsy", and was buried in the Carthusian Abbey of St John, Perth.

Issue of marriage:

1 *James*

He was born on 21st February, 1507 at Holyrood Palace, Edinburgh, and was Duke of Rothesay from birth. He died on 27th February, 1508 at Stirling Castle.

2 *Daughter (name not known).*

She was born on 15th July, 1508 at Holyrood Palace, Edinburgh, where she died the same day.

3 *Arthur*

He was born on 20th/21st October, 1509 at Holyrood Palace, Edinburgh, and was Duke of Albany from birth. He died on 14th/15th July, 1510 at Edinburgh Castle, and was buried in Holyrood Abbey, Edinburgh.

4 *James V (see page 241).*

5 *Daughter (name not known).*

She was born in November, 1512 at Holyrood Palace, Edinburgh, and died the same month.

6 *Alexander*

His father's posthumous son, he was born on 12th or 30th April, 1514 at Stirling Castle, and was styled Duke from birth: perhaps Duke of Ross. He died on 18th December, 1515 at Stirling Castle, and was buried in Cambuskenneth Abbey, Stirlingshire.

James IV also had the following **illegitimate issue:**

By Marion Boyd of Bonshaw:

1 Alexander Stewart, Archbishop of St Andrews (1493?–1513); he was killed at Flodden.

2 Katherine (d. after 1554); she married James Douglas, 3rd Earl of Morton (d.1548), and had issue.

By Janet Kennedy:

3 James Stewart, Earl of Moray (1499?–1544/5); he married Elizabeth, daughter of Colin Campbell, 3rd Earl of Argyll, and had issue.

4 Unnamed child (d. young).

5 Unnamed child (d. young).

By Margaret (murdered by poison, 1502), daughter of John, Lord Drummond:

6 Margaret (b.1497?); she married firstly John, Lord Gordon, Master of Huntly (d.1517), and had issue. She married secondly Sir John Drummond of Innerpeffray, and had issue.

By Isabella (d.1557), daughter of James Stewart, Earl of Buchan:

7 Janet or Joan (d.1560/63); she married Malcolm, 3rd Lord Fleming, and had issue.

JAMES IV
He was killed on 9th September, 1513 at the Battle of Flodden Field, Northumberland. He was perhaps buried in Sheen Abbey, Surrey, and his head may be interred in the Church of St Michael, Wood Street, City of London. A body said to be his was found at Hume Castle, but the identification is dubious. The only certain evidence of the fate of the King's body is the report that it was kept in a lumber room at Richmond Palace, Surrey, during the reign of Henry VIII. Reports that James IV was seen alive on the evening after Flodden and thereafter went on pilgrimage to the Holy Land, whence he never returned, are not to be trusted, although in 1527 Queen Margaret petitioned for a divorce from her second husband on the grounds that James was still alive in 1514 when her second marriage took place. James was succeeded by his son James.

Recommended reading
   R. L. Mackie: *King James IV of Scotland* (Oliver, 1958).
For Margaret Tudor, see:
   Hester W. Chapman: *The Sisters of Henry VIII* (Jonathan Cape, 1969).

JAMES V

FATHER: *James IV (see page 238).*
MOTHER: *Margaret Tudor (see page 238, under James IV).*
SIBLINGS: *(see page 239, under James IV).*

JAMES V
He was born on 10th, 11th or 15th April, 1512 at Linlithgow Palace, Fife, and was Duke of Rothesay from birth. He succeeded his father as King of Scotland on 9th September, 1513, and was crowned on 21st September, 1513 at the Chapel Royal, Stirling Castle. He was made a Knight of the Garter on 20th January, 1535.

James V married firstly, on 1st January, 1537 at the Cathedral of Notre Dame, Paris:

Madeleine
She was the daughter of Francis I, King of France, by Claude, daughter of Louis XII, King of France, and she was born on 10th August, 1520 at the Château of St Germain-en-Laye, Paris. She died on 2nd or 7th July, 1537 at Holyrood Palace, Edinburgh, and was buried in Holyrood Abbey, Edinburgh. There was no issue of the marriage.

James V married secondly, by proxy in May, 1538, and in person on 12th June, 1538 at St Andrews Cathedral, Fife:

Mary
She was the daughter of Claude I, Duke of Guise-Lorraine, by Antoinette, daughter of Francis de Bourbon, Duke of Vendôme, and she was born on 22nd November, 1515 at Bar-le-Duc, France. She married firstly Louis II, Duke of Longueville (d.1537) on 4th August, 1534, and had issue:

1 Francis, Duke of Longueville (1535–1551).
2 Louis (b.&d.1537).

241

Mary was crowned Queen Consort on 22nd February, 1540 at Holyrood Abbey, Edinburgh. She died on 10th/11th June, 1560 at Edinburgh Castle, and was buried in Rheims Cathedral, France.

Issue of marriage:

1 *James*

He was born on 22nd May, 1540 at St Andrews, Fife, and was Duke of Rothesay from birth. He died in April, 1541 at St Andrews, and was buried in Holyrood Abbey, Edinburgh.

2 *Arthur or Robert*

He was born in April, 1541 at Falkland Palace, Fife, where he died, aged 8 days, the same month. He was styled Duke of Albany during his lifetime. He was buried in Holyrood Abbey, Edinburgh.

3 *Queen Mary* (see page 243).

James V also had the following **illegitimate issue**:

By Elizabeth or Katherine, daughter of Sir John Carmichael:

1 John, Prior of Coldingham (1531/2–1563); he married Jean, daughter of Patrick Hepburn, 3rd Earl of Bothwell, and had issue.

By Margaret, daughter of John, 4th Lord Erskine:

2 James Stewart, Earl of Moray and Mar (1531?–murdered 1570); he married Agnes, daughter of William Keith, 3rd Earl Marischal, and had issue.

By Euphemia, daughter of Alexander, 1st Lord Elphinstone:

3 Robert, Earl of Orkney and Prior of Holyrood (1533–1591); he married Janet (d.1598), daughter of Gilbert Kennedy, 3rd Earl of Cassilis, and had issue.

By Elizabeth Shaw of Sauchie:

4 James Stewart, Abbot of Kelso and Melrose (1529?–1557).

By Christine Barclay:

5 James Stewart.

By Elizabeth, daughter of John Stewart, 3rd Earl of Lennox:

6 Adam, Prior of the Charterhouse (d.1606); he married Janet, daughter of William Ruthven.

By Elizabeth Bethune or Beaton:

7 Jean; she married Archibald Campbell, 5th Earl of Argyll (d.1573), from whom she was later divorced.

By unknown mothers:

8 Robert, Prior of Whithorn (d.1581).

9 Margaret.

JAMES V

He died on 14th December, 1542 at Falkland Palace, Fife, and was buried in Holyrood Abbey, Edinburgh.

He was succeeded by his daughter Mary.

Recommended reading
    C. Bingham: *James V, King of Scots* (Collins, 1971).
    R. K. Marshall: *Mary of Guise* (Collins, 1977).

QUEEN MARY

FATHER: *James V (see page 241).*
MOTHER: *Mary of Guise (see page 241, under James V).*
SIBLINGS: *(see page 242, under James V).*

QUEEN MARY

She was born on 7th or 8th December, 1542 at Linlithgow Palace. She succeeded her father as Queen of Scotland on 14th December, 1542, and was crowned on 9th September, 1543 at Stirling Castle. She became Queen Consort of France on 6th July, 1559 upon the accession of her first husband to the French throne.

Queen Mary married firstly, on 24th April, 1558 at the Cathedral of Notre Dame, Paris:

Francis II

He was the son of Henry II, King of France, by Catherine, daughter of Lorenzo de' Medici, Duke of Florence, and he was born on 16th January, 1544 at the Château of Fontainbleau-sur-Loire, France. He became King Consort of Scotland upon his marriage to Queen Mary. He succeeded his father as King of France on 6th July, 1559, and was crowned with Mary on 18th September, 1559, at Rheims Cathedral.

He died on 5th December, 1560 at Orléans, France, and was buried in the Cathedral of St Denis, Paris. There was no issue of the marriage.

Queen Mary married secondly, on 29th July, 1565 in the Chapel of Holyrood Palace, Edinburgh:

Henry

He was the son of Matthew Stewart, 4th Earl of Lennox, by Margaret, daughter of Archibald Douglas, 6th Earl of Angus by Margaret Tudor, daughter of Henry VII of England and widow of James IV. He was born on 7th December, 1545 at Temple Newsham, Yorkshire, and was styled Lord Darnley from birth. He was created Baron Ardmannoch and Earl of Ross on 15th May, 1565. He was proclaimed King of Scotland on 28th July, 1565, but was usually referred to as King Consort. He was created Duke of Albany on 20th July, 1565. He was murdered, possibly with Mary's connivance, on 10th February, 1567 at the Provost's House, Kirk o' the Field, Edinburgh, and was buried in Holyrood Abbey, Edinburgh.

Issue of marriage:

1 *James VI & I (see page 245).*

Queen Mary married thirdly, on 15th May, 1567, at Holyrood Palace, Edinburgh:

James

He was the son of Patrick Hepburn, 3rd Earl of Bothwell, and he was born in c.1535. He succeeded his father as 4th Earl of Bothwell in September, 1556. He married firstly Jean, daughter of George Gordon, 4th Earl of Huntly on 24th February, 1566; they were divorced on 3rd May, 1567 in the Protestant Commissary Court of Edinburgh, on grounds of his adultery; the marriage was also annulled on 7th May, 1567 on grounds of consanguinity. James was created Duke of Orkney and Earl of Shetland on 12th May, 1567. His titles and estates were all declared forfeit on 20th December, 1567. He died on 14th April, 1578 in prison at Dragsholm Castle, Denmark, and was buried in Faarevejle Church, Dragsholm, Denmark.

Issue of marriage:

2 & 3 *Stillborn twins*

They were born between 18th and 24th July, 1568 at Lochleven Castle.

QUEEN MARY

She was forced by the lords of Scotland to abdicate in favour of her son on 24th July, 1567. She fled to England, where she was kept a prisoner for 18 years by Elizabeth I. She plotted to take the English crown, and was executed on 8th February, 1587 at Fotheringhay Castle, Northants. She was buried in Peterborough Cathedral; her remains were removed to Westminster Abbey in 1612.

She was succeeded by her son James.

Recommended reading
There is a vast amount of material on Mary, Queen of Scots, but the best recent works are:

Antonia Fraser: *Mary, Queen of Scots* (Weidenfeld and Nicolson, 1969).

G. M. Thomson: *The Crime of Mary Stuart* (Hutchinson, 1967).

I. B. Cowan: *The Enigma of Mary Stuart* (Gollancz, 1971).

G. Donaldson: *Mary, Queen of Scots* (English Universities Press, 1974).

For Mary's husbands, see:

R. H. Mahon: *The Tragedy of Kirk o' Field* (1930).

R. Gore-Brown: *Lord Bothwell* (Collins, 1937).

JAMES VI

FATHER: *Henry Stewart, Lord Darnley (see page 244, under Queen Mary).*
MOTHER: *Mary, Queen of Scots (see page 243).*
SIBLINGS: *James VI did not have any siblings.*

JAMES VI

Christened James Charles, he was born on 19th June, 1566 at Edinburgh Castle, and was Duke of Rothesay from birth. He succeeded his father as Duke of Albany, Earl of Ross and Baron Ardmannoch on 10th February, 1567. He succeeded his mother as

King of Scotland on 24th July, 1567, and was crowned on 29th July, 1567 at the Church of the Holy Rood, Stirling.

JAMES VI
He succeeded Elizabeth I, last of the Tudor sovereigns, as King of England, on 24th March, 1603, thus founding the Royal House of Stuart (now using the French version of the name) and uniting for the first time the Crowns of England and Scotland under one monarch. Henceforth, the kingdom incorporating England and Scotland would be known as Great Britain.

For further details of the life of James VI and I, see under James I.

7. The House of Stuart

England and Scotland became one united kingdom in 1603 when James VI of Scotland became James I of England, and thus finally fulfilled Edward I's dream of the two countries being joined together.

The Stuart century was to see dramatic changes in the nature of the monarchy. James I believed in the Divine Right of Kings, a doctrine which held that the King was God's mouthpiece on earth, and could do and say no wrong. This was a view also held by James's son, Charles I, who, when thwarted by Parliament—a Parliament grown used to being consulted to a greater and greater degree by successive Tudor monarchs—tried to rule without it. He failed, and the country was plunged into a great civil war, which ended with the King's execution and the declaration of a Republic or "Commonwealth" under Oliver Cromwell, who became Lord Protector.

Of course, the monarchy did survive. Charles II lived in exile at the courts of Holland and France while Cromwell governed, but the Lord Protector's hold on the country died with him in 1658. His son Richard was weak and ineffectual, and it was not long before Parliament sent for Charles II, whose Restoration came about in May, 1660. Yet by then, the balance of power had been tipped firmly on the side of Parliament, and no British monarch after that date would ever enjoy the autonomy exercised by his predecessors. In fact, it was in the late 17th century that "constitutional" monarchy came into being in Britain; this meant that, instead of actually ruling the country, the sovereign reigned over it. The real power lay with an elected Parliament. In 1688, James II, a professed Catholic, realised that he could not hold the throne in the face of Protestant opposition, and fled the country. Parliament deemed that this act was tantamount to abdication, and invited William of Orange, husband of James' daughter Mary, to take the throne of Britain with his wife. In what was known as the "Bloodless" or "Glorious" Revolution, he accepted, and thus became the first "constitutional" monarch.

The unpopularity of James II, mainly due to his Catholicism, made King and Parliament realise that never again could Britain be successfully ruled by a monarch not of the Protestant faith of the Church of England. Thus, in 1701 was passed the Act of Settlement, barring a

Roman Catholic from ever ascending the throne of Britain, and a British sovereign from marrying a Roman Catholic. This same Act also settled the succession, in default of Stuart heirs, upon the successors of Sophia of Bohemia, a granddaughter of James I, who had married the Protestant Ernest Augustus, Elector of Hanover in Germany.

The Stuarts, like the Tudors, were not dynastically robust. Many of their children died young or were miscarried—poor Queen Anne suffering the most losses in this respect—and those who did grow to maturity died in the flower of youth of smallpox. Charles II's wife was barren, so was Mary II. Anne's children had all died by the time she ascended the throne. James II's only surviving son was rumoured, falsely, to have been a changeling, and spent his life in exile, plotting to regain the throne from which he, a Catholic, was debarred by the Act of Settlement. Therefore, when Queen Anne died in 1714, there was no suitable heir of the House of Stuart to succeed her. Thus it came about that Prince George, Elector of Hanover, a bucolic German who could speak no English, succeeded to the throne of Britain and founded the Hanoverian dynasty.

JAMES I

JAMES I
He succeeded Elizabeth I as King of England on 24th March, 1603, thus founding the Royal House of Stuart and uniting the crowns of England and Scotland under one monarch. (For details of his earlier life, see page 245, under James VI of Scotland in the previous chapter.) James was crowned on 25th July, 1603 in Westminster Abbey.

James VI & I married, by proxy on 20th or 24th August, 1589 at Kronborg Castle, Copenhagen, Denmark, and in person on 23rd

November, 1589 at Oslo, Norway, and again in person on 21st January, 1590 at Kronborg Castle:

Anne

She was the daughter of Frederick II, King of Denmark and Norway, by Sophia, daughter of Ulrich III, Duke of Mecklenburg-Güstrow. She was born on 14th October (date on coffin plate) (although the date is sometimes incorrectly given as 12th December), 1574 at Skanderborg Castle, Jutland, Denmark. She was crowned Queen Consort of Scotland on 17th May, 1590 at Holyrood Abbey, Edinburgh, and Queen Consort of England on 25th July, 1603 in Westminster Abbey. She died on 4th March (date on coffin plate) (although other sources state 1st or 12th March), 1619 at Hampton Court Palace, and was buried in Westminster Abbey.

Issue of marriage:

1 Henry Frederick

He was born on 19th February, 1594 at Stirling Castle, and was Duke of Rothesay, Earl of Carrick, and Lord of the Isles from birth. He became Duke of Cornwall upon the accession of his father to the throne of England on 24th March, 1603. He was made a Knight of the Garter on 14th June, 1603. He was created, and invested as, Prince of Wales and Earl of Chester on 4th June, 1610 at Westminster Abbey. He died on 6th (or, less probably, 12th or 16th) November, 1612 at St James's Palace, London, of typhoid, and was buried in Westminster Abbey.

2 Stillborn child

It was born at the end of July, 1595.

3 Elizabeth

She was born on 19th August, 1596 at Dunfermline Palace, Fife. She married Frederick Henry of Wittelsbach, Elector Palatine of the Rhine and later Frederick V, King of Bohemia (1596–1632) on 14th February, 1613 at the Chapel Royal, Whitehall Palace, London, and had issue:

1 Frederick Henry (1614–drowned 1629).
2 Charles Louis, Duke of Bavaria, Elector Palatine of the Rhine (1618–1680); he married firstly Charlotte (1627–1687), daughter of William V, Landgrave of Hesse-Cassel, and had issue, although they were later divorced. He married secondly, morganatically, Marie Susanne Louise (1634–1677), Raugräfin of Degenfeld, daughter of Baron Martin Christopher von Degenfeld, and had issue.
3 Elizabeth, Abbess of Hervorden (or Herford) (1618–1680).

4 Rupert, Duke of Cumberland (1619–1682); he married, morganatically, Frances Baird (d.1708). He also had illegitimate issue.

5 Maurice (1621–drowned 1654).

6 Louise Hollandine, Abbess of Maubisson, Pontoise (1622–1709).

7 Louis (1623–1624).

8 Edward (1625–1663); he married Anne (1616–1684), daughter of Charles I de Gonzaga, Duke of Nevers and Mantua, and had issue.

9 Henrietta Maria (1626–1651); she married Sigismund Ragotski, Prince of Siebenbürgen, Transylvania (1623?–1652).

10 John Philip Frederick (1627–killed 1650).

11 Charlotte (1628–1631).

12 Sophia; she married Ernest Augustus, Elector of Hanover, and became the mother of George I (see page 273, under George I).

13 Gustavus Adolphus (1632–1641).

Elizabeth became Queen Consort of Bohemia upon the accession of her husband to the throne of Bohemia on 27th August, 1619, and was crowned as such on 7th November, 1619 at Prague Cathedral, Bohemia. She was driven into exile with her husband in 1620 after he was deposed, and was afterwards known as "the Winter Queen". There is no foundation in the rumour that, after Frederick's death, she married secondly William Craven, Earl of Craven. She died on 3rd, 12th, 14th or 23rd February, 1662 at Leicester House, Leicester Fields, London, and was buried in Westminster Abbey.

4 Margaret

She was born on 24th December, 1598 at Dalkeith Palace, Scotland, and died in March, 1600 at Linlithgow Palace, Fife. She was buried in Holyrood Abbey, Edinburgh.

5 Charles I *(see page 252).*

6 Robert Bruce

He was born on 18th January or 18th February, 1602 at Dunfermline Palace, Fife. He was designated Duke of Kintyre and Lorne, Marquess of Wigtown, Earl of Carrick and Lord of Annerdail (Annandale?) on 2nd May, 1602. He died on 27th May, 1602 at Dunfermline Palace, Fife, and was buried in Dunfermline Abbey.

7 Stillborn son

He was born in May, 1603 at Stirling Castle.

8 *Mary*

She was born on 8th April, 1605 at Greenwich Palace, Kent. She died on 16th September or 16th December, 1607 at Stanwell Park, Staines, Middlesex, and was buried in Westminster Abbey.

9 *Sophia*

She was born on 22nd June, 1606 at Greenwich Palace, Kent, and died there on 23rd June, 1606. She was buried in Westminster Abbey.

Queen Anne also suffered at least three other miscarriages.

JAMES I & VI

He died on 27th March, 1625 at Theobalds Park, Herts., and was buried in Westminster Abbey.

He was succeeded by his son Charles.

Recommended reading

Antonia Fraser: *The Life and Times of King James* (Weidenfeld and Nicolson, 1973).

David Mathew: *King James I* (Eyre and Spottiswoode, 1967).

R. Ashton: *James I by his Contemporaries* (Hutchinson, 1969).

C. Bingham: *The Making of a King* (Collins, 1968).

A. G. R. Smith: *The Reign of James VI and I* (Macmillan, 1973).

G. P. V. Akrigg: *Jacobean Pageant* (Hamish Hamilton, 1962).

For James's family, see:

E. Carleton Williams: *Anne of Denmark* (Longmans, 1970).

Roy Strong: *Henry, Prince of Wales and England's Lost Renaissance* (1986).

J. Gorst-Williams: *Elizabeth, the Winter Queen* (Abelard, 1977).

Carola Oman: *Elizabeth of Bohemia* (Hodder and Stoughton, 1938, 1964).

CHARLES I

FATHER: *James I (see page 248).*
MOTHER: *Anne of Denmark (see page 249, under James I).*
SIBLINGS: *(see page 249, under James I).*

CHARLES I

He was born on 19th November, 1600 at Dunfermline Palace, Fife. He was created Duke of Albany, Marquess of Ormonde, Earl of Ross and Baron of Ardmannoch on 23rd December, 1600. He was created Duke of York and made a Knight of the Bath on 6th January, 1605. He was made a Knight of the Garter on 24th April, 1611. He succeeded his brother Henry as Duke of Cornwall and Rothesay on 6th November, 1612, and was created and invested as Prince of Wales and Earl of Chester on 4th November, 1616 at Whitehall Palace, London. He succeeded his father as King of Great Britain on 27th March, 1625, and was crowned on 2nd February, 1626 at Westminster Abbey. He was crowned in Scotland on 15th or 18th June, 1633 at Holyrood Abbey, Edinburgh.

Charles I married, by proxy on 1st or 11th May, 1625 at the Cathedral of Notre Dame, Paris, and in person on 13th June, 1625 at St Augustine's Church, Canterbury, Kent:

Henrietta Maria

She was the daughter of Henry IV (of Bourbon), King of France, by Mary, daughter of Francis I de' Medici, Grand Duke of Tuscany, and she was born on 26th November, 1609 at the Palace of the Louvre, Paris. She was not crowned Queen Consort; as a Roman Catholic, she would not allow herself to participate in the Anglican coronation ritual. She died on 21st August (O.S.) or 31st August (N.S.), 1669 at the Château of St Colombes, near Paris, and was buried in the Cathedral of St Denis, Paris.

Issue of marriage:

1 *Charles James*

He was born on 13th May, 1629 at Greenwich Palace, Kent, and was Duke of Cornwall and Rothesay from birth. He died the same day, and was buried in Westminster Abbey.

2 *Charles II (see page 255).*

3 *Mary Henrietta*

She married William II of Orange, and became the mother of William III. (See page 265, under William III).

4 *James II (see page 258).*

5 *Elizabeth*

She was born on 29th December, 1635 at St James's Palace, London. She died on 8th September, 1650 in prison at Carisbrooke Castle, Isle of Wight, and was buried in St Thomas's Church, Newport, Isle of Wight.

6 *Anne*

She was born on 17th March, 1637 at St James's Palace, London. She died on 5th November, 1640 at Richmond Palace, Surrey, of consumption, and was buried in Westminster Abbey.

7 *Katherine*

She was born on 29th June, 1639 at Whitehall Palace, London, and died the same day. She was probably buried in Westminster Abbey.

8 *Henry*

He was born on 8th July, 1640, probably at Oatlands Palace, Surrey, and was probably styled Duke of Gloucester from birth. He was made a Knight of the Garter on 4th April, 1653, and is said to have been created Duke of Gloucester and Earl of Cambridge on 13th May, 1659. He died on 13th (O.S.) or 23rd (N.S.) September, 1660 at Whitehall Palace, London, and was buried in Westminster Abbey.

9 *Henrietta Anne*

Known as "Minette", she was born on 16th June, 1644 at Bedford House, Exeter, Devon. She married Philip of Bourbon, Duke of Orléans (1640–1701) on 21st (O.S.) or 31st (N.S.) March, 1661 at the Chapel of the Palais Royale, Paris, and had issue:

1 Marie Louise (1662–1689); she married Charles II, King of Spain (1661–1700).

2 Miscarriage (1663).

3 Philip Charles, Duke of Valois (1664–1666).

4 Unnamed daughter (b.&d.1665).

5 Miscarriage (1666).

6 Miscarriage (1667).

7 Miscarriage (1668).

8 Anne Marie (1669–1728); she married Victor Amadeus II, Duke of Savoy and King of Sardina (1666–1732), and had issue, from whom descends the present day Stuart claimant to the throne of Great Britain (who is a Roman Catholic and therefore barred from the succession).

Henrietta Anne died on 15th or 30th June, 1670 at the Palace of St Cloud, near Paris, and was buried in the Cathedral of St Denis, Paris.

CHARLES I

He was tried and condemned to death by an illegally convened Parliament following the conclusion of the Civil War between the Cavaliers (supporters of the King) and the Roundheads (Parliamentarians), the latter being led by Oliver Cromwell. Charles I was convicted of treason against the state, and was executed on 30th January, 1649 outside Whitehall Palace, London. He was buried in St George's Chapel, Windsor. After his death, Britain was declared a Republic (for the only time in its history) with Oliver Cromwell as Lord Protector. Charles I was succeeded in name only by his son Charles, then in exile in France.

Recommended reading

John Bowle: *Charles the First* (Weidenfeld and Nicolson, 1975).

D. R. Watson: *Charles I* (Weidenfeld and Nicolson, 1972).

Christopher Hibbert: *Charles I* (Weidenfeld and Nicolson, 1968).

C. V. Wedgwood: *The King's Peace* (Collins, 1955), *The King's War* (Collins, 1958) and *The Trial of Charles I* (Collins, 1964)

Hugh Trevor-Roper: *The Trial and Execution of Charles I* (1966).

R. Lockyer: *The Trial of Charles I* (Longmans, 1959).

For Charles's family, see:

Elizabeth Hamilton: *Henrietta Maria* (Coward, McGann and Geoghegan, 1976).

Q. Bone: *Henrietta Maria, Queen of the Cavaliers* (Owen, 1973).

Carola Oman: *Henrietta Maria* (Hodder and Stoughton, 1936).

J. Doorn: *Mary Stuart, 1631–1660* (1966).

C. H. Hartmann: *The King, my Brother* (Heinemann, 1954), a biography of Henrietta Anne Stuart.

CHARLES II

FATHER: *Charles I (see page 252).*
MOTHER: *Henrietta Maria of France (see page 252, under Charles I).*
SIBLINGS: *(see page 253, under Charles I).*

CHARLES II

He was born on 29th May, 1630 at St James's Palace, London, and was Duke of Cornwall and Rothesay from birth. He was made a Knight of the Garter on 21st May, 1638, and around the same time was designated Prince of Wales and Earl of Chester, although he was never formally so created. He succeeded his father as King of Great Britain in name only on 30th January, 1649; Charles I was executed on that day, and Charles II was then an exile in France, whilst Cromwell took up the reins of government in Britain under the title Lord Protector. The Scots rallied to Charles' cause, and he was crowned on 1st January, 1651 at Scone Abbey, Perthshire. He was formally restored to the throne of Great Britain, Cromwell having died, on 29th May, 1660, and was crowned on 23rd April, 1661 at Westminster Abbey.

Charles II married, on 21st/22nd May, 1662 at the Church of St Thomas à Becket, Portsmouth:

Katherine Henrietta

She was the daughter of John IV, Duke of Braganza and King of Portugal, by Louisa Maria, daughter of John Manuel Domingo Perez de Guzman, 8th Duke of Medina-Sidonia, and she was born on 15th (O.S.) or 25th (N.S.) November, 1638, at Vila Viçosa, Lisbon, Portugal. She was never crowned as Queen Consort because she was a Roman Catholic and could not take part in the Anglican coronation ritual. She died on 30th November or 1st December, 1705 at Belém Palace or at Bemposta Palace, Lisbon, Portugal, and was buried in the monastery of Belém, Lisbon.

Issue of marriage:

1 *Miscarriage*

This occurred in 1662.

2 *Stillborn child*

It was born in February, 1666 at Oxford.

3 *Stillborn child*

It was born on 7th May, 1668.

4 *Stillborn child*

It was born on c.7th June, 1669.

Charles II also had the following **illegitimate issue**:

By Margaret de Carteret of Jersey:

1 James, a Jesuit (1646–1667?).

By Lucy (1630?–1658), daughter of Richard Walter of Haverford-west:

2 James Crofts, who took his wife's surname of Scott upon marriage, Duke of Monmouth (1649–executed 1685); he married Anne (1651–1732), daughter of Francis Scott, Earl of Buccleuch, and had issue.

Monmouth always claimed that his parents had been married, and that he was therefore legitimate; he also claimed to possess their marriage lines, but never produced them.

Lucy Walter bore another child, Mary, but Charles II was not her father.

By Elizabeth, afterwards Lady Shannon, daughter of Sir Robert Killigrew:

3 Charlotte Jemima Henrietta Maria FitzRoy (1650–1684); she married firstly James Howard, Earl of Suffolk (d.1669). She married secondly William Paston, 2nd Earl of Yarmouth (1653–1732), and had issue.

By Katherine, daughter of Thomas Pegge of Yeldersley, Derbyshire:

4 Charles FitzCharles, Earl of Plymouth (1657–1680); he married Bridget (d.1718), daughter of Thomas Osborne, 1st Duke of Leeds.

5 Katherine (1658–1759); she was a nun at Dunkirk, France.

6 Unnamed daughter (?) (Katherine?); her existence is conjectural. She is said to have died young.

By Barbara (1641–1709), daughter of William Villiers, 2nd Viscount Grandison, and wife of Roger Palmer, Earl of Castlemaine; she was later created Duchess of Cleveland in her own right:

7 Anne FitzRoy (1661–1722); she married Thomas Lennard, Earl of Sussex (1654–1715). She was possibly the daughter of Roger Palmer, although the King acknowledged her as his own.

8 Charles FitzRoy, Duke of Southampton and Cleveland (1662–1730); he married firstly Mary (1664–1680), daughter of Sir Henry Wood. He

married secondly Anne (1663–1745), daughter of Sir William Poultney of Misterton, Leics., and had issue.

9 Henry FitzRoy, Duke of Grafton (1663–1690); he married Isabella (d.1723), daughter of Henry Bennett, 1st Earl of Arlington, and had issue.

10 Charlotte FitzRoy (1664–1717); she married Edward Henry Lee, Earl of Lichfield (1663–1716), and had issue.

11 George FitzRoy, Duke of Northumberland (1665–1716); he married firstly Katherine (d.1714), daughter of Robert Wheatley of Bracknell, Berks., and secondly Mary (d.1738), daughter of Henry Dutton.

12 Barbara (who later assumed the name Benedicte when she entered the religious life) Prioress of Hôtel Dieu, Pontoise, France (1672–1737). She had illegitimate issue. Although Lady Castlemaine claimed that Charles II was Barbara's father, other evidence makes it more probable that she was the daughter of John Churchill, 1st Duke of Marlborough.

By Eleanor, known as "Nell" (1650–1687), daughter of Thomas Gwyn or Gwynne:

13 Charles Beauclerk, Duke of St Albans (1670–1726); he married Diana (d.1742), daughter of Aubrey de Vere, 20th Earl of Oxford, and had issue.

14 James, Lord Beauclerk (1671–1680).

By Louise Renée de Penencoët de Quérouialle (or Kérouaille), Duchess of Portsmouth in her own right (1649–1734):

15 Charles Lennox, Duke of Richmond, and Duke of Aubigny in France (1672–1723); he married Anne, daughter of Francis, Lord Brudenell, and had issue.

By Mary, or "Moll", Davies, an actress:

16 Mary Tudor (1673–1726); she married firstly Edward Ratcliffe, 2nd Earl of Derwentwater (1655–1705), and had issue. She married secondly Henry Graham of Levens (d.1707), and thirdly James Rooke.

CHARLES II

He died on 6th February, 1685 at Whitehall Palace, London, of the effects of a stroke, and was buried in Westminster Abbey.

He was succeeded by his brother James.

Recommended reading
   Antonia Fraser: *King Charles II* (Weidenfeld and Nicolson, 1979).
   Christopher Falkus: *Charles II* (Weidenfeld and Nicolson, 1972).

Maurice Ashley: *Charles II, the Man and the Statesman* (Weidenfeld and Nicolson, 1971).
Hebe Elsna: *Catherine of Braganza* (Robert Hale, 1967).

JAMES II

FATHER: *Charles I (see page 252).*
MOTHER: *Henrietta Maria of France (see page 252, under Charles I).*
SIBLINGS: *(see page 253, under Charles I).*

JAMES II

He was born on 14th (O.S.) or 24th (N.S.) October, 1633 at St James's Palace, London, and was designated Duke of York from birth. He was made a Knight of the Garter on 20th April, 1642. He was created Duke of York on 27th January, 1644, and Earl of Ulster on 10th May, 1659. He was created Duke of Normandy by Louis XIV of France on 31st December, 1660. He succeeded his brother Charles II as King of Great Britain on 6th February, 1685. Having converted to Roman Catholicism sometime previously, he was privately crowned by Catholic rites on 22nd April, 1685 at Whitehall Palace, London; he was crowned by the traditional Anglican ritual on 23rd April, 1685 at Westminster Abbey.

James II married firstly, in secret in November or on 24th December, 1659, at Breda, Holland (although doubts exist as to whether this ceremony ever took place), and publicly on 3rd September, 1660, at Worcester House, The Strand, London:

Anne

She was the daughter of Edward Hyde, 1st Earl of Clarendon, by Frances, daughter of Sir Thomas Aylesbury, and she was born on 12th or 22nd March, 1637 at Cranbourne Lodge, Windsor. She died on 31st March, 1671 at St James's Palace, London, of cancer, and was buried in Westminster Abbey.

Issue of marriage:

1 *Charles*

He was born on 22nd October, 1660 at Worcester House, The Strand, London, and was designated Duke of Cambridge. He died on 5th May, 1661 at Whitehall Palace, London, and was buried in Westminster Abbey.

2 *Mary II* *(see page 266).*

3 *James*

He was born on 11th or 12th July, 1663 at St James's Palace, London. He was created Duke and Earl of Cambridge and Baron of Dauntsey, Wilts. on 23rd August, 1664, and was made a Knight of the Garter on 3rd December, 1666. He died on 20th June, 1667 at Richmond Palace, Surrey, and was buried in Westminster Abbey.

4 *Queen Anne* *(see page 267).*

5 *Charles*

He was born on 4th July, 1666 at St James's Palace, London, and was designated Duke of Kendal, Earl of Wigmore and Baron Holdenby; there is no evidence of any formal creation. He died on 22nd May, 1667 at St James's Palace, London, and was buried in Westminster Abbey.

6 *Edgar*

He was born on 14th September, 1667 at St James's Palace, London. He was created Duke and Earl of Cambridge and Baron of Dauntsey, Wilts. on 7th October, 1667. He died on 8th June, 1671 at Richmond Palace, Surrey, and was buried in Westminster Abbey.

7 *Henrietta*

She was born on 13th January, 1669 at Whitehall Palace, London. She died on 15th November, 1669 at St James's Palace, London, and was buried in Westminster Abbey.

8 *Katherine*

She was born on 9th February, 1671, probably at Whitehall Palace, London (less probably at Richmond Palace, Surrey). She died on 5th December, 1671 at St James's Palace, London, and was buried in Westminster Abbey.

James II married secondly, by proxy on 20th (O.S.) or 30th (N.S.) September, 1673 at the Ducal Palace, Modena, Italy, and in person on 21st November, 1673 at Dover, Kent:

Mary Beatrice Eleanor Anne Margaret Isabella

Baptised Maria, but called Mary from the time of her marriage, she was the daughter of Alfonso d'Este III, Duke of Modena, by Laura, daughter of Girolamo Martinozzi, and she was born on 25th September (O.S.) or 5th October (N.S.), 1658 at the Ducal Palace, Modena, Italy. She was crowned Queen Consort by Catholic rites on 22nd April, 1685 at Whitehall Palace, London, and by Anglican rites on 23rd April, 1685 at Westminster Abbey. She died on 7th/8th May, 1718 at the Château of St Germain-en-Laye, Paris, of cancer, and was buried in the Abbey of the Visitation of St Mary, Chaillot, France (although her body was later destroyed during the French Revolution).

Issue of marriage:

1 *Stillborn child*

It was born in March or May, 1674.

2 *Katherine Laura*

She was born on 10th January, 1675 at St James's Palace, London. She died on 3rd October, 1675 at St James's Palace, London, of convulsions, and was buried in Westminster Abbey.

3 *Stillborn child*

It was born in October, 1675.

4 *Isabella*

She was born on 18th (O.S.) or 28th (N.S.) August, 1676 at St James's Palace, London. She died on 2nd or 4th March, 1681 at St James's Palace, and was buried in Westminster Abbey.

5 *Charles*

He was born on 7th November, 1677 at St James's Palace, London, and was designated Duke of Cambridge. He died on 12th December, 1677 at St James's Palace, of smallpox, and was buried in Westminster Abbey.

6 *Elizabeth*

She was born and died in c.1678.

7 *Stillborn child*

It was born in February, 1681.

8 *Charlotte Maria*

She was born on 16th August, 1682, either at St James's Palace, London, or at Windsor Castle. She died on 6th October, 1682 at St James's Palace, of convulsions, and was buried in Westminster Abbey.

9 *Stillborn child*

It was born in October, 1683.

10 Stillborn child
It was born in May, 1684.

11 James Francis Edward
Called "James III", according to Roman Catholic doctrine, he was also known as the "Chevalier de St George" or "The Old Pretender". He was born on 10th June, 1688 at St James's Palace, London. There were widespread rumours at the time that he was a changeling, smuggled into the Queen's bed in a warming pan, but this was mere political invention. What is certain is that the birth of a Catholic heir ensured that James II's days as King were numbered. James was Duke of Cornwall and Rothesay from birth, and was styled Prince of Wales and Earl of Chester from birth. His father abdicated when he was a baby, and he spent his life in exile in France or Italy. He was made a Knight of the Garter in 1692. He succeeded his father as Stuart pretender to the throne of Great Britain (from which he was barred by the Act of Settlement) on 16th September, 1701, and was proclaimed in France as "James III of England and VIII of Scotland". He was attainted by Act of Parliament on 2nd March, 1702, and forfeited all his British titles. He died on 1st January, 1766 in Rome, where he was buried in St Peter's Basilica in the Vatican.

James married, by proxy on 9th (O.S.) or 19th (N.S.) May, 1719 at Bologna, Italy, and in person on 1st or 3rd September, 1719 at Montefiascone Cathedral, Italy:
Maria Casimire Clementina
She was the daughter of Prince James Louis Henry Sobieski of Poland, by Hedwig Elizabeth Amelia, daughter of Philip William, Elector of Pfalz-Neuburg, and she was born on 6th (O.S.) or 17th/18th (N.S.) July 1702. She was called "Queen of Great Britain" by adherents of the Stuarts. She died on 12th or 18th January, 1735 at the Apostolic Palace, Rome, and was buried in St Peter's Basilica in the Vatican.
Issue of marriage:
(i) *Charles Edward Louis John Philip Casimir Sylvester Maria*
Called "Charles III" by his adherents, he was also known as the "Chevalier de St George", "The Young Pretender" and "Bonnie Prince Charlie". He was born on 31st December, 1720 at the Palazzo Muti, Rome, and was styled "Prince of Wales" from birth. He sometimes styled himself "Count of Albany". On the death of his father on 1st January, 1766, he succeeded him as Stuart pretender to the throne of Great Britain, styling

himself "Charles III". He died on 30th/31st January, 1788 at the Palazzo Muti, Papazurri, Rome, and was buried in Frascati Cathedral, Italy. His remains were later removed to St Peter's Basilica in the Vatican.

Charles had the following illegitimate issue:
By Clementina Maria Sophia Walkinshaw, Countess of Alberstroff (d.1802):

1 Charlotte, Countess of Albany in her own right (1753–1789). She had illegitimate issue.

Charles married, by proxy on 28th March, 1772, in Paris, and in person on 17th April, 1772 at the Chapel of the Palazzo Compagnani, Marefoschi, Macerata, Ancona, Italy:
Louise Maximiliana Caroline Emanuèle
She was the daughter of Gustavus Adolphus, Prince of Stolberg-Gedern, by Elizabeth Philippine Claudine, daughter of Maximilian Emanuel, Prince of Hornes and of the Empire. She was born on 20th or 21st September, 1752 at Mons, Hainault, Flanders. After her marriage, she was styled "Queen of Great Britain" by adherents of the Jacobite cause. It is possible, but not probable, that she made a second marriage, either with Count Vittorio Alfieri, or with Francis Xavier Fabre. She died on 29th January, 1824 at Florence, Italy, and was buried in the Church of Santa Croce, Florence.

(ii) *Henry Benedict Maria Clement Thomas Francis Xavier*
He was born on 6th or 21st March, 1725 at the Palazzo Muti, Papazurri, Rome, Italy, and was styled "Duke of York" from birth by adherents of the Jacobite cause. He entered the Roman Catholic Church, and was ordained Cardinal Deacon on 30th June, 1747 and Cardinal of Santa Maria, Portici on 3rd July, 1747, before being ordained as a priest on 1st September, 1748. He was known thereafter as "Cardinal York". He was provided to the Archbishopric of Corinth on 19th November, 1758, but was translated to the Bishopric of Frascati, Italy, on 13th July, 1761. He succeeded his brother Charles as Pretender to the throne of Great Britain on 30th/31st January, 1788, styling himself "Henry IX". He died on 13th July, 1807 at Frascati, Italy, and was buried in St Peter's Basilica in the Vatican, Rome, after being briefly laid to rest in the church of St Andrea della Valle, Rome.

12 *Louisa Maria Theresa*
She was baptised Louisa Maria, and received the name Theresa at

her confirmation. She was born on 18th (O.S.) or 28th (N.S.) June, 1692 at the Château of St Germain-en-Laye, Paris, and died there on 8th (O.S.) or 18th (N.S.) April, 1712. She was buried in the Chapel of St Edmund in the Church of the English Benedictines, Rue St Jacques, Paris, but later transferred to St Germain-en-Laye by order of George IV.

James II also had the following **illegitimate issue**:

By Arabella (1648–1730), daughter of Sir Winston Churchill and sister of John Churchill, 1st Duke of Marlborough:

1 Henrietta FitzJames (1667–1730); she married firstly Henry, 1st Baron Waldegrave of Chewton, Somerset (1661–1690), and had issue. She married secondly Piers Butler, 2nd Viscount of Galmoye (d.1740).

2 James FitzJames (1670–1734), Duke of Berwick; he married firstly Honora (1674–1697), daughter of William Bourke, Earl of Clanricarde, and had issue. He married secondly Anne (d.1751), daughter of Henry Bulkely, and had issue.

3 Henry FitzJames, Duke of Albemarle (1673–1702); he married Marie Gabrielle (1675–1741), daughter of John d'Audibert, Count of Lussan, and had issue.

4 Arabella (1674–1704); she became a nun at Pontoise, France, under the name Ignatia.

Arabella Churchill may have borne James other children who died young prior to 1670.

By Katherine, Countess of Dorchester (1657–1717), daughter of Sir Charles Sedley:

5 Katherine Darnley (1679/81–1743); she married firstly James Annesley, Earl of Anglesey (d.1702), but they later divorced. She married secondly John Sheffield, Duke of Buckingham and Normanby (1647–1721), and had issue.

6 James Darnley (1684–1685).

7 Charles Darnley (d. young).

JAMES II

He was deemed by Parliament to have abdicated on 11th December, 1688 by fleeing the country to exile in France. He was formally deposed by Parliament on 23rd December, 1688. He died on 16th September, 1701 at the Château of St Germain-en-Laye, near Paris. His body was temporarily buried in the Chapel of St Edmund in the Church of the English Benedictines in the Rue St Jacques, Paris, whilst hopefully awaiting eventual transportation to England for burial in Westminster Abbey. The body seems to have disappeared, however, during the French Revolution, although there are reports that it was found and reinterred at St Germain-en-Laye by order of George IV.

An Interregnum followed the deposition of James II, who was succeeded two months later by his son-in-law William of Orange and his daughter Mary as joint sovereigns.

Recommended reading

For James II, see:

Meriol Trevor: *The Shadow of a Crown* (Constable, 1988).

Maurice Ashley: *James II* (Dent, 1977).

Peter Earle: *James II* (Weidenfeld and Nicolson, 1972).

Jock Haswell: *James II: Soldier and Sailor* (Hamish Hamilton, 1972).

For James's family, see:

J. R. Henslowe: *Anne Hyde* (1915).

Carola Oman: *Mary of Modena* (Hodder and Stoughton, 1962).

B. Bevan: *I was James the Second's Queen* (Robert Hale, 1963).

M. Hopkirk: *Queen over the Water* (1953).

Peggy Miller: *James* (Allen and Unwin, 1971) (a biography of the Old Pretender).

B. Bevan: *King James III of England* (Robert Hale, 1962).

Peggy Miller: *A Wife for the Pretender* (Allen and Unwin, 1969).

Susan McClean Kybett: *Bonnie Prince Charlie* (Unwin Hyman, 1988).

H. Douglas: *Charles Edward Stuart* (Robert Hale, 1975).

M. McClaren: *Bonnie Prince Charlie* (Hart-Davis, 1972).

Eric Linklater: *The Prince in the Heather* (Macmillan, 1965).

H. M. Vaughan: *The Last Stuart Queen* (Methuen, 1910) (a biography of Louise of Stolberg).

Brian Fothergill: *The Cardinal King* (Faber, 1958).

WILLIAM III AND MARY II

WILLIAM III

FATHER: *William (II)*

He was the son of Frederick Henry, Prince of Orange, by Amalia, daughter of John Albert I, Count of Solms-Braunfels, and he was born on 27th May, 1626 at The Hague, Holland. He married Mary Stuart on 2nd May, 1641 at the Chapel Royal, Whitehall Palace, London. He was made a Knight of the Garter on 2nd March, 1645. He succeeded his father as William II, Stadtholder of the United Provinces of the Netherlands in March, 1647. He died on 6th November, 1650 at the Binnenhof Palace at The Hague, of small-pox, and was buried at Delft, Holland.

MOTHER: *Mary Henrietta*

She was the daughter of Charles I, King of Great Britain, by Henrietta Maria of France, and she was born on 4th or 29th November, 1631 at St James's Palace, London. She was designated Princess Royal in c.1642, thus establishing the tradition that the eldest daughter of a British sovereign bears the title Princess Royal. She died on 24th December, 1660 at Whitehall Palace, London, of smallpox, and was buried in Westminster Abbey.

SIBLINGS: *William III did not have any siblings.*

WILLIAM III

Baptised William Henry, he was born on 4th (O.S.) or 14th (N.S.) November, 1650 at the Binnenhof Palace, The Hague, Holland. He was Stadtholder of Holland from birth, his father having predeceased him, but was deprived of the title during his childhood. He was made a Knight of the Garter on 25th April, 1653. He was designated Count of Nassau-Dillenburg, and reinstated as Stadtholder of Holland in 1672. He acceded to the throne of Great Britain as joint sovereign with his wife Mary (the rightful heir) on 13th February, 1689, following the Interregnum after the abdication and deposition of his father-in-law James II. William was crowned on 11th April, 1689 at Westminster Abbey. He died on 8th March, 1702 at Kensington Palace, London, and was buried in Westminster Abbey.

William III married, on 4th November, 1677, either at St James's Palace or at Whitehall Palace, London:

MARY II
FATHER: *James II (see page 258).*
MOTHER: *Anne Hyde (see page 258, under James II).*
SIBLINGS: *(see page 259, under James II).*

MARY II
She was born on 30th April, 1662 at St James's Palace, London. She was proclaimed Queen of Great Britain on 13th February, 1689 following the deposition of her father and the Interregnum; she reigned as joint sovereign with her husband, with whom she was crowned on 11th April, 1689. She died on 28th December, 1694 at Kensington Palace, London, of smallpox, and was buried in Westminster Abbey.

Issue of marriage:
1 *Stillborn child*
   It was born in c. April, 1678 at Breda, Holland.
2 *Stillborn child*
   It was born in September, 1678 at Hanserlaersdyck, Holland.
3 *Stillborn child*
   It was born in February, 1680 at The Hague, Holland.

WILLIAM III
After **Mary II**'s death, **William III** reigned alone, the rightful heir, Anne Stuart, having given up her place in the succession to him for the term of his life.

William was succeeded by Anne in 1702.

Recommended reading
   H. and. B. Van Der Zee: *William and Mary* (Macmillan, 1973).
   J. Miller: *William and Mary* (Weidenfeld and Nicolson, 1974).
   S. B. Baxter: *William III* (Longmans, 1966).
   David Ogg: *William III* (Collins, 1956).

Maurice Ashley: *The Glorious Revolution of 1688* (Hodder and Stoughton, 1966).

Elizabeth Hamilton: *William's Mary* (Coward, McGann and Geoghegon, 1972).

Hester W. Chapman: *Mary II, Queen of England* (Jonathan Cape, 1953).

QUEEN ANNE

FATHER: *James II (see page 258).*
MOTHER: *Anne Hyde (see page 258, under James II).*
SIBLINGS: *(see page 259, under James II).*

QUEEN ANNE

She was born on 6th February, 1665 at St James's Palace, London. She succeeded her brother-in-law William III as Queen of Great Britain on 8th March, 1702, and was crowned on 23rd April, 1702 at Westminster Abbey. In 1707, she adopted the royal style Queen of Great Britain, France and Scotland, following the Act of Union.

Queen Anne married, on 28th July, 1683 at the Chapel Royal, St James's Palace, London:

George

He was the son of Frederick III of Oldenburg, King of Denmark, by Sophia Amelia, daughter of George, Duke of Brunswick-Lüneberg, and he was born on 2nd April (date on coffin plate), 29th February, 11th November or 21st April, 1653 at Copenhagen, Denmark. He was naturalised as an English subject on 20th September, 1683, and made a Knight of the Garter on 1st January, 1684. He was created Duke of Cumberland, Earl of Kendal and Baron Wokingham ("Ockingham") on 6th April, 1689. During Queen Anne's reign he was styled Prince George, never King Consort. He died on 28th

October, 1708 at Kensington Palace, London, and was buried in Westminster Abbey.

Issue of marriage:

1 *Stillborn daughter*

She was born on 12th May, 1684, and was buried in Westminster Abbey.

2 *Mary or Marie*

She was born on 2nd June, 1685 at Whitehall Palace, London. She died on 8th February, 1687 at Windsor Castle of "an acute infection", and was buried in Westminster Abbey.

3 *Anne Sophia*

She was born on 12th May, 1686 at Windsor Castle. She died there on 2nd February, 1687, and was buried in Westminster Abbey.

4 *Stillborn child*

It was born between 20th January and 4th February, 1687, probably on 21st January, and was buried in Westminster Abbey.

5 *Stillborn son*

He was born on 22nd October, 1687, and was buried in Westminster Abbey on the day of his birth.

6 *Miscarriage*

It occurred on 16th April, 1688.

7 *Stillborn child (?)*

It was perhaps born late in 1688.

8 *William Henry*

He was born on 24th July, 1689 at Hampton Court Palace, and was styled Duke of Gloucester from birth, although he was never formally so created. He was made a Knight of the Garter on 6th January, 1695. He died on 30th July, 1700 at Windsor Castle, of hydrocephalus, and was buried in Westminster Abbey.

9 *Mary*

She was born on 14th October, 1690 at St James's Palace, London, where she died, aged 2 hours, the same day. She was buried in Westminster Abbey.

10 *George*

He was born on 17th April, 1692 at Syon House, Brentford, Middlesex where he died, aged a few minutes, the same day. He was buried in Westminster Abbey.

11 *Stillborn daughter*

She was born on 23rd March, 1693 at Berkely House, St James's Street, London, and was buried in Westminster Abbey.

12 *Stillborn child*
It was born on 21st January, 1694, and may have been a daughter.
13 *Stillborn daughter*
She was born on 17th or 18th February, 1695.
14 *Stillborn son*
Of six months' growth, he was born on 25th March, 1696.
15 *Stillborn twins*
A male foetus of 2 or 3 months' growth and a male foetus of 7 months' growth were born on 25th March, 1697, and were buried in St George's Chapel, Windsor.
16 *Stillborn son*
He was born in early December (before 10th December), 1697.
17 *Stillborn son*
He was born on 15th September, 1698 at Windsor Castle, and was buried in St George's Chapel, Windsor.
18 *Stillborn son*
He was born on 25th January, 1700, and was buried in Westminster Abbey.

QUEEN ANNE
She died on 1st August, 1714 at Kensington Palace, London, and was buried in Westminster Abbey. Although she conceived 19 children, none survived her, and she was the last Stuart sovereign.

She was succeeded by her third cousin, Prince George of Hanover.

Recommended reading
Edward Gregg: *Queen Anne* (Routledge, 1980).
D. Green: *Queen Anne* (Collins, 1970).
Iris Butler: *Rule of Three* (Hodder and Stoughton, 1967).
Hester W. Chapman: *Queen Anne's Son* (Jonathan Cape, 1954).

8. The House of Hanover

When Queen Anne died in 1714, her nearest living Protestant relative was her third cousin, Prince George of Hanover, who was the grandson of Elizabeth Stuart, the Winter Queen of Bohemia and daughter of James I; Elizabeth's daughter Sophia had married the Elector of Hanover. When the Act of Settlement was passed in 1701, investing the succession in the House of Hanover, Sophia was still alive and hopeful of becoming Queen of Great Britain herself in the fullness of time; this was not to be, as she died only weeks before Queen Anne passed away, and it was her son George who succeeded instead.

There were, however, still living in France at that time, members of the House of Stuart, the children of James II, notably Prince James Francis Edward, the Old Pretender (as he later came to be called). He was a Roman Catholic, and therefore barred from the succession, yet he maintained all his life the belief that he was the rightful King of Great Britain, and his adherents, known as Jacobites, led an uprising on his behalf in 1715 in an ill-fated attempt to restore him to the throne. It failed miserably, and James never took up arms again in his cause. It was left to his son known to history as Bonnie Prince Charlie, to uphold the Jacobite claims, and in 1745 a further uprising saw the young Prince at first victorious. The bloody defeat of his supporters at Culloden, however, put an end once and for all to any hopes the Stuarts had of ever regaining the throne. In exile in Italy, they quietly continued to style themselves Kings of Great Britain: James III, Charles III, and lastly Henry IX (brother of Charles), but they were no longer a threat to the House of Hanover, and their line came to an end in 1807.

The Hanoverians reigned over Great Britain for nearly 200 years, with the succession passing peacefully from father to son, or grandson, and, finally, to the girl who became the illustrious Queen Victoria. Yet the sovereigns of this particular dynasty all manifested a peculiar resentment against their heirs designate: George I, George II and George III all disliked their eldest sons vehemently; George IV had a poor relationship with his only daughter, Princess Charlotte; and Queen Victoria never understood and was irritated by the future Edward VII. It was not, on a personal level, a happy dynasty.

Furthermore although it was a fruitful dynasty, it was fraught with marital scandals. George I divorced his wife for adultery, and shut her up in a castle for the rest of her life. Several brothers and sons of George III made morganatic, or unofficial, and therefore unsuitable, marriages, most notably the future George IV. Some Hanoverian males lived openly in sin with their mistresses, many for years. It was the marriages of his brothers that shocked George III, a moral-minded man, into passing the Royal Marriages Act in 1772. This Act, which still applies to the royal family today, provides that any marriage made by any of the descendants of George II without the consent of the sovereign automatically becomes null and void. Should the sovereign withhold consent to a projected marriage, the Prince or Princess wishing to make it may wait until he or she reaches the age of 25 and then apply to the Privy Council for assent. This being given, the marriage may be lawfully entered into. It will be seen in the following chapters what effect the Act had upon the personal lives of members of the House of Hanover.

Modern monarchy evolved during the Hanoverian period. Increasingly, the sovereign reigned, rather than ruled, over his/her people. The rights of the sovereign became confined to the rights of being informed, of advising, and of warning those in whom actual power was invested, i.e. the government.

The monarch came to be seen more as a figurehead than as a participant; George II was the last king to lead his troops into battle, at Dettington in 1747. Later sovereigns confined their martial activities to reviewing their armed forces, and undertaking military training. As Head of the Church of England, the monarch was expected to set a moral example. Few of the Hanoverians were capable of this. It was left to George III and Queen Charlotte, Queen Adelaide, and Queen Victoria and Prince Albert to set moral standards acceptable to their people, and which we now think of as Victorian. In this way, the monarchy became very much a domestic institution, and to this day a constitutional sovereign leading an exemplary family life has a very much better chance of achieving popularity than one who might be described as "playboy". One is reminded, when reflecting upon this, of the Victorian lady who went to watch a performance of Shakespeare's *Antony and Cleopatra*: "So unlike the home life of our own dear Queen!" she commented.

The Hanoverians were very much a German dynasty; even Queen Victoria spoke with a German accent. They married German princes or princesses. Apart from George IV and Victoria, they had little time for the arts, although George I and George II patronised Handel. They were not popular monarchs, and suffered scathing portrayals by the caricaturists of their time. They were licentious and uncouth; even Victoria was highly sexed, and in her youth revelled in being "decadent". George I and George II saw Britain as secondary in importance to Hanover, which did not endear them to their new subjects. Yet this dynasty, which began so unpromisingly with George I, ended in a blaze of glory as Victoria, the Queen-Empress, celebrated her Diamond Jubilee four years before her death in 1901, amidst scenes of unprecedented adulation and reverence. Thus was the monarchy pulled from the mire to the pinnacle of respectability where it has remained, almost constantly, to this very day.

GEORGE I

FATHER: *Ernest Augustus*

He was the son of George, Duke of Brunswick-Lüneberg, by Anne Eleanor, daughter of Louis, Landgrave of Hesse-Darmstadt, and he was born on 20th or 30th November, 1629/30 at Herzberg, Germany. He married Sophia of Bohemia on 30th September, 1658 at the Castle Chapel, Heidelberg, Germany. He was elected Prince Bishop of Osnabrück in 1661, and succeeded his father as Duke of Hanover and Brunswick-Lüneberg in 1679; he was created Elector of Hanover in 1692 (this conferred upon him the right to elect the German Emperor). He died on 23rd January, 1698 at Schloss Herrenhausen, Hanover, and was buried in the Chapel of the Leine Schloss, Hanover. His remains were later removed to the Chapel of Schloss Herrenhausen, Hanover.

Ernest perhaps had the following illegitimate issue:
By Clara Elizabeth Meisenburg, wife of Francis Ernest, Count von Platen:

1 Sophia Charlotte, Countess of Platen, Baroness von Kielmansegge, Countess of Leinster, Baroness of Brentford, and Countess of Darlington (1673?–1725). She later became the mistress of her half-brother, George I.

2 George Louis.

3 Charles Augustus.

4 Caroline

By the Marchesa Paleotti of Bologna:

5 Unnamed son.

6 Laura (?).

MOTHER: *Sophia*

She was the daughter of Frederick V, King of Bohemia and Elector Palatine of the Rhine, by Elizabeth, daughter of James I, and she was born on 13th/14th October, 1630 at the Wassenaer Court Palace, The Hague, Holland. She died on 8th or 14th June, 1714 at Schloss Herrenhausen, Hanover, and was buried in the Chapel of the Leine Schloss, Hanover. Her remains were later removed to the family vault in the Chapel of Schloss Herrenhausen, Hanover.

SIBLINGS:

1 *Frederick Augustus*

He was born on 3rd October, 1661 at Hanover, Germany. He was killed on 31st December, 1690 (O.S.) or 10th January, 1691 (N.S.) fighting the Turks at the Battle of St Georgen, Siebenbürgen, Transylvania.

2 *Stillborn twins*

They were born in February, 1664 at Heidelberg, Germany.

3 *Maximilian William*

He was born on 13th (O.S.) or 23rd (N.S.) December, 1666 at Schloss Iburg, Hanover, and died on 16th (O.S.) or 27th (N.S.) July, 1726 at Vienna, Austria.

4 *Stillborn son*

He was the twin of Maximilian, and was born in December, 1666 at Schloss Iburg, Hanover.

5 *Sophia Charlotte*

She was born on 12th October, 1668 at Schloss Iburg, Hanover. She married Frederick III of Brandenburg, later Frederick I King of Prussia (1657–1713) on 8th or 28th September, 1684 at Schloss Herrenhausen, Hanover, and had issue:

1 Frederick Augustus (1685–1686).

2 Unnamed son (b.&d.1687).

3 Frederick William I, King of Prussia (1688–1740); he married Sophia Dorothea, daughter of George I, and had issue.

Sophia died on 21st January (O.S.) or 1st February (N.S.), 1705 at Hanover, and was buried in the Royal Chapel, Berlin, Germany.

6 *Charles Philip*
He was born on 3rd or 13th October, 1669 at Schloss Iburg, Hanover. He was killed on 31st December, 1690 or 1st January, 1691, fighting the Turks at the Battle of Pristina, Albania.

7 *Christian*
He was born on 19th or 29th September, 1671 at Schloss Iburg, Hanover. He drowned on 31st July, 1703 in the River Danube, near Ulm, during the Battle of Munderkingen.

8 *Ernest Augustus*
He was born on 7th (O.S.) or 17th (N.S.) September, 1674 at Osnabrück, Hanover. He was elected Prince Bishop of Osnabrück in 1715. He was made a Knight of the Garter on 3rd July, 1716, and was created Duke of York and Albany and Earl of Ulster on 5th July, 1716. He died on 14th August, 1728 at Osnabrück, Hanover.

GEORGE I

Baptised George Louis, he was born on 28th May (O.S.) or 7th June (N.S.), 1660 at Osnabrück, Hanover. He succeeded his father as Duke and Elector of Hanover on 23rd January, 1698. He was made a Knight of the Garter on 18th June, 1701, and was naturalised as a British subject in 1705. He succeeded his third cousin, Queen Anne, as King of Great Britain on 1st August, 1714, and adopted the style King of Hanover also on the same day. He was crowned on 20th October, 1714 in Westminster Abbey.

George I married, on 21st November, 1682, at Celle Castle Chapel, Germany:

Sophia Dorothea
She was the daughter of George William, Duke of Brunswick-Lüneberg-Celle, by Eleanor, Countess of Williamsburg, daughter of Alexander II d'Olbreuse, Marquess of Desmiers, and she was born on 3rd February, 5th September or 15th September, 1666 at Celle Castle, Germany. She was divorced by Prince George on 28th December, 1694 on the grounds of her adultery with Count Philip Christopher von Königsmarck. She was forbidden to remarry, and was confined to the Castle of Ahlden for the rest of her life, being styled Duchess of Ahlden from February, 1695. She was never Queen of England. She died on 2nd (O.S.) or 13th (N.S.) November, 1726 at the Castle of Ahlden, Hanover, Germany, and was buried in Celle Church, Germany.

Issue of marriage:

1 *George II (see page 277).*

2 *Sophia Dorothea*

She was born on 16th (O.S.) or 26th (N.S.) March, 1685 or 1687 at Hanover. She married Frederick William of Prussia, later Frederick William I, King of Prussia (1688–1740) firstly on 17th November, 1706 at Hanover, and secondly on 28th November, 1706 at Berlin, Prussia, and had issue:

1 Frederick Louis (1707–1708).

2 Frederica Sophia Wilhelmina (1709–1758); she married Henry or Frederick, Margrave of Bayreuth (1711–1763), and had issue.

3 Frederick William, Prince of Orange (1710–1711).

4 (Charles) Frederick II "the Great", King of Prussia (1712–1786); he married Elizabeth Christina (1715–1797), daughter of Ferdinand Albert II, Duke of Brunswick-Wolfenbüttel.

5 Charlotte Albertine (1713–1714).

6 Frederica Louisa (1714–1784); she married Charles William Frederick, Margrave of Brandenburg-Ansbach (1712–1757), and had issue.

7 Philippina Charlotte (1716–1801); she married Charles I, Duke of Brunswick-Wolfenbüttel (1713–1780), and had issue.

8 Louis Charles William (1717–1719).

9 Sophia Dorothea Maria (1719–1765); she married Frederick William, Margrave of Brandenburg-Schwedt (1700–1771), and had issue.

10 Louisa Ulrica (1720–1782); she married Adolphus Frederick of Gottorp, King of Sweden (1710–1771), and had issue.

11 Augustus William (1722–1758); he married Louisa Amelia (1722–1780), daughter of Ferdinand Albert II, Duke of Brunswick-Wolfenbüttel, and had issue.

12 Anne Amalia, Abbess of Quedlinburg (1723–1787).

13 Frederick Henry Louis (1726–1802); he married Wilhelmina (1726–1808), daughter of Maximilian, Landgrave of Hesse-Cassel.

14 Augustus Ferdinand (1730–1813); he married Louisa (1738–1820), daughter of Frederick William, Margrave of Brandenburg-Schwedt, and had issue.

Sophia Dorothea died on 28th or 29th June, 1757 at Monbijou Palace near Berlin, Prussia, and was buried at Potsdam, Germany.

George I also had the following **illegitimate issue:**

By Ermengarde Melusina (1667–1743), Baroness von der Schulenberg, Duchess of Kendal, daughter of Gustavus Adolphus, Baron von der Schulenberg:

1 Petronilla Melusina, Baroness of Aldborough and Countess of Walsingham (1693?–1778); she married Philip Stanhope, Earl of Chesterfield (1694–1773).
2 Margaret Gertrude (1703–1773); she married Count von Lippe.

GEORGE I

He died on 28th May (O.S.) or 11th June (N.S.), 1727 near Osnabrück, Hanover, of the effects of a stroke. He was buried in the Chapel of the Leine Schloss, Hanover, but was transferred to the Chapel vaults of Schloss Herrenhausen after the Second World War.

He was succeeded by his son George.

Recommended reading
   Ragnald Marie Hatton: *George I, Elector and King* (Thames and Hudson, 1978).
   J. Marlow: *George I* (Weidenfeld and Nicolson, 1974).
   J. M. Beattie: *English Court Life in the Reign of George I* (Cambridge University Press, 1967).
There is no English biography of Ernest, Elector of Hanover. For George's mother and wife, see:
   Maria Kroll: *Sophie, Electress of Hanover* (Gollancz, 1973).
   F. E. Baily: *Sophia of Hanover and her Times* (Hutchinson, 1936).
   Hester W. Chapman: *Privileged Persons* (Jonathan Cape, 1966).
   Ruth Jordan: *Sophia Dorothea* (Constable, 1971).

GEORGE II

FATHER: *George I (see page 272).*
MOTHER: *Sophia Dorothea of Celle (see page 274, under George I).*
SIBLINGS: *(see page 275, under George I).*

GEORGE II

Baptised George Augustus, he was born on 30th October (O.S.) or 9th November (N.S.), 1683 at Schloss Herrenhausen, Hanover. He was naturalised as a British subject in 1705, and was made a Knight of the Garter on 4th April, 1706. He was created Duke and Marquess of Cambridge, Earl of Milford Haven, Viscount Northallerton and Baron of Tewkesbury on 9th November, 1706. He became Duke of Cornwall and Rothesay when his father succeeded to the throne of Great Britain on 1st August, 1714, and was created and invested Prince of Wales and Earl of Chester on 27th September, 1714 at the Palace of Westminster. He succeeded his father as King of Great Britain on 28th May (O.S.) or 11th June (N.S.), 1727, and was crowned on 11th October, 1727 at Westminster Abbey.

George II married, on 22nd August (O.S.) or 2nd September (N.S.), 1705 at Schloss Herrenhausen, Hanover:

(Wilhelmina Charlotte) Caroline
Known by her last Christian name, she was the daughter of John Frederick, Margrave of Brandenburg-Ansbach, by Eleanor Erdmuthe Louisa, daughter of John George, Duke of Saxe-Eisenach. She was born on 1st/2nd (O.S.) or 11th (N.S.) March, 1683, at Ansbach, Germany. She was crowned on 11th October, 1727 at Westminster Abbey. She died on 20th November, 1737 at St James's Palace, London, and was buried in Westminster Abbey.

Issue of marriage:
1 *Frederick Louis*
He was born on 20th January (O.S.) or 1st February (N.S.), 1707 at

Hanover, Germany. He was made a Knight of the Garter on 3rd July, 1716, and was created Duke of Gloucester on 10th January, 1717. He became Duke of Cornwall and Rothesay when his father succeeded to the throne of Great Britain on 11th June, 1727. He was created Duke of Edinburgh, Marquess of the Isle of Ely, Earl of Eltham, Viscount of Launceston, and Baron of Snowdon on 26th July, 1727. He was created Prince of Wales and Earl of Chester on 8th January, 1729. He died on 20th (O.S.) or 31st (N.S.) March, 1751, at Leicester House, St Martin's-in-the-Fields, London, and was buried in Westminster Abbey.

Frederick had the following illegitimate issue: By Anne (1705–36), daughter of Gilbert Vane, Baron Barnard: 1 FitzFrederick Vane (1732–36). By Margaret, Comtesse de Marsac, 2 Charles Marsack (1736–1820).

Frederick married, on 27th April (O.S.) or 8th May (N.S.), 1736, at the Chapel Royal, St James's Palace, London:

Augusta

She was the daughter of Frederick II, Duke of Saxe-Gotha-Altenburg, by Magdalena Augusta, daughter of Charles William, Prince of Anhalt-Zerbst, and she was born on 20th (O.S.) or 30th (N.S.) November, 1719 at Gotha, Germany. She died on 8th February, 1772 at Carlton House, London, of cancer, and was buried in Westminster Abbey.

Issue of marriage:

(i) *Augusta*

She was born on 31st July, 1737 at St James's Palace, London. She married Charles II (William Ferdinand), Duke of Brunswick-Wolfenbüttel (1735–1806) at the Chapel Royal, St James's Palace on 16th January, 1764, and had issue:

1 Augustina Caroline Frederica Louise (1764–1788); she married Frederick I (William Charles), King of Württemburg (1754–1816) (who afterwards married Charlotte, daughter of George III), and had issue.

2 Charles George Augustus (1766–1806); he married Frederica Louise Wilhelmina (1770–1819), daughter of William V, Prince of Orange.

3 Caroline Amelia Elizabeth; she married George IV, King of Great Britain (see page 301, under George IV).

4 George William Christian (1769–1811).

5 Augustus (1770–1820).

6 Frederick William, Duke of Brunswick-Wolfenbüttel

(1771–1815); he married Mary Elizabeth Wilhelmina (1782–1808), daughter of Prince Charles Louis of Baden, and had issue.

7 Amelia Caroline Dorothea Louise (1772–1773).

Augusta died on 23rd March, 1813 at her house in Hanover Square, London, and was buried in St George's Chapel, Windsor.

(ii) *George III (see page 285).*

(iii) *Edward Augustus*

He was born on 14th March, 1739 at Norfolk House, St James's Square, London. He was made a Knight of the Garter on 13th March, 1752, and was created Duke of York and Albany and Earl of Ulster on 1st April, 1760. He died on 17th September, 1767 at Monaco, and was buried in Westminster Abbey.

(iv) *Elizabeth Caroline*

She was born on 30th December, 1740 at Norfolk House, St James's Square, London. She died on 4th September, 1759 at Kew Palace, Surrey, and was buried in Westminster Abbey.

(v) *William Henry*

He was born on 14th November, 1743 at Leicester House, St Martin's-in-the-Fields, London. He was made a Knight of the Garter on 27th May, 1762, and was created Duke of Gloucester and Edinburgh and Earl of Connaught on 19th November, 1764. He died on 25th August, 1805 at Gloucester House, Grosvenor Street, London, and was buried in St George's Chapel, Windsor.

William had the following illegitimate issue:

By Lady Almeria Carpenter:

1 Louisa Maria (1762–1835); she married Godfrey Bosville MacDonald, 3rd Baron of Slate, and had issue.

William married, on 6th September, 1766, at her father's house in Pall Mall, London:

Maria

She was the illegitimate daughter of Sir Edward Walpole by Dorothy, daughter of Hammond Clement of Darlington or Durham, and she was born shortly before 10th July, 1736 at Westminster, London. She married firstly James Waldegrave, 2nd Earl Waldegrave (1714–1763) on 15th May, 1759 at her father's house in Pall Mall, London, and had issue:

1 Elizabeth Laura (1760–1816), Countess Waldegrave; she

married George Waldegrave, 4th Earl Waldegrave (1751–1789), and had issue.

2 Charlotte Maria (1761–1808); she married George Henry FitzRoy, Duke of Grafton (1760–1844), and had issue.

3 Anne Horatia (1762–1801); she married Admiral Sir Hugh Seymour (1759–1801), and had issue.

Maria died on 22nd/23rd August, 1807 at Oxford Lodge, Brompton, Middlesex, and was buried in St George's Chapel, Windsor.

Issue of marriage:

(a) *Sophia Matilda*

She was born on 29th May, 1773 at Gloucester House, Grosvenor Street, London. She died on 29th November, 1844 at the Ranger's House, Blackheath, Kent, and was buried in St George's Chapel, Windsor.

(b) *Caroline Augusta Maria*

She was born on 24th June, 1774 at Gloucester House, Grosvenor Street, London, and died there on 14th March, 1775. She was buried in St George's Chapel, Windsor.

(c) *William Frederick*

He was born on 15th January, 1776 at the Tedoli Palace, Rome, Italy. He was made a Knight of the Garter on 16th July, 1794. He succeeded his father as Duke of Gloucester and Edinburgh and Earl of Connaught on 25th August, 1805. He died on 30th November, 1834 at Bagshot Park, Surrey, and was buried in St George's Chapel, Windsor.

William married, on 22nd July, 1816, at the Private Chapel, Buckingham Palace, London:

Mary

She was the daughter of George III, King of Great Britain, by Charlotte of Mecklenburg-Strelitz, and she was born on 25th April, 1776 at Buckingham Palace. She died on 30th April, 1857 at Gloucester House, Piccadilly, London, and was buried in St George's Chapel, Windsor. There was no issue of the marriage.

(vi) *Henry Frederick*

He was born on 27th October, 1745 at Leicester House, St Martin's-in-the-Fields, London. He was created Duke of Cumberland and Strathearn and Earl of Dublin on 22nd

October, 1766, and was made a Knight of the Garter on 21st December, 1767. He died on 18th September, 1790 at Cumberland House, Pall Mall, London, and was buried in Westminster Abbey.

Henry is alleged, on circumstantial evidence, to have married privately, either on 4th March (?), 1767, or in 1770:

Olivia

She was the daughter of the Reverend D. James Wilmot. She died on 5th December, 1774.

Alleged issue of marriage:

(a) *Olivia*

Known as "Princess Olivia of Cumberland", she was born on 3rd April, 1772. She married John Thomas Serres on 1st September, 1791 and had issue:

1 Lavinia Janetta Horton (1797–1871); she married Antony Thomas Ryves, and had issue.

2 Daughter.

Olivia died before 3rd December, 1834 (date of burial), and was buried in St James's Church, Westminster.

Henry certainly did marry, on 2nd October, 1771, at her house in Hertford Street, Mayfair, London (the which marriage was bigamous if Henry had actually married Olivia Wilmot):

Anne

She was the daughter of Simon Luttrell, 1st Earl of Car-hampton, by Judith Maria, daughter of Sir Nicholas Lawes, and she was born on 24th January, 1742/3 in the Parish of St Marylebone, London. She married firstly Christopher Hor-ton of Catton Hall, Derbyshire on 4th August, 1765, and had issue:

1 Son (name not known) (d. young).

Anne died on 28th December, 1808, or in February, 1809 at Trieste, Italy. There was no issue of her marriage to Henry.

(vii) *Louisa Anne*

She was born on 8th March, 1749 at Leicester House, St Martin's-in-the-Fields, London. She died on 13th May, 1768 at Carlton House, Mayfair, London, and was buried in Westminster Abbey.

(viii) *Frederick William*

He was born on 13th May, 1750 at Leicester House, St

Martin's-in-the-Fields, London. He died there on 29th December, 1765, and was buried in Westminster Abbey.

(ix) *Caroline Matilda*

She was born on 11th July, 1751 at Leicester House, St Martin's-in-the-Fields, London. She married Christian VII, King of Denmark (1749–1808), by proxy on 1st October, 1766 at Carlton House, London, and in person on 8th November, 1766 at Schloss Frederiksberg, or at Christianborg, Denmark, and had issue:

1 Frederick VI, King of Denmark (1768–1839); he married Mary Sophia Frederica (1767–1852), daughter of Charles, Landgrave of Hesse-Cassel, and had issue.

2 Louise Augusta (1771–1843); she married Frederick Christian II, Duke of Schleswig-Holstein (1765–1814), and had issue. Although recognised as the legitimate daughter of Christian VII, Louise was without doubt the daughter of Queen Caroline by her lover, Count Struensee: her portraits bear this out most strikingly when compared to those of Struensee.

Caroline was crowned Queen Consort of Denmark on 1st May, 1767. She was divorced on 6th April, 1772 on the grounds of her adultery with Count John Frederick Struensee (1737–executed 1772). She died on 10th May, 1775 at Celle Castle, Hanover, and was buried in Celle Church.

2 Anne

She was born on 9th or 22nd (O.S.) October or 2nd November (N.S.), 1709 at Schloss Herrenhausen, Hanover. She was styled Princess Royal from c.30th August, 1727. She married William IV (Charles Henry Friso), Prince of Orange (1711–1751) on 14th (O.S.) or 24th/25th (N.S.) March, 1734 at the Chapel Royal St James's Palace, and had issue:

1 Unnamed son (b.&d.1735).

2 Unnamed daughter (b.&d.1736).

3 Unnamed daughter (b.&d.1739).

4 Wilhelmina Caroline (1743–1787); she married Charles Christian, Duke of Nassau-Weilburg (1735–1788), and had issue.

5 Anne Marie (b.&d.1746).

6 William V (Batavus), Prince of Orange (1748–1806); he married Frederica Sophia Wilhelmina (1751–1820), daughter of Prince Augustus William of Prussia, and had issue.

Anne died on 2nd (O.S.) or 12th (N.S.) January, 1759 at The Hague, Holland.

3 *Amelia Sophia Eleanor*

Known as Emily, she was born on 30th May (O.S.) or 10th June (N.S.), 1711 at Schloss Herrenhausen, Hanover. She died on 31st October, 1786 at her house in Cavendish Square, London, and was buried in Westminster Abbey.

4 *Caroline Elizabeth*

She was born on 30th May (O.S.) or 10th June (N.S.), 1713 at Schloss Herrenhausen, Hanover. She died on 28th December, 1757 at St James's Palace, London, and was buried in Westminster Abbey.

5 *Stillborn son*

He was born on 9th November, 1716 at St James's Palace, London.

6 *George William*

He was born on 2nd/3rd November, 1717 at St James's Palace, London. He is sometimes referred to as the Duke of Gloucester, but there is no evidence that he was ever so styled, designated or formally created. He died on 6th February, 1718 at Kensington Palace, London, and was buried in Westminster Abbey.

7 *Miscarriage*

This occurred in 1718.

8 *William Augustus*

He was born on 15th April, 1721, either at Leicester House, St Martin's-in-the-Fields, London, or—less probably—at St James's Palace, London. He was made a Knight of the Bath on 27th May, 1725, and was created Duke of Cumberland, Marquess of Berkhamstead, Earl of Kennington, Viscount Trematon, and Baron of Alderney on 27th July, 1726. He was made a Knight of the Garter on 18th May, 1730. He died unmarried on 31st October, 1765 at his house in Upper Grosvenor Street, London, and was buried in Westminster Abbey.

William is said, without reliable evidence, to have had three illegitimate children by the daughter of a Scottish soldier.

9 *Mary*

She was born on 22nd February (O.S.) or 5th March (N.S.), 1723 at Leicester House, St Martins-in-the-Fields, London. She married Frederick II, Landgrave of Hesse-Cassel (1720–1785), by proxy on 8th (O.S.) or 19th (N.S.) May, 1740 at St James's Palace, London, and in person on 28th June, 1740 at Cassel, Germany, and had issue:

1 William (1741–1742).
2 William IX, Landgrave and Elector of Hesse-Cassel (1743–1821); he married Wilhelmina Caroline (1747–1820), daughter of Frederick V, King of Denmark by Louisa, daughter of George II (see page 271), and had issue.
3 Charles, Landgrave of Hesse-Cassel (1744–1836); he married Louisa (1750–1831), daughter of Frederick V, King of Denmark by Louisa, daughter of George II (see below), and had issue.
4 Frederick III, Landgrave of Hesse-Cassel (1747–1837); he married Caroline Polyxena (1762–1823), daughter of Charles William, Prince of Nassau-Usingen, and had issue, including Augusta, wife of Adolphus, Duke of Cambridge, son of George III.

Mary died on 14th or 16th January, 1772 at Hanau, Germany.

10 *Louisa*

She was born on 7th December, 1724 at Leicester House, St Martin's-in-the-Fields, London. She married Frederick V, King of Denmark and Norway (1723–1766), by proxy on 27th or 30th October, 1743 at Hanover, Germany, and in person on 11th December, 1743 at Altona, near Hamburg, Germany, and had issue:
1 Christian (1745–1747).
2 Sophia Magdalena (1746–1813); she married Gustavus III, King of Sweden (1746–1792), and had issue.
3 Wilhelmina Caroline (1747–1820); she married William I, Elector of Hesse-Cassel (son of Mary, daughter of George II—see above) (1747–1821), and had issue.
4 Christian VII, King of Denmark (1749–1808); he married Caroline Matilda of Wales, granddaughter of George II (see page 282).
5 Louisa (1750–1831); she married Charles, Landgrave of Hesse-Cassel (1744–1836) (son of Mary, daughter of George II—see above), and had issue.

Louisa died on 8th or 19th December, 1751 at Christianborg Castle, Copenhagen, Denmark.

George II may have had the following illegitimate issue, although the King never acknowledged him as such:

By Amalia Sophia Marianne, Countess von Walmoden and Countess of Yarmouth (1704–1765):
1 John Louis, Count von Walmoden-Gimborn (1736–1811).

GEORGE II

He died on 25th October, 1760 at Kensington Palace, London, and was buried in Westminster Abbey.

He was succeeded by his grandson George.

Recommended reading

Charles Chevenix Trench: *George II* (A. Lane, 1973).

Horace Walpole: *Memoirs of the Reign of George II* (Henry Colburn, 1846).

For George's family, see:

P. Quennell: *Caroline of England* (Collins, 1939).

R. L. Arkell: *Caroline of Ansbach* (Oxford University Press, 1939).

Morris Marples: *Poor Fred and the Butcher* (Michael Joseph, 1970).

Charles Neilson Gattey: *Farmer George's Black Sheep: The Lives and Loves of George III's Siblings* (Kensal Press, 1985).

Hester W. Chapman: *Caroline Matilda, Queen of Denmark* (Jonathan Cape, 1971).

GEORGE III

FATHER: *Frederick, Prince of Wales (see page 277, under George II).*
MOTHER: *Augusta of Saxe-Gotha (see page 278, under George II).*
SIBLINGS: *(see page 278, under George II).*

GEORGE III

Baptised George William Frederick, he was born on 24th May (O.S.) or 4th June (N.S.), 1738, at Norfolk House, St James's Square, London. He was made a Knight of the Garter on 22nd June, 1749. He succeeded his father as Duke of Cornwall and Rothesay, Duke of Edinburgh, Marquess of the Isle of Ely, Earl of Eltham, Viscount of Launceston and Baron of Snowdon on 20th March, 1751. He was created Prince of Wales and Earl of Chester on 20th April, 1751. He succeeded his grandfather George II as King of Great Britain on 25th October, 1760, and was crowned on 21st/22nd September, 1761 at Westminster Abbey. On 1st January, 1801 he relinquished for ever the title "King of France", held by English Kings since Edward III laid claim to the French crown in 1340.

George III is alleged to have married secretly, on 17th April, 1759, a Quakeress called Hannah Lightfoot, daughter of a Wapping shoemaker, who is said to have borne him three children. Documents relating to the alleged marriage, bearing the Prince's signature, were impounded and examined in 1866 by the Attorney General. Learned opinion at that time leaned to the view that these documents were genuine. They were then placed in the Royal Archives at Windsor; in 1910, permission was refused a would-be author who asked to see them. If George III did make such a marriage when he was Prince of Wales, before the passing of the Royal Marriages Act in 1772, then his subsequent marriage to Queen Charlotte was bigamous, and every monarch of Britain since has been an usurper, the rightful heirs of George III being his children by Hannah Lightfoot, if they ever existed.

George III married, bigamously or not, on 8th September, 1761 at the Chapel Royal, St James's Palace, London:

(Sophia) Charlotte
Known as Charlotte, she was the daughter of Charles Louis Frederick, Duke of Mecklenburg-Strelitz, by Elizabeth Albertine of Saxe-Hildburghausen, and she was born on 19th May, 1744 at Mirow, Mecklenburg-Strelitz, Germany. On 7th March, 1760, she was invested as a Protestant canoness of Herford (or Hervorden) in Westphalia, Germany. She was crowned Queen Consort on 21st/22nd September, 1761. She died on 17th November, 1818 at Kew Palace, Surrey, and was buried in St George's Chapel, Windsor.

Issue of marriage:

1 *George IV (see page 300).*

2 *Frederick Augustus*
He was born on 16th August, 1763 at St James's Palace, London (or, less probably, at Buckingham Palace). He was elected Prince Bishop of Osnabrück on 27th February, 1764, and was made a Knight of the Garter on 19th June, 1771. He was created Duke of

York and Albany and Earl of Ulster on 29th November, 1784. He died on 5th January, 1827 at Rutland House, Arlington Street, London, and was buried in St George's Chapel, Windsor.

Frederick had the following illegitimate issue (?):

1 Charles, Captain Hesse. There is no certain proof that Frederick actually was his father, although he was generally reputed to be. Charles was killed in a duel with Count Léon, bastard son of Napoleon I, Emperor of the French.

Frederick married, on 28th September, 1791 at Charlottenburg, Berlin, Prussia, and again on 23rd November, 1791 at Buckingham Palace:

Frederica Charlotte Ulrica Katherine

She was the daughter of Frederick William II, King of Prussia, by Elizabeth Christine Ulrica, daughter of Charles, Duke of Brunswick-Wolfenbüttel, and she was born on 7th May, 1767, either at Charlottenburg or at Potsdam, Prussia. She died on 6th August, 1820 at Oatlands Park, Weybridge, Surrey, and was buried in Weybridge Churchyard, Surrey. There was no issue of the marriage.

3 *Miscarriage*

This occurred in the summer of 1764 at Richmond Lodge, Surrey.

4 *William IV (see page 303).*

5 *Charlotte Augusta Matilda*

She was born on 29th September, 1766 at Buckingham Palace, and was styled Princess Royal from October, 1766; she was officially designated Princess Royal on 22nd June, 1789. She married Frederick William Charles, Duke of Württemburg, afterwards Frederick I, King of Württemburg (1754–1816) on 18th May, 1797 at the Chapel Royal, St James's Palace, London, and had issue:

1 Stillborn daughter; she was born on 27th April, 1798.

Charlotte became Queen Consort when her husband acceded to the throne of Württemburg on 1st January, 1806, and was crowned as such on the same day at Stuttgart, Germany. She died on 6th October, 1828 at Ludwigsburg Palace, Stuttgart, Germany, and was buried there in the Ludwigsburg family vault.

6 *Edward Augustus*

He was born on 2nd November, 1767 at Buckingham Palace. He was made a Knight of the Garter on 2nd June, 1786, and was created Duke of Kent and Strathearn and Earl of Dublin on 23rd or 24th April, 1799. He died on 23rd January, 1820 at Woodbrook Cottage, Sidmouth, Devon, and was buried in St George's Chapel,

Windsor. His remains were later removed to the Kent Mausoleum, Frogmore, Windsor.

Edward had the following illegitimate issue:

By Adelaide Dubus:

1 Adelaide Victoria Augusta (1789–1790).

By Julie de St Laurent (?):

2 A son or sons, said to have been adopted at birth in Canada (?).

Edward married, on 29th May, 1818 at Schloss Ehrenburg, Coburg, Germany, and again on 13th July, 1818 at Kew Palace, Surrey:

(Mary Louisa) Victoria

Known as Victoria, she was the daughter of Francis I (Frederick Anthony), Duke of Saxe-Coburg-Saalfield, by Augusta Caroline Sophia, daughter of Henry XXIV, Count of Reuss-Ebersdorf, and she was born on 17th August, 1786 at Coburg, Germany. She married firstly Emich Charles, 2nd Prince of Leiningen (1763–1814) on 21st December, 1803, and had issue:

1 Charles Frederick William Ernest, 3rd Prince of Leiningen (1804–1856); he married Mary, Countess of Kleklesburg (1806–1880), daughter of Maximilian, Count of Kleklesburg, and had issue, although they were afterwards divorced.

2 Anne Feodora Augusta Charlotte Wilhelmina (1807–1872); she married Ernest, Prince of Hohenlohe-Langenburg (1794–1860), and had issue.

Victoria died on 16th March, 1861 at Frogmore House, Windsor, and was buried in St George's Chapel, Windsor. Her remains were later removed to the Kent Mausoleum, Frogmore, Windsor.

Issue of marriage:

(i) *Queen Victoria (see page 305).*

7 *Augusta Sophia*

She was born on 8th November, 1768 at Buckingham Palace. She perhaps married Major General Sir Brent Spencer (d.1828) in c.1811, but there is no substantiating evidence for this. She died on 22nd September, 1840 at Clarence House, London, and was buried in St George's Chapel, Windsor.

8 *Elizabeth*

She was born on 22nd May, 1770 at Buckingham Palace. Some documentary evidence exists to suggest that she either married or was the mistress of a page called George Ramus in c.1785, and that they had a daughter Eliza, born in c.1786/7, who married a man called James Money. Although such a marriage would have been illegal under the Royal Marriages Act 1772, other evidence would seem to indicate that it did not take place at all, and that there was no connection whatsoever between Elizabeth and "George Ramus": among 6 or 7 pages surnamed Ramus, not one was called George. Furthermore, the known details of the Princess's illness in 1786/7 are not identifiable with the symptoms of pregnancy. Elizabeth did marry Frederick (Joseph) VI, Landgrave and Prince of Hesse-Homburg (1769–1829) on 7th April, 1818 at the Private Chapel, Buckingham Palace. She died on 10th January, 1840 at Frankfurt-am-Main, Germany, and was buried in the Mausoleum of the Landgraves at Homburg, Germany.

9 *Ernest Augustus*

He was born on 5th June, 1771 at Buckingham Palace. He was made a Knight of the Garter on 2nd June, 1786, and was created Duke of Cumberland and Teviotdale and Earl of Armagh on 24th April, 1799. He succeeded his brother William IV as King of Hanover on 20th June, 1837, adopting the style Ernest I; the Salic Law governed the Hanoverian succession, thus preventing the accession of Queen Victoria. Ernest died on 18th November, 1851 at Schloss Herrenhausen, Hanover, and was buried there in the Chapel vaults.

Ernest had the following illegitimate issue:

1 George FitzErnest (d.1828)

Ernest married, on 29th May, 1815 at the parish church of Neu Strelitz, Germany, and again on 29th August, 1815 at Carlton House, London:

Frederica Louisa Caroline Sophia Alexandrina

She was the daughter of Charles Louis Frederick V, Grand Duke of Mecklenburg-Strelitz, by Frederica Caroline Louise, daughter of George William, Landgrave of Hesse-Darmstadt, and she was born on 2nd March, 1778 at Hanover, Germany. She married firstly Prince Frederick Louis Charles of Prussia (1773–1796) on 26th December, 1793 at the Royal Palace, Berlin, Prussia, and had issue:

1 Frederick William Louis (1794–1863); he married Louise (1799–1882), daughter of Alexis, Duke of Anhalt-Bernbourg, and had issue.
2 Charles George (1795–1798).
3 Frederica Wilhelmina Louise (1796–1850); she married Leopold Frederick, Duke of Anhalt-Dessau (1794–1871).

Frederica was divorced from her first husband in 1796. She married secondly Frederick William, Prince of Solms-Braunfels (1770–

1814) on 7th or 10th January, 1798/9 or 10th December, 1798 at Berlin, Prussia, and had issue:

4 Frederick William Henry Casimir George Charles Maximilian (1801–1868); he married Mary Anne (1809–1892), daughter of Francis, Count of Kinsky, and had issue.

5 Son (name not known); (b.1801; d. young).

6 Augusta Louisa Theresa Matilda (1804–1865); she married Albert, Prince of Schwarzbourg-Roudolstadt (1798–1869).

7 Alexander Frederick Louis (1807–1867); he married Louise (b.1835), daughter of Engelbert, Baron Landsberg-Steinfürt, and had issue.

8 Frederick William Louis George Alfred Alexander (1812–1875); he married Marie Josephine Sophie, daughter of Prince Constantine of Löwenstein-Wertheim-Rochefort, and had issue.

Frederica became Queen of Hanover upon the accession of her third husband, Prince Ernest, to the throne of Hanover, on 20th June, 1837. She died on 29th June, 1841 at Hanover, and was buried in the Chapel at Schloss Herrenhausen, Hanover.

Issue of marriage:

(i) *Frederica*
She was stillborn on 27th January, 1817 at St James's Palace, London. She was buried in Westminster Abbey, but was later removed to St George's Chapel, Windsor.

(ii) *Stillborn Daughter*
She was born in April, 1818. There is no record of her burial.

(iii) *George Frederick Alexander Charles Ernest Augustus*
He was born on 27th May, 1819 in a house on the Unter-den-Linden Strasse, Berlin, Prussia. He was made a Knight of the Garter on 15th August, 1835. He succeeded his father as King of Hanover, Duke of Cumberland and Teviotdale, and Earl of Armagh on 18th November, 1851; he was styled George V of Hanover. He was deposed on 20th September, 1866 by the Prussians, and formally abdicated on the same day. He died on 12th June, 1878 at 7, Rue Presbourg, Paris, and was buried in St George's Chapel, Windsor.
(Note: King George went blind following an accident in 1834).
George married, on 18th February, 1843, at Hanover, Germany:
(Alexandrina) Mary Wilhelmina Katherine Charlotte Theresa Henrietta Louisa Pauline Elizabeth Frederica Georgina
Known as Mary, she was the daughter of Joseph George

Frederick Ernest Charles, Duke of Saxe-Altenburg, by Amelia Theresa Louise Wilhelmina Philippina, daughter of Louis Alexander, Duke of Württemburg, and she was born on 14th April, 1818 at Hildburghausen, Germany. She died on 9th January, 1907 at Gmunden, Austria, where she was buried.

Issue of marriage:

(a) *Ernest Augustus William Adolphus George Frederick*

He was born on 21st September, 1845 at Hanover, and was Crown Prince of Hanover until his father's abdication on 20th September, 1866. He succeeded his father as Duke of Cumberland and Teviotdale and Earl of Armagh on 12th June, 1878, and was made a Knight of the Garter on 23rd June, 1878. He was created Duke of Brunswick-Lüneberg on 18th October, 1884. He died on 14th November, 1923 at Gmunden, Austria.

Ernest married, on 21st December, 1878, at Copenhagen, Denmark:

Thyra Amelia Caroline Charlotte Anne

She was the daughter of Christian IX, King of Denmark, by Louise Wilhelmina Frederica Caroline Augusta Julie, daughter of William X, Landgrave of Hesse-Cassel, and she was also sister to Alexandra, Queen of Edward VII. She was born on 29th September, 1853 at Copenhagen, Denmark. She died on 26th February, 1933 at Gmunden, Austria, where she was buried.

Issue of marriage:

(i) *Marie Louise Victoria Caroline Amelia Alexandra Augusta Frederica*

She was born on 11th October, 1879 at Gmunden, Austria. She married Maximilian, Prince and Margrave of Baden (1867–1929) on 10th July, 1900 at Gmunden, Austria, and had issue:

1 Marie Alexandra Thyra Victoria Louisa Carola Hilda (1902–1944); she married Wolfgang Moritz, Prince of Hesse (b.1896).

2 Berthold Friedrich William Carl, Margrave of Baden (1906–1963); he married Theodora (b.1906), daughter of Prince Andrew of Greece and Denmark, and sister of Prince Philip, Duke of Edinburgh, and had issue.

291

Marie died on 31st January, 1948 at Salem Castle, Germany.

(ii) *George William Christian Albert Edward Alexander Frederick Waldemar Ernest Adolphus*
He was born on 28th October, 1880 at Gmunden, Austria, and was styled Duke of Armagh. He was killed on 20th May, 1912 in a motor accident at Nackel, Brandenburg, Germany.

(iii) *Alexandra Louise Marie Olga Elizabeth Theresa Vera*
She was born on 29th September, 1882 at Gmunden, Austria. She married Frederick Francis IV, Grand Duke of Mecklenburg-Schwerin (1882–1945) on 7th June, 1904 at Gmunden, Austria, and had issue:
1 Frederick Francis V, Grand Duke of Mecklenburg-Schwerin (b.1910); he married Karen Elizabeth (b.1920), daughter of Walter von Schaper.
2 Christian Louis, Grand Duke of Mecklenburg-Schwerin (b.1912); he married Barbara (b.1920), daughter of Prince Sigismund of Prussia, and had issue.
3 Thyra (b.1919).
4 Anastasia (b.1922); she married Frederick Ferdinand, Prince of Schleswig-Holstein-Sonderburg-Glücksburg (b.1913), and had issue.
Alexandra died on 30th August, 1963 at Glücksburg Castle, Germany.

(iv) *Olga Adelaide Louise Marie Alexandrina Agnes*
She was born on 11th July, 1884 at Gmunden, Austria, and died on 21st September, 1958, either at Linz, or at Hubertibus, Gmunden, Austria.

(v) *Christian Frederick William George Peter Waldemar*
He was born on 4th July, 1885 at Gmunden, Austria, and died there on 3rd September, 1901.

(vi) *Ernest Augustus Christian George*
He was born on 17th November, 1887 at Penzing Hall, near Vienna, Austria. He succeeded his father as Duke of Brunswick-Lüneberg on 14th November, 1923. He died on 30th January, 1953 at Marienburg Castle, Hanover, Germany.

Ernest married, on 24th May, 1913, at Berlin, Germany:

Victoria Louise

She was the daughter of William II, Emperor of Germany, by Augusta Victoria, daughter of Frederick, Duke of Schleswig-Holstein-Sonderburg-Augustenburg, and she was born on 13th September, 1892 at the Marble Palace, Potsdam, Germany. She died in 1980.

Issue of marriage:

1 Ernest Augustus George William Christian Louis Francis Joseph Nicholas (b.1914); he married firstly Ortrud (1925–1980), daughter of Prince Albert of Schleswig-Holstein-Sonderburg-Glücksburg, and had issue. He married secondly Monica (b.1929), daughter of George Frederick, Duke of Solms-Laubach.

2 George William Ernest Augustus Frederick Axel (b.1915); he married Sophia (b.1914), daughter of Prince Andrew of Greece and Denmark, and sister of Prince Philip, Duke of Edinburgh, and had issue.

3 Frederica Louise Thyra Victoria Margaret Sophia Olga Cecilia Isabella Christa (1917–1981); she married Paul I, King of Greece (1901–1964), and had issue.

4 Christian Oscar Ernest Augustus William Victor George Henry (1919–1981); he married Mireille (b.1946), daughter of Armand Dutry, and had issue, although they were divorced in 1976.

5 Welf Henry Ernest Augustus George Christian Berthold Frederick William Louis Ferdinand (b.1923); he married Alexandra (b.1938), daughter of Otto Frederick, Fürst of Ysenburg and Büdingen.

(b) *Frederica Sophia Marie Henrietta Amelia Theresa*

She was born on 9th January, 1848 at Hanover, Germany. She married Liutbert Alexander George Lionel Alphonse, Baron von Pawel-Rammingen (1843–1932) on 24th April, 1880 at St George's Chapel, Windsor, and had issue:

1 Victoria Georgina Beatrice Maud Anne, Baroness von Pawel-Rammingen (b.&d.1881).

Frederica died on 16th October, 1926 at Biarritz, France.

(c) *Mary Ernestine Josephine Adolphine Henrietta Theresa Elizabeth Alexandra*

She was born on 3rd December, 1849 at Hanover,

Germany, and died on 4th June, 1904 at Gmunden, Austria, where she was buried.

10 *Augustus Frederick*

He was born on 27th January, 1773 at Buckingham Palace. He was made a Knight of the Garter on 2nd June, 1786, and was created Duke of Sussex, Earl of Inverness and Baron Arklow on 27th November, 1801. He died on 22nd April, 1843 at Kensington Palace, London, and was buried in Kensal Green Cemetery, London.

Augustus had the following illegitimate issue:

By Miss Tranter of Windsor:

1 Lucy Beaufoy Tranter; she married Charles George Tranter, and had issue, from whom was descended the actress, Dame Anna Neagle.

Augustus married firstly, privately, and in contravention of the Royal Marriages Act 1772, on 4th April, 1793 at the Hotel Sarmiento, Rome, and again on 5th December, 1793, at St George's Church, Hanover Square, London:

Augusta

She was the daughter of John Murray, 4th Earl of Dunmore, by Charlotte, daughter of Alexander Stewart, 6th Earl of Galloway, and she was born on 27th January (?), 1763 (or, less probably, 1768), in London. Her marriage to Augustus was declared null and void by the Arches Court of Canterbury on 14th July, 1794, and again by the Prerogative Court on 3rd August, 1794, although she did not separate from Augustus until 1801. She assumed the style "Duchess of Sussex" in 1801. On 13th October, 1806, she assumed instead, by Royal Licence, the surname and title Lady de Ameland. She died on 5th March, 1830 at her house on the East Cliff, Ramsgate, Kent, and was buried in St Lawrence's Church, Isle of Thanet, Kent.

Issue of marriage:

(i) *Augustus Frederick*

He was born on 13th January, 1794 at 16, Lower Berkeley Street, London. He adopted the surname "d'Este", and was knighted. He died on 28th December, 1848, at Ramsgate, Kent, of disseminated sclerosis, and was buried in St Lawrence's Church, Isle of Thanet, Kent.

(ii) *Augusta Emma*

She was born on 9th August, 1801 in Grosvenor Street, London, and was styled "Mademoiselle d'Este". She married Thomas Wilde, 1st Baron Truro of Bowes (1782–1855) on 13th

August, 1845 in London. She died on 21st May, 1866 at 83, Eaton Square, London, and was buried in St Lawrence's Church, Isle of Thanet, Kent.

Augustus married secondly, also privately and in contravention of the Royal Marriages Act 1772, on c.2nd May, 1831, at Great Cumberland Place, London:

Cecilia Laetitia

She was the daughter of Arthur Saunders Gore, 2nd Earl of Arran, by Elizabeth, daughter of Richard Underwood of Dublin, and she was born in 1778, or 1785, or 1788, or 1789. She married firstly Sir George Buggin of Thetford, Norfolk (1760–1825) on 14th May, 1815 at her father's house in Dover Street, London. She assumed her mother's maiden surname of Underwood by Royal Licence on 2nd May, 1831, the day her second marriage is thought to have taken place. She was created Duchess of Inverness in her own right on 5th April, 1840. She died on 1st August, 1873 at Kensington Palace, London, and was buried in Kensal Green Cemetery, London. There was no issue of the marriage.

11 *Adolphus Frederick*

He was born on 24th February, 1774 at Buckingham Palace. He was made a Knight of the Garter on 2nd June, 1786, and was created Duke of Cambridge, Earl of Tipperary, and Baron of Culloden on 27th November, 1801. He died on 8th July, 1850 at Cambridge House, Piccadilly, London, and was buried at Kew. His remains were later removed to St George's Chapel, Windsor.

Adolphus married, on 7th May, 1818 at Cassel, Prussia, and again on 1st June, 1818 at Kew Palace, Surrey:

Augusta Wilhelmina Louisa

She was the daughter of Frederick III, Landgrave of Hesse-Cassel (son of Mary, daughter of George II), by Caroline Polyxena, daughter of Charles William, Prince of Nassau-Usingen, and she was born on 25th July, 1797 at Rumpenheim Castle, Cassel, Germany. She died on 6th April, 1889 at St James's Palace, London, and was buried at Kew. Her remains were later removed to St George's Chapel, Windsor.

Issue of marriage:

(i) *George William Frederick Charles*

He was born on 26th March, 1819 at Cambridge House, Hanover, Germany. He was made a Knight of the Garter on 15th August, 1835, and succeeded his father as Duke of

Cambridge, Earl of Tipperary and Baron of Culloden on 8th July, 1850. He died on 17th March, 1904 at Gloucester House, Piccadilly, London, and was buried in Kensal Green Cemetery, London.

George married, privately and in contravention of the Royal Marriages Act 1772, on 8th January, 1847, at St John's Church, Clerkenwell, London:

Sarah Louisa

She was the daughter of John Fairbrother by an unnamed daughter of Thomas Freeman of Wylcot, Shrewsbury, and she was born in 1816 at Bow Street, Covent Garden, London. An actress, she was known as "Mrs FitzGeorge" after her marriage. She died on 12th January, 1890 at 6, Queen Street, Mayfair, London, and was buried in Kensal Green Cemetery, London.

Sarah Louisa had the following illegitimate issue:

1 Charles Manners Sutton Fairbrother (?) (1836–1901).
2 Louisa Katherine (b.1839?); she married a Captain Hamilton.

Issue of marriage, all surnamed "FitzGeorge" (the first two were actually born before their parents entered wedlock):

(a) *George William Adolphus*

He was born on 27th August, 1843 in London. He died on 2nd September, 1907 at Lucerne, Switzerland.

George married, on 28th November, 1885, in Paris:

Rosa Frederica

She was the daughter of William Baring of Norman Court, Hants., by Elizabeth Hammersley, and she was born on 9th March, 1854 at Norman Court, Hants. She married firstly Frank Wigsell Arkwright of Sanderstead Court, Surrey on 29th August, 1878, and had issue:

1 Mabel Iris (b.1886); she married firstly Robert Shekelton Balfour (1869–1942), and had issue, and secondly Vladimir Emanuellovitch, Prince Galitzine (1884–1954).
2 George Daphné (1889–1954); she married Sir George Foster Earle (1890–1965), although they later divorced.
3 George William Frederick (1892–1960); he married firstly Esther Vignon (1888–c.1935), from whom he was later divorced, and secondly Frances (b.1911), daughter of Robert Bellenger.

Rosa was divorced from her first husband, prior to marrying George FitzGeorge. She died on 10th March,

1927, either at Cannes or in London. There was no issue of her marriage to George.

(b) *Adolphus Augustus Frederick*
He was born on 30th January, 1846 in London, and rose to the rank of knight. He died on 17th December, 1922 in London.

Adolphus married firstly, on 21st September, 1875, either at Hull or at Hessle, Yorkshire:

Sophia Jane
She was the daughter of Thomas Holden of Winestead Hall, Hull, and she was born in 1857 at Hull. She died on 3rd February, 1920 in London.

Issue of marriage:

(i) *Olga Mary Adelaide*
She was born in 1877. She married firstly Sir Archibald Hamilton (1876–1939), and had issue: 1 George Edward Archibald Augustus FitzGeorge (1898–killed in action 1918). She was divorced from her first husband in 1902, and married secondly Robert Charlton Lane (1873–1943), and had issue, although again, I have been unable to obtain details of such. She died in 1920.

Adolphus married secondly, on 28th October, 1920, at Pimlico, London:

Margaret Beatrice Daisy
She was the daughter of John Watson, and she was born in 1863. She died on 26th February, 1934 in London. There was no issue of the marriage.

(c) *Augustus Charles Frederick*
He was born on 12th June, 1847 in London, and rose to the rank of knight. He died unmarried on 30th October, 1933 in London.

(ii) *Augusta Caroline Charlotte Elizabeth Mary Sophia Louise*
She was born on 19th July, 1822 at the Palace of Montbrilliant, Hanover. She married Frederick William, Grand Duke of Mecklenburg-Strelitz (1819–1904) on 28th June, 1843 at Buckingham Palace, and had issue:

1 Unnamed son (b.&d.1845).

2 George Adolphus Frederick Augustus Victor Ernest Adalbert Gustavus William Wellington, Grand Duke of Mecklenburg-Strelitz (1848–1914); he married Elizabeth

Marie Frederica Amelia Agnes of Anhalt (1857–1933), and had issue.

Augusta died on 4th/5th December, 1916 at Neustrelitz, Germany, where she was buried.

(iii) *Mary Adelaide Wilhelmina Elizabeth*

She was born on 27th November, 1833 at Hanover, Germany. She married Francis Paul Charles Louis Alexander, Duke of Teck (1837–1900) on 12th June, 1866 at Kew Church, Surrey, and had issue:

1 Queen Mary, wife of George V. (See page 322, under George V.)
2 Adolphus Charles Alexander Albert Edward George Philip Louis Ladislaus, 1st Marquess of Cambridge (1868–1927); he married Margaret Evelyn (1873–1929), daughter of Hugh Lupus Grosvenor, 1st Duke of Westminster, and had issue.
3 Francis Joseph Leopold Frederick (1870–1910).
4 Alexander Augustus Frederick William Alfred George, Earl of Athlone (1874–1957); he married Princess Alice of Albany, daughter of Prince Leopold, Queen Victoria's youngest son, and had issue.

Mary Adelaide died on 27th October, 1897 at White Lodge, Richmond Park, Surrey, and was buried in St George's Chapel, Windsor.

12 *Mary*

She was born on 25th April, 1776 at Buckingham Palace. She married her cousin, William Frederick, Duke of Gloucester (see page 280, under George II) (1776–1834) on 22nd July, 1816 at the Private Chapel, Buckingham Palace. She died on 30th April, 1857 at Gloucester House, Piccadilly, London, and was buried in St George's Chapel, Windsor.

13 *Sophia Matilda*

She was born on 3rd November, 1777 at Buckingham Palace. She died on 27th May, 1848 at her house in Vicarage Place, Kensington, London, and was buried in Kensal Green Cemetery.

Sophia had the following illegitimate (?) issue:

By General Thomas Garth (d.1829):

1 Thomas Garth (1800–after 1839). He left issue. He was born before August, 1800 in Weymouth, Dorset. It is possible that Sophia and General Garth had been married soon after her arrival in Weymouth that year, as his family lived nearby. However, there is no evidence to

298

support a story that they were married in Puddletown Church, Dorset. A portrait of Sophia in old age shows her wearing a wedding ring.

14 *Octavius*

He was born on 23rd February, 1779 at Buckingham Palace. He died on 3rd May, 1783 at Kew Palace, Surrey, and was buried in Westminster Abbey. His remains were later removed to St George's Chapel, Windsor.

15 *Alfred*

He was born on 22nd September, 1780 at Windsor Castle. He died on 20th August, 1782 at Windsor Castle, and was buried in Westminster Abbey. His remains were later removed to St George's Chapel, Windsor.

16 *Amelia*

She was born on 7th August, 1783 at The Lodge, Windsor Castle. It is possible that she married, at some unknown date, the Hon. Charles FitzRoy (1762–1831), but the evidence is conflicting. She died on 2nd November, 1810 at Augusta Lodge, St Albans Street, Windsor, of erysipelas, and was buried in St George's Chapel, Windsor.

GEORGE III

He suffered from the disease porphyria, which led his contemporaries to believe he was mad. The death of his youngest daughter Amelia in 1810 broke his health for good, and he became unfit to reign. In 1811, his son George was created Prince Regent, and remained so until his father's death, when he succeeded him.

George III died on 29th January, 1820 at Windsor Castle, and was buried in St George's Chapel, Windsor.

He was succeeded by his son George.

Recommended reading

Stanley Ayling: *George the Third* (Collins, 1972).
I. Macalpine and R. Hunter: *George III and the Mad Business* (Allen Lane, 1969).
A. Andrews: *The King who lost America* (1976).
A. Lloyd: *The Wickedest Age: The Life and Times of George III* (David and Charles, 1971).
For George's family, see:
Olwen Hedley: *Queen Charlotte* (John Murray, 1975).
Morris Marples: *Wicked Uncles in Love* (Michael Joseph, 1972).

Morris Marples: *Six Royal Sisters: The Daughters of George III* (Michael Joseph, 1969).

Dorothy Margaret Stuart: *The Daughters of George III* (Macmillan, 1939).

Roger Fulford: *Royal Dukes* (Duckworth, 1933).

A. H. Burne: *The Noble Duke of York* (Staples, 1949).

David Duff: *Edward of Kent* (Muller, 1938).

Mollie Gillen: *The Prince and his Lady* (Sidgwick and Jackson, 1970).

M. Porter: *Overture to Victoria* (1961).

Dulcie M. Ashdown: *Queen Victoria's Mother* (Robert Hale, 1974).

Dorothy Margaret Stuart: *The Mother of Queen Victoria* (Macmillan, 1941).

G. M. Willis: *Ernest Augustus, Duke of Cumberland and King of Hanover* (1954).

Mollie Gillen: *Royal Duke* (Sidgwick and Jackson, 1976).

G. St Aubyn: *The Royal George* (Constable, 1963).

L. Felderman: *The House of Teck* (1911).

Lucille Iremonger: *Love and the Princess* (about Princess Sophia and Princess Amelia) (Faber, 1958).

W. S. Childe-Pemberton: *The Romance of Princess Amelia* (1910).

GEORGE IV

FATHER: *George III (see page 285).*

MOTHER: *Charlotte of Mecklenburg-Strelitz (see page 286, under George III).*

SIBLINGS: *(see page 286, under George III).*

GEORGE IV

Baptised George Augustus Frederick, he was born on 12th August, 1762 at St James's Palace, London, and was Duke of Cornwall and Rothesay, Earl of Carrick, Baron Renfrew and Lord of the Isles from birth. He was created Prince of Wales and Earl of Chester on 17th or 19th August, 1762. He was created Prince Regent of the United Kingdom by Act of Parliament on 5th February, 1811, because of his father's incapacity; he held this title until his accession. He succeeded his father as King of Great Britain on 29th January, 1820, and was crowned on 19th July, 1821 at Westminster Abbey.

George IV married firstly, privately and in contravention of the Act of Settlement 1701 and the Royal Marriages Act 1772, on 15th September, 1785, at her house in Park Lane, Mayfair, London:

Maria Anne

She was the daughter of Walter Smythe of Brambridge, Hants., by Mary, daughter of John Errington of Red Rice, Andover, Hants., and she was born on 26th July, 1756 at Brambridge, Hants. She married firstly Edward Weld (d.1775) of Lulworth Castle, Dorset in 1775, and secondly Thomas FitzHerbert of Norbury, Derby and Swynnerton, Staffs. (d.1781) in 1778. Her marriage to the Prince of Wales was invalid under British Law, but was recognised by Papal Brief in 1800 (Mrs FitzHerbert was a Roman Catholic). Maria formally adopted the following children:

1 Mary ("Minnie") Seymour, orphaned daughter of Lord Hertford, who later married Colonel Dawson Darner.

2 Mary Anne Smythe, the illegitimate daughter of Maria's brother; she later married Captain Jerningham.

Maria spent most of her married life living apart from her husband. She died on 27th or 29th March, 1837 at Brighton, Sussex, and was buried in the R.C. Church of St John the Baptist, Brighton, Sussex. There was no issue of her marriage to George IV.

George IV married secondly, on 8th April, 1795 at the Chapel Royal, St James's Palace, London:

Caroline Amelia Elizabeth

She was the daughter of Charles II (William Ferdinand), Duke of Brunswick-Wolfenbüttel, by Princess Augusta of Wales, granddaughter of George II. She was born on 17th May, 1768 at Brunswick, Germany. The King tried unsuccessfully to divorce her for adultery (then a treasonable crime on the part of his Consort), and she was refused admission to his coronation in 1821. She died on 7th August,

1821, at Brandenburg House, Hammersmith, London, and was buried at Brunswick.

Issue of marriage:

1 *Charlotte Augusta*

She was born on 7th January, 1796 at Carlton House, London. She married Prince Leopold George Frederick of Saxe-Coburg-Saalfield (1790–1865) (later to become Leopold I, King of the Belgians) on 2nd May, 1816 at Carlton House, London, and had issue:

1 Miscarriage; this occurred in July, 1816 at Camelford House, London.

2 Stillborn son; he was born on 5th November, 1817 at Claremont House, Esher, Surrey, and was buried in St George's Chapel, Windsor.

Charlotte died on 6th November, 1817 at Claremont House, Esher, Surrey, in childbed, and was buried in St George's Chapel, Windsor.

George IV also had the following **illegitimate issue**:

By Grace Darymple, Mrs Elliott:

1 Georgina Frederica Augusta (?) (b.1782). She may have been the daughter of Lord Cholmondeley.

By Elizabeth Milbanke, Viscountess Melbourne (d.1818):

2 George (b.1784). Perhaps died young.

GEORGE IV

He died on 26th June, 1830 at Windsor Castle, and was buried in St George's Chapel, Windsor.

He was succeeded by his brother William.

Recommended reading

Christopher Hibbert: *George IV, Prince of Wales* (Longmans, 1972) and *George IV, Regent and King* (Longmans, 1973).

A. Palmer: *George IV* (Weidenfeld and Nicolson, 1972).

Joanna Richardson: *George IV: A Portrait* (Sidgwick and Jackson, 1966).

J. B. Priestley: *The Prince of Pleasure* (Heinemann, 1969).

For George's family, see:

A. Leslie: *Mrs FitzHerbert* (Hutchinson, 1960).

Joanna Richardson: *The Disastrous Marriage* (Jonathan Cape, 1960).

Roger Fulford: *The Trial of Queen Caroline* (Batsford, 1968).

Thea Holme: *Prinny's Daughter* (Hamish Hamilton, 1976).

Dorothy Margaret Stuart: *Daughter of England* (1951).

WILLIAM IV

FATHER: *George III (see page 285)*

MOTHER: *Charlotte of Mecklenburg-Strelitz (see page 286, under George III).*

SIBLINGS: *(see page 286, under George III).*

WILLIAM IV

Baptised William Henry, he was born on 21st August, 1765 at Buckingham Palace. He was made a Knight of the Thistle on 5th April, 1770, and a Knight of the Garter on 19th April, 1782. He was created Duke of Clarence and St Andrews, and Earl of Munster on 20th May, 1789. He succeeded his brother George IV as King of Great Britain on 26th June, 1830, and was crowned on 8th September, 1831 at Westminster Abbey.

William IV married, on 13th July, 1818 at Kew Palace, Surrey:

Adelaide Louisa Theresa Caroline Amelia

She was the daughter of George I (Frederick Charles), Duke of Saxe-Meiningen, by Louisa Eleanor, daughter of Christian Albert Louis, Prince of Hohenlohe-Langenburg, and she was born on 13th August, 1792 at Meiningen, Thuringia, Germany. She was crowned Queen Consort on 8th September, 1831 at Westminster Abbey. She died on 2nd December, 1849 at Bentley Priory, Stanmore, Middlesex, and was buried in St George's Chapel, Windsor.

Issue of marriage:

1 *Charlotte Augusta Louise*

She was born on 27th March, 1819 at the Fürstenhof Palace, Hanover, and died the same day. She was buried at Hanover, Germany.

2 *Stillborn child*

It was born on 5th September, 1819 at Dunkirk, France.

3 *Elizabeth Georgina Adelaide*

She was born on 10th December, 1820 at St James's Palace, London, where she died on 4th March, 1821. She was buried in St George's Chapel, Windsor.

4 *Stillborn child*

It was born in the spring of 1822 at Bushey Park, Middlesex.

5 *Stillborn twins*

They were born in 1824.

William IV also had the following **illegitimate issue**:

By Caroline von Linsingen (who alleged that William married her in 1784/5 or c.1790, in secret; this is very unlikely, although not impossible):

1 William (1784/5–drowned 1807).

By Dorothea Bland, Mrs Jordan (1761–1816):

2 George Augustus Frederick FitzClarence, Earl of Munster (1794–committed suicide 1842); he married Mary, illegitimate daughter of George Wyndham, 3rd Earl of Egremont, and had issue.

3 Henry Edward FitzClarence (1795–1817).

4 Sophia FitzClarence (1796–1837); she married Philip Charles Sidney, 1st Baron de Lisle and Dudley of Penshurst (1800–1851).

5 Mary FitzClarence (1798–1864); she married Charles Richard Fox.

6 Frederick FitzClarence (1799–1854); he married Augusta Boyle.

7 Elizabeth FitzClarence (1801–1856); she married William George Hay, 18th Earl of Erroll (1801–1846), and had issue.

8 Adolphus FitzClarence (1802–1856).

9 Augusta FitzClarence (1803–1865); she married firstly John Kennedy Erskine, and had issue, and secondly John, Lord Gordon.

10 Augustus FitzClarence, Rector of Mapledurham (1805–1854); he married Sarah Elizabeth Katherine Gordon.

11 Amelia FitzClarence (1807–1858); she married Lucius Bentinck Carey, 10th Viscount Falkland (1803–1884), and had issue.

WILLIAM IV

He died on 20th June, 1837 at Windsor Castle, and was buried in St George's Chapel, Windsor.

He was succeeded by his niece Victoria.

Recommended reading

Philip Ziegler: *William IV* (Collins, 1971).

W. G. Allen: *King William IV* (1960).

M. Hopkirk: *Queen Adelaide* (John Murray, 1946).

QUEEN VICTORIA

FATHER: *Edward, Duke of Kent (see page 287, under George III).*

MOTHER: *Victoria of Saxe-Coburg-Saalfield (see page 288, under George III).*

SIBLINGS: *Queen Victoria did not have any full siblings.*

QUEEN VICTORIA

Baptised Alexandrina Victoria, she was born on 24th May, 1819 at Kensington Palace, London. She succeeded William IV, her uncle, as Queen of Great Britain on 20th June, 1837, and was crowned on 28th June, 1838 at Westminster Abbey. She was declared Empress of India on 1st May, 1876, and proclaimed as such on 1st January, 1877 at Delhi, India.

Queen Victoria married, on 10th February, 1840, at the Chapel Royal, St James's Palace, London:

Albert Francis Charles Augustus Emmanuel

He was the son of Ernest I, Duke of Saxe-Coburg and Gotha, by Louise of Saxe-Gotha-Altenburg, and he was born on 26th August, 1819 at the Marble Hall, Schloss Rosenau, Coburg, Germany. He was made a Knight of the Garter on 16th December, 1839. He was created Prince Consort by Letters Patent on 26th June, 1857, and proclaimed as such the same day. He died on 14th December, 1861 at Windsor Castle, of typhoid, and was buried in St George's Chapel Windsor (in the Albert Memorial Chapel). His remains were later removed to the Royal Mausoleum, Frogmore, Windsor.

Issue of marriage:

1 *Victoria Adelaide Mary Louise*

She was born on 21st November, 1840 at Buckingham Palace, and was designated Princess Royal from birth. She married Prince Frederick William Nicholas Charles of Prussia, afterwards Frederick III, Emperor of Prussia (1831–1888) on 25th January, 1858 at the Chapel Royal, St James's Palace, London, and had issue:

1 William II (Frederick William Albert Victor), Emperor of Germany (1859–1941); he married Augusta Victoria Louisa Feodora Jenny (1858–1921), daughter of Frederick, Duke of Schleswig-Holstein, and had issue. He married secondly, Hermine (1887–1947), daughter of Henry XXII, Duke of Reuss.

2 Victoria Elizabeth Augusta Charlotte (1860–1919); she married Bernhard III, Duke of Saxe-Meiningen (1851–1928), and had issue.

3 Albert William Henry (1862–1929); he married Irene Louise Mary Anne (1866–1953), daughter of Louis IV, Grand Duke of Hesse-Darmstadt, by Alice, daughter of Queen Victoria (see page 307, below), and had issue.

4 Francis Frederick Sigmund (1864–1866).

5 Frederica Wilhelmina Amelia Victoria (1866–1929); she married firstly Prince Adolphus William of Schaumburg-Lippe (1856–1916), and secondly Alexander Alexandrovich Zubka (1900–1936).

6 Joachim Frederick Ernest Waldemar (1868–1879).

7 Sophia Dorothea Ulrica Alice (1870–1932); she married Constantine I, King of Greece (1868–1923), and had issue.

8 Margaret Beatrice Feodora (1872–1954); she married Frederick Charles, Landgrave of Hesse (1868–1940), and had issue.

Victoria died on 5th August, 1901 at the Friedrichshof Palace, Krönberg, Germany, of cancer, and was buried in the Friedenskirche, Potsdam, Germany.

2 *Edward VII* *(see page 319)*.

3 *Alice Maud Mary*

She was born on 25th April, 1843 at Buckingham Palace. She

married Louis IV, Grand Duke of Hesse-Darmstadt and the Rhine, and Duke of Saxony (1837–1892) on 1st July, 1862 at Osborne House, Isle of Wight, and had issue:

1 Ernest Louis Albert Charles William (1868–1937), Grand Duke of Hesse-Darmstadt and the Rhine; he married Princess Victoria of Edinburgh (1876–1936), granddaughter of Queen Victoria (see page 309, below), and had issue, although they were afterwards divorced. He married secondly Eleanor Ernestine Marie of Solms-Hohensolmslich (1871–1937), and had issue. Both he and his second wife were killed in air crashes.

2 Frederick William Augustus Victor Leopold Louis (1870–1873). He was killed falling out of an upstairs window.

3 Victoria Alberta Elizabeth Matilda Mary (1863–1950); she married Prince Louis Alexander of Battenberg (who changed his name to Mountbatten in 1917), 1st Marquess of Milford Haven (1854–1921), and had issue, including Lord Louis Mountbatten, 1st Earl Mountbatten of Burma (1900–assassinated by the I.R.A. in 1979).

4 Elizabeth Alexandra Louise Alice (assumed name Elizabeth Federovna upon marriage) (1864–assassinated 1918 during the Russian Revolution); she married Grand Duke Serge of Russia (1857–murdered 1905).

5 Irene Louise Marie Anne (1866–1953); she married Prince Albert William Henry of Prussia (1862–1929), son of the Princess Royal, eldest daughter of Queen Victoria (see page 306, above), and had issue.

6 Alice Victoria Helena Louise Beatrice (assumed name Alexandra Federovna upon marriage) (1872–1918: murdered during the Russian Revolution); she married Nicholas II, Tsar of all the Russias (1868–assassinated 1918 by the Bolsheviks), and had issue, all of whom were assassinated during the Russian Revolution.

7 Mary Victoria Feodora Leopoldine (1874–1878); she died of diphtheria.

Alice died on 14th December, 1878, at Darmstadt, of diphtheria, and was buried in the Mausoleum of Rosenhöhe, Hesse-Darmstadt, Germany.

4 *Alfred Ernest Albert*

He was born on 6th August, 1844 at Windsor Castle. He was made a Knight of the Garter on 24th May, 1863, and was created Duke of Edinburgh, Earl of Kent and Earl of Ulster on 24th May, 1866. He succeeded his father's brother Ernest as reigning Duke of Saxe-Coburg and Gotha on 22nd August, 1893. He died on 30th July, 1900 at Schloss Rosenau, Coburg, Germany, of cancer, and was buried in the cemetery of Coburg.

Alfred married, on 23rd January, 1874, at the Winter Palace, St Petersburg, Russia:

Marie Alexandrovna

She was the daughter of Alexander II, Tsar of all the Russias, by Marie Alexandrovna, daughter of Louis II, Grand Duke of Hesse and the Rhine, and she was born on 5th or 17th October, 1853 at Tsarskoie-Selo, Russia (or, less probably, at St Petersburg, Russia). She died on 5th or 24th October, 1920 at Zürich, Switzerland.

Issue of marriage:

(i) *Alfred Alexander William Ernest Albert*

He was born on 15th October, 1874, either at Buckingham Palace, or at Eastwell Park, Kent. He became a Prince of Saxe-Coburg and Gotha upon the accession of his father to the ducal throne on 22nd August, 1893, and he was made a Knight of the Garter on 23rd April, 1894. He never married. He shot himself on 6th February, 1899, at Meran, in the Austrian Tyrol (or, much less probably, at Coburg), and was buried in the Castle church at Friedenstein, near Gotha, Germany.

(ii) *Marie Alexandra Victoria*

She was born on 29th October, 1875 at Eastwell Park, Kent. She married Ferdinand I (Albert Meinrad) King of Romania (1865–1927) on 10th January, 1893 at Sigmaringen Castle, Romania, and had issue:

1 Charles II, King of Romania (1893–1953); he married firstly Joanna Maria Valentina (known as Zizi) (1898–1953), daughter of Constantine Lambrino; they were divorced in 1919. He married secondly Helen (1896–1982), daughter of Constantine I, King of Greece, and had issue; they were divorced in 1928. He married thirdly Elena Magda (1902–1977), daughter of Nicholas Lepescu.

2 Elizabeth Charlotte Josephine Victoria Alexandra (1894–1956); she married George II, King of Greece (1890–1947), but they were divorced in 1935.

3 Marie (1900–1961); she married Alexander I, King of Yugoslavia (1891–murdered 1934), and had issue.

4 Nicholas (b.1903); he married firstly Joanna Dolete (1909–1963), daughter of John Dumitrescu-Tohani, and secondly Theresa Lisboa Figueria (b.1913), daughter of Jeronymo de Avellar Figueira de Mello.

5 Ileana (b.1909); she married firstly Anton, Archduke of Austria-Tuscany (b.1901), and had issue; they were divorced in 1954. She married secondly Stephen Issarescu (b.1906). She is now a nun, and is known as Mother Alexandra of the Monastery of the Transfiguration, Ellwood City, P.A., U.S.A.

6 Mircea (1913–1916).

Marie died on 18th July, 1938 at Peles Catle, Sinaia, Romania.

(iii) *Victoria Melita*

She was born on 25th November, 1876 at the Palace of San Antonio, Malta. She married firstly Ernest Louis, Grand Duke of Hesse-Darmstadt and the Rhine (1868–1937) (son of Alice, daughter of Queen Victoria—see above) on 19th April, 1894 at Schloss Ehrenburg, Coburg, Germany, and had issue:

1 Elizabeth Mary Alice Victoria (1895–1903).

2 Unnamed son (b.&d.1900).

3 Miscarriage.

Victoria was divorced from Ernest on 21st December, 1901. She married secondly Grand Duke Kyrill Vladimirovitch of Russia (1876–1938) on 8th October, 1905 at Tegernsee, and had issue:

1 Marie Kirillovna (1907–1951); she married Frederick Charles Edward Erwin, 6th Fürst of Leiningen (1898–1946), and had issue.

2 Kira Kirillovna (1909–1967); she married Louis Ferdinand, Prince of Prussia (b.1907), and had issue.

3 Vladimir Kirillovitch (b.1917); he married Leonida Georgievna, Princess Bagration-Monkhransky (b.1913), and had issue.

Victoria died on 2nd March, 1936 at Amorbach, Germany.

(iv) *Alexandra Louise Olga Victoria*

She was born on 1st September, 1878 at Coburg, Germany. She married Ernest William Frederick Charles Maximilian, 7th Prince of Hohenlohe-Langenburg (1863–1950) on 20th April, 1896 at Coburg, and had issue:

1 Godfrey Victor Hermann Alfred Paul Maximilian, 8th Prince of Hohenlohe-Langenburg (1897–1960); he married

Margaret (1905–1981), daughter of Prince Andrew of Greece and Denmark and sister of Prince Philip, Duke of Edinburgh, and had issue.

2 Marie Melita Leopoldine Victoria Feodora Alexandra Sophia (1899–1967); she married William Frederick, Duke of Schleswig-Holstein-Glücksburg, and had issue.

3 Alexandra Beatrice Leopoldine (1901–1963).

4 Irma Helena (b.1902).

5 Alfred (b.&d.1911).

Alexandra died on 16th April, 1942 at Schwäbisch-Hall, Württemburg, Germany.

(v) *Unnamed daughter*

She was born on 13th October, 1879 at Eastwell Park, Kent, and died the same day. She may have been stillborn.

(vi) *Beatrice Leopoldine Victoria*

She was born on 20th April, 1884 at Eastwell Park, Kent. She married Alfonso Maria Francisco Antonio Diego, Infante of Spain and 3rd Duke of Galliera (1886–1975) on 15th July, 1909 at Schloss Rosenau, Coburg, Germany, and had issue:

1 Alvaro Antonio Fernando Carlos Felipe, Prince of Orléans (b.1910); he married Carla Delfino (b.1909), and had issue.

2 Alonso Maria Cristino Justo (1912–killed 1936).

3 Ataulfo Alejando Isabelo Carlos (b.1913).

Beatrice died on 13th July, 1966 at Sanlucar de Barrameda, Spain.

5 *Helena Augusta Victoria*

She was born on 23rd or 25th May, 1846 at Buckingham Palace. She married Christian, Prince of Schleswig-Holstein-Sonderburg-Augustenburg (1831–1917) on 5th July, 1866 at the Private Chapel, Windsor Castle, and had issue:

1 Christian Victor Albert Louis Ernest Anthony (1867–1900).

2 Albert John Charles Frederick Alfred George, Duke of Schleswig-Holstein (1869–1931).

3 Victoria Louise Sophia Augusta Amelia Helena (1870–1948).

4 Franzisca Josepha Louise Augusta Marie Christina Helena (known as Princess Marie Louise) (1872–1956); she married Aribert Joseph Alexander, Prince of Anhalt (1864–1933); they were divorced in 1900.

5 Frederick Christian Augustus Leopold Edward Harold (b.&d.1876).

6 Unnamed son (b. & d.1877).

Helena died on 9th June, 1923 at Schomberg House, Pall Mall, London, and was buried in the Royal Mausoleum, Frogmore, Windsor.

6 _Louise Caroline Alberta_

She was born on 18th March, 1848 at Buckingham Palace. She married John George Edward Henry Douglas Sutherland Campbell, Marquess of Lorne, later 9th Duke of Argyll (1845–1914) on 21st March, 1871 at St George's Chapel, Windsor. She died on 3rd December, 1939 at Kensington Palace, London, and was cremated at Golders Green Crematorium, her ashes being buried in the Royal Mausoleum, Frogmore, Windsor.

7 _Arthur William Patrick Albert_

He was born on 1st May, 1850 at Buckingham Palace. He was made a Knight of the Garter on 24th May, 1867, and a Knight of the Thistle on 24th May, 1869. He was created Duke of Connaught and Strathearn and Earl of Sussex on 24th May, 1874. He died on 16th January, 1942 at Bagshot Park, Surrey, and was buried in the Royal Mausoleum, Frogmore, Windsor.

Arthur married, on 13th March, 1879, at St George's Chapel, Windsor:

Louise Marguerite Alexandra Victoria Agnes

She was the daughter of Prince Frederick Charles Nicholas of Prussia by Mary Anne, daughter of Leopold Frederick, Duke of Anhalt-Dessau, and she was born on 25th July, 1860 at Marmorpalais (Marble Palace), near Potsdam, Germany. She died on 14th March, 1917 at Clarence House, London, and was buried in the Royal Mausoleum, Frogmore, Windsor.

· Issue of marriage:

(i) _Margaret Victoria Augusta Charlotte Norah_

She was born on 15th January, 1882 at Bagshot Park, Surrey. She married (Oscar Frederick William Olaf) Gustavus Adolphus VI, King of Sweden (1882–1973) on 15th June, 1905 at St George's Chapel, Windsor, and had issue:

1 Gustavus Adolphus Oscar Frederick Arthur Edmund (1906–1947); he married Sybilla Calma Marie Alice Bathildis Feodora of Saxe-Coburg (1908–1972), and had issue.

2 Sigvard Oscar Frederick, Duke of Upland (b.1907); he married firstly Erika Maria Regina Rosalie Patzeck; they were later divorced. He married secondly Sonia Helen Robbert (b.1909), and had issue.

311

3 Ingrid Victoria Sophia Louise Margaret (b.1910); she married Frederick IX, King of Denmark, and had issue.

4 Bertil Gustavus Oscar Charles Eugene, Duke of Holland (b.1912).

5 Charles John Arthur, Duke of Dalecarlia (b.1916); he married Ellen Christine Margaret Wijkmark (b.1910).

6 Unnamed daughter (d. young).

Margaret died on 1st May, 1920 at Stockholm, Sweden.

(ii) *Arthur Frederick Patrick Albert*
He was born on 13th January, 1883 at Windsor Castle. He was made a Knight of the Garter on 15th July, 1902. He died on 12th September, 1938 at Belgrave Square, London.

Arthur married, on 15th October, 1913, at the Chapel Royal, St James's Palace:

Alexandra Victoria Alberta Edwina Louise
She was the daughter of Alexander William George Duff, Duke of Fife, by Louise, daughter of Edward VII, and she was born on 17th May, 1891 at East Sheen Lodge, Surrey. She succeeded her father as Duchess of Fife in her own right in 1912. She died on 26th February, 1959 at her house in Avenue Road, London, and was cremated at Golders Green Crematorium, London.

Issue of marriage:

(a) *Alastair Arthur*
He was born on 9th August, 1914 in Mount Street, London, and was styled Earl of MacDuff from birth. He succeeded his grandfather Arthur as Duke of Connaught and Strathearn and Earl of Sussex on 16th January, 1942. He died on 26th April, 1943 at Government House, Ottawa, Canada, and was buried in Mar Lodge Chapel, Braemar, Aberdeenshire.

(iii) *Victoria Patricia Helen Elizabeth*
She was born on 17th March, 1886 at Buckingham Palace. She married Sir Alexander Robert Maule Ramsay (1881–1972) on 27th February, 1919 at Westminster Abbey (this was the first royal wedding to take place in the Abbey since Tudor times). She renounced her title of Princess, and assumed the style Lady Patricia Ramsay upon marriage. She had issue:

1 Alexander Arthur Alfonso David Maule (b.1919); he mar-

ried Marjorie Flora (b.1930), daughter of Alexander Arthur Fraser, 19th Earl of Saltoun, and had issue.

Lady Patricia died on 12th January, 1974.

8 *Leopold George Duncan Albert*

He was born on 7th April, 1853 at Buckingham Palace. He was made a Knight of the Garter on 24th May, 1869, and created Duke of Albany, Earl of Clarence and Baron Arklow on 14th May, 1881. A haemophiliac, he died after an accident on 28th March, 1884 at the Villa Nevada, Cannes, France, and was buried in St George's Chapel, Windsor.

Leopold married, on 27th April, 1882, at St George's Chapel, Windsor:

Hélène Frederica Augusta

She was the daughter of George Victor, Prince of Waldeck-Pyrmont, by Helena Wilhelmina Henrietta Pauline Marianne, daughter of George William Augustus Henry, Duke of Nassau-Weilburg, and she was born on 17th February, 1861 at Arolsen, Waldeck, Germany. She died on 1st September, 1922 at Hinterris in the Austrian Tyrol, and was buried in Austria.

Issue of marriage:

 (i) *Alice Mary Victoria Augusta Pauline*

She was born on 25th February, 1883 at Windsor Castle. She married Alexander of Teck, Earl of Athlone (1874–1957) (great-grandson of George III and brother of Queen Mary, wife of George V) on 10th February, 1904 at St George's Chapel, Windsor, and had issue:

1 May Helen Emma (b.1906); she married Colonel Sir Henry Abel Smith (b.1900), and had issue.

2 Rupert Alexander George Augustus, Viscount Trematon (1907–killed in a car accident 1928).

3 Maurice Francis George (b.&d.1910).

In 1917, Alexander of Teck adopted the surname Cambridge, which has since been used by his family. Princess Alice died on 3rd January, 1981 at Kensington Palace, London, and was buried at Frogmore, Windsor.

 (ii) *(Leopold) Charles Edward George Albert*

Known as Charles, he was born on 19th July, 1884 at Claremont House, Esher, Surrey, his father's posthumous son. He therefore succeeded at birth as Duke of Albany, Earl of Clarence and Baron Arklow. He succeeded his uncle Alfred as Duke of Saxe-Coburg-Gotha on 30th July, 1900. He was made a Knight of the Garter on 15th July, 1902. He supported Kaiser William II during the First World War, and was consequently struck off the register of the Knights of the Garter in 1915. He abdicated as Duke of Saxe-Coburg-Gotha on 14th November, 1918, and his English titles were formally removed by order of King George V in Council on 28th March, 1919. He died on 6th March, 1954 at Coburg, Germany.

Charles married, on 11th October, 1905, at Glücksburg Castle, Holstein, Germany:

Victoria Adelaide Helena Louise Marie Frederica
She was the daughter of Frederick Ferdinand George Christian Charles William, Duke of Schleswig-Holstein-Sonderburg-Glücksburg, by Victoria Frederica Augusta Marie Caroline Matilda, daughter of Frederick Christian Augustus, Duke of Schleswig-Holstein-Sonderburg-Glücksburg. She was born on 31st December, 1885 at Grünholz, Holstein, Germany. She died on 3rd or 5th October, 1970, either at Coburg, Germany, or at Greinburg, Austria.

Issue of marriage:

(a) John Leopold William Albert Ferdinand Victor (1906–1972); he married firstly Feodora Mary Alma Margaret (b.1907), daughter of Baron Bernard von der Horst, and had issue; they were divorced in 1962. He married secondly Maria Theresa Elizabeth (1908–72), daughter of Max Reinde.

(b) Sybilla Calma Mary Alice Bathildis Feodora (1908–1972); she married Prince Gustavus Adolphus of Sweden (1906–killed 1947), and had issue.

(c) Dietmar Hubert Frederick William Philip (1909–1943).

(d) Caroline Matilda Louisa Eleanor Augusta Beatrice (b.1912); she married firstly Frederick Wolfgang, Count of Castell-Rudenhausen (1906–1940), and had issue; they were divorced in 1938. She married secondly Max Schnirring (1896–1944), and had issue, and thirdly Jim Andree (b.1912); they were divorced in 1949.

(e) Frederick Josias Charles Edward Ernest Cyril Harold (b.1918); he married firstly Victoria Louisa Frederica Caroline Matilda (b.1921), daughter of Hans, Count of Solmsbaruth, and had issue; they were divorced in 1946. He married secondly Denise Henrietta (b.1923), daughter of Gaston Robert de Muralt, and had issue; they were divorced in 1964. He married thirdly Katherine (b.1940), daughter of Dietrich Charles Bremme.

9 *Beatrice Mary Victoria Feodore*

She was born on 14th April, 1857 at Buckingham Palace. She married Prince Henry Maurice of Battenberg (1858–1896) on 23rd July, 1885 at Whippingham Church, Isle of Wight, and had issue:

1 Alexander Albert, Marquess of Carisbrooke (1886–1960); he married Irene Frances Adza (1890–1956), daughter of William Denison, 3rd Earl of Londesbrough, and had issue.

2 Victoria Eugénie Julia Ena (who took the additional names Maria Christina upon entering the Roman Catholic Faith) (1887–1969); she married Alfonso XIII, King of Spain (1886–1941), and had issue.

3 Leopold Arthur Louis (1889–1922).

4 Maurice Victor Donald (1891–killed at the Battle of Mons, 1914).

Beatrice died on 26th October, 1944 at Brantridge Park, Balcombe, Sussex, and was buried in St George's Chapel, Windsor. Her remains were later removed to St Mildred's Church, Whippingham, Isle of Wight.

QUEEN VICTORIA

She died on 22nd January, 1901 at Osborne House, Isle of Wight, and was buried in the Royal Mausoleum, Frogmore, Windsor.

She was succeeded by her son Albert, who styled himself Edward VII.

Recommended reading

There have been two outstanding biographies of Queen Victoria in recent years:

Elizabeth Longford: *Victoria R. I.* (Weidenfeld and Nicolson, 1964).

C. Woodham-Smith: *Queen Victoria: Her Life and Times Vol. 1* (Hamish Hamilton, 1972).

See also:

Joanna Richardson: *Victoria and Albert* (Dent, 1977).

David Duff: *Albert and Victoria* (Muller, 1977).

Dulcie M. Ashdown: *Queen Victoria's Family* (Robert Hale, 1975).

Nina Epton: *Victoria and her Daughters* (Weidenfeld and Nicolson, 1971).

Tom Cullen: *The Empress Brown* (The Bodley Head, 1969).

Roger Fulford (editor): *Dearest Child* (1964), *Dearest Mama* (1968) and *Your Dear Letter* (1971), (a trilogy of letters between Queen Victoria and the Princess Royal).

For the Queen's family, see:

Daphne Bennett: *King without a Crown* (Heinemann, 1977).

Hector Bolitho: *Albert, Prince Consort* (Parrish, 1964).

G. and M. Scheele: *The Prince Consort* (1977) (with superb illustrations).

Roger Fulford: *The Prince Consort* (Macmillan, 1949).

Daphne Bennett: *Vicky* (Collins Harvill, 1971).

David Duff: *Hessian Tapestry* (Muller, 1967).

G. Noel: *Princess Alice, Queen Victoria's Forgotten Daughter* (Constable, 1974).

Jehanne Wake: *Princess Louise* (Collins, 1988).

David Duff: *The Life Story of H.R.H. Princess Louise, Duchess of Argyll* (Stanley Paul, 1940).

H.R.H. Princess Alice, Countess of Athlone: *For My Grandchildren* (Evans, 1966).

Theo Aronsen: *Princess Alice* (1982).

David Duff: *The Shy Princess* (Muller, 1958), a biography of Princess Beatrice.

9. The House of Saxe-Coburg-Gotha becomes the House of Windsor

The Hanoverian line officially ended with the death of Queen Victoria. Her son, Edward VII, was the first sovereign of the short-lived royal House of Saxe-Coburg-Gotha, as the son of the Prince Consort. At the turn of the 20th century, the British royal family was enjoying its greatest pinnacle of prestige, with the British Empire —which had vastly expanded during the reign of Victoria—covering much of the globe. The Monarchy now had imperial status, and Victoria herself embodied all its highest ideals.

This state of affairs could not last. The 20th century has seen the most sweeping changes in our history, as well as two world wars. The great Empire did not long survive the Second World War, and became the British Commonwealth of Nations, although many have since become independent.

It was one of the supreme ironies of history that the monarchy which led Britain and the Empire through two wars against Germany should itself be of German origin, and its members closely intermarried with high-ranking supporters of Kaiser William II or Adolf Hitler. Queen Victoria herself spoke English with a strong German accent, and German at home with Albert. The royal family of Hanover and that of Saxe-Coburg-Gotha were British by birth, closely related to the British royal house. Yet so strong was the monarchy's identification with its people, and so anti-German was the popular feeling of its subjects, that in 1917 King George V decided to expunge all German names and titles from his House and family. Thus the House of Saxe-Coburg-Gotha became the House of Windsor; their Serene Highnesses the Prince and Princess of Teck became transformed by the surname Cambridge; and Battenberg —the name of one of the most illustrious families of 19th- and 20th-century Europe—became Mountbatten.

Thirty years later, Mountbatten and Windsor were to become linked by marriage, when the present Queen married Lieutenant Philip Mountbatten. Since Elizabeth II's accession, it has become clear that, while the Queen's House and family are still known as

Windsor, her children are surnamed Mountbatten-Windsor. George V decreed also that the title Prince or Princess might be borne, not only by the sons and daughters of the monarch, but also by the children of sons of the sovereign. Great-grandchildren in the male line are styled Lord (name) or Lady (name) Windsor. Primogeniture, as practised by the Plantagenets centuries ago, is still used to determine the order of succession to the throne.

Of course, the monarchy has adapted to change, and also to an age in which media intrusion has—rather dangerously—on occasions reduced it to the level of a soap opera. This is perhaps the greatest threat it has faced since 1936, when Edward VIII abdicated for love, to marry a twice-divorced woman. That event shook the throne, and it was only the dedication and devotion to duty of King George VI and the present Queen Mother that set it back on an even keel. Her Majesty Queen Elizabeth II continues that tradition, and has been rewarded with the love and respect of her people, with her commitment to tradition and to family life. As sovereign, she embodies all the domestic virtues that made Queen Victoria so successful a monarch; yet, unlike Victoria in her later years, Elizabeth II is a very visible monarch, seen to be performing her duties with sincerity and dedication, in full glare of the media. She is a constitutional monarch *par excellence*, whose long experience in politics and public life has earned her the respect of political leaders worldwide.

For all the rumours, it is unthinkable that the Queen will abdicate. The memory of Edward VIII is too fresh in the public mind. The succession is assured well into the 21st century, and we may confidently hope that the traditions of a thousand years of British monarchy will continue long into the future.

EDWARD VII

FATHER: *Albert, Prince Consort (see page 305, under Queen Victoria).*
MOTHER: *Queen Victoria (see page 305).*
SIBLINGS: *(see page 306, under Queen Victoria).*

EDWARD VII

Baptised Albert Edward, he was born on 9th November, 1841 at Buckingham Palace, and was Duke of Cornwall and Rothesay, Earl of Carrick, Lord of the Isles and Baron Renfrew from birth. He was created Prince of Wales and Earl of Chester on 8th December, 1841, and Earl of Dublin on 17th January, 1850. He was made a Knight of the Garter on 9th November, 1858. In 1863, he renounced his courtesy title, Duke of Saxe-Coburg-Gotha, inherited from his father. He was made a Knight of the Thistle of 24th May, 1867. He succeeded his mother as King of Great Britain and Emperor of India on 22nd January, 1901, and was crowned on 9th August, 1902 at Westminster Abbey.

Edward VII married, on 10th March, 1863, at St George's Chapel, Windsor:

Alexandra Caroline Marie Charlotte Louise Julie
She was the daughter of Christian IX, King of Denmark, by Louise Wilhelmina Frederica Caroline Augusta Julie, daughter of William X, Landgrave of Hesse-Cassel, and she was born on 1st December, 1844 at the Amalienborg or "Gule" (Yellow) Palace, Copenhagen, Denmark. She was made a Lady of the Garter in 1901. She was crowned Queen on 9th August, 1902 at Westminster Abbey. She died on 20th November, 1925 at Sandringham House, Norfolk, and was buried in St George's Chapel, Windsor.

Issue of marriage:

1 *Albert Victor Christian Edward*
He was born on 8th January, 1864 at Frogmore House, Windsor.

319

He was made a Knight of the Garter on 3rd September, 1883, and was created Duke of Clarence and Avondale and Earl of Athlone on 24th May, 1890. He died on 14th January, 1892 at Sandringham House, Norfolk, of pneumonia, and was buried in St George's Chapel, Windsor.

The Duke of Clarence is said to have married one Annie Crook of Cleveland Street, London (d. 1920) during the 1880s, and is said to have had issue:

1 Alice Margaret Crook; she is said to have had a liaison with the painter, Walter Sickert, and to have had a son, Joseph Sickert, who is the source of this information, which should, however, be treated with extreme caution.

Historically, the Duke of Clarence was betrothed to Mary of Teck, who later married George V.

2 *George V (see page 322)*.

3 *Louise Victoria Alexandra Dagmar*

She was born on 20th February, 1867 at Marlborough House, London. She married Alexander William George Duff, Marquess of MacDuff, afterwards 1st Duke of Fife (1849–1912) on 27th July, 1889 in the Private Chapel, Buckingham Palace, and had issue:

1 Alastair (stillborn 1890).

2 Alexandra, Duchess of Fife (1891–1959); she married Prince Arthur of Connaught, grandson of Queen Victoria, and had issue.

3 Maud Alexandra Victoria Georgina Bertha (1893–1945); she married Charles Alexander Carnegie, 11th Earl of Southesk (b. 1893), and had issue.

Louise was designated Princess Royal on 9th November, 1905. She died on 4th January, 1931 at her house in Portman Square, London, and was buried in St George's Chapel, Windsor. Her remains were later removed to the Private Chapel, Mar Lodge Mausoleum, Braemar, Aberdeenshire.

4 *Victoria Alexandra Olga Mary*

She was born on 6th July, 1868 at Marlborough House, London. She died on 3rd December, 1935 at Coppins, Iver, Bucks., and was buried in the Royal Mausoleum, Frogmore, Windsor.

5 *Maud Charlotte Mary Victoria*

She was born on 26th November, 1869 at Marlborough House, London. She married Prince Christian Frederick Charles George Waldemar Axel of Denmark, afterwards Haakon VII, King of

Norway (1872–1957) on 22nd July, 1896 at the Private Chapel, Buckingham Palace, and had issue:

1 Olav V (Alexander Edward Christian Frederick), King of Norway (b.1903); he married Martha Sophia Louisa Dagmar Thyra (1901–1954), daughter of Carl, Prince of Sweden and Duke of Västergötland, and had issue.

Queen Maud died on 20th November, 1938 in London.

6 *Alexander John Charles Albert*

He was born on 6th April, 1871 at Sandringham House, Norfolk, and died there the following day. He was buried in Sandringham Church, Norfolk.

EDWARD VII

He died on 6th May, 1910 at Buckingham Palace, and was buried in St George's Chapel, Windsor.

He was succeeded by his son George.

Recommended reading

Keith Middlemas: *Edward VII* (Weidenfeld and Nicolson, 1972).
Christopher Hibbert: *Edward VII* (1976; Penguin, 1982).
Philip Magnus: *King Edward VII* (John Murray, 1964).
J. Maas: *The Prince of Wales' Wedding* (1977).
Graham and Heather Fisher: *Bertie and Alix* (Robert Hale, 1974).
Anita Leslie: *Edwardians in Love* (Hutchinson, 1972).
G. Brook-Shepherd: *Uncle of Europe* (Collins, 1975).
J. Brough: *The Prince and the Lily* (Hodder and Stoughton, 1975).
For Edward's family, see:
Georgina Battiscombe: *Queen Alexandra* (Constable, 1969).
M. Harrison: *Clarence* (W. H. Allen, 1972).
There are no biographies of Edward's daughters.

GEORGE V

FATHER: *Edward VII (see page 319).*
MOTHER: *Alexandra of Denmark (see page 319, under Edward VII).*
SIBLINGS: *(see page 319, under Edward VII).*

GEORGE V

Baptised George Frederick Ernest Albert, he was born on 3rd June, 1865 at Marlborough House, London. He was made a Knight of the Garter on 4th April, 1884, and was created Duke of York, Earl of Inverness and Baron Killarney on 24th May, 1892. He became Duke of Cornwall and Rothesay when his father succeeded to the throne on 22nd January, 1901, and was created Prince of Wales and Earl of Chester on 9th November, 1901. He succeeded his father as King of Great Britain and Emperor of India on 6th May, 1910, and was crowned on 22nd June, 1911 at Westminster Abbey. He was crowned Emperor of India on 11th December, 1911 at New Delhi, India. In 1917, George V changed the name of his House from Saxe-Coburg-Gotha to Windsor, which it remains today.

George V married, on 6th July, 1893, at the Chapel Royal, St James's Palace:

(Victoria) Mary Augusta Louise Olga Pauline Claudia Agnes
Known as Mary (or May within her family), she was the daughter of Francis Paul Charles Louis Alexander, Duke of Teck, by Princess Mary Adelaide of Cambridge, a granddaughter of George III. She was born on 26th May, 1867 at Kensington Palace, London, and was first betrothed to her future husband's elder brother, the Duke of Clarence, before his death. She was made a Lady of the Garter in 1910. She was crowned on 22nd June, 1911 at Westminster Abbey; she was also crowned Empress of India on 11th December, 1911 at New Delhi, India. She died on 24th March, 1953 at Marlborough House, London, and was buried in St George's Chapel, Windsor.

Issue of marriage:

1 *Edward VIII (see page 327).*
2 *George VI (see page 329).*
3 *(Victoria Alexandra Alice) Mary*

Known as Mary, she was born on 25th April, 1897 at Sandringham, Norfolk. She married Henry George Charles Lascelles, 6th Earl of Harewood (1882–1947) on 28th February, 1922 at Westminster Abbey, and had issue:

1 George Henry Hubert, 7th Earl of Harewood (b.1923); he married firstly Maria Donata Nanette Pauline Gustava Erwina Wilhelmina (known as Marion) (b.1926), daughter of Erwin Stein, and had issue; they divorced in 1967 (Marion later married the Liberal M.P. Jeremy Thorpe). He married secondly Patricia Elizabeth (b.1926), daughter of Charles Tuckwell, by whom he has issue.

2 Gerald David (b.1924); he married firstly Angela (b.1919), daughter of Charles Stanley Dowding, and had issue; they were divorced in 1978. He married secondly Elizabeth Colvin, née Collingwood (b.1924), by whom he has issue.

Mary was designated Princess Royal on 1st January, 1932. She died on 28th March, 1965 at Harewood House, Leeds, Yorkshire, and was buried at Harewood.

4 *Henry William Frederick Albert*

He was born on 31st March, 1900 at York Cottage, Sandringham, Norfolk. He was made a Knight of the Garter in 1921, and was created Duke of Gloucester, Earl of Ulster and Baron Culloden on 31st March, 1928. He died on 10th June, 1974 at Barnwell Manor, Northants., and was buried in St George's Chapel, Windsor.

Henry married, on 6th November, 1935, at the Private Chapel, Buckingham Palace:

Alice Christabel

She is the daughter of John Charles Montagu-Douglas-Scott, 7th Duke of Buccleuch and 10th Duke of Queensberry, by Margaret Alice, daughter of George Cecil Orlando Bridgeman, 4th Earl of Bradford, and she was born on 25th December, 1901 in London. Since her husband's death, she has been styled H.R.H. Princess Alice, Duchess of Gloucester.

Issue of marriage: **(i)** Miscarriage, late in 1937. **(ii)** Miscarriage, Autumn 1938. **(iii)** *William Henry Andrew Frederick*

He was born on 18th December, 1941 at Barnet, Herts. He

never married. He was killed on 28th August, 1972 in an air crash at Halfpenny Green, Wolverhampton, Staffs., and was buried in the Royal Mausoleum, Frogmore, Windsor.

(iv) *Richard Alexander Walter George*
He was born on 26th August, 1944 at Barnwell Manor, Peterborough, Northants. He succeeded his father as Duke of Gloucester, Earl of Ulster and Baron Culloden on 10th June, 1974.

Richard married, on 8th July, 1972, at the Parish Church of St Andrew, Barnwell, Northants.:
Birgitte Eva
She is the daughter of Asgar Preben Wissing Henrikson by Vivian, daughter of Waldemar Oswald van Deurs of Copenhagen, Denmark, and she was born on 20th June, 1946 at Odense, Isle of Funen, Denmark. Prior to her marriage, she used her mother's maiden surname "van Deurs".
Issue of marriage:

(a) *Miscarriage*
This occurred in 1973.

(b) *Alexander Patrick Gregers Richard*
He was born on 24th October, 1974 at St Mary's Hospital, Paddington, London, and has been styled Earl of Ulster from birth.

(c) *Davina Alice Elizabeth Benedikte*
She was born on 19th November, 1977 at St Mary's Hospital, Paddington, London, and is styled Lady Davina Windsor.

(d) *Rose Victoria Birgitte Louise*
She was born on 1st March, 1980 at St Mary's Hospital, Paddington, London, and is styled Lady Rose Windsor.

5 *George Edward Alexander Edmund*
He was born on 20th December, 1902 at Sandringham, Norfolk. He was made a Knight of the Garter in 1923, and was created Duke of Kent, Earl of St Andrews and Baron Downpatrick on 10th or 12th October, 1934. He was killed on 25th August, 1942 when his R.A.F. plane crashed into a hillside at Borgue or Morven, near Caithness, Scotland, whilst he was on active service during the Second World War. He was buried in St George's Chapel, Windsor, but his remains were later removed to the Kent Mausoleum, Frogmore, Windsor.

George married, on 29th November, 1934 at Westminster

Abbey, and again—by Greek Orthodox rites—on the same day at the Private Chapel, Buckingham Palace:
Marina
She was the daughter of Prince Nicholas of Greece and Denmark by Helen Vladimirovna, Grand Duchess of Russia, and she was born on 30th November or 13th December, 1906 at Athens, Greece. She died on 27th August, 1968 at Kensington Palace, London, of a brain tumour, and was buried in the Kent Mausoleum, Frogmore, Windsor.
Issue of marriage:

(i) *Edward George Nicholas Paul Patrick*
He was born on 9th October, 1935 at 3, Belgrave Square, London. He succeeded his father as Duke of Kent, Earl of St Andrews and Baron Downpatrick on 25th August, 1942.

Edward married, on 8th June, 1961 at York Minster:
Katharine Lucy Mary
She is the daughter of Sir William Arthrington Worsley, Bt., of Hovingham Hall, Yorkshire, by Joyce Morgan, daughter of Sir John Fowler Brunner, Bt., and she was born on 22nd February, 1933 at Hovingham Hall, Yorkshire.

Issue of marriage:

(a) *George Philip Nicholas*. Born on 26th June, 1962 at Coppins, Iver, Bucks., and has been styled Earl of St Andrews from birth. Married on 9th January, 1988, at Leith Register Office, Edinburgh: *Sylvana Palma*. She is the daughter of Max Tomaselli and Josiane Demers, and was born on 28th May, 1957, at Placentia, Newfoundland, Canada and has issue: 1 Edward, Baron Downpatrick; born on 2nd December 1988. 2 Marina; born on 30th September 1992.

(b) *Helen Marina Lucy*. Born on 28th April, 1964 at Coppins, Iver, Bucks., and is styled Lady Helen Windsor. Married in 1992 at St George's Chapel, Windsor, Timothy Taylor and has issue: 1 Columbus (b.1994).

(c) *Nicholas Charles Edward Jonathan*. Born on 25th July, 1970 at University College Hospital, London, and is styled Lord Nicholas Windsor.

(d) *Stillborn child*. Born on 5th October, 1977 at the King Edward VII Hospital for Officers, Marylebone, London.

(ii) *Alexandra Helen Elizabeth Olga Christabel*
She was born on 25th December, 1936 at 3, Belgrave Square,

London. She married Sir Angus James Bruce Ogilvy (b.1928) on 24th April, 1963 at Westminster Abbey, and has issue: 1 James Robert Bruce (b.1964); married to Julia (b.1965), daughter of Charles Rawlinson, and has issue. 2 Marina Victoria Alexandra (b.1966); married to Paul Mowatt (b.1962) and has issue.

(iii) *Michael George Charles Franklin*
He was born on 4th July, 1942 at Coppins, Iver, Bucks.

Michael married, on 30th June, 1978, at a civil ceremony at the Rathaus, Vienna, Austria (and in so doing renounced his place in the succession, as his bride is a Roman Catholic):
Marie Christine Anne Agnes Hedwig Ida
She is the daughter of Baron Gunther Hubertus von Reibnitz by Marianne, Countess Szapary, and she was born on 15th January, 1945 at Karlsbad, Bohemia (now Czechoslovakia). She married firstly Thomas Troubridge (b.1939) on 14th September, 1971 at Chelsea Old Church, London, but this marriage was formally annulled by the Roman Catholic Church in May, 1978, on undisclosed grounds.
Issue of marriage:
(a) *Frederick Michael George David Louis*
He was born on 6th April, 1979 at St Mary's Hospital, Paddington, London, and is known as Lord Frederick Windsor.
(b) *Gabriella Marina Alexandra Ophelia*
She was born on 23rd April, 1981 at St Mary's Hospital, Paddington, London, and is known as Lady Gabriella Windsor.

6 *John Charles Francis*
He was born on 12th July, 1905 at York Cottage, Sandringham, Norfolk. An epileptic who was kept away from the public eye, he died on 18th January, 1919 at Wood Farm, Wolferton, Norfolk, and was buried in Sandringham Church, Norfolk.

GEORGE V
He died on 20th January, 1936 at Sandringham House, Norfolk, and was buried in St George's Chapel, Windsor.

He was succeeded by his son Edward.

Recommended reading
Kenneth Rose: *King George V* (Weidenfeld and Nicolson, 1983).
Dennis Judd: *George V* (Weidenfeld and Nicolson, 1973).

Harold Nicolson: *George V: His Life and Reign* (Constable, 1952) (the official biography).
For George's family, see:
Anne Edwards: *Matriarch: Queen Mary and the House of Windsor* (Hodder and Stoughton, 1984).
James Pope-Hennessy: *Queen Mary* (Allen and Unwin, 1959) (the official biography).
Christopher Warwick: *George and Marina, Duke and Duchess of Kent* (Weidenfeld and Nicolson, 1988).
Richard Hough: *Born Royal: The Lives and Loves of the Young Windsors* (André Deutsch, 1988).
Princess Alice, Duchess of Gloucester: Memoirs (Collins, 1983).
G. St Aubyn: *William of Gloucester, Pioneer Prince* (1977).
Helen Cathcart: *The Duchess of Kent* (W. H. Allen, 1971).
Peter Lane: *Princess Michael of Kent* (Robert Hale, 1985).

EDWARD VIII

FATHER: *George V (see page 322).*
MOTHER: *Mary of Teck (see page 322, under George V).*
SIBLINGS: *(see page 323, under George V).*

EDWARD VIII

Baptised Edward Albert Christian George Andrew Patrick David, he was born on 23rd June, 1894 at White Lodge, Richmond, Surrey. He became Duke of Cornwall and Rothesay, Earl of Carrick, Lord of the Isles and Baron Renfrew upon his father's accession to the throne on 6th May, 1910. He was made a Knight of the Garter on 23rd June, 1910, and was created Prince of Wales and Earl of Chester on the same day, being invested as such on 13th July, 1911 at Caernarvon Castle, Wales. He was made a Knight of the Bath in January, 1936.

He succeeded his father as King of Great Britain and Emperor of India on 20th January, 1936. He was never crowned. He abdicated on 11th December, 1936 because he wished to marry a twice-divorced woman, the American Mrs Simpson (see below), and because this could not be consistent with his position as Head of the Church of England, an institution which does not recognise divorce. Edward was created Duke of Windsor on 8th March, 1937, having been so designated since 12th December, 1936. He spent the rest of his life in exile in France, apart from occasional visits to England and America, and a wartime spell as Governor of the Bahamas.

Edward VIII married, after his Abdication, on 3rd June, 1937, at Château de Candé, Maine-et-Loire, France:

Bessiewallis

Known as Wallis, she was the daughter of Teackle Wallis Warfield by Alice M. Montague, and she was born on 19th June, 1896, at Square Cottage, the Monterey Inn, Blue Ridge Summit, Pennsylvania, U.S.A. She married firstly Earl Winfield Spencer (1888–1950) on 8th November, 1916 at the Christ Protestant Episcopal Church, Baltimore, Maryland, U.S.A.; they were divorced on 10th December, 1927. She married secondly Ernest Aldrich Simpson of New York (d.1958) on 21st July, 1928 at Chelsea Register Office, London; they were divorced on 27th October, 1936. She resumed her maiden name of Warfield on 7th May, 1937 by Deed Poll. Her marriage to the Duke of Windsor has been seen by some as morganatic (i.e. in contravention of the Royal Marriages Act 1772), but this was not so; neither did the fact that she was deprived of the style Her Royal Highness by George VI's Letters Patent of March, 1937, have any basis in law. She died on 24th April, 1986 at her house in the Bois de Boulogne, Paris, and was buried at Frogmore, Windsor. There was no issue of any of her marriages.

EDWARD VIII

He died on 28th May, 1972, at his house in the Bois de Boulogne, Paris, of cancer, and was buried at Frogmore, Windsor.

He was succeeded, after his Abdication in 1936, by his brother Albert, who assumed the style George VI.

Recommended reading

Anything written prior to 1974 when Frances Donaldson's definitive biography *Edward VIII* was published by Weidenfeld and Nicolson (it has recently been revised) is now out of date.

H.R.H. The Duke of Windsor: *A King's Story* (1951; Reprint Society, 1983) and The Duchess of Windsor: *The Heart has its Reasons* (Michael Joseph, 1956) were both ghost-written and have since been discredited in many respects.

See also the following, although it is worth noting that the author is biased in favour of his subjects:

Michael Bloch: *The Duke of Windsor's War* (Weidenfeld and Nicolson, 1982), *Wallis and Edward: Letters, 1931–1937* (Weidenfeld and Nicolson, 1986) and *The Secret File of the Duke of Windsor* (Bantam, 1988).

Charles Higham's *Wallis* (Sidgwick and Jackson, 1988) is also controversial, and somewhat sensational.

GEORGE VI

FATHER: *George V (see page 322).*
MOTHER: *Mary of Teck (see page 322, under George V).*
SIBLINGS: *(see page 323, under George V).*

GEORGE VI

Baptised Albert Frederick Arthur George, he was born on 14th December, 1895 at York Cottage, Sandringham, Norfolk. He was made a Knight of the Garter in 1916, and was created Duke of York, Earl of Inverness and Baron Killarney on 4th June, 1920. He succeeded his brother Edward VIII as King of Great Britain and Emperor of India on 11th December, 1936, and was crowned on 12th May, 1937 at Westminster Abbey. He relinquished the title Emperor of India on 22nd June, 1947 when India was granted independence.

George VI married, on 26th April, 1923, at Westminster Abbey:
Elizabeth Angela Marguerite
She is the daughter of Sir Claude George Bowes-Lyon, 14th Earl of

Strathmore and Kinghorne, by Nina Cecilia, daughter of the Rev. Charles William Frederick Cavendish-Bentinck, and she was born on 4th August, 1900, either at Belgrave Mansions, Grosvenor Gardens, London, or in a London ambulance on the way to a London maternity home (the available evidence suggests that the Queen Mother herself believes she was born in an ambulance). She was made a Lady of the Garter in 1936. She was crowned Queen Consort and Empress of India on 12th May, 1937 in Westminster Abbey. On the death of the King on 6th February, 1952, she assumed the style of H.M. Queen Elizabeth the Queen Mother.

Issue of marriage:

1 *Elizabeth II* (see page 331).

2 *Margaret Rose*

She was born on 21st August, 1930 at Glamis Castle, Angus, Scotland. She married Antony Charles Robert Armstrong-Jones, 1st Earl of Snowdon (b.1930) on 6th May, 1960, at Westminster Abbey, and has issue: 1 David Albert Charles, Viscount Linley (b.1961); married to the Hon. Serena Stanhope (b.1970), daughter of Viscount Petersham. 2 Sarah Frances Elizabeth (b.1964); married to Daniel Chatto (b.1957).

Princess Margaret and Lord Snowdon were divorced in May, 1978, having lived apart since March, 1976.

GEORGE VI

He died on 6th February, 1952, at Sandringham House, Norfolk, of cancer, and was buried in the King George VI Memorial Chapel, St George's Chapel, Windsor.

He was succeeded by his daughter Elizabeth.

Recommended reading

Patrick Howarth: *George VI* (Hutchinson, 1987).

Keith Middlemas: *George VI* (Weidenfeld and Nicolson, 1974).

Frances Donaldson: *George VI and Queen Elizabeth* (1977).

Peter Townshend: *The Last Emperor* (Weidenfeld and Nicolson, 1975).

Sir John Wheeler-Bennett: *The Life and Reign of George VI* (Macmillan, 1958) (the official biography).

See also:

Anne Morrow: *The Queen Mother* (Granada, 1984).

Robert Lacey: *God Bless Her! Queen Elizabeth, The Queen Mother* (Century, 1987).

Helen Cathcart: *The Queen Mother: Fifty Years a Queen* (W. H. Allen, 1986).
Douglas Liversidge: *The Queen Mother* (Barker, 1987).
Christopher Warwick: *Princess Margaret* (Magna, 1985) (with which the author was given some assistance by the Princess herself).

ELIZABETH II

By the Grace of God, of the United Kingdom of Great Britain and Northern Ireland, and of Her other Realms and Territories, Queen, Head of the Commonwealth, Defender of the Faith.

FATHER: *George VI (see page 329)*.
MOTHER: *Elizabeth Bowes-Lyon (see page 329, under George VI)*.
SIBLINGS: *(see page 330, under George VI)*.

ELIZABETH II

Baptised Elizabeth Alexandra Mary, she was born on 21st April, 1926 at 17, Bruton Street, London. She succeeded her father as Queen of Great Britain on 6th February, 1952, and was crowned on 2nd June, 1953 at Westminster Abbey.

Elizabeth II married, on 20th November, 1947, at Westminster Abbey:

Philip

He is the son of Prince Andrew of Greece and Denmark (of the House of Schleswig-Holstein-Sonderburg-Glücksburg) by Victoria Alice Elizabeth Julia Marie, daughter of Louis, Prince of Battenberg, Marquess of Milford-Haven, and he was born on 10th June, 1921 at Villa Mon Repos, Isle of Corfu, Greece. On 28th February, 1947, he renounced his Greek nationality and became a British subject, at the same time adopting the surname Mountbatten. He was made a

Knight of the Garter in 1947, and was created Duke of Edinburgh, Earl of Merioneth and Baron Greenwich on 19th November, 1947. He was made a Knight of the Thistle in 1952. On 27th February, 1957, he was granted the style of H.R.H. The Prince Philip, with precedence over all other male members of the Royal Family.

Issue of marriage:

1 *Charles Philip Arthur George*

He was born on 14th November, 1948 at Buckingham Palace. He became Duke of Cornwall and Rothesay, Earl of Carrick, Lord of the Isles and Baron Renfrew upon his mother's accession to the throne on 6th February, 1952. He was created Earl of Chester and Prince of Wales on 26th July, 1958, being invested as such on 1st July, 1969 at Caernarvon Castle, Wales. He was made a Knight of the Garter in 1968, and a Knight of the Bath in 1976.

Prince Charles married, on 29th July, 1981, at St Paul's Cathedral, London:

Diana Frances

She is the daughter of Edward John, 8th Earl Spencer, by the Hon. Frances Ruth Burke, daughter of Edmund Maurice Roche, 4th Baron Fermoy, and she was born on 1st July, 1961 at Park House, Sandringham, Norfolk.

Issue of marriage:

(i) *William Arthur Philip Louis*. Born on 21st June, 1982 at St Mary's Hospital, Paddington, London, and is styled Prince William of Wales.

(ii) *Henry Charles Albert David*. Known as Harry; born on 15th September, 1984 at St Mary's Hospital, Paddington, and is styled Prince Henry of Wales.

2 *Anne Elizabeth Alice Louise*

She was born on 15th August, 1950 at Clarence House, London. She married Captain Mark Anthony Peter Phillips (b.1948) on 14th November, 1973 at Westminster Abbey, and has issue:

1 Peter Mark Andrew (b.1977). 2 Zara Anne Elizabeth (b.1981). Princess Anne was designated Princess Royal on 1st June, 1987. She was divorced in 1992 and married secondly Commander Timothy Laurence (b.1955) in December 1992 at Crathie Church, Scotland.

3 *Andrew Albert Christian Edward*

He was born on 19th February, 1960 at Buckingham Palace. He was created Duke of York, Earl of Inverness and Baron Killalee on 23rd July, 1986.

Prince Andrew married, on 23rd July, 1986, at Westminster Abbey:

Sarah Margaret

She is the daughter of Major Ronald Ivor Ferguson by Susan Mary, daughter of Fitzherbert Wright of Corbisdale Farm, Ardgay, Co. Ross, and she was born on 15th October, 1959 at 27, Welbeck Street, London, W.1.

Issue of marriage: **(i)** *Beatrice Elizabeth Mary.* Born on 8th August, 1988 at the Portland Hospital, Great Portland Street, London, W.1. **(ii)** *Eugenie Victoria Helena.* Born on 23rd March, 1990 at the Portland Hospital.

4 *Edward Antony Richard Louis*

He was born on 10th March, 1964 at Buckingham Palace, and is styled H.R.H. The Prince Edward.

Recommended reading

There have been three excellent biographies of the Queen in recent years:

Robert Lacey: *Majesty* (Hutchinson, 1977).

Elizabeth Longford: *Elizabeth II* (Weidenfeld and Nicolson, 1982).

Anne Morrow: *The Queen* (Granada, 1983).

See also:

Peter Lane: *Prince Philip* (Robert Hale, 1980).

Basil Boothroyd: *Philip, an Informal Biography* (Longmans, 1971).

Penny Junor: *Charles* (Sidgwick and Jackson, 1987).

Anthony Holden: *Charles, Prince of Wales* (Weidenfeld and Nicolson, 1980); the updated version (1988) is controversial.

Ingrid Seward: *Diana* (Weidenfeld and Nicolson, 1988).

Penny Junor: *Diana, Princess of Wales* (Sidgwick and Jackson, 1983).

Helen Cathcart: *Anne, the Princess Royal* (W. H. Allen, 1988).

Paul James: *Anne, the Working Princess* (Piatkus, 1987).

Brian Hoey: *H.R.H. The Princess Anne: A Biography* (Country Life, 1984).

Andrew Morton: *Duchess* (Michael O'Mara, 1988), about the Duchess of York.

Select Bibliography

The works consulted during the 22 years it has taken me to research this book are too numerous to mention. What follows is a list of the most important sources. Books marked * are especially recommended for researching royal genealogy. Every effort has been made to trace a publisher for each book listed; unfortunately, this was not possible in every case.

Adam of Usk: *Chronicon* (ed. E. M. Thompson, 1876).
Adamson, D. & Dewar, P. B.: *The House of Nell Gwynn* (Kimber, 1974).
Akrigg, G. P. V.: *Jacobean Pageant, or the Court of King James I* (Hamish Hamilton, 1962).
Albert, M. A.: *The Divorce* (Harrap, 1965).
Alderman, C. L.: *Blood Red the Roses: The Wars of the Roses* (Bailey and Swinfen, 1973).
Alexander, Marc: *The Outrageous Queens* (1977).
H.R.H. Princess Alice, Countess of Athlone: *For My Grandchildren* (Evans, 1966).
Altschul, M.: *A Baronial Family in Mediaeval England: The Clares, 1217–1314* (Johns Hopkins, 1965).
Ancient Charters, Royal and Private, prior to A.D. 1200 (ed. J. H. Round, Pipe Roll Society, 1888).
Andrews, A.: *The Royal Whore* (Hutchinson, 1971).
The Anglo-Saxon Chronicle (ed. G. N. Garmonsway, Dent, 1954).
Anominalle Chronicle (ed. V. H. Galbraith, 1967).
Appleby, J. T.: *England without Richard* (Bell, 1965).
Appleby, J. T.: *Henry II, the Vanquished King* (Bell, 1962).
Appleby, J. T.: *The Troubled Reign of King Stephen* (Bell, 1969).
Archaeologia (102 vols., Society of Antiquaries of London, 1773–1969).
Argy, J. & Riches, W.: *Britain's Royal Brides* (Sphere Books, 1977).
Armitage-Smith, S.: *John of Gaunt* (Constable, 1904).
Ashdown, D. M.: *Ladies in Waiting* (Arthur Barker, 1976).
Ashdown, D. M.: *Princess of Wales* (John Murray, 1979).
Ashdown, D. M.: *Queen Victoria's Mother* (Robert Hale, 1974).
Ashley, M.: *Charles II, the Man and the Statesman* (Weidenfeld and Nicolson, 1971).
Ashley, M.: *The Glorious Revolution of 1688* (Hodder and Stoughton, 1966).
Ashley, M.: *James II* (Dent, 1977).
Ashley, M.: *King John* (Weidenfeld and Nicolson, 1972).
Ashley, M.: *The Stuarts in Love* (Hodder and Stoughton, 1963).
Ashley, M.: *William I* (Weidenfeld and Nicolson, 1973).
Ashton, R.: *James I by his Contemporaries* (Hutchinson, 1969).
Asser, Bishop: *Life of King Alfred* (ed. W. M. Stevenson, Oxford University Press, 1904).
Ayling, S.: *George the Third* (Collins, 1972).
Bacon, Francis: *The Life of Henry VII* (1622; ed. J. R. Lumby, Cambridge University Press, 1902).
Bagley, J. J.: *Henry VIII* (Batsford, 1962).
Bagley, J. J.: *Margaret of Anjou, Queen of England* (Herbert Jenkins, 1948).
Baker, Geoffrey le: *Chronicon* (ed. E. M. Thompson, Oxford University Press, 1889).

Baker, Richard: *A Chronicle of the Kings of England from the Time of the Romans' Government unto the Death of King James* (1643).

Baker, T.: *The Normans* (Cassell, 1966).

Barber, R.: *Henry Plantagenet: A Biography of Henry II of England* (Boydell Press, 1972).

Barlow, F.: *Edward the Confessor* (Eyre and Spottiswoode, 1970).*

Barlow, F.: *The Feudal Kingdom of England* (Eyre and Spottiswoode, 1961).

Barlow, F.: *William I and the Norman Conquest* (Eyre and Spottiswoode, 1965).

Battiscombe, G.: *Queen Alexandra* (Constable, 1969).

Baxter, S. B.: *William III* (Longman, 1966).

Bayley, J.: *History and Antiquities of the Tower of London* (Jennings and Chaplin, 1830).

Beamish, T.: *Battle Royal* (Muller, 1965).

Beaverbrook, Lord: *The Abdication of King Edward VIII* (Hamish Hamilton, 1966).

Beckingsale, B. W.: *Elizabeth I* (Batsford, 1963).

Bennett, D.: *King without a Crown* (Heinemann, 1977).

Bennett, D.: *Vicky* (Collins and Harvill, 1971).

Berry, P.: *By Royal Appointment* (Femina, 1970).

Bevan, B.: *Charles the Second's French Mistress* (Robert Hale, 1972).

Bevan, B.: *I was James the Second's Queen* (Robert Hale, 1963).

Bevan, B.: *King James III of England* (Robert Hale, 1962).

Bevan, B.: *Nell Gwyn* (Robert Hale, 1969).

Bingham, C.: *Edward II* (Weidenfeld and Nicolson, 1973).

Bingham, C.: *James V, King of Scots* (Collins, 1971).

Bingham, C.: *The Kings and Queens of Scotland* (Weidenfeld and Nicolson, 1976).*

Bingham, C.: *The Stewart Kingdom of Scotland* (Weidenfeld and Nicolson, 1974).

Black, J. B.: *The Reign of Elizabeth* (Oxford University Press, 1959).

Blackman, John: *Collectarium Mansuetudinum et Bonorium Morum Regis Henrici VI* (ed. M. R. James, 1919).

Bloom, U.: *The House of Kent* (Robert Hale, 1969).

Bloom, Ursula: *Princesses in Love* (Robert Hale, 1973).

Bone, Q.: *Henrietta Maria, Queen of the Cavaliers* (Owen, 1973).

The Book of Burials of True Noble Persons (MS. in the Royal College of Arms).

Borrow, G. W. S.: *Robert the Bruce and the Community of the Realm of Scotland* (Eyre and Spottiswoode, 1965).

Bowle, J.: *Charles the First* (Weidenfeld and Nicolson, 1975).

Bowle, J.: *Henry VIII* (Allen and Unwin, 1964).

Brooke, C.: *The Saxon and Norman Kings* (Batsford, 1963).

Brooke, J.: *King George III* (Constable, 1972).

Brooke-Little, J. P.: *Boutell's Heraldry* (Frederick Warne, 1973).

Bruce, M. L.: *Anne Boleyn* (Collins, 1972).

Bruce, M. L.: *The Making of Henry VIII* (Collins, 1977).

The Brut, or The Chronicles of England (ed. F. Brie, Early English Texts Society, 1906, 1908).

Bryant, A.: *The Age of Chivalry* (Collins, 1963).

Brysson-Morrison, N.: *The Private Life of Henry VIII* (Robert Hale, 1964).

Burke's Guide to the Royal Family (Burke's Peerage, 1973).*

Burke's Peerage (various editions).*

Butler, I.: *Rule of Three* (Hodder and Stoughton, 1967).

Byrne, M. St. Clair: *The Letters of King Henry VIII* (Cassell, 1936).

Calendar of Charter Rolls preserved in the Public Record Office (6 vols., H.M.S.O., 1903).

Calendar of Documents preserved in France, illustrative of the History of Great Britain and Ireland, Vol. 1, 918–1206 (ed. J. H. Round, 1899).

Calendar of entries in the Papal Registers relating to Great Britain and Ireland: Papal Letters (ed. W. H. Bliss, 1893).

Calendar of Letters, Despatches and State Papers relating to Negotiations between England and Spain (ed. G. A. Bergenroth, 13 vols., H.M.S.O., 1862–1954).

Calendar of Letters and Papers, Foreign and Domestic, of the Reign of Henry VIII (ed. J. S. Brewer, J. Gairdner, and R. H. Brodie, 21 vols., H.M.S.O., 1862–1932).
Calendar of Patent Rolls preserved in the Public Record Office (H.M.S.O., 1906).
Calendar of State Papers: Milan (ed. A. B. Hinds, H.M.S.O., 1913).
Calendar of State Papers: Venice (ed. R. Brown and A. B. Hinds, 38 vols., Longman, 1864–1937).
Capgrave, John: *The Book of the Illustrious Henries* (ed. F. C. Hingston, Longman, Brown, Green, 1858).
Carpenter, E. (ed.): *A House of Kings: The History of Westminster Abbey* (Baker, 1966).
Cassavetti, E.: *The Lion and the Lilies: The Stuarts and France* (MacDonald and Jane's, 1977).
Cathcart, H.: *Anne and the Princesses Royal* (W. H. Allen, 1973).
Cathcart, H.: *The Duchess of Kent* (W. H. Allen, 1971).
Cathcart, H.: *Her Majesty* (W. H. Allen, 1962).
Chandos Herald: *Life of the Black Prince* (ed. M. K. Pope and E. C. Lodge, Clarendon Press, 1910).
Chapman, H. W.: *Anne Boleyn* (Jonathan Cape, 1974).
Chapman, H. W.: *Caroline Matilda, Queen of Denmark* (Jonathan Cape, 1971).
Chapman, H. W.: *Lady Jane Grey* (Jonathan Cape, 1962).
Chapman, H. W.: *The Last Tudor King* (Jonathan Cape, 1958).
Chapman, H. W.: *Mary II, Queen of England* (Jonathan Cape, 1953).
Chapman, H. W.: *Privileged Persons* (Jonathan Cape, 1966).
Chapman, H. W.: *Queen Anne's Son* (Jonathan Cape, 1954).
Chapman, H. W.: *The Sisters of Henry VIII* (Jonathan Cape, 1969).
Chapman, H. W.: *The Tragedy of Charles II* (Jonathan Cape, 1964).
Chapman, H. W.: *Two Tudor Portraits* (Jonathan Cape, 1960).
Cheetham, A.: *Richard III* (Weidenfeld and Nicolson, 1972).
Chevenix-Trench, C.: *The Royal Malady* (Longmans, 1964).
Chrimes, S. B.: *Henry VII* (Eyre Methuen, 1972).
Chrimes, S. B.: *Lancastrians, Yorkists, and Henry VII* (Macmillan, 1964).
A Chronicle of England during the reigns of the Tudors (ed. W. Douglas-Hamilton, 2 vols., Camden Society, 1875).
Chronicle of the Grey Friars of London (ed. J. Nichols, Camden Society, 1852).
Chronicle of London, 1089–1483 (ed. H. Nicholas, Society of Antiquaries of London, 1827).
Chronicles and Memorials of the Reign of Richard I (ed. W. Stubbs, 2 vols., Rolls Series, H.M.S.O., 1864–5).
Chronicles of the Reigns of Edward I and Edward II (ed. W. Stubbs, Rolls Series, H.M.S.O., 1882).
Chronicles of the Reigns of Stephen, Henry II and Richard I (ed. R. Howlett, Rolls Series, H.M.S.O., 1885).
Chronicles of the White Rose (ed. J. O. Halliwell, Camden Society, 1835).
Chronicum Monasterii de Abingdon (ed. J. Stevenson, Rolls Series, H.M.S.O., 1858).
Chronique de la Traison et Mort de Richard II (ed. B. Williams, English Historical Society, 1846).
Chroniques des Comtes d'Anjou (ed. L. Halphen and R. Poupardin, 1913).
Clarke, J.: *George III* (Weidenfeld and Nicolson, 1972).
Clear, C.: *Royal Children* (Arthur Barker, 1984).
Clive, M.: *This Sun of York: A Biography of Edward IV* (Macmillan, 1973).
Cobbett's Complete Collection of State Trials (1809; Routledge and Kegan Paul, 1972).
Cole, H.: *The Black Prince* (Granada, 1976).
Cole, H.: *The Wars of the Roses* (Hart-Davis MacGibbon, 1973).
A Collection of the Wills of the Kings and Queens of England from William the Conqueror to Henry VII (ed. J. Nichols, 1780).
Commines, Philippe de: *Mémoires* (ed. M. Jones, Penguin, 1972).
The Complete Peerage of England, Scotland, Ireland, Great Britain and the United Kingdom (ed. G. H. White, 13 vols., St. Catherine's Press, 1910–59).*

SELECT BIBLIOGRAPHY

Costain, T. B.: *Three Edwards* (Doubleday, 1958).

Cowan, I. B.: *The Enigma of Mary Stuart* (Gollancz, 1971).

Cowan, M.: *The Six Wives of Henry VIII* (Frewin, 1968).

Creston, D.: *The Youthful Queen Victoria* (Macmillan, 1952).

Creton, Jean: *Histoire de Roy d'Angleterre, Richard* (ed. J. A. C. Buchon, Collection des Chroniques Françaises, Paris, 1826).

Cronne, H. A.: *The Reign of Stephen, 1135–1154: Anarchy in England* (Weidenfeld and Nicolson, 1970).

Cullen, T.: *The Empress Brown* (The Bodley Head, 1969).

Dart, John: *The History and Antiquities of the Abbey Church of Westminster* (2 vols., 1723).

Davis, H. W. C.: *England under the Normans and Angevins, 1066–1272* (Methuen, 1905).

Davis, R. H. C.: *King Stephen* (Longmans, 1967).

Delderfield, E. R.: *Kings and Queens of England and Great Britain* (Raleigh Press, 1966).*

Denholm-Young, N.: *Richard of Cornwall* (Blackwell, 1947).

Dewhurst, J.: *Royal Confinements* (Weidenfeld and Nicolson, 1980).

Dictionary of National Biography (ed. L. Stephen and S. Lee, 63 vols., Oxford University Press, 1885–1900).

Donaldson, F.: *Edward VIII* (Weidenfeld and Nicolson, 1974).

Donaldson, G.: *Mary, Queen of Scots* (English Universities Press, 1974).

Donaldson, G.: *Scottish Kings* (Batsford, 1967).

Douglas, D. C.: *William the Conqueror* (Eyre and Spottiswoode, 1964).*

Duff, D.: *Albert and Victoria* (Muller, 1977).

Duff, D.: *Edward of Kent* (Muller, 1938).

Duff, D.: *Hessian Tapestry* (Muller, 1967).

Duff, D.: *The Shy Princess* (Muller, 1958).

Duggan, A.: *Devil's Brood: The Angevin Family* (Faber and Faber, 1957).

Durant, H.: *Sorrowful Captives: The Tudor Earls of Devon* (Griffin Press, 1960).

Dutton, R.: *English Court Life from Henry VII to George II* (Batsford, 1963).

Eadmer: *Historia Novorum* and *Vita Sancti Anselmi* (ed. M. Rule, Longman, 1884).

Earle, P.: *Henry V* (Weidenfeld and Nicolson, 1972).

Earle, P.: *James II* (Weidenfeld and Nicolson, 1972).

Edwards, Anne: *Matriarch: Queen Mary and the House of Windsor* (Hodder and Stoughton, 1984).

Elmham, Thomas: *Gesta Henrici Quinti* (ed. B. Williams, English Historical Society, 1850).

Elsberry, T.: *Marie of Roumania* (Cassell, 1973).

Elsna, H.: *Catherine of Braganza* (Robert Hale, 1967).

Elton, G. R.: *England under the Tudors* (Methuen, 1955).

Emerson, B.: *The Black Prince* (Weidenfeld and Nicolson, 1976).

An English Chronicle of the Reigns of Richard II, Henry IV, Henry V and Henry VI (ed. J. S. Davies, 1856).

Epton, N.: *Victoria and her Daughters* (Weidenfeld and Nicolson, 1971).

Erickson, C.: *Anne Boleyn* (Dent, 1984).

Erickson, C.: *Bloody Mary* (Dent, 1978).

Erickson, C.: *Great Harry: A Life of King Henry VIII* (Dent, 1980).

Erlanger, P.: *Margaret of Anjou, Queen of England* (Elek Books, 1970).

Fabyan, Robert: *The Concordance of Histories: The New Chronicles of England and France* (ed. H. Ellis, Rivington, 1811).

Falkus, C.: *Charles II* (Weidenfeld and Nicolson, 1972).

Farjeon, E. and H.: *Kings and Queens* (Dent, 1953, 1983).

The Fifteenth Century Chronicles (ed. J. Gairdner, 1880).

The First English Life of Henry V (ed. C. L. Kingsford, Clarendon Press, Oxford, 1911).

Florence of Worcester: *Chronicon ex Chronicis* (ed. B. Thorpe, English Historical Society, 1848–9).

Fothergill, B.: *Mrs. Jordan* (Faber and Faber, 1965).

Fowler, K. A.: *The King's Lieutenant: Henry of Grosmont, First Duke of Lancaster, 1300–1361* (Elek Books, 1969).

Fraser, A.: *The Life and Times of King James* (Weidenfeld and Nicolson, 1974).

Fraser, A. (ed.): *The Lives of the Kings and Queens of England* (Futura, 1977).

Fraser, A.: *Mary, Queen of Scots* (Weidenfeld and Nicolson, 1969).

Freeman-Grenville, G. S. P.: *The Queen's Lineage* (Rex Collings, 1977).*

Friedmann, P.: *Anne Boleyn* (2 vols., Macmillan, 1884).

Froissart, John: *Chronicles of England, France and Spain* (ed. J. Jolliffe, Harvill Press, 1967).

Fryer, M. B., Bousfield, A. and Toffoli, G.: *Lives of the Princesses of Wales* (Dundurn Press, 1983).

Fulford, R.: *From Hanover to Windsor* (Batsford, 1960).

Fulford, R.: *Royal Dukes* (Duckworth, 1933).

Fulford, R.: *The Trial of Queen Caroline* (Batsford, 1968).

Gaimar, Geoffrey: *L'Estoire des Engles* (ed. T. Hardy and C. T. Martin, Rolls Series, H.M.S.O., 1888–9).

Geoffrey of Monmouth: *History of the Kings of Britain* (ed. S. Evans and C. W. Dunn, Dent, 1963).

Gervase of Canterbury: *Historical Works* (ed. W. Stubbs, Rolls Series, H.M.S.O., 1879–80).

Gillen, M.: *The Prince and his Lady* (Sidgwick and Jackson, 1970).

Gillen, M.: *Royal Duke* (Sidgwick and Jackson, 1976).

Gillingham, J.: *Richard the Lion Heart* (Weidenfeld and Nicolson, 1973).

Given-Hilson, C. and Curteis, A.: *The Royal Bastards of Mediaeval England* (Routledge and Keegan Paul, 1984).*

Gorst-Williams, J.: *Elizabeth, the Winter Queen* (Abelard, 1977).

Grafton, Richard: *Continuation of Hardyng's Chronicles* (ed. Sir H. Nicholas, Society of Antiquaries of London, 1809).

The Great Chronicle of London (ed. A. H. Thomas and I. D. Thornley, Alan Sutton, 1983).

Great Dynasties (Various authors; Windward, New York, 1976, 1979).

Green, D.: *Queen Anne* (Collins, 1970).

Green, M. A. E.: *The Lives of the Princesses of England* (6 vols., London, 1849–55).*

Green, V. H. H.: *The Later Plantagenets* (Edward Arnold, 1955).*

Grinnell-Milne, D.: *The Killing of William Rufus* (David and Charles, 1968).

Hackett, F.: *Henry the Eighth* (1929; Chivers edition 1973).

Hall, Edward: *The Triumphant Reign of King Henry the Eighth* (ed. C. Whibley, 2 vols., T. C. and E. C. Jack, 1904).

Hall, Edward: *The Union of the Two Noble and Illustrious Families of Lancaster and York* (ed. H. Ellis, Rivington, 1809).

Hamilton, E.: *Henrietta Maria* (Coward, McGann and Geoghegan, 1976).

Hamilton, E.: *William's Mary* (Coward, McGann and Geoghegan, 1972).

Hamilton, R.: *Now I Remember: A Holiday History of England* (Pan, 1964).

Handbook of British Chronology (ed. F. M. Powicke and E. B. Fryde, Royal Historical Society, 1961).*

Harrison, M.: *Clarence* (W. H. Allen, 1972).

Harvey, J.: *The Plantagenets* (Batsford, 1948).

Hassall, W. O.: *Who's Who in History, Vol. 1, 55 B.C. to 1485* (Blackwell, 1960).

Haswell, J.: *The Ardent Queen* (Peter Davies, 1976).

Hatton, R.: *George I, Elector and King* (Thames and Hudson, 1978).

Hedley, O.: *Queen Charlotte* (John Murray, 1975).

Henry of Huntingdon: *Historia Anglorum* (ed. T. Arnold, Rolls Series, H.M.S.O., 1879).

Hibbert, C.: *Charles I* (Weidenfeld and Nicolson, 1968).

Hibbert, C.: *The Court at Windsor* (Longmans, 1964).

Hibbert, C.: *Edward VII* (1976; Penguin edition, 1982).

Hibbert, C.: *George IV, Regent and King* (Longmans, 1975).

Hichens, P.: *The Royal Baby Book* (Octopus Books, 1984).

Higden, Ranulph: *Polychronicon* (ed. C. Babington and J. R. Lumby, Rolls Series, H.M.S.O., 1865–6).

Histoire des Ducs de Normandie et des Rois d'Angleterre (ed. Francis-que-Michel, Société de l'Histoire de France, Paris, 1840).

Histoire de Guillaume le Maréchale (ed. P. Meyer, Société de l'Histoire de France, Paris, 1891–1901).

Historiae Croylandensis Continuato (cd. W. Fulman, 1684; trans. T. Rilcy, Bohn's Library, no date).

Historiae Vitae et Regni Ricardi Secundi (ed. T. Hearne, 1729).

History of the Arrival of Edward IV in England and the Final Recovery of his Kingdoms from Henry VI, A.D. MCCCCLXXI (ed. J. Bruce, 1838).

Hoey, B.: *H.R.H. The Princess Anne: A Biography* (Country Life, 1984).

Holden, A.: *Charles, Prince of Wales* (Weidenfeld and Nicolson, 1979).

Holinshed, Raphael: *Chronicles of England, Scotland and Ireland* (ed. H. Ellis, 6 vols., Dent, 1927).

Holme, T.: *Prinny's Daughter: A Biography of Princess Charlotte of Wales* (Hamilton, 1976).

Holt, J. C.: *King John* (Cambridge University Press, 1963).

Hopkirk, M.: *Queen Adelaide* (John Murray, 1946).

Hough, R.: *Louis and Victoria: The First Mountbattens* (Hutchinson, 1974).

Howard, P.: *The Royal Palaces* (Hamilton, 1970).

Hume, M. A. S.: *The Wives of Henry VIII* (Eveleigh Nash, 1905).

Hutchison, H. F.: *Edward II, the Pliant King* (Eyre and Spottiswoode, 1971).

Hutchison, H. F.: *Henry V* (Eyre and Spottiswoode, 1967).

Hutchison, H. F.: *The Hollow Crown: A Life of Richard II* (Eyre and Spottiswoode, 1961).

Incertie Scriptoris Chronicon Angliae de Regnis Henrici IV, Henrici V et Henrici VI (ed. J. A. Giles, 1848).

Inglis, B.: *Abdication* (Hodder and Stoughton, 1966).

Ingulph's Chronicle of the Abbey of Croyland (ed. H. T. Riley, 1854; this contains the Third Continuation of the Chronicle, of which the original no longer exists).

Iremonger, L.: *Love and the Princess* (Faber, 1958).

Itinerarium et Peregrinorum et Gesta Regis Ricardi (ed. W. Stubbs, Rolls Series, H.M.S.O., 1864).

Jacob, E. F.: *The Fifteenth Century, 1399–1485* (Oxford University Press, 1961).

Jean le Beau: *Chronique de Richard II* (ed. J. A. C. Buchon, 1826).

Jenkins, E.: *Elizabeth the Great* (Gollancz, 1958).

Jenkins, E.: *The Princes in the Tower* (Hamish Hamilton, 1978).

Jenner, H.: *Royal Wives* (1967).*

Jocelin of Brakelond: *Chronicle* (ed. G. Rokewoode, Camden Society, 1840).

Joelson, A.: *Heirs to the Throne* (Heinemann, 1966).

Johnson, P.: *Edward III* (Weidenfeld and Nicolson, 1973).

Jolliffe, J. E. A.: *Angevin Kingship* (Adam and Charles Black, 1955).

Jones, F.: *The Princes and Principality of Wales* (University of Wales, Cardiff, 1969).

Jordan, R.: *Sophia Dorothea* (Constable, 1971).

Jordan, W. K.: *Edward VI: The Young King* (Allen and Unwin, 1968).

Jordan, W. K.: *Edward VI: The Threshold of Power* (Allen and Unwin, 1970).

Judd, D.: *The House of Windsor* (MacDonald and Jane's, 1973).

Junor, P.: *Diana, Princess of Wales* (Sidgwick and Jackson, 1983).

Kay, F. G.: *Lady of the Sun: The Life and Times of Alice Perrers* (Muller, 1966).

Keepe, Henry: *Monumenta Westmonasteriensia* (1683).

Kelly, A.: *Eleanor of Aquitaine and the Four Kings* (Harvard University Press, 1952).

Kendall, P. M.: *Richard III* (Allen and Unwin, 1955).

Kendall, P. M.: *Warwick the Kingmaker* (Allen and Unwin, 1957).

Kenyon, F. P.: *The Stuarts: A Study in English Kingship* (Collins, 1958).

Kirby, J. L.: *Henry IV of England* (Constable, 1970).

Knighton, Henry: *Chronica* (ed. J. R. Lumby, 2 vols., Rolls Series, H.M.S.O., 1889–95).

Kroll, M.: *Sophia, Electress of Hanover: A Personal Portrait* (Gollancz, 1973).
Labargé, M. W.: *Henry V: The Cautious Conqueror* (Secker and Warburg, 1975).
Labargé, M. W.: *Simon de Montfort* (Eyre and Spottiswoode, 1962).
Lacey, R.: *Henry VIII* (Weidenfeld and Nicolson, 1972).
Lacey, R.: *Majesty: Elizabeth II and the House of Windsor* (Hutchinson, 1977).
Laird, D.: *Queen Elizabeth the Queen Mother* (Hodder and Stoughton, 1966).
Lancaster, O.: *Our Sovereigns* (1937).
Lander, J. R.: *The Wars of the Roses* (Secker and Warburg, 1965).
Lane, H. M.: *The Royal Daughters of England* (2 vols., Constable, 1910).*
Lane, P.: *Princess Michael of Kent* (Robert Hale, 1985).
Langdon-Davies (ed.): *Richard III and the Princes in the Tower* (Jackdaw Series, 1965).
Larson, L. M.: *Canute the Great and the Rise of Danish Imperialism* (1912).
Leary, F.: *The Golden Longing* (John Murray, 1959).
Leland, John: *Collectanea* (ed. T. Hearne, 6 vols., 1774; Chetham Society).
Lenz-Harvey, N.: *Elizabeth of York, Tudor Queen* (Arthur Barker, 1973).
Letters and Papers illustrative of the Reigns of Richard III and Henry VII (ed. J. Gairdner, 2 vols., Rolls Series, H.M.S.O., 1861, 1863).
Letters and Papers of the Reign of Henry VIII (ed. J. S. Brewer, J. Gairdner and R. H. Brodie, 21 vols., H.M.S.O., 1862–1932).
Lindsay, P.: *King Henry V* (Howard Baker, 1934).
Lindsay, P.: *Kings of Merry England* (Howard Baker, 1936).
Lindsay, P.: *The Secret of Henry VIII* (Howard Baker, 1953).
Linklater, E.: *The Royal House of Scotland* (Macmillan, 1970).
Lloyd, A.: *King John* (David and Charles, 1973).
Lloyd, A.: *The Year of the Conqueror* (Longmans, 1966).
Lockyer, R.: *Henry VII* (Longmans, 1968; revised edition 1983).
Lofts, N.: *Anne Boleyn* (Orbis, 1979).
Lofts, N.: *Queens of Britain* (Hodder and Stoughton, 1977).
Longford, E.: *Elizabeth II* (Weidenfeld and Nicolson, 1982).
Longford, E.: *The Royal House of Windsor* (Weidenfeld and Nicolson, 1974).
Longford, E.: *Victoria R. I.* (Weidenfeld and Nicolson, 1964).
Louda, J. and MacLagan, M.: *Lines of Succession: Heraldry of the Royal Families of Europe* (Orbis, 1981).*
Luke, M. M.: *Catherine the Queen* (Muller, 1967).
Luke, M. M.: *A Crown for Elizabeth* (Muller, 1971).
Macalpine, I. and Hunter, R.: *George III and the Mad Business* (Allen Lane, 1969).
MacGibbon, D.: *Elizabeth Woodville, 1437–1492* (1938).
Mackie, J. D.: *The Earlier Tudors, 1485–1558* (Oxford University Press, 1952).
Magnus, P.: *King Edward VII* (John Murray, 1964).
Mancini, Dominic: *The Usurpation of Richard III* (ed. C. A. J. Armstrong, Oxford University Press, 1936).
Map, Walter: *De Nugis Curialum* (ed. T. Wright, Camden Society, 1850).
Marlow, J.: *George I* (Weidenfeld and Nicolson, 1974).
Marlow, J. and Mackay, E.: *Kings and Queens of Britain* (1977).
Marples, M.: *Poor Fred and the Butcher* (Michael Joseph, 1970).
Marples, M.: *Six Royal Sisters: The Daughters of George III* (Michael Joseph, 1969).
Marples, M.: *Wicked Uncles in Love* (Michael Joseph, 1972).
Marshall, D.: *The Life and Times of Victoria* (Weidenfeld and Nicolson, 1972).
Marshall, R. K.: *Mary of Guise* (Collins, 1977).
Martiensson, A.: *Queen Katherine Parr* (Secker and Warburg, 1973).
Martin, R. G.: *The Woman He Loved* (W. H. Allen, 1974).
Materials for a History of the Reign of Henry VII (ed. W. Campbell, 2 vols., Rolls Series, H.M.S.O., 1873–7).
Mathew, D.: *The Courtiers of Henry VIII* (Eyre and Spottiswoode, 1970).
Mathew, D.: *King James I* (Eyre and Spottiswoode, 1967).
Mathew, D.: *Lady Jane Grey: The Setting of the Reign* (Eyre Methuen, 1972).
Matthew, D. J. A.: *The Norman Conquest* (Batsford, 1966).

Mattingley, G.: *Catherine of Aragon* (Jonathan Cape, 1942).
Maynard-Smith, D.: *Henry VIII and the Reformation* (Henry VIII, 1962).
McElwee, W.: *The Wisest Fool in Christendom* (Faber, 1958).
McKisack, M.: *The Fourteenth Century, 1307–1399* (Oxford University Press, 1959).
The Metrical Chronicle of Robert of Gloucester (ed. W. A. Wright, 1887).
Middlemas, K.: *Edward VII* (Weidenfeld and Nicolson, 1972).
Middlemas, K.: *George VI* (Weidenfeld and Nicolson, 1974).
Miller, J.: *William and Mary* (Weidenfeld and Nicolson, 1974).
Miller, P.: *James* (Allen and Unwin, 1971).
Molinet, Jean: *Chroniques des Ducs de Bougogne, 1476–1506* (ed. J. A. Buchon, Paris, 1827–8).
The Monarchy in Britain (Central Office of Information, 1977).
Montague-Smith, P.: *The Country Life Book of the Royal Silver Jubilee* (Country Life, 1977).
Montague-Smith, P.: *The Royal Line of Succession* (Pitkin, 1967).*
Montgomery-Massingberd, H.: *Burke's Guide to the British Monarchy* (Burke's Peerage, 1977).
More, Sir Thomas: *History of King Richard III* (ed. R. S. Sylvester, Yale University Press, 1965).
Morris, C.: *The Tudors* (Batsford, 1966).
Morrow, A.: *The Queen* (Granada, 1983).
Morrow, A.: *The Queen Mother* (Granada, 1984).
Mumby, F. A.: *The Youth of Henry VIII* (Constable, 1913).
Murimeth, Adam: *Continuato Chronicarum* (ed. E. M. Thompson, Rolls Series, H.M.S.O., 1889).
Neale, J. E.: *Queen Elizabeth I* (Jonathan Cape, 1934).
Neilson, M.: *Matilda of Scotland* (in The Lady, November, 1968).
Nicholson, R.: *Edward III and the Scots, 1327–35* (Oxford University Press, 1965).
Nicolson, H.: *George V: His Life and Reign* (Constable, 1952).
Noel, G.: *Princess Alice: Queen Victoria's Forgotten Daughter* (Constable, 1974).
Oman, C.: *Elizabeth of Bohemia* (Hodder and Stoughton, 1938, 1964).
Oman, C.: *Henrietta Maria* (Hodder and Stoughton, 1936).
Oman, C.: *Mary of Modena* (Hodder and Stoughton, 1962).
Ordericus Vitalis: *Historia Ecclesiastica* (ed. A. le Prèvost, 5 vols., Société de l'Histoire de France, Paris, 1838–55).
Pain, N.: *Empress Matilda: Uncrowned Queen of England* (Weidenfeld and Nicolson, 1978).
Palmer, A.: *George IV* (Weidenfeld and Nicolson, 1972).
Palmer, A.: *Kings and Queens of England* (Peerage, 1976).
Paris, Matthew: *Chronica Majora* (ed. H. R. Luard, 7 vols., Rolls Series, H.M.S.O., 1872–3).
Paris, Matthew: *Flores Historiarum* (ed. H. R. Luard, 3 vols., Rolls Series, H.M.S.O., 1890).
Paris, Matthew: *Historia Anglorum* (ed. F. H. Madden, 3 vols., Rolls Series, H.M.S.O., 1866–9).
Parmiter, G. de C.: *The King's Great Matter* (Longmans, 1967).
Paul, J. E.: *Catherine of Aragon and her Friends* (Burns and Oates, 1966).
Pearson, H.: *Charles II: His Life and Likeness* (Heinemann, 1960).
Peers, C.: *Berkhamstead Castle* (H.M.S.O., 1948).
Pepys, Samuel: *Diary* (ed. W. Matthews, vols. 1–7, Bell, 1970–72).
Pernoud, R.: *Blanche of Castile* (Collins, 1975).
Pernoud, R.: *Eleanor of Aquitaine* (Collins, 1967).
Petrie, C.: *The Stuarts* (Eyre and Spottiswoode, 1958).
Picard, B. L.: *The Tower and the Traitors* (Batsford, 1961).
Picknett, L.: *Royal Romance* (Marshall Cavendish, 1980).
Pierre de Langtoft: *Chronicle* (ed. W. A. Wright, 2 vols., Rolls Series, H.M.S.O., 1846–8).

Pine, L. G.: *Heirs of the Conqueror* (Herbert Jenkins, 1965).
Pine, L. G.: *Princes of Wales* (Herbert Jenkins, 1959).
Platts, B.: *A History of Greenwich* (David and Charles, 1973).
Plowden, A.: *The Young Elizabeth* (Macmillan, 1971).
Plumb, J. H.: *The First Four Georges* (Batsford, 1956).
Pollard. A. F.: *Henry VIII* (Longmans, 1902).
Poole, A. L.: *From Domesday Book to Magna Carta, 1087–1216* (Oxford University Press, 1951).
Pope-Hennessey, J.: *Queen Mary* (Allen and Unwin, 1959).
Porter, M.: *Overture to Victoria* (1961).
Powicke, F. M.: *King Henry III and the Lord Edward* (2 vols., Oxford University Press, 1947).
Powicke, F. M.: *The Thirteenth Century, 1216–1307* (Oxford University Press, 1962).
Prebble, J.: *The Lion in the North* (Penguin, 1973).
Prescott, H. F. M.: *Mary Tudor* (Constable, 1940).
Priestley, J. B.: *The Prince of Pleasure and his Regency, 1811–20* (Heinemann, 1969).
Ralph of Coggeshall: *Chronica Anglicanum* (ed. J. Stevenson, 1875).
Ralph de Diceto: *Imagines Historiarum* (ed. W. Stubbs, Rolls Series, H.M.S.O., 1876).
Ramsay, J. H.: *Lancaster and York* (2 vols., Clarendon Press, Oxford, 1892).*
Recueil d'Annales Angevines et Vendômoises (ed. L. Halphen, 1903).
Redman, Alvin: *The House of Hanover* (Alvin Redman, 1960).
The Reign of Henry VII from Contemporary Sources (ed. A. F. Pollard, 3 vols., Longmans, 1913–14).
Richardson, J.: *The Disastrous Marriage* (Jonathan Cape, 1960).
Richardson, J.: *George IV: A Portrait* (Sidgwick and Jackson, 1966).
Richardson, J.: *Victoria and Albert* (Dent, 1977).
Richardson, W. C.: *Mary Tudor, the White Queen* (Peter Owen, 1970).
Ridley, J.: *Mary Tudor* (Weidenfeld and Nicolson, 1973).
Rishanger, William: *Chronica* (ed. H. T. Riley, Rolls Series, H.M.S.O., 1865).
Rival, P.: *The Six Wives of Henry VIII* (Heinemann, 1937).
Robb, N.: *William of Orange* (2 vols., Heinemann, 1966).
Roche, T. W. E.: *The King of Almayne* (John Murray, 1966).
Roger of Hovedon: *Chronica* (ed. W. Stubbs, 4 vols., Rolls Series, H.M.S.O., 1868–71).
Roger of Hoveden: *Gesta Henrici Secundi and Gesta Ricardi* (ed. W. Stubbs, Rolls Series, H.M.S.O., 1867).
Roger of Wendover: *Flores Historiarum* (ed. H. O. Coxe, English Historical Society, 1841–4).
Ross, C.: *Edward IV* (Eyre Methuen, 1974).
Roulstone, M.: *The Royal House of Tudor* (Balfour, 1974).
Round, J. H.: *The Early Life of Anne Boleyn* (1886).
Rous, John: *Historia rerum Angliae* (ed. T. Hearne, 1716).
Routh, C. R. N.: *Who's Who in History, Vol. 2, 1485–1603* (Blackwell, 1964).
Rowse, A. L.: *Bosworth Field and the Wars of the Roses* (Macmillan, 1966).
Rowse, A. L.: *The Tower of London in the History of the Nation* (Weidenfeld and Nicolson, 1972).
Rowse, A. L.: *Windsor Castle in the History of the Nation* (Weidenfeld and Nicolson, 1974).
Russell of Liverpool, Lord: *Caroline, the Unhappy Queen* (Robert Hale, 1967).
Rymer, Thomas: *Foedora* (ed. T. Hardy, Records Commission, 1816–69).
Salzman, L. F.: *Edward I* (Constable, 1968).
Sandford, Francis: *A Genealogical History of the Kings and Queens of England and Monarchs of Great Britain, 1066–1677* (1677), continued by Samuel Stebbings (1707; Newcombe, 1707).*
Saunders, B.: *Henry the Eighth* (Alvin Redman, 1963).
Scarisbrick, J.: *Henry VIII* (Constable, 1968).
Scofield, C. L.: *The Life and Reign of Edward IV* (2 vols., Frank Cass, 1923, 1967).
The Scots Peerage (9 vols., 1904–14).

Scott-Moncrieff, M. C.: *Kings and Queens of England* (Blandford Press, 1966).

Sergeant, P.: *The Life of Anne Boleyn* (Hutchinson, 1923).

Seton, A.: *Katherine* (Hodder and Stoughton, 1954).

Seward, D.: *Prince of the Renaissance* (Constable, 1973).

Seymour, W.: *Ordeal by Ambition: An English Family in the Shadow of the Tudors* (Sidgwick and Jackson, 1972).

Sitwell, E.: *Fanfare for Elizabeth* (Macmillan, 1946).

Sitwell, E.: *The Queens and the Hive* (Macmillan, 1962).

Slocombe, G.: *Sons of the Conqueror* (Hutchinson, 1960).

Smith, L. B.: *The Elizabethan Epic* (Jonathan Cape, 1966).

Smith, L. B.: *Henry VIII, the Mask of Royalty* (Jonathan Cape, 1971).

Smith, L. B.: *A Tudor Tragedy: The Life and Times of Catherine Howard* (Jonathan Cape, 1961).

Softly, B.: *The Queens of England* (David and Charles, 1976).

St. Aubyn, G.: *The Royal George* (Constable, 1963).

Steele, A.: *Richard II* (Cambridge University Press, 1941).

Stenton, F. M.: *Anglo-Saxon England* (Oxford University Press, 1943, 1971).

Stones, E. L. G.: *Edward I and the Throne of Scotland* (Oxford University Press, 1978).

Storey, R. L.: *The End of the House of Lancaster* (Barrie and Rockliff, 1966).

Stow, John: *The Survey of London* (1598; Dent, 1956).

Strickland, A.: *Lives of the Queens of England* (8 vols., Henry Colburn, 1851; reprinted by Portway, 1973).*

Strong, R.: *The House of Tudor* (H.M.S.O., 1967).

Tauté, A., Brooke-Little, J. and Pottinger, D.: *Kings and Queens of Great Britain: A Genealogical Chart Showing their Descent, Relationships and Coats of Arms* (Elm Tree Books, 1970, revised edition 1986).*

Thomas, D.: *The Royal Baby Album* (Arlington, 1984).

Thompson, C. J. S.: *The Witchery of Jane Shore* (Grayson, 1933).

Thomson, G. M.: *The Crime of Mary Stuart* (Hutchinson, 1967).

Thornton, M.: *Royal Feud: The Queen Mother and the Duchess of Windsor* (Michael Joseph, 1985).

Thornton-Cook, E.: *Kings in the Making: The Princes of Wales* (1931).

Titus Livius Forojuliensis: *Vita Henrici Quinti* (ed. T. Hearne, 1716).

The Tower of London: Official Guide (H.M.S.O., 1966).

Trease, G.: *Seven Queens of England* (Heinemann, 1953).

Turner, F. C.: *James II* (Eyre and Spottiswoode, 1948).

Turton, G. E.: *The Dragon's Breed* (1969).

Turton, W. H.: *The Plantagenet Ancestry of Elizabeth of York* (1928).*

Van Der Zee, H. and B.: *William and Mary* (Macmillan, 1973).

Vergil, Polydore: *Anglica Historia* (ed. D. Hay, Camden Series, 1950).

Vita Edwardi Secundi (ed. N. Denholm-Young, Nelson, 1957).

Wakeford, G.: *The Princesses Royal* (Robert Hale, 1973).*

Wakeford, G.: *Three Consort Queens* (Robert Hale, 1971).

Waldman, M.: *The Lady Mary* (Collins, 1972).

Walsingham, Thomas: *Annales Ricardi Secundi* (ed. H. T. Riley, Rolls Series, H.M.S.O., 1866).

Walsingham, Thomas: *Chronicon Angliae* (ed. E. M. Thompson, Rolls Series, H.M.S.O., 1874).

Walsingham, Thomas: *Gesta Abbatum Monasterii St. Albani* (ed. H. T. Riley, 3 vols., Rolls Series, H.M.S.O., 1867–9).

Walsingham, Thomas: *Historiae Anglicana* (ed. H. T. Riley, 2 vols., Rolls Series, H.M.S.O., 1863–4).

Walter of Guisborough: *Chronica* (ed. H. C. Hamilton, 2 vols., English Historical Society, 1848–9).

Warkworth, John: *A Chronicle of the First Thirteen Years of the Reign of Edward IV* (ed. J. O. Halliwell, Camden Society, 1839).

Warren, W. L.: *Henry II* (Eyre Methuen, 1977).

Warren, W. L.: *King John* (Eyre and Spottiswoode, 1962).

Warwick, C.: *Princess Margaret* (Magna, 1985).

Watson, D. R.: *Charles I* (Weidenfeld and Nicolson, 1972).

Wedgewood, C. V.: *The King's Peace, 1637–41* (Collins, 1955).

Wedgewood, C. V.: *The King's War, 1641–47* (Collins, 1958).

Wedgewood, C. V.: *The Trial of Charles I* (Collins, 1964).

Weever, John: *Ancient Funeral Monuments within the United Monarchy of Great Britain, Ireland, and the Islands adjacent, their Founders, and what Eminent Persons have been in the Same Interred* (Thomas Harper, 1631).

Wentworth-Day, J.: *Princess Marina, Duchess of Kent* (Robert Hale, 1969).

Westminster Abbey: Official Guide (Jarrold, Norwich, 1966).

Wheeler-Bennett, J.: *The Life and Reign of George VI* (Macmillan, 1958).

Wilkins, J. H.: *Caroline the Illustrious* (Longmans Green, 1904).

Wilkinson, B.: *The Later Middle Ages in England* (Longmans, 1977).

William of Jumièges: *Gesta Normannorum Ducum* (ed. J. Marx, Société de l'Histoire de Normandie, 1914).

William of Malmesbury: *Chronicle of the Kings of England* (ed. J. A. Giles, 1866).

William of Malmesbury: *Historia Regum and Historia Novella* (ed. W. Stubbs, Rolls Series, H.M.S.O., 1887–9).

William of Newburgh: *Historia rerum Anglicarum* (ed. R. Howlett, 1884–5).

William of Poitiers: *Gesta Willelmi Ducis Normannorum et Regis Anglorum* (incorporated in *The Bayeux Tapestry and the Norman Invasion* ed. by L. Thorpe, Folio Society, 1973).

William of Worcester: *Annales rerum Anglicarum* (included in *Letters and Papers illustrative of the War with France*, ed. J. Stevenson, Rolls Series, H.M.S.O., 1864).

Williams, E. C.: *Anne of Denmark* (Longmans, 1970).

Williams, E. C.: *My Lord of Bedford* (Longmans, 1963).

Williams, N.: *Elizabeth I* (Weidenfeld and Nicolson, 1972).

Williams, N.: *Elizabeth I, Queen of England* (Weidenfeld and Nicolson, 1967).

Williams, N.: *Henry VII* (Weidenfeld and Nicolson, 1972).

Williams, N.: *Henry VIII and his Court* (Weidenfeld and Nicolson, 1971).

Williamson, H. R.: *The Butt of Malmsey* (Michael Joseph, 1967).

Williamson, H. R.: *The Marriage made in Blood* (Michael Joseph, 1968).

Williamson, H. R.: *A Matter of Martyrdom* (Michael Joseph, 1969).

Woodham-Smith, C.: *Queen Victoria: Her Life and Times, Vol. 1* (Hamish Hamilton, 1972).

Woodward, G. W. O.: *King Richard III* (Pitkin, 1972).

Ziegler, P.: *William IV* (Collins, 1971).

Special thanks are due to Anne Tauté for generously lending me some very rare books so that many gaps in the information included in Britain's Royal Families could be filled just prior to going to press.

Index

Elizabeth of Pomerania, Emps. of the Holy
Roman Empire 117
Elizabeth of Romania, Q. of Greece 308
Elizabeth of Valois, Q. of Spain 161
Elizabeth of York, Q. of England 121, 138,
145, 146, 149, 151, 238
Elizabeth I, Q. of England 146, 147; 148,
153, 159, 161, 162, 164, 244, 246, 248
Elizabeth II, Q. of Great Britain 2, 152,
317, 318, 330, 331–333
Ellen, nat. dr. of Jaspar Tudor see Helen
Elphinstone, Alexander, 1st Lord 242
Elphinstone, Euphemia 242
Elswitha, wife of Ealdorman Elthelholm
12
Emanuellovitch, Vladimir, P. Galitzine
296
Emich Charles, 2nd P. of Leiningen 288
Emma, nat. dr. of Henry I 49
Emma of Anjou, Ps. of East Gwynedd 57
Emma of Blois, Cs. of Maine 50
Emma of Conteville, Vcnts. of Avranches
41
Emma of Mortain, Cs. of Toulouse 40
Emma of Normandy, Q. of England 23,
24, 29, 31, 33, 39
Eneda see Ethelfleda
Engelbert, B. Landsberg-Steinfürt 290
Enguerrand III, C. of Ponthieu 40
Enguerrand II, Lord of Coucy, E. of
Bedford 94
Enguerrand III, Lord of Coucy 60, 199
Eochaid, K. of Scotland 166, 168, 169
Eochaid IV, K. of Scotland 165
Eochaid, s. of K. Indulf 172
Eppo, C. of Nellenburg 29
Eric II, K. of Norway 200, 201, 207
Eric VI, K. of Sweden 26
Eric of Pomerania, K. of Sweden, Denmark
and Norway 126
Erland Ugni, Jarl of Orkney 181
Erlend, Jarl of Orkney 184
Ermentrude of Clermont, Cs. of Chester
41
Ermentrude of Orléans, Q. of the Franks 5
Ernest Augustus, D. of Cumberland, K. of
Hanover 289–294
Ernest Augustus, Elector of Hanover 248,
250, 272, 274
Ernest Augustus of Hanover 293
Ernest Augustus of Hanover, D. of
Brunswick-Lüneberg 292, 293
Ernest Augustus of Hanover, D. of
Cumberland, D. of
Brunswick-Lüneberg 291–293
Ernest Augustus of Hanover, D. of York
and Albany 274

Ernest I, D. of Saxe-Coburg-Gotha 305
Ernest Louis, Grand D. of
Hesse-Darmstadt and the Rhine 307,
309
Ernest, P. of Hohenlohe-Langenburg 288
Ernest William, 7th P. of Hohenlohe-
Langenburg 309
Errington, John 301
Errington, Mary 301
Erskine, Alice 214
Erskine, Helen 207
Erskine, Janet 217
Erskine, Sir John 207, 214
Erskine, John Kennedy 304
Erskine, John, 4th Lord 242
Erskine, Margaret 242
Erskine, Sir Robert 217
Erskine, Robert, Lord 225
Erskine, Robert, 8th Lord 219
d'Este, Alfonso III, D. of Modena 260
d'Este, Augusta 294, 295
d'Este, Sir Augustus 294
d'Este, Maria Beatrice see Mary of
Modena
d'Estouteville, Henry 53
Estrith see Astrid
Ethelbald, K. of Wessex 5, 6, 7
Ethelbert, Ealdorman 22
Ethelbert, K. of Wessex 5, 7, 8
Ethelfleda, Abbess of Romsey 20
Ethelfleda of Damerham, Q. of England
16, 17
Ethelfleda of Wessex, Lady of the
Mercians 9, 10
Ethelfleda of Wessex, St., Abbess of
Romsey 14
Ethelfleda, Q. of England, wife of K.
Edgar 19, 21
Ethelfrida, dr. of K. Canute see Gunhilda,
Emps. of Germany
Ethelgiva, mother of Q. Elgiva, wife of K.
Edwy 18
Ethelgiva of Wessex, St., Abbess of
Shaftesbury 10
Ethelhelm, Ealdorman 12
Ethelhelm, s. of Ethelred I 8
Ethelhilda, dr. of Edward the Elder, K. of
Wessex 14
Ethelred, Ealdorman of Mercia 9
Ethelred, E. of Fife, Abbot of Dunkeld 185
Ethelred I, K. of Wessex 5, 7, 8, 9
Ethelred II, K. of England 20, 21, 22, 23,
24, 25, 26, 27, 29, 31, 32, 33, 39, 46, 178
Ethelreda of Northumbria, Q. of Scotland
179, 187
Ethelswitha of Gainsborough, Q. of
Wessex 9, 11

358

INDEX